CANADA
AND THE
AMERICAN REVOLUTION

THE DISRUPTION OF THE FIRST BRITISH EMPIRE

by
GEORGE M. WRONG

COOPER SQUARE PUBLISHERS, INC.
NEW YORK
1968

Originally Published 1935
Published by Cooper Square Publishers, Inc.
59 Fourth Avenue, New York, N. Y. 10003
Library of Congress Catalog Card No. 68-31300

Printed in the United States of America
by Noble Offset Printers, Inc., New York, N. Y. 10003

PREFACE

I OWE and now offer acknowledgement and thanks to many friends. I am indebted to Dr. A. G. Doughty of the Canadian Archives at Ottawa for many courtesies and to Mr. D. C. Harvey of Halifax, Archivist of Nova Scotia, for helpful suggestions. Mr. W. L. Grant, Principal of Upper Canada College, Toronto, and Professors Chester Martin and George W. Brown of the University of Toronto, have read and commented on the whole of the manuscript. Professor W. J. Alexander, of University College, has read a portion of the manuscript. My latest obligation is to Professor Ralph Flenley, of the University of Toronto, to Mr. H. H. Langton, former Librarian, and to Mr. W. S. Wallace, the present Librarian, for the laborious service of reading the whole of the book in proof. I have profited greatly by their aid.

While describing military operations within the frontiers of Canada, I have passed lightly over those in the English Colonies as beyond the purpose of the narrative. Hence there is only passing reference to the loyalist regiments serving there.

G. M. W.

TORONTO,
October, 1934.

722624

CONTENTS

CHAPTER I

CHAPTER II

CHAPTER III

CHAPTER IV

vii

CHAPTER XIII

CHAPTER XIV

CHAPTER XV

CHAPTER XVI

CANADA AND
THE AMERICAN REVOLUTION

CHAPTER I

AFTER the victorious peace of 1763, George III was the sovereign of North America from the Arctic to the Gulf of Mexico, as far westward as to the Mississippi. His sway in the north reached not only beyond this to the broad prairies claimed by the Hudson's Bay Co. but, as time was to show, even farther, over the mountains to the Pacific coast where Drake had raised the English flag nearly two centuries earlier. Thus inevitably the end of the war brought in America new and complex problems, problems related to the French in Canada and to the English colonies, already restless and assertive of their rights. Insight, constructive imagination, even genius, were needed to guide the nation in its new responsibilities. All these qualities Pitt had given to the winning of the war, but after him during the next twenty years those who directed British policy, except for brief intervals, were men oblivious of the law of change in political life and devoted to the old routine in governing colonies. To their unimaginative minds colonies must remain always subordinate to the mother country with the right to her, should she so decide, to tax them at will.

The culture of France was deeply rooted on the banks of the St. Lawrence, now become British territory. Canada had two considerable cities, Montreal and Quebec, and many villages. While the French were fewer than four score thousand in number, they were a fruitful people who have since multiplied to nearly four million, many of them now

1

in the United States. In race, religion, and language they were in almost humorous contrast with their new English masters. Since this small Catholic people had been abandoned by France, naturally the English hoped that in time they would accept the religion and the language of their conquerors. It was a vain hope. Time was to show that alien pressure only solidified this enduring France of the new world. With the parish curé as the guardian of its traditions, it is unshaken to this day.

The British inherited from France another new and difficult problem. There were many tribes in the new territory in the west and south, regions that included the great valley of the Ohio and also Florida just taken from Spain. The tribes were suspicious of any menace to their ancient rights. Each of them considered itself a sovereign nation and each was so wayward and childlike that the fantastic dream of a squaw might be interpreted as a call to attack and massacre neighbours with whom there was nominal peace. The control of scores of such tribes, in itself difficult, had a further complication. Since the English colonies fronting on the Atlantic had the west as a hinterland, they had claimed the right to expand so illimitably that the broad strip of frontage on the Atlantic of Connecticut, for instance, should reach across the continent to an equal frontage on the Pacific. Virginia and Pennsylvania pressed similar claims in that far-spreading land of broad rivers, of forests, and of open fertile prairies, where, in vast numbers, the buffalo roamed. In it were possibilities, since realized, of homes for many millions.

While the tribes were restless and treacherous they were a source of wealth. They exchanged their furs for what, after contact with Europeans, had come to be their urgent needs—firearms, steel axes to replace those of stone, blankets, tawdry ornaments that appealed to barbaric taste, last and worst, the rum and brandy—fire-water—for which they had a tragic craving. The European coveted, however, more than their trade in furs. Frontiersmen were realizing the fertility of their lands and pressing in to occupy them, while others who were not frontiersmen but speculators had watchful eyes for grants from government of thousands of acres that should increase in value as settlers pressed in. Not only in America but across the ocean in London men of influence desired such favours.

After the conquest of Canada Britain's place in the world had seemed secure. In her majesty, said Horace Walpole, she might now dictate to all Europe, while her private citizens might have more than the haughtiness of an Asiatic monarch. The hour of victory may be, however, that of greatest danger in a nation's life. This was true of Britain in 1763 as it was later of Napoleon in 1808, of Germany in 1871 and of the United States in the economic pride of 1929. The rule of Britain had in 1763 such elements of decay that within a score of years she barely escaped ruin. Her colonial system contained many germs of strife revealed only the more clearly by victorious war. It has been said of the relations of nations that, owing to rivalries and discontents, the pot is always boiling, while the aim of statesmanship is to keep it from boiling over. This homely illustration may be applied to England and the colonies during many years before the American Revolution. It was always held in England that colonial legislatures were subordinate bodies under charters or other instruments with rights limited by the terms of the grant. To claim that they had powers like those of the august assembly at Westminster was constitutional blasphemy. But though Whigs and Tories agreed in deriding such pretensions the colonies had a different outlook. Their popular assemblies often claimed the powers, privileges and sometimes even the name of the House of Commons. Men in the colonies of English blood, reared in deep reverence for

the traditions of their ancestry, were as sensitive in respect
of their rights as Hampden and Pym had been in the days
of the Stuart dynasty.

As time passed this sense of equality grew. In 1687 the
lower house in Maryland had asserted authority equal to
that of the House of Commons in England with the same
privileges for its members. In 1736 the assembly of Virginia claimed the full powers of the House of Commons,
unchecked by instructions that might be sent to the
governor from England and this was increasingly the note
of all the legislatures. It was marked in the colonies most
decisively English, such as Virginia and Massachusetts.
Thus while protest against Britain's claim to tax the
colonies furnished them with an effective slogan, the deeper
causes of the American Revolution lay in the sense of manly
independence matured during a century and a half of
colonial life and based upon an inevitable tendency in
human nature. Men whose fathers, grandfathers and even
great-grandfathers had faced and solved their own problems were too well aware of the traditions of English liberty
to yield to outside dictation. Equality with England was in
their mind as it was also in that of Canada a century and a
half later when in 1926 in the one hundred and fiftieth
anniversary year of the American Declaration of Independence in 1776 Great Britain and the British Dominions made
the Declaration of Equality that they form a group of self-
governing communities "within the British Empire, equal
in status, in no way subordinate one to another in any aspect of their domestic or external affairs, though united
by a common allegiance to the crown." There would have
been no American Revolution had a similar pronouncement
been made in 1776.

The social outlook of England differed widely from that
of the colonies. In spite of the expansion of trade and the
ambitions in politics of the newly rich from gains in India

and in the West Indies, the old landowning families still
controlled the House of Commons and looked down upon
traders. Burke rebuked this pride by saying that each class
was necessary to the other and "what God has joined together let no man put asunder." In America, on the other
hand, the merchant might move in the best society and be
the colonial aristocrat. Though in Virginia, indeed, and
farther south, there were great landowners who affected
contempt for trade, they might be themselves tradors in
tobacco and rice and were usually in debt to commercial
houses in England. Revolutions may spring, perhaps usually they do spring, from antagonisms of class, and there
was this cleavage between English and colonial society.
Whatever their pride, barely half a dozen of the influential
families in Virginia were derived from the upper rank of
England. The middle class and the classes below them had
chiefly peopled the colonies and they had few ties with
the ruling elements in the motherland. It was across a
social gulf that this class in England, headed by the king,
claimed the right to control the affairs of proud men in
America whose outlook they had no gleam of imagination
to lead them to understand.

The peace of 1763 proved to be no peace so far as
America was concerned. During the thirteen years that
lay between the peace and the Declaration of Independence
divisions matured from which came, in the end, two great
English-speaking federations in North America, each extending from the Atlantic to the Pacific and each in enduring contrast to the other in political outlook. We may
well be surprised at the rapidity with which these new
tendencies developed. Though in 1763 the English colonies
celebrated with joyous pealing of bells, with sermons of
elated thanksgiving, and with demonstrations of loyalty
to King George III, the triumphant peace that had made
him ruler from the Arctic Ocean to the Gulf of Mexico,

barely two years later the legislature of Virginia was protesting hotly against taxation by the Stamp Act, New York and Boston were in an uproar for the same reason and already were heard murmurs that might mean a final break with the mother country. In consequence Britain was soon at war with her own colonies. France joined them to avenge her recent defeat, in time Spain allied herself with France, and at last Great Britain had to accept the only great defeat in her proud record. She lost the former English colonies and she lost Florida ceded back to Spain. She retained, however, the whole north; Hudson Bay was hers with the prairie country, now the Canadian west, annexed by Charles II in 1671 and now the part of Canada that has been longest British; she retained Nova Scotia ceded by France in 1713 and Canada, the New France, ceded in 1763.

Since the key to the problems that affected Canada and the American Revolution is found in London, political methods and opinions in England are inevitably linked with the American scene. Horace Walpole describes Westminster Abbey on the night of November 11, 1760, when George II was laid beside other royal dust in Henry VII's chapel. The bright lighting of the great cathedral, Walpole says, made impressive the fretted roof, the rows of tombs and the long aisles. That burial scene marked a change in the kingship. George II had died at the mature age of seventy-seven. While this dapper little king was vain and so hot-tempered that sometimes in a fury he would kick his hat or his wig about the room, he was industrious, straightforward, and truthful and experience had made him cautious. Though he prided himself on his courage in war as a soldier who had fought in person against the French at Dettingen, in politics he was so timid and haunted by the fear of the Stuart claimant to the throne that he accepted the judgment of his ministers. The future of the

British race might well have been different had a ruler, able enough, old enough, and pliant enough to have learned political wisdom, succeeded George II. His eldest son Frederick, Prince of Wales, who died in 1751, had shown so little promise that his mother described him as "the greatest ass, and the greatest liar, and the greatest canaille [scoundrel] and the greatest beast in the whole world," whose death she hoped for daily. This hope was realized before his father died, and the throne came to a youth, Frederick's eldest son George, at the age of twenty-two. Assuredly the young king was not an ass, nor a liar, nor a scoundrel, nor a beast, but a young man of good moral character, great industry and a high sense of duty to the nation. It was, however, a misfortune for England that a youth, without experience or adequate education and with the instincts of a despot, should have become king at a critical period when England was arrogant because of great victories; when France and Spain were bent on revenge for recent defeat; and when forces were maturing in both America and Europe that were to bring far-spreading revolution. There was little in the honest narrow mind of George to help him to understand such forces and yet for too many years the destiny of the British Empire was in a real sense in his hands.

The Whigs who had put the House of Hanover on the throne had had their reward in fifty years of power. It is a melancholy rule in politics that power prolonged leads to faction and usually to corruption. The Whigs divided into groups, each aspiring to office, and all so sure of Whig hold upon the nation that they had pushed the king into a secondary place. While heir to the throne, Prince George had watched this Whig game and now when he reigned he was resolved that the king, the head of the nation, should have real authority. Naturally, kingly prestige had been lowered under the two first Georges who were foreigners and showed more love for petty Hanover than for the great nation of which an accident of birth had made them the sovereigns. Now, however, the new king broke the tradition, declared himself proud to be a Briton, and proved so anxious to disarm suspicions of partiality to Hanover that, though its ruler, he never saw it and indeed never set foot out of England even in his other dominions, Scotland and Ireland.

When George III came to the throne he found Pitt the nation's hero as the organizer of victory over France and bent on terms of peace that should end forever French rivalry. Naturally Pitt's supremacy was welcome neither to his colleagues nor to the king and their resolve to make a moderate peace soon led to Pitt's resignation. When, long before, in 1739, the clamour of Walpole's opponents had compelled war with Spain, he had made the remark, now become classic, that the ringing of bells would be followed by the wringing of hands. The statesmen who bring on war usually become keen to end it, since it is they who bear the heavy burden of its cost and uncertainty. George III found Pitt's colleagues weary of the war and bent on a mild peace. To make Britain too great, it was said, would so arouse the envy of the other nations as to bring downfall like that of Spain. Thus it happened that, while the nation clamoured for the fullest fruits of victory, the ministry, guided by the king, moved steadily towards moderation. In 1761 Pitt withdrew; in 1762 Newcastle was driven out; and then the Earl of Bute had the task of ending the war.

While Bute had fine qualities, a one-time friend, the Earl of Shelburne, who became an enemy, described him as proud, pompous and insolent, a would-be philosopher with "a very false taste in everything," "never natural," "always upon stilts," "the greatest political coward I ever knew," on the verge of "a sort of gloomy madness." Though lacking real ability Bute imagined himself a new Duc de Sully, the great reformer in France under Henry IV. His enemies, on the other hand, not only called him by the obnoxious name of the king's favourite but whispered scandal about his relations with the king's mother. Since Bute was a Scot that nation came in for scurrilous attacks. When he taxed cider, his opponents paraded in the cider counties a donkey wearing a crown led about by a man in a Scots plaid—the king led by Bute. John Wilkes, the son of a magnate in the city, had been an active supporter of Pitt. He hated Bute, who, he thought, had baulked his hopes to be made governor of Quebec, and in 1762 he founded a paper that he called *The North Briton,* a derisive name for the Scot. Its attacks had much to do with Bute's unpopularity. While clever Charles Townshend, of whom we shall hear much later, called the peace " a damned good one," Wilkes, with irreverent wit, assailed it as like the peace of God "for it passeth understanding." In No. 45 Wilkes said that the king's speech from the throne, describing the peace as honourable to the crown and beneficial to the nation, endorsed "an abominable lie" and was "an abandoned instance of ministerial effrontery." When Bute negotiated the peace with France, it was widely believed that he accepted an enormous bribe. In consequence London clamoured against Bute and all Scots; against their austere Presbyterian religion, hated in English society ever since the return of Charles II; their strange accent; the overweening pride of their nobles, despite such poverty that some were even out at elbows in dress; the corruption of their members of Parliament; and their exploiting of England for their own benefit. The Scots in Parliament were, in truth, a group that held together, just as did the Grenville, the Bedford, and the old Whig factions. A Scots member said that their leader in the House should always be a tall man so that the other Scots could see him go in

the crowd to the division lobby and thus the more readily
know how to vote.

It was in this crisis that young and obstinate George III
learned his first lessons in securing control of Parliament.
We are astounded at his certainty of himself. Backed by
his approval, Bute's ministry dismissed from office every
opponent of the peace. The disreputable and ruthless
Henry Fox, induced by Bute to change his party, became
leader of the House of Commons. Fox was at least straightforward and truthful. "I'll do him justice," said George II;
"I don't believe he ever told me a lie . . . But if he did
not he's the only man that ever came into my closet that
did not." To George III, however, Fox was a bad man, to
be used, as the king added, to overthrow bad men. To intimidate opposition the king now approved of the dismissal
from office of great and humble on a scale never before
known in England. "Leave none of them," Fox wrote to
Bute. The politics of the United States are familiar with
the doctrine that to the victor belong the spoils of office,
but even there it can rarely have been applied with Fox's
thoroughness. The date, December 20, 1762, was called
"Execution Day." Fox, in his fury to destroy the Whigs root
and branch, seemed like one possessed. It was even proposed
to cancel the patents of nobility granted by George II to
Whig peers. Dukes and obscure coastguards shared a common scourge. Part of Fox's reward was to be a peerage, in
order, as he said, that "his family should stand before Pitt's
in the list of peers." Newcastle was dismissed from the lord-
lieutenancy of three counties. The Marquis of Rockingham, the Duke of Devonshire and other Whig magnates
were turned out of posts of honour. The young king had
not yet learned that he could not treat with contempt
leaders who opposed his policy and, after years of struggle,
they were able to force their will upon him. Now, however,
when the Duke of Devonshire, a great noble and former

prime minister, went to court on October 18, 1762, and asked as usual to see the king, a page brought a message that the king would not see him, but later would send orders to him to return his staff of office as lord chamberlain. While the affront was unprecedented, greed for office brought support from those who desired favours from the ministry. In spite of popular clamour the majority in both houses of Parliament supported a moderate peace.

Little as it was understood at the time, this treaty signed at Paris on February 10, 1763, marked the end of an old and the beginning of a new and amazing era in colonial history. Hitherto colonies had been only the more or less docile children of the parent states, but by 1763 the whole colonial world was on the eve of change. Holland and Portugal were already negligible as rivals of the great powers; the grip of Spain on America was weak; France had received a blow to her colonial empire, all but mortal; and Britain herself, the seeming victor, was nearing the greatest disaster in her history, the revolt and loss of the American colonies. Unexampled changes were also imminent in Europe. Though Great Britain's convulsion came first, it was followed quickly by revolution in France that completed the ruin of the European colonial system. France then lost San Domingo, her richest colony, and when the armies of Napoleon invaded Spain and put upon its throne an alien king, the Spanish colonial empire collapsed. Unlike the English colonies the revolted Spanish colonies created no great union. Breaking from Spain one by one, as they did, they lost their former unity under Spanish sovereignty and set up many separate republics, often, as time was to show, at war with each other and weak compared with the powerful union created in the north by the former English colonies. Few contrasts could, indeed, be more vivid than that to-day between South America with many republics and North America with three great federations each stretching from the Atlantic to the Pacific and one of them, like Britain herself, a world power.

We are now so aware of a world-wide British Empire with great territories in every continent that we are slow to realize how few in 1763 were the British in the colonial world. The loss of her colonies took from Great Britain nearly all the people of her own blood who lived overseas. India was not a colony but an experiment in the rule of alien Asiatic peoples. Not a hundred thousand people of British origin lived in the West Indies and not two thousand in newly conquered Canada. As yet there was no British Australia nor South Africa. Fewer than twenty million people, of whom barely three million lived overseas, habitually spoke English while now some two hundred million use it. Nothing in the previous history of mankind, not Greece nor Rome nor changes in Asia or Europe, had such deep significance as the movements in the British world that began soon after George III came to the throne. Half of the wealth and of the political power of the world is now within the boundaries of the parent British and the daughter states of that period.

Looking forward beyond the American Revolution we may well wonder that after so crushing a disaster Great Britain had the energy to create a new empire and in Europe itself, through defeating Napoleon, to become by 1815 the most notable power in the world with London as perhaps its most splendid capital. Because driven from her former colonies, she had turned to a new field and founded Australia. France that had helped to ruin the first British Empire was, indeed, a chief cause of the expansion of the second. When Napoleon mastered Holland, Britain, at war with him, was free to take Holland's colony of South Africa, which she did in order to protect the route to India. It was Napoleon's dominance that ruined Spain, Great

Britain's only remaining rival in the colonial field, while the anticlericalism of revolutionary France made the Catholic French in Canada the more content that their destiny had taken them from France and made them British.

Each of the four nations that have made the history of North America claimed the whole continent. From the first Spain asserted a sweeping but vain claim to the two Americas, except what went by papal decree to Portugal. After Spain France proclaimed North America her own and fought valiantly to win it. By defeating France and Spain Britain seemed to make good her own resolve to have the continent. When her colonies broke from her to create a new nation, they too boasted that the United States must be continental and include what lay between the Arctic Ocean and the Gulf of Mexico. They did not succeed. Canada remained apart; a neglected Cinderella in the days of French rule; a colony half-forgotten in the early days of British rule; later a great region of forest and plain that seemed easy of absorption by the triumphant republic; to-day a nation that has played perhaps the most important part in shaping the political institutions of the modern British Commonwealth of Nations.

Canada's position has been unique. It is the only important country in the new world to retain a political tie with Europe and with it an outlook half European, and also, in the wider sense of the word, half American. In Canada, too, in close contact, are the civilizations of England and France, the double culture of a Protestant and a Catholic world. While all the other nations of the British Commonwealth have grown up in isolation from peoples of the same origin and language, Canada has lived side by side with a great foreign nation speaking the English tongue but at the same time long inspired by bitter anatagonism to the British parent from which it broke away. It is truly a romance of history that, when Britain's own colonists warred on her, a French colony should become for the time the guarantee of an enduring British North America. Romances, however, are not always happy. The tragic element in this romance is the long-enduring cleavage in spirit between the empire that remained and the republic formed by the colonies that broke away. United they might have led the world, perhaps, though one may not say certainly, for the world's good, since history has not proved that aims at world power by one people have made for the well-being of either the ruler or the ruled.

The position of Canada to-day shows that the ruin of the first British Empire was not necessary. Canada's ten million people—four times as many as those who created the United States—form a nation as complete in its liberties as are the peoples of Great Britain or the United States. While anomalies still exist in the great British commonwealth, containing half a dozen nations, the tie of allegiance to the crown and of mutual confidence holds them together. There is no one central authority. To-day Great Britain would no more claim authority in the affairs of Canada than she would in those of France or the United States. Clearly time might have brought in the first empire what it has brought to Canada. The break was due chiefly to the insistence of George III and his ministers on the unchangeable subordination of the colonies and to the resolve to coerce them should they refuse obedience. Unwise though this was, we can understand it. To ministers in England, ill-informed, the strife was due to a few malcontents and had no hold on right-thinking people in either England or America. It should not, however, be imagined that even the British statesmen who opposed the coercion of the colonies were ready to admit that they had the right to equality in freedom. Warships in their harbours and soldiers in their streets should, Chatham said, enforce Britain's right to control their external trade. Throughout the struggle Burke held that Britain's supremacy over the colonies should be maintained and that London must remain the seat of power in regard both to the colonies and to conquered Ireland. No right to secede existed. This view, if mistaken, was also natural. No state is likely to consent to its own disruption. A century after George III came to the throne the northern states in the American Union denied the right to secede claimed by the south, denounced it as treason, and made good the denial in a civil war that cost perhaps a million lives. To Burke the secession of the colonies had no more justification. Events were to prove his a vain opinion but in it there was nothing sinister.

CHAPTER II

THE CANADIANS AT HOME

THE territory in Asia and in America acquired by Great Britain in 1763 presents striking contrasts. The India won by Clive had an ancient civilization and was densely populated while the conquests in America lay still for the most part in primitive barbarism. Florida, a flat land of forest and savannah, was then inhabited by warlike tribes and by a few Spaniards who, almost to a man, withdrew when the country was ceded to Britain. Her sway was destined to be brief. Triumphant in 1763, she was forced twenty years later to return Florida to decadent Spain. During the short twenty years of her rule some twenty-five thousand British had found homes there and they did more to develop the country than Spain had done in the two hundred years of her indolent sway. In the West Indies, Grenada and Dominica, tropical islands taken from France in 1763, still remain British. Grenada had some twelve hundred French and ten times as many negroes. Sugar was the chief product; to-day it is cocoa, and the one-time negro slaves have now become peasant proprietors. Most of them retain the ancient faith taught by the early French missionaries and some still speak a French *patois*. The island has prospered under British rule and is now one of the happiest of the West Indies. Dominica has a similar history. The two islands now have more than a hundred thousand inhabitants. The new territory won in the north was baffling in extent. The Gulf of St. Lawrence is an arm of the sea so wide that there is room across the entrance for an island,

16

good soldiers, but they had found the discipline of the military camp irksome and had deserted in such numbers that, in the last stage of the war, the army defending Montreal contained a mere handful of Canadians. We may be sure that none of those who had slipped away to their farms made any claim to be carried to France. Though French, they were proud to call themselves not Frenchmen but Canadians. A little later we find exact parallels in the American Revolution. Though George Washington was English he was not an Englishman but a Virginian.

A visitor might have thought Canada well peopled. The farms fronting on the great highway, the St. Lawrence, consisted usually of long narrow strips running back from the river, with the dwellings near each other. A few villages had well-built stone churches. The strain of a long war had, however, brought many Canadians to a pitiable condition. Stretching eastward on both sides of the St. Lawrence below Quebec were the blackened ruins of farm houses and villages destroyed by Wolfe's order as a military necessity. The churches alone had been left; and now near them and along the primitive roads the inhabitants, free at last from war, were building rough shelters for their wives and their swarming children and once more ploughing their fields.

Though each of the two cities, Quebec and Montreal, had then fewer than ten thousand people, they made an impressive appearance. The Castle of St. Louis, on the edge of the cliff at Quebec, had been the scene of a court that had preserved something of the stateliness and formal manners of the old world. There were two Quebecs; the upper town, approached by a road of all but impossible steepness, was the chief scene of social life, while in the lower town, stretching along the river and along the great basin into which the river broadens, were the quays and

Newfoundland, three hundred miles long. The gulf narrows into a mighty river, "the finest in the Universe," as General Murray, the first British governor, called it. Though these waters stretch westward from the entrance for a thousand miles to Montreal, this town lay only at the gate to the country. The great interior beyond it had broad rivers and great lakes vast like the sea.

When Pitt left office in 1761 he had been offered the post of governor of Canada at a salary of five thousand pounds. On the face of it the proposal to send the greatest statesman of the time to rule the conquered country seems to show appreciation of a difficult situation. There was, however, no thought that Pitt should cross the ocean; he was assured that he might remain in England and rule by a deputy, while those who had driven him from power should have their reward in muzzling a pensioner on their bounty. Had Pitt accepted the proposal, he might have mastered the vital questions involved in the conquest that was due to his genius, and in consequence might have made happier the history of North America. Though he declined the offer, he was, in truth, muzzled, since he accepted a pension of three thousands pounds and, for a time, gave the ministry a half contemptuous support. John Wilkes, soon to be engaged in his prolonged struggle with George III, aspired to be governor of Quebec and seems to have had the support of Pitt. No more than Pitt would he have gone to Canada; while he should have the prestige and the salary of the office, others would have done the work.

The problem of wise government in Canada called for liberal training. To learn how best to rule the French was important and in addition events soon showed that relations with the English colonies required special tact and insight. While it was not to be expected that a statesman of Pitt's rank would give his years to a task so obscure, a lesser man trained in politics might have done the needed work. Instead, however, military officers, admirable in character, it is true, but with the limited outlook of their type of mind, were sent to rule a conquered country and this unhappy practice continued during four score years. The first two governors, Murray and Carleton, had fought in Wolfe's last battle. When, in the late autumn of 1760, most of the British forces were withdrawn from Canada, three officers were left in charge of the three areas into which Canada had been divided during the French régime. General Thomas Gage commanded at Montreal, Colonel Burton, a mediocrity, at Three Rivers, and General James Murray remained as military governor of Quebec which he had defended during the year between its surrender to the British and the final fall of French power. As the capital, it was the most important place in Canada. When military rule ended in 1764, Murray became civil governor of all Canada with the task, heavy for a soldier untrained in civil affairs, of reconciling a French people to rule on the model of England.

Unlike the Acadians, so ruthlessly removed in 1755 from Nova Scotia, the Canadians had received a specific pledge that, while they might retire to France, they might also stay in Canada, hold their property, and have, as the event proved, the free exercise of their religion. A few went to France and we hear from these exiles plaintive appeals to the French king for aid. He made them some allowances and they formed a society of *émigrés* in or near towns in Touraine and Berry. Scanty records have made it difficult to learn the extent of this exodus from conquered Canada. It was long believed that most persons of position and property migrated and that Canada was left with an ignorant and backward population chiefly of peasants and artizans. We may well ask, however, what prospect either seigneur or habitant who sold or abandoned land in Canada

would confront in France. Many of its peasantry were on the border land of starvation, with discontent so acute that it soon led to revolution. The trading classes had seen their commerce driven from the sea by the maritime power of Britain; and the upper classes, themselves greedy for pensions and other favours of the court, were not likely to show sympathy for new-comers from a despised colony that, in their view, had always been a burden and was now seen to have been rooted in corruption. The two chief classes who left Canada were the officials of the French government and the soldiers, neither of them with any lasting stake in the country. Perhaps beyond any other nation the French are attached to their own soil, the soil of France. Amid the rigours of the winter at Quebec, Montcalm had pined for the warmth and sunshine of his home in that south of France which now lures so many visitors in the winter. Naturally few of the soldiers who served under him and had claims for employment at home or for a pension wished to remain in a forlorn colony now to be ruled by a victorious and hated rival nation. For those, however, whose home had always been Canada, the outlook was different. Canadian officers, hoping to be welcomed in the motherland as restored sons, were soon embittered by neglect. Their chief means consisted in the paper money issued under the French régime for both supplies and military pay. Though it was in the end redeemed, but at a discount, it long seemed valueless and was so regarded in France.

It is broadly true that the Canadians remained in their former homes and accepted the fortunes of war and the new allegiance to the British king. Colonel Haldimand, for a time in command at Three Rivers, reported that perhaps not ten wished to go from there to France and General Murray in command at Quebec says that ships were provided for six times as many as desired to sail. The Canadians were, as both French and British officers testified, naturally

Newfoundland, three hundred miles long. The gulf narrows into a mighty river, "the finest in the Universe," as General Murray, the first British governor, called it. Though these waters stretch westward from the entrance for a thousand miles to Montreal, this town lay only at the gate to the country. The great interior beyond it had broad rivers and great lakes vast like the sea.

When Pitt left office in 1761 he had been offered the post of governor of Canada at a salary of five thousand pounds. On the face of it the proposal to send the greatest statesman of the time to rule the conquered country seems to show appreciation of a difficult situation. There was, however, no thought that Pitt should cross the ocean; he was assured that he might remain in England and rule by a deputy, while those who had driven him from power should have their reward in muzzling a pensioner on their bounty. Had Pitt accepted the proposal, he might have mastered the vital questions involved in the conquest that was due to his genius, and in consequence might have made happier the history of North America. Though he declined the offer, he was, in truth, muzzled, since he accepted a pension of three thousands pounds and, for a time, gave the ministry a half contemptuous support. John Wilkes, soon to be engaged in his prolonged struggle with George III, aspired to be governor of Quebec and seems to have had the support of Pitt. No more than Pitt would he have gone to Canada; while he should have the prestige and the salary of the office, others would have done the work.

The problem of wise government in Canada called for liberal training. To learn how best to rule the French was important and in addition events soon showed that relations with the English colonies required special tact and insight. While it was not to be expected that a statesman of Pitt's rank would give his years to a task so obscure, a

lesser man trained in politics might have done the needed
work. Instead, however, military officers, admirable in
character, it is true, but with the limited outlook of their
type of mind, were sent to rule a conquered country and
this unhappy practice continued during four score years.
The first two governors, Murray and Carleton, had fought
in Wolfe's last battle. When, in the late autumn of 1760,
most of the British forces were withdrawn from Canada,
three officers were left in charge of the three areas into
which Canada had been divided during the French régime.
General Thomas Gage commanded at Montreal, Colonel
Burton, a mediocrity, at Three Rivers, and General James
Murray remained as military governor of Quebec which he
had defended during the year between its surrender to the
British and the final fall of French power. As the capital,
it was the most important place in Canada. When military
rule ended in 1764, Murray became civil governor of all
Canada with the task, heavy for a soldier untrained in civil
affairs, of reconciling a French people to rule on the model
of England.

Unlike the Acadians, so ruthlessly removed in 1755 from
Nova Scotia, the Canadians had received a specific pledge
that, while they might retire to France, they might also stay
in Canada, hold their property, and have, as the event
proved, the free exercise of their religion. A few went to
France and we hear from these exiles plaintive appeals to
the French king for aid. He made them some allowances
and they formed a society of *émigrés* in or near towns in
Touraine and Berry. Scanty records have made it difficult
to learn the extent of this exodus from conquered Canada.
It was long believed that most persons of position and
property migrated and that Canada was left with an
ignorant and backward population chiefly of peasants and
artizans. We may well ask, however, what prospect either
seigneur or habitant who sold or abandoned land in Canada

would confront in France. Many of its peasantry were on the border land of starvation, with discontent so acute that it soon led to revolution. The trading classes had seen their commerce driven from the sea by the maritime power of Britain; and the upper classes, themselves greedy for pensions and other favours of the court, were not likely to show sympathy for new-comers from a despised colony that, in their view, had always been a burden and was now seen to have been rooted in corruption. The two chief classes who left Canada were the officials of the French government and the soldiers, neither of them with any lasting stake in the country. Perhaps beyond any other nation the French are attached to their own soil, the soil of France. Amid the rigours of the winter at Quebec, Montcalm had pined for the warmth and sunshine of his home in that south of France which now lures so many visitors in the winter. Naturally few of the soldiers who served under him and had claims for employment at home or for a pension wished to remain in a forlorn colony now to be ruled by a victorious and hated rival nation. For those, however, whose home had always been Canada, the outlook was different. Canadian officers, hoping to be welcomed in the motherland as restored sons, were soon embittered by neglect. Their chief means consisted in the paper money issued under the French régime for both supplies and military pay. Though it was in the end redeemed, but at a discount, it long seemed valueless and was so regarded in France.

It is broadly true that the Canadians remained in their former homes and accepted the fortunes of war and the new allegiance to the British king. Colonel Haldimand, for a time in command at Three Rivers, reported that perhaps not ten wished to go from there to France and General Murray in command at Quebec says that ships were provided for six times as many as desired to sail. The Canadians were, as both French and British officers testified, naturally good soldiers, but they had found the discipline of the military camp irksome and had deserted in such numbers that, in the last stage of the war, the army defending Montreal contained a mere handful of Canadians. We may be sure that none of those who had slipped away to their farms made any claim to be carried to France. Though French, they were proud to call themselves not Frenchmen but Canadians. A little later we find exact parallels in the American Revolution. Though George Washington was English he was not an Englishman but a Virginian.

A visitor might have thought Canada well peopled. The farms fronting on the great highway, the St. Lawrence, consisted usually of long narrow strips running back from the river, with the dwellings near each other. A few villages had well-built stone churches. The strain of a long war had, however, brought many Canadians to a pitiable condition. Stretching eastward on both sides of the St. Lawrence below Quebec were the blackened ruins of farm houses and villages destroyed by Wolfe's order as a military necessity. The churches alone had been left; and now near them and along the primitive roads the inhabitants, free at last from war, were building rough shelters for their wives and their swarming children and once more ploughing their fields.

Though each of the two cities, Quebec and Montreal, had then fewer than ten thousand people, they made an impressive appearance. The Castle of St. Louis, on the edge of the cliff at Quebec, had been the scene of a court that had preserved something of the stateliness and formal manners of the old world. There were two Quebecs; the upper town, approached by a road of all but impossible steepness, was the chief scene of social life, while in the lower town, stretching along the river and along the great basin into which the river broadens, were the quays and the business houses. Since the war-ships in the river could do little damage against the upper town and were themselves an easy mark for its defenders, Wolfe had planted two batteries on the opposite shore at Point Levi, and they had knocked to pieces the buildings within range. Some of these had been set on fire and now their walls stood gaunt and roofless. For years still the débris made Quebec seem a cheerless memorial of the devastation of war.

Montreal had escaped this ruin and by contrast with Quebec seemed to the British, who occupied it in 1760 without striking a blow, to possess greater beauty and charm. "For delightfulness of situation," says Captain John Knox, "I think I never saw any town to equal it. The great stone buildings, the charming gardens within the walls, and the people, some of them as well-dressed as if on promenade in a European capital, gave it a striking dignity." No doubt this effect was partly due to the contrast with ruined Quebec which remained, however, and is still the seat of government, while Montreal has become the chief commercial city of Canada with more than a million people.

This community of French people was now to be governed by a long-hated enemy. Each nation believed its civilization superior to the other's and each could claim past triumphs. England had been conquered by Normans from France who, during hundreds of years, had imposed their customs and language on the English court; later, on the other hand, an English king had mastered France and had caused to be burned at the stake Joan of Arc, whom the French made their national heroine. Dozens of battlefields from Crécy and Agincourt to scenes of the Seven Years' War had been stained with mingled French and English blood. The two peoples seemed perversely different; they spoke different languages; in religion one was

Protestant, the other Roman Catholic; one had shaken off
feudalism and the relation of lord and vassal, while the
other had still the customs of the feudal age; the British
were a sea-faring people, the French had won their chief
glories on land. And now branches of these people, so
strangely variant, had to learn to work together in a common British citizenship. While most Canadians had little
affection for the France that had ruled them, they loved
the culture of that chivalrous, self-centred France, which
believed that her civilization fitted her to lead the world.

James Murray, the younger son of the Scottish Earl of
Elibank, to whom was committed the task of governing
Canada, had fought under Wolfe and had been left in command at Quebec during its first winter under British rule.
In the spring that followed he had had the humbling
experience of complete defeat before its walls on the ground
where a few months earlier Wolfe had gained the victory
that meant the fall of French power in North America. In
spite of this lost battle of Sainte-Foy Murray, unlike Quebec's defenders against Wolfe, defied the victor on the plains
before it and held out until the arrival of a British fleet in
May, 1760, caused the quick flight of the besieging French
army. The merits and defects of Murray's character had
already become apparent before he was left in the autumn
of 1760 to the lonely and thankless task of governing an
alien people in a land devastated by war and of giving a
just rule both to the old inhabitants and to the British
new-comers. He had a quick and rash temper and a gift of
invective that he used too freely. For trade and traders he
had the scorn of the aristocrat of the time and there was
almost no villainy that he was not ready to attribute to
those from England and from the English colonies who,
after 1760, sought fortune in Canada, an unexplored field
hitherto closed to them. He was, on the other hand, tactful

and generous in his relations with the depressed and anxious people whom France had abandoned. During the last campaign he had denounced to French officers, his prisoners, the dilatory methods of his leader, Amherst, who took three years for a victory that, Murray said, ought to have been gained in one. With this keen sympathy for the vanquished people, he resented the tone of some of the thoughtless victors who seemed to wish to treat them as slaves.

In those days of abuses in high places some governors of English colonies drew large salaries but did nothing to earn them. During some years General Amherst was governor of Virginia which he never saw. Murray himself retained the military post of governor of Quebec long after he had left Canada. While there, however, he was zealous to do his duty. He liked the country. Though to many of his fellow officers it seemed a cheerless land of biting cold, the climate and other conditions so suited him that he wished never to leave Canada. "The conquered country," he wrote to his brother, "is a noble one indeed—infinitely beyond what any Briton imagined it to be, whether for the fertility of its soil, or number of its inhabitants." He borrowed money from his brother Lord Elibank to buy estates, among them the great seigniory of Lauzon, across the river from Quebec, which to-day contains the town of Levis and many pleasant villages. He hoped that his beautiful and attractive English wife would join him at Quebec where she might well have supplied a gentle tact to soften his bluster, but she would not cross the sea. Though Murray wrote, promising magnificent clothes, and a "handsome showy coach," the lady, while protesting that she loved him as much as a woman ever loved a man, could not be induced to brave the discomforts of an ocean voyage that might last three months.

Murray describes the working of the old French administration and the corrupt extravagance of its later days.

Agriculture had suffered because, for private gain, "greedy and avaricious" officials had withdrawn the farmers from their proper tasks. In any case the fascination of the free life of the forest had tended to draw men away from the farms. This would now be changed, since the British had taken away the fire-arms required in hunting. There was material for industries in the iron at Three Rivers, and in the ash, hickory, walnut, maple and other hard woods of the forest. Murray passes lightly over the rich fur trade, in reality so important that for many years it dominated British policy in the great west. Under the French régime it had been a source of corruption as the monopoly of a few favourites of the governor. To Murray, son of a maritime nation, the fisheries seemed more important. The chill northern waters gave them the best quality in all the world. There were breeding places and natural harbours in many sheltered bays and inlets. The least encouragement would, he says, make every man a fisherman and a sailor and thus add to British maritime power. On the smaller rivers there was salmon fishing that gave profit to the fisherman and delight to the sportsman. The cod fishery in the great river and gulf of St. Lawrence might "in time prove an inexhaustible source of wealth and power." The whale fishery could be carried on "with less risk and expense than in any other seas." Had the French attended to this "with as much eagerness as they grasped at the insignificant Fur Trade, how formidable might this colony have proved to be!"

The fur trade was not really insignificant. By it during the next half century large fortunes were made in Montreal, New York and London. It was the link between the older society from Europe and the many Indian tribes who roamed in the vast spaces of the interior. They needed the fire-arms and other products of Europe and paid for them with the furs of wild animals. Inevitably adventurous spirits in the Canadian village turned from the cramped life of the farm to the rugged adventure of the *coureur-de-bois*. It had colour and change, long days of paddling on lake and river past forest-clad shores, sport in hunting and fishing, nervous contact with the caprices of savage tribes, the lure of dusky native women who reared families of half-breed children, tired lounging by camp fires after the day's work; with song and story and, not rarely, wild revels inspired by the fire-water that was almost the coinage of trade. The *coureur-de-bois* was himself half Indian in dress and outlook and sometimes in primitive savagery. When he returned to his native village he might be a restless menace to its peace, apt to spend his earnings with reckless abandon and then to be off again, perhaps inducing to go with him other adventurous spirits chafing at their dull routine. Usually he was hardy, cheerful, unawed by danger. To this day the French Canadian is the best guide in the wilds, the most skilful trapper and voyageur on inland waters. He and his leaders scattered over a continent where many French names still endure as memorials of their wanderings. Their easy-going fellowship with the natives, their freedom from the racial aloofness of the English, helped to make the tribes friendly to the French. They had done little, however, to build up Canada. While the English created on or near the sea-coast colonies strong in agriculture and trade and supporting some two million people, the *coureur-de-bois* remained a wanderer in the wilderness and New France had only a few inhabitants.

The Canadian habitant was robust, ignorant, for few could read, ingenious in his handiwork, self-reliant in his daily tasks and inured to rugged toil, fatigue and cold. He built his own house. He made its furniture, and also the *charette* which was his waggon and the *calèche,* his carriage. There was a spinning-wheel in every house and the housewife's homespun clothed the family. The warm tuque with a tassel dangling at the side of the man's head; his habit held in at the waist by a sash of bright colour; the dresses of the women; underclothing of linen from home-grown flax; the coverlet on the bed; the rag carpet on the floor; the soap and the candles; even the straw hats worn in the field; all were home products. The habitant was his own butcher and he tanned with lye from the ashes of his fire the hides of his own cattle to make his harness and the *bottes sauvages* still seen in rural parts. The wooden rakes, buckets and bowls, the baskets and brooms in use, might be made by him. If he carried his grain to be ground in the seigneur's mill, he paid for the service in this product. He might have his own forge to shoe his horses and for other work in iron. What food agriculture failed to supply was to be secured by hunting and fishing. The Canadians were such smokers of home-grown tobacco that children went about with pipes in their mouths. Murray says that the severity of the climate had led to drinking habits even among women and children. He describes the Canadian women as lively but not beautiful, the men as quarrelsome and easily offended.

At the top of the social scale was the seigneur, in some cases descended from the lesser *noblesse* of France. He was the owner of an estate often vast, to whom feudal dues were paid, the magistrate by whom offenders were tried. In priest and seigneur centred the chief authority that touched the daily life of the Canadian village. That of the priest was, however, the greater. Since the seigneur had been often absent, perhaps in the train of the governor at Quebec, or on military service, or in command at some post in the interior reaping what fortune he could from the fur trade, his relations with his people might be distant. When at home the poorest seigneur might without loss of dignity plough his own fields, or even keep an inn, while at the same time professing an aristocratic scorn for the shopkeeper and despising the paid labour of the mechanic. The more prosperous seigneur tended to look upon the manor house as the mansion of a lord with his vassals about him; the priest, on the other hand, shared the intimate life of the humblest of his people. When, after the conquest, some seigneurs sold their grants to new English owners, Protestants, out of sympathy with the people's faith, the curé was alone as the universal friend and teacher.

Though the upper clergy, born in France, would, Murray reported, find it hard to live under British rule, the lower clergy, Canadian by birth, of restricted vision, but with roots in the country, would easily acquiesce. They were devoted to their spiritual duties, and the village curés had vast parishes. Naturally, with a population so scattered, schools were few and the long war had increased this defect. There were, however, schools in the towns, under nuns and under members of the Jesuit and other orders. In Quebec there was an excellent seminary for boys. Most of the people in rural parts were illiterate, as indeed they were still in both France and England. There were few books and no newspapers. Agriculture was primitive. Sometimes to get rid of manure the farmers would throw it on ice-covered streams that it might be carried away by the floods in the spring. Murray thought that they kept too many horses and should rather breed horned cattle. But, whatever their defects, the Canadians were a virile race, active, healthy and moral. "No people can be more at their ease", said a later traveller, who was so critical as to call them "a cheerful, lazy, dirty, ignorant, happy people" working in a leisurely way and much given to friendly dissipation. They were too fond of disputes at law, an outcome perhaps of the obscurities of their legal system, feudal in character. The census taken by the victors showed only seventy-six thousand people in the country. But because the women were prolific, Murray ventured a prophecy to be abundantly fulfilled that they "will produce a vast increase of people."

There was a time-honoured patriarchal family life. While the father commanded veneration and respect, the mother, often the better educated, led in the family worship, carefully observed in many households; planned, if any one did, for the training and education of the children, and was the guardian of the family purse. The sense of the unity of the family is strong to this day; always the door must be open to receive returning members ill or unfortunate. Families are still so large that sometimes the rule that the curé must provide for the twenty-sixth child actually brings him such a ward, perhaps as some return for the twenty-sixth of the grain as his tithe. Often the house contains two families, that of the patriarch father and that of one of his sons who will inherit the family property and carry on its traditions. Not usually is he the eldest son since he, while the family is growing up, would have to go out to make his own place and leave the younger members to aid in the work of the farm. Life in the village was and remains friendly; an old French proverb asks what can be dearer to a man, after his family, than his neighbour. If a neighbour's house should burn, the villagers would help to rebuild it. They gather freely at each other's houses for diversions that have behind them a long tradition. The curé's counsel is always respected if not always obeyed. By an old custom the right of sanctuary of mediæval times is still valid for the wrong-doer who may take refuge in the house of the curé.

About two-thirds of the population of Canada knew only their own village life and, primitive though it might be, it had its charm. Neighbours so visited each other that on a Sunday the country roads in the more settled parts were alive with calèches or carrioles. The people were all of one religion. Of a Sunday morning all went to mass, heard at the church door public notices of parochial interest, and loitered to exchange news and gossip and perhaps to consult

régime. On Sundays they read the public notices at the church doors where the people gathered and they were now ordered to hear complaints and to settle disputes on the basis of the laws and customs with which the people were familiar. Should this method fail, the officer commanding the troops in the district was to act and in serious cases the governor himself. Some of the British officers spoke French and had this means of understanding the conquered people. The soldiers were told that they must live "in harmony and good fellowship" with the inhabitants. To ease the scarcity due to war the traders of the neighbouring British colonies were invited to bring to Canada "all sorts of provisions and supplies." So conciliatory to the Canadians were the new British rulers that English civilians complained that they were under the heel of the French. One of them writing from Montreal on November 1, 1763, says that they are summoned in French to a French court, where they do not understand the language and must employ an interpreter. Their property is subject to a captain of militia, who treats them with contempt and scurrility. "We labour under the Galling Yoke of the Oppressor," they said, and added that when they complained they were told they had no right to be in Canada, that France would soon retake it.

The Canada of to-day would in some respects dismay and in some console its French founders. The fiery governor, Frontenac, looking out upon the St. Lawrence from the Castle of St. Louis, had thought the scene one of the most striking in all the world and had pictured a day when the tide that surges now inward now outward in a mighty flood should carry the commerce of an expanded France and make Quebec a busy French seaport. We may imagine the inner fury of Frontenac could he have seen in 1759 the flag of a rival nation fluttering high over the fortress where

he had defied English attack. Hardly a stone's throw from
the castle arose soon an enduring monument of British
victory, a modest church, in the Georgian style, that ranks
as the cathedral of the Church of England in Quebec. A
little farther inland are now great buildings that house a
Parliament where the traditions and rules of the Parliament
of England are applied in full force. Yet, none the less, in
this seat of government, France survives in great vigour.
The debates are almost wholly in French and the sons of
France are supreme in this political world. In that of religion, too, the France of the old régime still prevails. The
first bishop, surveying modern Quebec, might find that he
had laid here enduring foundations. At the head of the road
from the lower to the upper town now stands a colossal
statue of Laval as if welcoming a visitor to a Catholic city.
Close at hand are the massive buildings of a university that
bears his name and the great school for boys founded by
him with its quadrangle unmistakably of the France of
Louis XIV. The lectures in the philosophical faculty of the
university are still given in Latin. The literature chiefly
studied is not in the tongue of Shakespeare but in the
French of Bossuet and Racine. The cathedral nearby is
on the spot where Laval went to the unheated church before
daylight on winter days and remained so long absorbed in
devotion that at last the frail body perished from the deadly
chill. In the neighbouring episcopal palace rules still a
prelate whose tongue is French and who preserves in his
diocese the traditions of France, first brought here more
than three hundred years ago. Great convent buildings,
schools, hospitals and churches crowd on the sight in Quebec. At the cathedral is communion plate given by Louis
XIV; in the chapel of the Ursulines is shown the skull of
Montcalm, a grim reminder of man's mortality in contrast
with the sparkling vitality of this son of the radiant south.
The most treasured memorials are all French.

Montreal, too, is still chiefly a French and Catholic city. The influential English minority have, indeed, their great university, their churches and clubs. In one of their vast hotels a visitor might fancy himself remote from French Canada, for the wider business of Montreal and the bustle of its travel are chiefly English. But this English element, always a minority, forms in reality a separate community. In Montreal more than two-thirds of the people are French in speech, in religious life and in social customs. Here, as in Quebec, great Catholic churches, monastic buildings, schools, hospitals, are among the most striking features of the city. Religious orders, proscribed in France, are here active and rich; one of them, the Sulpicians, remains the chief owner of land in Montreal. Its wealth is used for the wide purposes of the order; little of it goes to priests and teachers. These serve for no worldly gain. The celibate professors in Laval University receive in money a meagre hundred dollars a year. It happened at least once that, in need of money to aid a friend, the rector at its head was able to earn a few dollars by copying manuscripts for the Canadian Archives.

The Roman Church is not the church of one but of many nations. Its head claims to be the Vicar of Christ on earth and its mission is to the whole world. Accordingly, when the British had secured Canada, it was not hard for the church to accept, in place of Louis XV of France, George III of England. It seemed indeed happy in the hour of transfer for then the French monarchy, the church's bulwark, was on the eve of the resounding fall that brought disaster to both church and monarchy. France confiscated the property of the church and sent to death many of its priests. In contrast with these events in France the church in the Canada that had just come under the alien British ruler soon enjoyed the fullest liberty, untrammeled by the state in respect of either its property or its teaching. It has so prospered under a Protestant king that to-day it is even freer in Canada that it had been in the age of Louis XIV, since that king, as the eldest son of the church, had some authority in church affairs. His favourites became bishops, the revenues of convents and abbeys rewarded his nominees, often more secular than spiritual in outlook. A civil court, the Parlement of Paris, exercised a certain jurisdiction respecting marriage, excommunication, and even absolution for the dying. To this day in republican France a priest in clerical dress may not enter the municipal school. On the other hand in the Canada that was New France the church preserves wide privileges. The pope appoints the bishops and these name the curés. The parish priest has the legal right to the tithe on grain. What he receives is not large for his tithe is only one twenty-sixth of the crop, but this right gives him a real security in the village and a measure of authority in secular affairs. If the majority in a parish decide to levy a tax for new church buildings or for improvements, or even to buy the land for a cemetery, the state will enforce the right on all the Catholic parishioners as it enforces its own levies for schools, roads or police. The schools in Quebec are either Protestant or Catholic but, while those of the Protestant minority are few, those of the Catholic majority include most of the population and in them every child is instructed by teachers, paid by the state, in the beliefs and traditions of the Roman Church. No wonder that, to preserve this system, the bishops keep watch over what the people read, and prefer for them a certain isolation from the English-speaking society with a different outlook.

France is the conqueror in spirit, not the conquered, in the valley of the St. Lawrence. In most rural districts English is rarely heard. It is true that in town and village there is something English for the people have now what was unknown under French rule, the excitement of electing those who shall govern them. The habitant takes this interest seriously, crowds to great meetings and is likely to be a fervent party man. While in politics he may be so aggressive in asserting his liberty as to warn his spiritual leaders to attempt no dictation in that field, in the world of religion he is submissive. It is, he believes, the priest's task to instruct him in its solemn mysteries and to tell him with authority what a Christian should believe and do. In contrast with the Anglo-Saxon world many of the people have a frank belief in saints who protect and devils who molest them and they find guidance and comfort in the curé's teaching. He keeps before them ultimate things, sin and repentance, the love and the severity of God, the meaning of sacrifice, the certainty of death and the need to prepare for it. On Sunday he is up often before dawn for services and confessions and sometimes he fasts until well on in the day.

The mark of the church is on the country itself. Along quiet country roads are wayside crosses like those so numerous in Brittany. Sometimes standing close to the swift waters of the majestic St. Lawrence, sometimes high on a cliff overlooking it, sometimes inland with a background of blue mountains, but everywhere at short intervals, the traveller finds a church usually of grey stone surmounted by a steeple. Huge convent buildings are found even in small villages. In the churchyard may stand three tall crosses on which are figures showing the agony of Christ on the cross with the two malefactors at his side. Social life centres in the church and the adjoining presbytery. The parishes are large but, at least once a year, the priest visits every household and often he is accompanied on his survey by a church-warden. It is rare that even a seemingly careless parishioner should fail to take the communion at Easter. On Sunday mornings the roads are alive with people going to or from mass.

Enter the church at, it may be, the dusk of the evening. In the poorest of them some light glimmers night and day before the altar and perhaps at stations of the cross, symbols of reverence for the Light of the World. In the twilight dim figures may be seen kneeling; old men or women, peering into and preparing for the mystery of death; troubled souls asking for hope and strength; youth trying here to tame an emotion to the will of God. Even in the early morning of a week day one will find that religion plays an impressive part in the village. There is much coming and going at the presbytery. The curé advises, rebukes, encourages those in perplexity or contrition; he is consulted about family relations, about a project in business or the making of a will. In the confessional he hears the well-worn tale of human frailty. He is supreme in the village school. When he is called to the bedside of a dying parishioner and carries with him the host, a warning bell is rung in the moving vehicle and the people kneel reverently by the wayside as he passes. Whatever the murmurs, should he dabble in politics, there is little sign in the parish of revolt against his spiritual authority. The women are his faithful allies. Trained often with the refining discipline of the convent, they manage the affairs of the household with an alert economy like that found in the peasant and the bourgeois families of France. The farmer in Canada as in France clings to the land. Many families have been on the same land during two hundred years or more. The families are large. In a single parish in the diocese of Quebec there were fifteen families with from twelve to nineteen children. While in Canada a childless family is a reproach, by contrast France has some two million households without children and more than three million with only one child.

Rénan said of the clergy in France "I have never known any but good priests" and this would be the general testimony of the people in Quebec. Often, perhaps usually, the curés are men of humble origin, but sometimes they have the refined bearing of the aristocrat of the old régime. A curé may spend his leisure in studying the fascinating story of French martyrs and explorers in founding this Catholic society or in writing the annals of his parish. If few reach literary distinction, it is still true that Quebec has records of its past more complete perhaps than those of any other part of North America. Hardly a prominent family but has its printed history. Quebec, a French outpost in the English-speaking continent, is preserved by its traditions and discipline from the absorbing influence of a potent alien culture. The people strike the observer as gay in spirit. They are fond of music and delight in folk-songs. If they read little they have much social diversion. There is enjoyment in the village. Of an evening neighbours come together and may divide into three groups. In the salon the young dance, checked from too great *abandon* by the curé; in the kitchen the middle-aged play cards; while in the grand salon the elders listen in awed silence to the *conteur* who repeats the tale of strange events, of mysterious beasts such as the loup-garou, and of wonders from the world of spirits in which most have an intense belief. The *chanteur* has sometimes a collection of hundreds of songs chiefly from the past of France. A favourite relates to the death of Marlborough whose victories over France startled and alarmed the whole nation. Often the housewife sings *chansons* to the tune of the shuttle in her weaving, and the habitant, beating his arms to keep warm on a winter day as he walks behind his cart for protection from the wind, will pour out songs on the frosty air. Perhaps there is in the minds of the villagers little of the broodings of those who

> "watched the sorrow of the evening sky
> And smelt the sea, and the earth and the warm clover,
> And heard the waves and the sea-gulls, mocking cry."

They are not a melancholy but a cheerful people, well content with the daily round of life and they form a stable, well-organized element in this New France that has become British.

This Canada is in truth an older France, a France of the age of faith and an undivided church. In some respects conditions in the villages have hardly changed since 1763. We have still, though sometimes with a relapse into more vulgar modernity, the long low houses built close to the village street. Over the village towers the church spire, its tin covering flashing in the sunlight. The talk of the Paris boulevard is so far away that French Canada, though of the shifting new world, changes less in outlook than does France herself, that most conservative of modern nations. Yet, though the parish is half remote from the skeptical questionings of modern thought, some of these filter in. The village curé who passes along the street in his black *soutane* is often troubled by some new unrest. His position is, however, still secure. He is absorbed in his own world and gives entire devotion to his tasks. He has travelled as far as Quebec or Montreal, often even to Rome or Paris. He has had contact with the English that enables him to speak their language brokenly. With charming courtesy he will converse, if necessary, in that tongue, but the world that speaks English and crowds into great cities is remote from his thought. Mention Canadian places such as Toronto or Winnipeg and he may murmur "Ah, that is very far away." Not even the Jews surpass him and his people in tenacious adherence to their customs. Though France has made no effort to draw them back to herself, in them too is the spirit of that France where, so she likes to think, during two thousand years she has established a nation the most firmly cemented in spirit of any in the world. The Canadians maintain their national character in an alien world of another tongue and faith. They have a firm belief that

"Un peuple peut changer de nom et de allegeance,
Mais de mère jamais . . . si sa mère est La France." *

*A people may change name and allegiance, but mother never,—if the mother is France.

CHAPTER III

THE PERPLEXITIES OF THE FIRST BRITISH GOVERNOR
OF CANADA

THE imagination of General James Murray might well have been staggered by his complex task in 1763 not only of defending Britain's new conquest but of bringing content under British rule to the former subjects of the King of France. Murray had the outlook and the prejudices of the soldier. He lived in a scene where military pomp, bugle calls, drill on the parade ground, sentries on guard and officers and men in uniform were part of the daily routine of life. No hostess graced his receptions and dinners, and usually it was fellow officers who sat with him at table and drank his wine. The talk, we may be sure, was more of past campaigns and military plans and dangers than of the wider problems of the mind on which, in this same period, Boswell was so eagerly noting the wisdom of Dr. Johnson.

Military dangers, in truth, there were. The Indian tribes of the interior were so restless at the change from French to British sovereignty that even before peace was signed in 1763 they were holding the secret conferences that resulted in treacherous and savage massacre on the western frontier. Nor was this the only danger. If in London Horace Walpole could boast of British victories that rivalled those of Rome's greatest generals, across the Channel in France was a military nation embittered by defeat and soon planning the revenge that within a score of years humbled Britain's pride. France would be likely to appeal and soon did ap-

42

peal to her sons in Canada to cure the ignominy of their conquest by a hated rival nation. Though in this situation Murray would be under orders from the British Commander-in-Chief at New York, a wilderness separated the two leaders and Murray had to make his own plans.

Unlike the English colonies, Canada had been won by the sword and was destined during nearly eighty years to be governed by men of the sword. Those who in this long period ruled Canada were veterans of the Seven Years' War, or of the Revolutionary War, or of the later struggle with France. As late as in 1837 when, owing to delay in concessions to the people, armed rebellion broke out, the governor was a soldier who had fought with Wellington at Waterloo. Inevitably this type of ruler had slight instinct and less knowledge to shape with sympathy the evolution of a political society. In consequence, those in power in Canada tried for the most part to hold colonial life in enduring control from London and denounced as disloyal rebels those who favoured the growth of liberal ideas in which England herself was setting the example. Demands of the masses of the people in Canada for political power met with anathema. Democracy was satanic.

The contrast with the United States is striking and helps to explain the economic stagnation that observers noted in Canada. The earlier presidents of the United States were well versed in the problems of civil life, far removed from the soldier's tone of discipline and obedience. Though Washington had led the armies of the republic he was much less soldier than statesman, while his successors, Adams, Jefferson and Madison, were deeply learned in the literature of politics and had an enthusiastic share in the triumphs of a democratic republic. To-day we are not convinced that democracy has yet found the key to social well-being, but it served for the rapid development of a great nation. The city of Washington became a stirring political centre while Quebec under its military governor long remained little more than a fortress.

At Quebec Murray's metal was tested in the autumn of 1763. The soldier of the time remained long in foreign service and had so broken with family ties that the life of the barracks was his all. Often, during many months, and even for two or three years, his pay might be in arrears. Since at best it was meagre and at Quebec prices were high, he naturally resented any new charges. In England, however, Grenville, who had just come into office, was, on the one hand, sowing the seeds of the American Revolution by his efforts to increase revenue through new taxes levied on the colonies while, on the other hand, he was trying to enforce a rigid economy. Accordingly, just at the moment when a great empire had been won by the soldier, a new burden was laid upon him. During the war free rations had been issued, but this allowance was now stopped and, out of his shilling a day, the soldier must either pay fourpence for the daily ration of food, or feed himself. The order was issued at Quebec on September 18, 1763, and was to take effect the next day. The men were reminded that they were happily situated, in comparison with the troops at the remoter posts in the interior, exposed to the horrors of treachery and massacre by Indians. The order provided that each regiment should have a plot of ground in which to grow vegetables, but this had only remote promise, as winter was just coming on.

Disorder broke out at once. The men secured their arms and, with drums beating, marched to the St. John's gate. Some of the men struck their officers and, as night came on, Murray feared that they might sack the town. When he tried to reason with them they replied that, while they respected and loved their officers, "they could not live without victuals" and intended to go with two pieces of

artillery to lay their complaints at the feet of the commander-in-chief at New York, an impossible project considering the route and the distance. Next day Murray
paraded the garrison, urged the men, file by file, to behave
as soldiers, and at the same time warned the officers that
they must secure obedience or perish, since mutiny at Quebec, the strongest British fortress in America, would spread
to the other garrisons. On the twentieth, after Murray had
harangued each battalion, some of the men wavered. Next
morning he ordered a general parade at ten o'clock, read to
the men the articles of war, told Amherst's grenadiers that
he would kill the first man who disobeyed, and gave the
order to march back to barracks. There was a moment
of suspense, but discipline won the day and the regiment
marched away quietly. It is gratifying to know that, in the
end, the obnoxious order was rescinded. Lord Halifax wrote
to Murray: "I am commanded by His Majesty to express
to you in the strongest terms, His Royal Appreciation of
your distinguished Conduct, upon that trying Occasion."

The British government had had a long experience in
appointing colonial governors and Murray's commission,
dated November 21, 1763, gave adequate powers. With the
consent of his council, nominated by himself, he might
create courts, civil and criminal; appoint judges; pardon
offenders, except in cases of murder and treason; spend
public money; make grants of public lands; and name to
ecclesiastical benefices. He might levy troops and wage war
against "enemies, pirates and rebels" and "put to death or
keep and preserve alive" such persons. He might build forts
and castles. In respect of religion he was to give members
of the Roman church every right guaranteed by the treaty
of peace, but he was to permit no recognition of the authority of the pope in Canada.

Following Murray's commission came his amusingly

elaborate Instructions, dated December 7, 1763. They are based upon the Instructions to Governors in the English Colonies and contain eighty-two clauses, couched in the best official style, and requiring of him the virtues of an angel. Murray was to suppress "every Species of Vice and Immorality"; to enforce all laws against adultery, polygamy, profanation of the Lord's Day, swearing, drunkenness and other evils; to exclude from public office persons "whose ill-fame and conversation may occasion scandal"; and to take care "that God Almighty be dovoutly and duly served" throughout his government. To further these admirable ends the Church of England was to be established in Canada. Though Scotland, too, had a state church and many Scots found their way to Canada, Scottish Presbyterianism counted for so little in government circles that now every Protestant minister in Canada must have a certificate from the Bishop of London that he conformed to the doctrine and practice of the Church of England. Even a schoolmaster must have the bishop's licence while all other teachers than those in schools must have a licence from the governor.

Murray was to encourage the growing of hemp and flax to which the country seemed favourable. Timber for masts for the royal navy was to be specially reserved. He was to make careful enquiries into the state and numbers of the Indian tribes; to treat with them tactfully, and from time to time to give them presents. Since, in that age, one of the chief tasks of the king's government was to provide berths for its friends, Murray was solemnly warned "not to grant or dispose of any office or place" that the home government might choose to reserve for its own nominees. It was then and long after a settled policy to discourage manufactures in the colonies. "Upon pain of our highest displeasure," Murray was not, "upon any pretext whatever," to give his consent to the setting up of manufactures, or the carrying on of trade that might be prejudicial to Great Britain.

By the Treaty of Paris made on February 16, 1763, the French in Canada were to be allowed a year and a half to withdraw from the country and in consequence civil law was not introduced until August 10, 1764. Meanwhile to replace the French officials who had been carried back to France came new officials from England. They illustrate, perhaps, the worst feature of British rule at the time. Hangers-on of those in power clamoured for posts, in return for real or supposed services, with the result that in India and in Canada men were placed in authority who had no fitness for their work. It is true that, within a few years, in both India and Canada, the evil was corrected and systems based on justice and integrity were set up, but meanwhile unworthy officials disgraced the British name. The chief offices in Canada, Murray declared, had been put in the gift of a politician in England who sold them to the highest bidder. Canada became in a small way what Ireland had long been, a refuge for officials of a type too scandalous to be appointed in England. Gregory, the Chief Justice, was taken from jail where he was held for debt. This in itself in that age involved no moral disgrace but the Chief Justice, while a man of integrity, knew no French and was ignorant of French law. Both he and Suckling, the Attorney-General, had no training for the difficult task of ruling an alien people. Legal skill was needed to evolve what Canada required—law courts and the method of government suited to the needs of the country—and Murray should have had men trained in the institutions of both England and France. He describes the public coroner sent out, as "the most thorough-paced villain that ever existed." A civil system framed by a harassed soldier, to be worked by officials ignorant, or slothful, or corrupt, was not likely to be a marvel of wisdom. In fact Murray's

straightforward integrity—"I am a plain honest man"—
guided him to results better than might have been expected. While he showed little tact in dealing with the
English traders, for to his class trade was degrading, he
had much in common with the Canadian seigneurs, landowners and often, like himself, soldiers. He received them
at his table and paid tribute to their courage in the late
war. On the other hand, we may doubt whether any traders
at Quebec were honoured by such invitations. Some of
these engaged in the fur trade were men of education and
integrity. There was no free newspaper press. While the
English colonies had some two-score newspapers, they had
been unknown in Canada during the French régime. Though
in June, 1764, Murray permitted the issue of the *Quebec
Gazette,* half in French, half in English, it was a small
sheet, well under control, but at the same time the symbol
in Canada of a new era of public discussion.

It is a melancholy fact that in England in the year 1763,
when the problem of Canada had to be faced, a minister
came into power whose policy was destined to wreck the
first British Empire. George Grenville's mind ran in a
groove and his colleagues too had few gleams of imagination
that should enable them to frame for Canada a system
requiring, in truth, nice discrimination. This Grenville
ministry was called a triumvirate. Three men dominated
it, Grenville himself and the two secretaries of state, one
his brother-in-law, the Earl of Egremont, the other the
Earl of Halifax. The cabinet of the time was small, with
only seven or eight members. In theory there was but
one office of secretary of state to serve the king. While in
early days one person performed the duty, seven or eight
are now needed. In 1763 there were two; one had the
northern department, the other the southern department.
Egremont, secretary for the southern department, had

charge of foreign affairs in Western Europe, especially with France and Spain, restive since their defeat in the late war. He had also India and all the colonies, clearly too wide a range of duties for one man. Egremont's enemies have said hard things against him. He is accused of an arrogant pride by which indeed he might have come quite naturally, since, in addition to being the owner of great estates, he had as maternal grandfather the "proud Duke of Somerset." This epithet is due to the Duke's comic arrogance of birth and rank. On one occasion, when his second wife ventured to tap his arm with her fan to attract his attention, he turned to her and said, "Madam, my first wife was a Percy and she never took such a liberty." When he drove through his own part of the country he had the roads cleared so that vulgar people might not gaze at him. Perhaps we ought not to take too seriously Horace Walpole's vindictive description of the Duke's grandson, Egremont, as a mixture of "ill-nature, avarice and good-breeding, incapable on even the most trivial subject of speaking the truth." He must have impressed some of his contemporaries for one of the leaders of the time, Earl Temple, spoke of him as "destined to be another Pitt." He had the courage at times to oppose the will of George III who, we are told, "spoke daggers" to him on one occasion.

Clearly, though the despatches of the time relating to Canada are signed by Egremont, he himself knew little of its problems. These were in charge of a young member of the cabinet, the Earl of Shelburne who, as president of the Board of Trade, carried on the business of the colonies but was obliged, to his chagrin, to report to Egremont who insisted on his superior authority as secretary. Shelburne was destined to play a considerable part in colonial affairs and, twenty years later, to be the prime minister who had the bitter task of making the treaty that accepted the independence of the colonies to form the

United States. During this long period Shelburne was much occupied in the affairs of Canada, where now a county and more than one town are called by his name. That was so much a golden age for young men of rank and of capacity for politics that our own time, counting itself receptive of the fresh vigour of youth, has little to equal it. In 1763, in his twenty-sixth year, Shelburne was a member of the cabinet and twenty years later the younger Pitt was prime minister when still in his twenty-fifth year. It is true that both were derided for their youth. In 1763 Shelburne's youth hampered his influence with older colleagues and in 1783, when, a few months after Shelburne had been driven from office as prime minister, Pitt announced to the House of Commons that he had taken this office, he was received with astonished laughter. In joining the cabinet in 1763 Shelburne had expected the rank of secretary that would have freed him from the control of Egremont, but Grenville would not concede this position to a man whose family, as he said, had only recently been raised to the peerage and whose inexperience would arouse jealousy in other aspirants. As only president of the Board of Trade, he could not deal directly with the colonies.

Shelburne had barely taken office when Egremont sent to him a copy of the treaty of peace and other papers and asked him to report on the best mode of dealing with the new possessions. The voluminous reports that followed show this, at least, that the Board studied the problem carefully, no matter what lack of imagination its labours reveal. Shelburne had a strange belief of the time that the older colonies were already so crowded as no longer to have room for more people. In view of their large tracts of untamed forest it is amusing to find them described as already "overstocked with inhabitants." In consequence new settlers should go to empty Florida and to an enlarged Nova Scotia. To Canada, it seemed, not many English

would go, since it was already so well peopled. In fact only
a few went until, after twenty years, many loyalists were
forced into exile in Canada. Though it contained only about
one quarter as many people as Virginia, reports described
it as having "a very great number of French inhabitants and
settlements." Shelburne wished to treat them generously.
They should retain their own French laws and remain
compact French community enclosed within a rather n
area, since their province of Quebec should extend
short distance west of Montreal. Farther east th
settlers were to be encouraged to go to Nova
left partly unpeopled by the expulsion of
though already many settlers from New
cupied vacated farms. Its frontier was
ward to include part of the peninsul
enlarge the area for English settle
St. Lawrence, under the kindly
cil named by the British m
laws and preserve their c
Shelburne thought, to
French population,
heard of such a s

Shelburne ha
when a crisi
a glutton
that he
for c
ea

o
II
pre
be
revol
Shelbu
of Sept
share in
but rathe
tary in cha
able official.
Halifax h
paired by diss
Like the repro
versed in the c
though he was ne
rank of lieutenant
precocity of youth
the Board of Trade

burne told the king that he found the work at the Board of
Trade unpleasant, the difficulties many and the claims upon
his time too exacting. Accordingly he soon resigned. The
Earl of Halifax changed from the northern to the southern department, which gave him charge of the colonies, and
the Earl of Hillsborough succeeded Shelburne at the Board
of Trade. It was not a happy change. We shall meet Hillsborough later as the persistent supporter of the coercion of
the rebellious colonies. Even censorious Horace Walpole
describes him, however, as a man of honour who kept his
word. He was a good speaker and well-read and he cannot
be accused of neglecting his duties for he was present at
every one of the meetings of the Board of Trade in 1763
after he took office and at 128 out of 131 in 1764. This
zeal had, no doubt, some connection with the payment of
a fee for each attendance, in addition to the liberal salary
of the post. At court he made a splendid figure, but George
I said that he knew no one of less judgment. He had
judices so violent that later he thought Shelburne should
mpeached for his liberal attitude to the colonies in

Since Hillsborough did not take up his duties as
rne's successor at the Board of Trade until the end
ember, 1763, it was hardly he who had the chief
the final decision as to the government of Canada,
the Earl of Halifax, his superior, the new secre-
rge of the colonies.
d had experience in colonial affairs and was an
Though he died at fifty-five, his faculties im-
pation, in his time he had done useful work.
bate Wilkes, he was a good scholar, well
ssics. He was so much of a soldier that,
ver on active service, he attained the high
general. He also had something of the
for at thirty-two he was president of
an office that he held from 1748 to

1761. After this he was lord-lieutenant of Ireland. He had what was rare in that age, a sense of decency in regard to taking all the money that could be squeezed from government. Though it was largely due to his urgency that the salary of the lord-lieutenant was increased from twelve to sixteen thousand pounds, he refused for himself, while in the office, the extra four thousand pounds; the benefit should go only to his successors. His elaborate dress, his imposing appearance and affable manners, and his knowledge of trade impressed his contemporaries. Early in his career he had improved his fortune by marrying the heiress of a Mr. Dunk who had grown rich in the clothing trade. Halifax even added to his family name of Montague that of Dunk and he occupied himself in affairs of trade, for his wife had inherited her fortune on the condition that her husband should be in touch with commerce. The lady died young to the deep sorrow of Halifax. His later life was marked by licence in both manners and finance. It shows the fury of rival groups in the politics of the time that in 1768, in a struggle for supremacy in the borough of Northhampton, long dominated by Halifax's family, he is said to have spent a hundred and fifty thousand pounds and his opponents, Lords Spencer and Northhampton, between them, two hundred and fifty thousand. It is hard to imagine how any fortune could bear so great a strain. As Northampton had hardly more than a thousand voters one would suppose that each of the venal ones must have been enriched.

The memory of Halifax is preserved in Canada in the name of the capital of Nova Scotia. He had been the real creator of that colony in 1749 during his term of office as president of the Board of Trade. His insight into the needs of trade earned for him the title of "Father of the Colonies." He had encouraged settlers from New England to go to Nova Scotia to occupy the farms from which the unhappy

Acadians had been driven in 1755, and he had been the instrument of creating there in 1758, just after Louisbourg had fallen to Amherst and Wolfe, the one colonial legislature in North America that preserved its loyalty to the British king during the troubled period of the American Revolution. As early as in 1752 Nova Scotia had had that mark of progress, a newspaper.

The experience of Halifax in Nova Scotia had settled his conviction that the new British conquests should all be ruled on the model of that colony, with an appointed governor and an elected assembly; and now he was prepared to apply to the new possessions this system that lay at the root of the sensitive demand in the English colonies for liberty as complete as that of the Englishman in the mother country. Ever since an assembly "broke out" in the early days of the oldest colony, Virginia, an elected legislature had been linked with English law as the normal equipment of a colony. Even small West Indian islands had such assemblies. Clearly, to the official mind, running in a groove, a colony without an assembly and with French law such as Shelburne had planned for Canada, would not do. Yet the fact remained that Canada was all but wholly French and that its people were devoted to French traditions. Some of the members of the Board of Trade had given close attention to the puzzling problems of the new possessions, though others were more intent on the salary of a thousand pounds a year and the fees for attendance. At the later time of the American Revolution the historian Gibbon sat on the Board for three years, drew salary and fees, but gave more thought to the decline and fall of the Roman Empire than to his duty in regard to the fate of the new British Empire. Both tact and imagination were needed for the difficult task of reconciling to British rule a people whom the fortune of war had separated from their proud parent, France.

would go, since it was already so well peopled. In fact only
a few went until, after twenty years, many loyalists were
forced into exile in Canada. Though it contained only about
one quarter as many people as Virginia, reports described
it as having "a very great number of French inhabitants and
settlements." Shelburne wished to treat them generously.
They should retain their own French laws and remain a
compact French community enclosed within a rather narrow
area, since their province of Quebec should extend only a
short distance west of Montreal. Farther east the incoming
settlers were to be encouraged to go to Nova Scotia, still
left partly unpeopled by the expulsion of the Acadians,
though already many settlers from New England had occupied vacated farms. Its frontier was to be pushed northward to include part of the peninsula of Gaspé and thus to
enlarge the area for English settlement. The French on the
St. Lawrence, under the kindly rule of a governor and council named by the British ministry, should have their own
laws and preserve their own customs. It would be absurd,
Shelburne thought, to set up an elected assembly for a
French population, most of whom had probably never even
heard of such a system.

Shelburne had been in the cabinet for only a few months
when a crisis came in the ministry. Egremont was such
a glutton at table that, as Walpole says, "every one knew
that he would die suddenly" and the prophecy was justified,
for on August 21, 1763, he died of apoplexy. A day or two
earlier he had said, according to Walpole, "Well, I have but
three turtle dinners to come and if I survive them, I shall
be immortal." He did not survive them and his death
caused confusion. By this time, for reasons not clear, Shelburne was drawing away from the Grenville ministry. He
was always so difficult a colleague that twenty years later,
rather than sit in the same cabinet with him, Charles James
Fox wrecked Whig prospects for some forty years. Shel-

burne told the king that he found the work at the Board of
Trade unpleasant, the difficulties many and the claims upon
his time too exacting. Accordingly he soon resigned. The
Earl of Halifax changed from the northern to the southern department, which gave him charge of the colonies, and
the Earl of Hillsborough succeeded Shelburne at the Board
of Trade. It was not a happy change. We shall meet Hillsborough later as the persistent supporter of the coercion of
the rebellious colonies. Even censorious Horace Walpole
describes him, however, as a man of honour who kept his
word. He was a good speaker and well-read and he cannot
be accused of neglecting his duties for he was present at
every one of the meetings of the Board of Trade in 1763
after he took office and at 128 out of 131 in 1764. This
zeal had, no doubt, some connection with the payment of
a fee for each attendance, in addition to the liberal salary
of the post. At court he made a splendid figure, but George
III said that he knew no one of less judgment. He had
prejudices so violent that later he thought Shelburne should
be impeached for his liberal attitude to the colonies in
revolt. Since Hillsborough did not take up his duties as
Shelburne's successor at the Board of Trade until the end
of September, 1763, it was hardly he who had the chief
share in the final decision as to the government of Canada,
but rather the Earl of Halifax, his superior, the new secretary in charge of the colonies.

Halifax had had experience in colonial affairs and was an
able official. Though he died at fifty-five, his faculties im-
paired by dissipation, in his time he had done useful work.
Like the reprobate Wilkes, he was a good scholar, well
versed in the classics. He was so much of a soldier that,
though he was never on active service, he attained the high
rank of lieutenant-general. He also had something of the
precocity of youth for at thirty-two he was president of
the Board of Trade, an office that he held from 1748 to

1761. After this he was lord-lieutenant of Ireland. He had what was rare in that age, a sense of decency in regard to taking all the money that could be squeezed from government. Though it was largely due to his urgency that the salary of the lord-lieutenant was increased from twelve to sixteen thousand pounds, he refused for himself, while in the office, the extra four thousand pounds; the benefit should go only to his successors. His elaborate dress, his imposing appearance and affable manners, and his knowledge of trade impressed his contemporaries. Early in his career he had improved his fortune by marrying the heiress of a Mr. Dunk who had grown rich in the clothing trade. Halifax even added to his family name of Montague that of Dunk and he occupied himself in affairs of trade, for his wife had inherited her fortune on the condition that her husband should be in touch with commerce. The lady died young to the deep sorrow of Halifax. His later life was marked by licence in both manners and finance. It shows the fury of rival groups in the politics of the time that in 1768, in a struggle for supremacy in the borough of Northhampton, long dominated by Halifax's family, he is said to have spent a hundred and fifty thousand pounds and his opponents, Lords Spencer and Northhampton, between them, two hundred and fifty thousand. It is hard to imagine how any fortune could bear so great a strain. As Northampton had hardly more than a thousand voters one would suppose that each of the venal ones must have been enriched.

The memory of Halifax is preserved in Canada in the name of the capital of Nova Scotia. He had been the real creator of that colony in 1749 during his term of office as president of the Board of Trade. His insight into the needs of trade earned for him the title of "Father of the Colonies." He had encouraged settlers from New England to go to Nova Scotia to occupy the farms from which the unhappy

Acadians had been driven in 1755, and he had been the instrument of creating there in 1758, just after Louisbourg had fallen to Amherst and Wolfe, the one colonial legislature in North America that preserved its loyalty to the British king during the troubled period of the American Revolution. As early as in 1752 Nova Scotia had had that mark of progress, a newspaper.

The experience of Halifax in Nova Scotia had settled his conviction that the new British conquests should all be ruled on the model of that colony, with an appointed governor and an elected assembly; and now he was prepared to apply to the new possessions this system that lay at the root of the sensitive demand in the English colonies for liberty as complete as that of the Englishman in the mother country. Ever since an assembly "broke out" in the early days of the oldest colony, Virginia, an elected legislature had been linked with English law as the normal equipment of a colony. Even small West Indian islands had such assemblies. Clearly, to the official mind, running in a groove, a colony without an assembly and with French law such as Shelburne had planned for Canada, would not do. Yet the fact remained that Canada was all but wholly French and that its people were devoted to French traditions. Some of the members of the Board of Trade had given close attention to the puzzling problems of the new possessions, though others were more intent on the salary of a thousand pounds a year and the fees for attendance. At the later time of the American Revolution the historian Gibbon sat on the Board for three years, drew salary and fees, but gave more thought to the decline and fall of the Roman Empire than to his duty in regard to the fate of the new British Empire. Both tact and imagination were needed for the difficult task of reconciling to British rule a people whom the fortune of war had separated from their proud parent, France.

By October, 1763, the Board had made its report on a policy and on the seventh of that month was issued with formal ceremony what is known as "The Proclamation of 1763" providing that the new possessions taken from France and Spain should be governed on the pattern of the older English colonies. In order that printed copies might be prepared and forwarded to the colonial governors, the usual ship was delayed until, on October 11, she sailed away with news for all the colonies of great moment for their future. The governor and the nominated council in each of the four conquests, Canada, East and West Florida and Grenada might, as soon as circumstances should permit, summon an Assembly on the model of the "Colonies and Provinces in America which are under our immediate Government." All were to have the benefit of the "Laws of our Realm of England . . . as well Criminal as Civil," and courts were to be created to administer the law. The French were thus, it seemed, to have only English law, though later this purpose was denied. The truth seems to be that in declaring for English law in Canada the framers of the Proclamation had not envisaged the injustice that such a change would mean. It would involve a radical departure from the merciful custom in the past, even of the Roman conqueror, to leave to a conquered people at least the comfort of their own laws. When Lord Chief Justice Mansfield examined this feature of the Proclamation, he declared that "the history of the world don't furnish an instance of so rash and unjust an act by any conqueror whatever." Lord Chancellor Northington called the Proclamation "very silly" while Lord Chancellor Thurlow said it involved an act "of the grossest and absurdest and cruellest tyranny." Whatever the injustice Murray understood that he was at once to apply English law in Canada.

In order, after the long war, to meet the problem of reducing the army and of providing for disbanded soldiers, the Proclamation offered them large grants of land. The existing Canadian owners were to have their titles scrutinized and the limits of their holdings defined. New townships might be laid out of about twenty thousand acres in each of which should be a town, situated, if possible, either on a navigable river or on the sea coast. A convenient site was to be set apart for a church, together with four hundred acres of land for the support of a Protestant minister and two hundred for a schoolmaster. Of those who had served in North America in the late war a field officer might have five thousand acres; a captain three thousand; a subaltern two hundred. The highest non-commissioned officer might have two hundred acres, the private a beggarly fifty. Since, however, most of the available land in settled Canada was already parcelled into seigneuries, the openings were few for large grants to new settlers. Some officers either bought seigneuries, as did Murray himself, or were granted those that had reverted to the crown. Some disbanded soldiers remained in the country. Since there were few women of their own race, they usually married Canadian wives and their children were reared in the Roman Catholic faith, and spoke the language of their mothers. To this day there are in Quebec families of Frasers, Scotts, McLeans and similar names, with no trace, except in physical type, of their British ancestry, and in tastes and ideals wholly French. Under the Proclamation Canada suffered a great loss of territory. The whole Atlantic coast of Labrador from the Gulf of St. Lawrence to Hudson Straits was annexed permanently to Newfoundland, as were also, for the time, the island of Anticosti and lesser islands within the Gulf. For the time too a part of the peninsula of Gaspé remained to Nova Scotia.

In the farther interior there were acute problems. "Great frauds and abuses have been committed against the Indians," the Proclamation declared. Colonial traders and

settlers were pushing into regions formerly closed to them.
They were debauching the natives by drink and were claiming Indian lands secured by guile from perhaps a drunken
chief. The French had checked such evils. Every French
trader or hunter who went among the Indians must have a
licence; to go without one might involve the penalty of
death. Now, however, under the English, rough frontiersmen were going where they liked and doing what they
liked. The tribes were already so restive under the change
from France to Britain that at the moment when the clauses
of the Proclamation were being framed England was hearing of barbarous war with the Indians in which hundreds
of settlers and soldiers lost their lives. The problem was
vast; Florida, Nova Scotia, Canada and all the English
colonies were affected by it. The Indians, for their part,
wished an exact frontier to be drawn, beyond which no
settlement should be made, so that they might be free to
pursue their own mode of life, aided, as was now inevitable,
by such things from Europe as fire-arms, knives, kettles and
blankets to be bought in exchange for furs. To ensure
peace, a central control seemed necessary. Since the problem was largely military, this control was vested by the
Proclamation in the commander-in-chief at New York who
was to have the aid of the governor in each colony concerned.

While it was not easy to draw an exact frontier, the
Proclamation decreed that no one should claim Indian
lands or make any settlement beyond the sources of the
rivers flowing into the Atlantic Ocean. This excluded lands
in the Valley of the Ohio which flows westward to the
Mississippi and so to the Gulf of Mexico; lands in the Illinois country farther north; and also lands farther south lying east of the Mississippi itself. No governor of a colony,
nor the commander-in-chief himself, was to presume "upon
any Pretense whatever" to permits surveys or to pass titles

for lands beyond the defined frontier. Intruders on lands not conceded by the Indians were "to remove themselves from such Settlements." Every one going to trade with the Indians must have a licence from the governor of his colony or from the commander-in-chief and he must give security for good conduct.

We admire the humane spirit of these regulations. The Indians should be protected from the brutalities of lawless traders and from the greedy seizure of their lands. But both opinion and conditions in the colonies themselves aroused protests against this policy. The framers of the Proclamation did not realize the extent of the vested interests of the English colonies in the forbidden territory. Nearly every one of them had made claim to western lands. Virginia had promised many hundred thousands of acres of lands bordering on the Ohio to soldiers as a reward for service in the late war. Early in 1762 the Ohio Company demanded the confirmation of earlier grants of land and on June 3rd, 1763, just when Shelburne had been giving thought to the question, the Mississippi Company was founded and asked for two and a half million acres in which it would place two hundred families. Each of the promoters of this company was to have fifty thousand acres and one of them was that keen speculator in western lands, George Washington, already the champion of the rights promised to the Virginian soldiers who had served under him in the war.

Inevitably this new strictness, dictated from London, brought mutterings from men in Pennsylvania, Virginia, New York and other colonies. A whole promised land was now closed to adventurous ambition and naturally the frontiersmen cursed the far-away government that checked them. A despotic mother country, they began to say, now shut out the colonies from their natural expansion westward, and made herself the special protector of savages who had devastated their homes and murdered their wives and children. On nothing are men more readily and deeply embittered than on claims to land. A dozen years later a Congress of the English colonies at Philadelphia was debating angrily the supposed sinister intent of this policy to cripple colonial life.

At Quebec, meanwhile, a harassed soldier-governor, who knew little of law, English or French, was left to make sweeping changes. There was little difficulty about applying English criminal law. Though it was so severe that hanging was the penalty for stealing only a few shillings, the French law was even more brutal. It permitted torture; murder was punished with slow and painful death upon the wheel or rack; while the penalty for a second offence of blasphemy was to have the lips seared by a hot iron and, in extreme cases, to have the tongue cut out. Even unpremeditated homicide involved hanging, changed in the case of those of noble rank to the lesser degradation of beheading. While the English criminal law would give some relief from this barbarity, the civil law was another matter. To change it would involve a revolution in social life. The parish priest would lose his privileged position and be no longer entitled to the support of the tithe. As time passed he might, so some English hoped, give way to a Protestant clergyman, with a wife and children in the former celibate presbytery, while in the church the altar, the stations of the cross, the lights and statues and incense, might yield to the austere simplicity of an English parish church or even of a nonconformist meeting-house. The seigneur too would lose his feudal rights and become a mere owner or seller of land. "One must be upon the spot," Murray wrote on March 2, 1765, to the Lords of Trade, "to form a judgment of the difficulties which occur in establishing the English law in this colony, the body of the people from education and religion are averse to them." He was expressly forbidden to select men on the spot to aid in his task. Such jobs, carrying a salary, the ministry in England reserved for its own hangers-on and they sent out, as we have seen, two ignorant, needy lawyers who proved "so unfit for their duties as to be wholly useless." Murray chose a council of seven or eight members who, in truth, gave little help and with this equipment he issued on September 17, 1764, the fifth anniversary of the fall of Quebec, an Ordinance bringing into force on October 1 English law: courts of King's Bench and Common Pleas on the English model, and trial by juries on which, stretching and even defying English law as it stood, he decided that, since there were so few Protestant freeholders, Roman Catholics might act, a concession that gave great offence to bigoted Protestant elements at Quebec. Murray soon found that to bring English law into force on October 1, 1764, involved consequences laughable, except for the serious issues that it raised. If a French landowner should die on September 30 of that year his real property would be divided among his children, under the French law; but if he should linger until the next day it would, under English law, go to his eldest son. Such was the difficulty that, after a few weeks, on November 6, 1764, Murray issued a second Ordinance continuing for the time the French system of inheritance among the Canadians, though it was not to apply to the British newcomers.

Murray's attempt to ease the position of the French aroused bitter fanaticism among the English traders. Since Canada, they argued, had become British by conquest, the whole British system should be applied. If the laws of England said that no Roman Catholic might sit in a legislature, or hold public office, or plead in a law court, or practise medicine, or be an apothecary (presumably lest he might poison his customers) why should they not apply to the

Canadians? To let Roman Catholics sit on a jury was "an open Violation of our most sacred laws and Libertys." Their religion was frivolous. They gave balls and played cards on the Sabbath day and this Murray himself, his critics added, was quite too lax in rebuking. "The Gospel in its primitive purity" was needed for this people and clergy able to preach it in both English and French should be secured; Murray, aiming to be a despot, was taking it on himself to make laws, something that only chosen representatives might do. Accordingly when he summoned a grand jury composed chiefly of traders, they told him that, since there was no legislature, they alone could speak for the people and he must submit his measures to them for approval.

We may imagine Murray's wrath at such claims by people whom he called licentious fanatics, abandoned men, the offscouring of the earth, the most immoral people in all the world, cruel, ignorant, rapacious; bullies who professed to despise the soldiers as slaves, by their own act of enlistment, and the Canadians as slaves, by conquest. On one occasion he summoned them to his presence, told them that they were a set of damned villains and that, if they did not behave better, he should expel them. No wonder, he said, that officers and the better class of Canadians alike showed contempt for them; "the genteel people of this country despise merchants and, of course, esteem the officers who shun them most." This rabble, he said, insulted him and his officers, their betters by birth and education, and they were trying to trample upon the Canadians, the losers, but the honourable losers, in the great game of war. If accused, he would plead guilty of not being willing to persecute the king's Roman Catholic subjects. Those whom he displeased for not trampling "on the poor Canadians" were, he said, "Quakers, Puritans, Anabaptists, Presbyterians, Atheists, Infidels and even Jews." This comprehensive list in which Presbyterians and Atheists rank side by side shows the range of Murray's invective. By contrast the Canadians seemed to him "the bravest and the best race upon the globe"; "the most faithful and useful set of men in this American Empire."

Until October 1, 1764, Canada had been ruled under military law and now the change to civil law, under which no longer the military officer but the civilian magistrate tried accused persons, brought a crisis in the relations of the civil population with the soldiers. The officer of the time, apt in any case to be contemptuous of trade, was especially aloof from the colonial traders, some of whom were little more than pedlars who had come in the wake of the conquering army. When the officers at Quebec gave a ball in 1763 they invited only the wives of the merchants without their husbands. During the military régime the well-to-do trader might have an officer quartered in his house whether he liked it or not. In England the quartering of soldiers in private houses had been one of the causes of the civil war. It also haunts the history of the English colonies during the ten years prior to the Declaration of Independence and caused such strife that the new constitution of the United States expressly forbids it. Conditions were such, under military rule in Canada, that a dignified civilian, for some breach of regulations of which he was ignorant, might be brought before a court presided over by a stiff officer resolved to show who it was that had authority. Four years of this military rule over civilians had made the soldier unpopular. Since the ranks were filled by men often of a degraded class, brutalized by camp life and prone to crimes of violence, the military code was severe. Officers of the 62nd regiment sentenced a soldier to one hundred and seventy-five strokes and he was actually flogged to death. Three soldiers were hanged for taking part in theft. It was natural that the soldier, himself inured to such severity, should be exacting to civilians in a garrison town such as Montreal, when he was on guard in the streets and responsible for order. It was equally natural that a trader from the English colonies who had never seen a court with an officer in uniform as the judge should resent the penalties of military law.

Thomas Walker, an Englishman, who had lived for some ten years in Boston and there imbibed the spirit of that turbulent city, had hurried to Montreal to engage in the fur trade and had become prominent in the commercial world. He soon made himself odious to Colonel Burton, who succeeded in the command at Montreal, when General Gage was moved to New York as commander-in-chief, and Burton's fellow officers had not been slow to show their resentment and contempt. In the strife that ensued civilians complained of arbitrary fines and imprisonments by the military and made violent charges against them. The tension became acute and was increased by bickering among the higher officers. Burton had wished to be not only military but civil governor at Montreal and when civil law was proclaimed he resented Murray's authority over him. Murray for his part believed that Burton was slack in holding the soldiers in check, despised him as of low birth—"the spawn of a Yorkshire attorney"—and accused him of lack of consideration for "the poor Mercantile Devils" for whom at Quebec Murray himself had little but scorn. So aroused was Murray that he declared Burton should be tried for conduct that, in the end, caused a savage outrage. Walker was an unpleasant person of whom later, when Montreal was held by the revolted colonies, Benjamin Franklin said that no matter where he and his wife might live they would soon make the place too hot to hold them. Since Walker had complained about his treatment under military rule, Murray, on setting up civil law, made him a magistrate, perhaps in an excess of generosity to give the civilian point of view a fair chance, probably also as a rebuke to Burton.

The houses of magistrates were exempt from the quartering of soldiers, but it was not clear that a house would be exempt in which a magistrate was not the householder but only a lodger. In the late autumn of 1764, with winter at hand, a certain Captain Payne was quartered in one of the best houses. A civilian magistrate who had rooms in the house claimed that he had engaged those occupied by Payne and had thus a prior claim. When Payne refused to leave, he was thrown into the common jail, on a warrant issued by Walker and four other magistrates. Walker's advice to householders to refuse firing and furniture to persons billeted upon them brought the quarrel to a head. Nearly every one took sides, Murray, far away, summoned Walker to Quebec but, before he could obey, the soldiers carried out a brutal outrage.

On Thursday, December 6, 1764, at about nine o'clock of a bright moonlight night, when Walker was at supper, half a dozen masked men forced their way into his house while a score of others stood on guard in the street to prevent interruption. They seemed so bent on murder that Mrs. Walker ran shrieking from the room, followed by the two guests and three servants. In the struggle Walker received what he thought a mortal wound. As he lay prostrate, beaten into insensibility, the men cut off his ear and then went away muttering, "The villain is dead; damn him, we've done for him." Not many minutes later, a group of soldiers opened the door of the room of the adjutant of the 28th regiment and threw on the table a small packet that was found to contain Walker's ear. A hat and a bayonet of the 28th regiment, left in Walker's house, seemed to make clear the source of the outrage. He declared that he could identify certain officers as his assailants. When arrests followed, soldiers stormed the jail and released the prisoners. Though the government offered two hundred pounds and the inhabitants three hundred pounds for the discovery of Walker's assailants no one was ever convicted. Fear of a massacre by soldiers so spread in Montreal that civilians carried arms in the streets and laid their pistols on the table when they sat down to dinner. A soldier entering a shop was likely to have a pistol presented to him to warn him against attempting outrage. Murray, who went to Montreal and remained a month enquiring into the case, declared that a stranger would think that the town contained two hostile armies ready to fall upon each other. The incident occurred just when the quartering of troops became an acute problem for the British army in the English colonies. General Gage, with headquarters in New York, induced the British government to pass in April, 1765, a Quartering Act requiring the colonies to provide not only housing and bedding, but also salt, vinegar, and beer or cider for the comfort of the troops quartered in any community. The outrage upon Walker inflamed opposition in New York, Boston and elsewhere and the agitation thus fortified endured for years.

It fell in the end to Carleton, Murray's successor, to close the incident relating to Walker. Two years after the event, when, in November, 1766, MacGovack, a former soldier in the 28th regiment, came forward with testimony against half a dozen persons, four of them officers socially prominent in Montreal, Chief Justice Hey, newly arrived and competent, issued a warrant for their arrest and in the dead of night they awoke to find men with fixed bayonets at their bedsides. "All manner of delicacy and decency" was absent, the prisoners complained. They were housed with other prisoners in a common jail so out of repair and bitterly cold as to endanger their lives. In order to apply in person to the Chief Justice for bail, they made, in custody, a long

cold journey to Quebec. The suspicion was abroad that
Murray had been unduly lenient to the soldiers. Now he
was gone and Carleton, for his part, discouraged any indulgence to officers accused of gross crime. Since the law
for felony of this kind forbade bail and Walker declared that
his life would not be worth a day's purchase if any of the
accused were free, the Chief Justice ordered that the accused should be kept in prison. In consequence, though
their friends threatened violence, they were returned in
custody to Montreal and remained in jail during many
weeks. In the end the Grand Jury found a true bill against
only one of them, Captain Disney whom, after trial, a jury
found not guilty. Such an incident, in itself of no great importance, was so precisely of the kind to attract attention
that it long disturbed Canada. Probably the offenders were
soldiers whose officers feared mutiny if too zealous in hunting down the criminals.

Meanwhile a change came in England. In July, 1765,
George III, weary of austere dictation from the prime
minister, George Grenville, suddenly dismissed him and
called upon a young nobleman of high rank, the Marquis of
Rockingham, to form a ministry. Though, a few months
earlier, George III had forced the dismissal of General
Conway from his posts because he had dared to oppose
measures favoured by the king, now Conway, whom every-
one respected, came back to the important office of secretary
of the southern department that included the charge of the
colonies. The Earl of Dartmouth, a man of fine character
though he lacked the firm courage of Conway, took Shelburne's former post at the Board of Trade and the prospect
for wise rule at Quebec was brightened. Murray's opponents
in Canada carried the issue to London, engaged a barrister
to push their interests and enlisted the support of traders
from whom they bought their goods. Murray's aristocratic

scorn of trade had incensed the merchants and the jealousy and rather low mentality of this class are evident in the angry endorsement by the London firms of the venom of Murray's enemies. Opposing them, the Canadians, for their part, appealed to the king against an intolerance under which, as they said, some thirty English merchants persecuted ten thousand heads of families. When Murray's recall was imminent the seigneurs mourned that "our protector, our father is taken from us. Like a father he listened to our complaints." They said that they would be "unworthy to live" if they did not tell the king of their debt to him in protecting them from ignorant men of low birth who wished to trample on them.

In the end the merchants drew up a formidable petition demanding the recall of Murray. A minister such as Conway, the enemy of abuses, could hardly fail to notice the unrest in Canada and to seek a remedy. The traders at Quebec charged that Murray was using his authority to impose oppressive ordinances "injurious to Civil liberty and the Protestant cause." They complained that he showered on them contempt and rage and rudeness; that he seized property illegally and was enriching himself; that he was partial in administering the law; that, though the guardian of public virtue, he never attended church and was guilty of blasphemy. The result of such misgovernment, they added, was that trade languished and that the oppressed British were leaving the country. Accordingly, the petitioners asked that a governor should be appointed who knew something besides the life of a soldier and that a House of Representatives should be established. On September 2, 1765, after enquiry by the Board of Trade, Dartmouth made an elaborate report to Conway. It condemned the violent charges against Murray as unjust, uncandid and indecent. The law officers of the crown supported Murray's tolerance in refusing to apply to Catholics in Canada the disabilities of the laws of England. These oppressive laws, they said, did not run in Canada where Catholics were free to hold public office and to plead in the courts and where the French law of property should be followed. On the other hand, though the Board did not impugn Murray's good intentions, it condemned the inadequacy of his ordinances and supported the plan of an elected legislature in which, however, to the annoyance of English traders, the French ought to have equal rights.

Murray's enemies had powerful support in London. Among those who signed the petition against him were the Lord Mayor, four aldermen, and four members of Parliament. George III was himself impressed and in March, 1766, told General Conway that Murray should come home in order to reply to the "many heavy charges laid against him." The Board of Trade said more gently that he should be summoned to give an account of the colony. This really so meant recall that the incendiary Walker boasted at Montreal that Dartmouth backed the protests of the merchants. Murray fumed and protested against the credence given to "four hundred and fifty contemptible sutlers and traders." Base men, "intoxicated with the unexpected powers put into their hands," were heard against the man who had tried to protect British officials from insult and a helpless people from tyranny. While deploring possible errors of judgment, he wished, he said, no forgiveness for lack of benevolence and justice: "I defy all the earth to accuse me of one harsh, unjust or oppressive action." He gloried, he said, in having been accused of warmth and firmness in protecting the king's Canadian subjects, persecuted by "the most cruel, ignorant, rapacious Fanatics who ever existed." Clearly Murray had further matured his fine gift of invective but it did not avert the blow that he was summoned to London. His recall to explain the situation was part of

Conway's plan for reform in Canada. In 1766 the Rockingham ministry dismissed summarily the incompetent Chief
Justice and the Attorney-General and named two men of
fine character, Hey and Masères, to succeed them.

Before the beginning of this new and better order Murray,
however, was gone. He reached London in the summer of
1766 and there with fire and indignation he denounced the
charges against him. Since it was clear that he would not
be sent back to Canada, the traders baulked at the demand
that they should put up security for costs and did not press
their charges. After full consideration, an Order in Council,
dated in April, 1767, declared them to be groundless and
scandalous. There was no stain on Murray's honour. He
long drew his emoluments as governor of Quebec, but never
again did he see Canada. Friends told him that he was
happy in not returning to "the frozen Regions of Canada,"
a place fit only for exiles sent there to be punished for ill-
spent lives. Lord Despencer declined to buy Murray's
seigniory of Lauzon because it was "too near the North
Pole." Murray had a property in Sussex and there he built
a mansion, which he called Beauport after the village near
Quebec. He kept up a friendly correspondence with his old
enemy Lévis. Later he exchanged the post of military
governor of Quebec for that of Minorca and the day came
when he suffered a second defeat by the French. He defended Minorca during the American War, but he had not
the good fortune, like that at Quebec, of rescue by a British
fleet. Thus it happened that on February 5, 1782, his "six
hundred old decrepit soldiers" with other remnants of an
army, surrendered after a long siege, marched out of Fort
St. Philips with the honours of war due to a brave foe, and
passed through the long line of fourteen thousand French
and Spanish troops. On that day France had revenge to
ease the sting of the British victory at Quebec. Murray's
remaining years were spent at Beauport. He married a

young second wife, aged eighteen, when he was nearly sixty, and has many surviving descendants. His name is on the map of Canada in Murray Bay, a fashionable summer resort.

CHAPTER IV

THE INDIAN RISING AGAINST THE BRITISH

THE scene changes to the primeval forest in the far interior of North America. In this vast region the British victory over France meant that at lonely trading posts it should henceforth be English and not French with whom the native tribes must traffic. They were savage and warlike and were easily made suspicious and resentful. French missionaries and traders had pictured the King of France as the tribes' kindly father, who sent among them priests to teach the true way of life, and who from time to time showed how he valued their friendship by giving them presents. Gradually, during the long war, the Indians had become aware of the weakening of French power. Presents had ceased, traders at the posts no longer had goods to exchange for furs, and the slow decline had ended in September, 1760, in the fall of French power in North America. When this happened, anxiety spread among the tribes as to what they might expect from the victor. They had heard from their French friends nothing to reassure them. Unscrupulous traders told them that not only were the English cheaters in trade; they were traffickers in human flesh who would spread deadly diseases such as smallpox among the Indians and sell them poisonous rum, in order to kill them off and take their lands. Thousands of armed men in Virginia and the Carolinas were ready, it was said, to join others from Canada to carry out these dark designs.

During more than a century French explorers, French priests, and French traders had worked among the tribes. At

71

points of vantage on the Great Lakes, on straits connecting
these lakes, on the Wabash, the Ohio, the Mississippi and
other rivers, at old meeting places of the Indians, adventurous Frenchmen had built posts over which floated the white
flag with the lilies of France. Priests in black robes, soldiers in uniform, traders in leather and homespun, had
lived among the Indians and won from them a fitful confidence. The French *coureur-de-bois* was gay and friendly
and sometimes the father of a family of half-breed children.
With all sincerity these agents of France had described
their age-long enemies, the English, as darkened heretics in
religion and so greedy and cruel in secular affairs that they
would enslave the native tribes. The flaming red of the
British flag that should replace the *fleur-de-lis* was the
symbol of ruthless power. Little wonder that the Indians
of the Illinois country who had been on the French side
declared that they had rather die than make peace with
the victors at Quebec.

The surrender of Canada gave the British the title to
all the French posts in the interior westward to the
Mississippi River; among them Fort Frontenac at the east
end of Lake Ontario; Fort Niagara at the west end; Detroit
commanding the passage from Lake Erie to the upper lakes,
Huron, Michigan and Superior; Michilimackinac at the
entrance to Lake Michigan; and at that to Lake Superior, Sault Ste. Marie, where barely a century earlier the
French with impressive pomp had formally taken possession of the whole west in the name of Louis XIV. These
posts, remote as they may seem from the new seat of British
power at Quebec, were only at the beginning of a vaster
domain that spread westward to the mountains. Even on
the far Saskatchewan whose waters drained the rolling
prairies and reached Hudson Bay, the claims made by hardy
French explorers were extinguished and the French flag was
now replaced by the British. Though the change was to

involve the destiny of the many millions who now inhabit the regions concerned, at the time only a few Europeans of one nation replaced a few of another, while the native tribes, owners from time immemorial, looked on, puzzled to know what it all meant, many of them fearful that it might be a new menace to their wild freedom.

One vital interest, the fur trade, dominated the life of this region. The coming of the European with his implements of steel had made all but useless the bows and arrows and the stone axes of native life. The Indians must have muskets, powder and ball; if one tribe secured these they would be easily superior to enemies with only the bow and arrow. Indian labour had been eased by the implements of Europe, since, for both war and the daily life of plain and forest, stone axes and hatchets were clumsy tools compared with those of tempered steel. Light kettles of brass and copper that could be put on the fire and easily carried from place to place made all but useless the clay pottery in which hot stones were dropped to heat the water. The Indians had become so dependent that they would travel hundreds of miles to procure a little powder. Whether clumsy or only indolent, they could not even repair the musket necessary to their well-being. Since they must have supplies from the Europeans they had to find the means to procure them. The Indian's primitive agriculture provided little for exchange. There was no industry in which he could serve for wages and since the European was ready to buy from him only one commodity, furs, the result was to intensify his efforts as a trapper. Furs became the money of the natives and their life depended on the supplies that furs would buy.

The Indian tribes had denied that they were subjects of either France or Britain. The land was theirs and they intended to hold it. In their diplomacy they had tried sometimes to play off one European nation against another.

So fickle had been their friendship with the French that, when Montreal surrendered, the Canadians had asked the British general for protection against their former allies. When he answered that "there never have been any cruelties committed by the Indians of our army and good order shall be preserved," he intended this not only as an assurance to the French, but as a warning to the Indians. One whom he caught stealing he promptly hanged. To the Indian the thought was hateful that, since the British were now masters, he must accept their control. If, however, so he pondered, the tribes could learn to act together, they would be powerful and command respect, as either friends or enemies. It is a fact that during more than fifty years still their unrest involved war, first with Britain herself, and then with the revolted colonies. It added to the perplexity of the new British rule that some military leaders showed little tact in conciliating the tribes and, indeed, by their tone, justified what French agents said about the sinister aim of British policy. While Amherst knew how to awe Indians by a display of power, he made little effort to win their affection and confidence. When it was suggested to him that the British should continue the French practice of making presents to the Indians, he replied that he was not going to win them by fair words or to bribe them to behave, but would punish them if they did not. He refused at first to believe that any trouble with them would be serious. It was of little consequence, he said, what the Indians might think; they knew they had better keep quiet; kind acts would only lead them to imagine that the British were moved by fear. "I am firmly resolved," he wrote to Sir William Johnson, "whenever they give me an occasion, to extirpate them, root and branch." Those who knew the Indians better were aware that this tone meant prolonged strife and massacre. "The Indians," wrote George Croghan, Johnson's chief lieutenant, "will not consider consequences if too much distressed, tho' Sir Jeffery Amherst thinks they will."

To the British soldier, steeped in the conventions of war, the methods of the Indians were shocking. Their code, learned in primitive conditions, justified anything in order to kill the enemy. They saw no guilt in entering a post as pretended friends and in murdering defenders thrown off their guard. Sometimes they lured envoys for peace into their camps and killed them. Even to terms of peace solemnly accepted, they might pay no heed. They tortured to death and even ate prisoners. All this caused in the British officers the angry conviction that the only good Indian was a dead Indian. Colonel Bouquet, the fine Swiss officer in the British service who, in the end, suppressed the rising, thought the Indians "infernal wretches," "the vilest of brutes," and that they should be destroyed like vermin, possibly by hunting them with dogs and mounted scouts. Amherst agreed that it was desirable to "extirpate that execrable race" and proposed to give them blankets tainted by smallpox, a disease peculiarly fatal to them. Though General Gage, who succeeded Amherst, showed tact in dealing with the Indians, after a long experience he thought that the only way to deal with them was to knock them on the head.

A few on the British side understood them better. Sir William Johnson, an Irish gentleman by birth and a soldier by profession, showed adaptability and tact. Though neither he nor Amherst has the classic fame of Wolfe, each has left an enduring mark on North America where Amherst, the soldier, won British dominance, while Johnson made what proved to be enduring peace between the British and the native tribes. Like so many of his fellow countrymen, Johnson had found abroad what was denied in Ireland, an adequate field for remarkable talents. His mother was the sister of the admiral commemorated by an ornate monument in Westminster Abbey, Sir Peter Warren, the commander of the fleet that had aided the New England colonies to capture Louisbourg in 1745. When, by marriage with Miss De Lancey of New York, Warren obtained a great tract of land on the Mohawk River which flows into the Hudson at Albany, his nephew was just the man to develop this great estate. Though most of it was still forest it could be cleared for agriculture. Moreover, its situation offered advantages for trade with the Iroquois tribes, the Six Nations, the most stable of them, the Mohawks, being the nearest neighbours. The Mohawk River gave the best means of communication between the northern English colonies and the west. While farther south mountains barred the way, boats could go up the Hudson to Albany and then up the Mohawk River to the source of waters flowing to Lake Ontario and to fertile flat lands stretching westward to Niagara.

Johnson, young, handsome, with an imposing presence and boundless energy, saw the advantages of this situation and made himself ruler of a great feudal estate. On the south bank of the Mohawk, three miles from the site of the present industrial city of Amsterdam, he created the village of Johnstown, near which still stands his fine mansion. He built a church, a school, a court house, and a jail. The Indians learned to trust him for he was honest and had quick sympathy to understand their character. He could speak the language of the Mohawks; sometimes he wore their native dress and he received from them the rank of chief that he highly valued. He liked and even imitated the ways and manners of his barbaric neighbours. He knew how to humour the vanity of chiefs who, with only the standards of the forest, thought themselves among the great of the earth, while, in truth, more like children swayed by the passions of the moment. With them Johnson carried on a great trade; trade in muskets, powder and shot; in hatchets, knives, razors and awls; in blankets and bright-coloured cloth; in ribbons and mirrors,—in any and everything that Indian need and vanity demanded.

Much of Johnson's trade was less innocent for he sold freely to the Indians rum and other fire-water. They would not trade unless they could get this alluring product of the Europeans. Though to distil a fiery liquor from grain is an easy process, the natives had never learned the secret. The rum and brandy of Europe was to them new and wonderful, with lure so irresistible that they would have them at any cost. Though the results were appalling, those who howled and fought and gnawed each other did not feel disgraced when quiet came the next day. Rather was it an honour thus to have shown the fruits of the culture of Europe. A chief in Johnson's neighbourhood was proud of the title of The Drunkard. If, indeed, the Indians got drunk, so also did Johnson himself; the many healths on one St. Patrick's day left him, he says, scarcely able to write next morning. Hardly more than the Indian was civilized man then ashamed of such excesses. The famous governor Pownall wrote to Johnson in 1755 that he had been "exceedingly drunk" at the festivities when he was made lieutenant-governor of New Jersey. It is true that few such excesses are recorded in the more austere annals of New England and Johnson's manner of life, his love of horse-racing, his fox-hunting, his wine and his concubines so shocked the Puritans that no love was lost between Boston and Johnstown.

At Johnson's village where civilization and barbarism met there was incessant coming and going, European guests at his table wondered that on this edge of the wilderness they were served with imported delicacies and rare wines. They wondered too at meeting there Indian chiefs in European dress bearing themselves with solemn gravity. Indians in hundreds lounged about Johnson's mansion and grounds. They swarmed into every corner of his house, watching for a chance to air to him their needs and their grievances. They dirtied his rooms and spoiled his garden. Near the house were cabins for the negro slaves that remind us of the thatched cottages under the shadow of the mediæval castle. Johnson kept in his great feudal household a personal physician, a dwarf as a jester, a secretary, a tailor, a butler, and many other servants. When land-grabbers came to him with their schemes it is to his credit that he carried on with fine integrity a daily combat against the avarice, cruelty, and dishonesty of plans to beguile the Indians and secure their lands. In this confusion Johnson moved, tactful, alert, coarsened by his barbaric life and not squeamish in taste. After the death of his first wife, who bore him the lawful heir, who later as Sir John Johnson was a loyalist, exiled to Canada, Johnson lived loosely, chiefly with native women. It is said that he had a hundred natural children. When Mary Brant, sister of Joseph Brant, the famous chief of the Mohawks during the American Revolution, was only sixteen, Johnson took her to his house. She bore him many children and he could study native character at his own turbulent fireside. But even in this domestic life he did not treat the natives on terms of equality by marrying this Indian woman. In truth, however Johnson might flatter the Indians, they needed his masterful hand.

In 1750 Johnson became a member of the governor's council of New York, and until his death in 1775 he had a part in most of the great colonial events of his time. In 1754 he attended the conference at Albany that tried, but failed, to unite for common purposes all the English colonies and might have created an enduring and vaster British North America than that of to-day. In 1755 he was with Braddock in Virginia and no doubt gave that ill-fated leader sound advice for dealing with the Indians.

Later in the same year Johnson was fighting the French on Lake Champlain where he defeated and captured Montcalm's predecessor in the command in Canada, General Dieskau, an exploit for which he received the thanks of the British Parliament and a gift of five thousand pounds. In addition he was made a baronet and also superintendent of the Six Nations and all other northern Indians. Johnson was with the defeated British army at Ticonderoga in 1758 when Montcalm won an astounding but fruitless victory. Next year Johnson was in command when the British took the French fort at Niagara and cut communications with the west. That same year Quebec fell to the British and in September, 1760, Johnson was with the victorious army that completed the conquest of Canada. No doubt it was his control over the Indians that justified Amherst's boast of their good conduct, in contrast with the massacre of British prisoners by Indians on the French side that Montcalm had not been able to prevent. Such was Sir William Johnson, upon whom, after the cession of Canada, fell the task of reconciling the tribes to the change from France to Britain. Though he was not able to avert a barbarous war on the frontiers, in the end he made peace so enduring that never since have the British in North America been at war with the Indians.

The defect of the Indian was rather of education than of nature. The fur-traders who knew the better side knew also that his worse side was partly due to vices, such as drunkenness, learned from Europeans. The trader, Alexander Henry, a native of New Jersey, who had been with Amherst's victorious army, made in the next year his way to Michilimackinac. His sympathetic mind was alive to the beauties and enjoyments of the free life of the forest. He describes vividly the outfit and habits of the voyageurs who set out from Lachine, near Montreal. No detail is omitted, down to the pest of black flies and mosquitoes, and the "smudges" of smoke made for driving them away. Henry found the Indians alarmed at the dangers of starvation, if with the French gone they could not get from the British ammunition and other necessities for hunting. Should these be denied, they would not, they said, allow a single Englishman to remain in their country. Henry saw many good traits in the Indians. "I did not quit the lodges," he says after a captivity among them, "without the sincerest respect for the virtues I have seen." When they went hunting they gave him the lightest burden to carry and, he adds, "to the women the heaviest." Jonathan Carver, a famous traveller, who was among the Indians in the regions of the Great Lakes in 1766, tells of uniformly hospitable and courteous treatment. He was persuaded that, until corrupted by the whites, they were friendly. They so restrained their passions that violence to white female captives is never charged against them and they were capable of generous deeds. They had indulgent affection for children and a cheerful, if often malicious, sense of humour. On the other hand some tribes practised revolting cruelties and it was true of most Indians that they were lazy, dirty, vain and arrogant. The Indians' dignity of bearing in council was a sham; they were emotional and unstable.

After the fall of Montreal in 1760, Amherst had lost no time in taking possession of the west. On September 12, only four days after the surrender, Major Robert Rogers set out with two hundred men in fifteen great whale boats to raise the British flag over distant French posts. Though of rather dubious character Rogers was a tried leader in irregular warfare and knew the outlook of the Indian. While he had only a small force to assert British rule over almost a continent, he expected no fighting since he carried a letter from the French governor, the Marquis de Vaudreuil, ordering the commanders at the posts to hand them over. Rogers's account of his journey is interesting to the sportsman. He is the first known Briton to describe the wild northern shore of Lake Ontario with its abundant game. Where now stands the great city of Toronto, "a most convenient place for a factory," something well known to the French, who had had a trading post on the spot and had just abandoned it, the deer were plentiful; there were many wild fowl; and the fishing of half an hour sufficed to fill a bark canoe with salmon. At the approach of Rogers the Indians fled; but they soon came back and, no doubt in return for liquor in which to drink the health of the British king, "testified their joy," as Rogers says, "at the news of our success against the French."

The French had long used the route from Montreal to the west, past the Falls of Niagara, but only now, with the fall of Canada, was it freely open to the British. Since French influence was still strong with neighbouring tribes alarmed and suspicious at the change, we may imagine mutterings among the Indians as Rogers's party carried their canoes over the height at Niagara and launched them on the swift and dangerous waters above it that swept down to the great cataract. As he pushed on along the south shore of Lake Erie he was often storm-bound by the heavy seas on the vast and shallow lake. It was already late autumn; winter ends navigation on these waters and he advanced only slowly. At Presqu'isle, from which the upper waters of the Ohio were reached, he halted his party and himself went on with despatches from Amherst to Fort Pitt on the site of the modern great city of Pittsburgh. Not, it seems, till late October, was he again on his way to take over Detroit, the most important French post on the Great Lakes. He had now reinforcements. George Croghan, deputy of Sir William Johnson, joined the party with a band of Indian scouts as did also a company of Royal Americans, led by

Captain Campbell, destined to meet a dire fate in the impending war with the native tribes.

The Indians had watched with anxious curiosity the advance into their country of this formidable little army. The French they knew; they had traded with them at Detroit and other posts. Though lately the French had little with which to trade, they had assured the Indians who needed powder, blankets, rum and a hundred other things, that France would be victor in the war and that better days would come soon and meanwhile they had impressed on the Indians the danger from the malignant designs of the British. Consequently now, jealous of their rights and too ready at all times to be moved like children by any idle tale, the Indians decided to intimidate Rogers. When he halted at the mouth of a little river on the south shore of Lake Erie, perhaps the site of the present city of Cleveland, he was challenged by a band of Indians. They must know, they said, why he was invading their country and he must go no farther until he had met their great chief and explained his designs.

The leader, thus announced, soon appeared. He was Pontiac, chief of the Ottawa tribe that had a village near the French settlement of Detroit. In some respects he was a remarkable man. While a primitive savage in treachery and cruelty and in wild orgies when he could get rum or brandy, he had the ability of a statesman of the forest. His prestige at the time among the Indians was due to his fame as a warrior. He had been with the French when in 1755 they had defeated the British army and killed its leader, General Braddock. Later he had fought under Montcalm and on great occasions he still wore a French uniform, the gift of Montcalm. He was now the chief of a loose Indian confederacy friendly to French and hostile to British interests. Though unrest among the Indians in half a continent went far beyond the obscure plottings of such a chief as Pontiac, for the moment he was leader at the point where the British position was most critical, and he met Rogers with the tone of a sovereign. As "King and Lord of the Country" he demanded an explanation of this invasion. If the British were to remain they must acknowledge his authority. In many a rough campaign Rogers had learned the workings of the native mind, and now he soothed Pontiac with such skill that he turned back and really guided the British force for the rest of the journey to Detroit. The Indians well knew that if the French power had fallen in Canada they could be saved from starvation in only one of two possible ways; by supplies from the British in the east or from the French on the Mississippi in the west. Though Pontiac preferred the French, he was shrewd enough to see that the British had been victorious.

Meanwhile at Detroit there was much searching of heart. Captain Belêtre, the French officer in command, though well aware of the surrender at Montreal, kept up a tone of defiance. The Indians, too, seemed ready to attack the boats as they advanced up the eighteen miles of the broad strait that carries to Lake Erie the mighty waters of the upper lakes. For the moment, however, Pontiac's influence was for peace, and he checked hostile designs. The river, always called by the French a strait, was dotted with islands charming to the eye. Croghan says that later the most beautiful of them, Grosse Isle, eight miles long, was offered to him by the Indians as a gift, but adds that he refused it because, at this critical time, he did not wish to seem a land-grabber. He wrote, however, to Johnson that "if your Honour wish to have a Small Estate in that country I will gett itt for you."

It is by no accident that on this river has grown up a great city, for its situation gives it command of the traffic by water between the east and the west. In earlier days the English in New York had seen its importance and had had some design to occupy it, but it continued to be within the French sphere of influence. In 1701, La Mothe Cadillac, a picturesque French soldier turned fur-trader, and later governor of Louisiana, seeing the advantage of this situation, made a toilsome journey, lasting forty-nine days, from Montreal by way of the Ottawa River, a journey that involved carrying his canoes over more than thirty portages. When he reached Lake Huron he paddled along its rocky coast to the Detroit, the strait, leading to Lake Erie. Cadillac had with him fifty soldiers and also fifty voyageurs, skilled in the task before them of clearing the forest to make room for the first settlement in that region. He halted at the narrowest part of the river and there, on perhaps the best site for trade in all the west, he began not only the building of Fort Detroit, but also the clearing of fields for the farms that soon attracted settlers whose descendants remain in that region to this day. When the news of his coming spread, the Indians, full of curiosity, came to watch the creation of a post in their midst where they might get needed supplies. At first Detroit was chiefly a fort and no women came. The settlement grew slowly. Cadillac, an out-spoken, highhanded man, so sure of himself as to defy even the Jesuits then supreme in Canada, had influence enough to secure a monopoly of the fur trade of the whole region. Three tribes, the Wyandots (the former Hurons), the Potawatamies and the Ottawas founded villages near the fort.

By 1760 Detroit was the most important French post in the west. The small fort, set a little back from the river on the right bank, was surrounded by palisades twenty-five feet high, with a bastion at each corner, and a few mounted cannon. There were about a hundred houses, with roofs of thatched straw, or of birchbark, peculiarly liable to take fire. Though the streets were narrow there was on the south side a spacious parade. Récollet friars served the parish church. Opposite the fort, on the present Canadian side, the Jesuits had a mission station. Stretching along both sides of the swift river were houses, fields and orchards of apples, plums, pears and even peaches, making a pleasing break in the monotony of the forest. The settlement was a copy of the country-side about Quebec. The farmer had the calèche for use in summer, the carriole for winter, an excellent breed of horses from French Canada, oxen for ploughing, and other live stock. By the way-side were crosses, the *calvaires* still numerous in Quebec. Detroit was the only agricultural settlement in the region of the Great Lakes. There were some two thousand five hundred Canadians in and about the place, five hundred of them capable of bearing arms. In addition to farming they carried on profitable trade with the Indians. By 1760, however, owing to the war, supplies were lacking. Traders had little to sell, prices were high, and it was not unlikely that, to both settlers and Indians, even their former enemies, the British, would be welcome if their coming would ensure the needed goods.

When Rogers's clumsy whale-boats arrived before the fort he landed and pitched his tents in a green field on the opposite side of the river. Though Captain Belêtre, in command at the fort, had been notified by Rogers of his approach and of the fall of French power, he chose to show a mordant humour. He put up on a pole a roughly carved head of a man with a crow pecking at it,—himself, as he explained to the Canadians and Indians, scratching out the brains of the British leader. Why, he asked, if New France had fallen, had not a French officer been sent with Rogers as was the practice in Europe? Soon, however, when convinced that he must yield, he summoned the Indians in the neighbourhood to a conference on November 28. They came to his house with, as they said, tearful eyes though, they added, weeping should end in the spring when all the Indian nations would join the king of France, their father, to drive out the English. With some asperity Belêtre told them that they were the authors of their own downfall by drinking English rum. The new English master, he added, would not be as gentle as the French. They had better move westward to the Illinois country where French aid was still available.

On November 29, 1760, a striking ceremony took place, watched by some seven hundred Indian warriors. Two British officers with a squad of thirty-six soldiers, in what impressive military array they could command, crossed the river to the fort and demanded surrender. The French garrison marched out and laid down their arms. The white flag of France was hauled down and in its place floated the red flag of Britain, while perhaps for the first time in that region was heard "God save the King." Rogers had been so lavish in promises to the Indians of the good things to come with British rule that they greeted the change with yells of seeming delight. After lean days under the French, visions of relief from the new king caused them to shout "that they would always for the future fight for the nation thus favoured by Him that made the world." To the surprise of their warlike Indian friends, the French settlers readily accepted the situation. In due course the French garrison marched to waiting boats and departed down the river, prisoners of war, bound for Philadelphia. Then the Indian tribes were left alone with the British.

What happened at Detroit happened at Michilimackinac and other French posts now occupied by the British. For a time the alluring hopes of a paradise, to be created by the newcomers, checked native unrest. Rivers of rum should flow; presents from the British king should be unlimited; goods should be so plentiful that the Indians might buy a warm blanket for two beaver skins. The Indians looked upon the expected presents as a kind of ground rent for the use of the lands of which they themselves were the owners. Inevitably disillusion soon followed. Presents were not forthcoming. The French were gone and the British clearly intended to rule. They seemed, however, so weak, so remote from support, that, inspired chiefly by Pontiac, the Indians soon came to believe that a deadly blow, struck before the British had grown strong, might ensure that the tribes should be again supreme in their own land. Some leaders among them were hoping for a return to the simple life of the days before they had been tainted by the corruption of Europe, a vain hope since, when once undermined by a more complex culture, the simple life is never revived.

A rare gift which those of British origin may well envy inheres in the French. Though they are sure that they lead the world in the finest products of culture, they are in large measure free from the arrogance of race. With them to be French is what matters; granted this the skin may be white, yellow or black. Just as, on the condition of baptism, the Roman Catholic Church is ready to receive all races, so does France welcome on a basis of equality all those of whatever colour who owe allegiance to her. They all have the right to be at home in France's capital. On the other hand the people of England and of the United States have an acute consciousness of racial differences that often offends alien peoples. The Englishman may have, perhaps usually he has, a fine sense of justice but it is not easy for him to accept others than the white races as equals. To this day in London a black man is not received in some of the good hotels, while in Paris if he saunters into a fashionable restaurant or registers at a great hotel he is accepted without reserve as to race. Among the tribes in North America this French characteristic had won friends, while the British tone of superiority had caused suspicion. Sir William Johnson was, indeed, as tactful as any Frenchman, partly perhaps

because he was Irish, but the average English soldier or
trader was more likely to adopt the tone of General Amherst that the Indians, a debased breed, must pay the penalty of annihilation if they proved troublesome.

Unlike the French the British had never controlled their
traders among the Indians. Each English colony did what
it liked, while the French had always declared, if not always
with success, that the whole west was under single control
from Quebec and that no trader might go to the interior
without the governor's licence. For remaining in the forest
during more than twenty-four hours, without such a licence,
Governor Frontenac had made the penalty death, and had
hanged at least one trader who had defied this rule. The
system of licence led to abuses. Behind it lay the spirit of
monopoly, and French officials and their friends grew rich
because they, and they alone, might reap the profits of the
Indian trade. Nevertheless single control gave the French
the real advantage that they could shape and direct a
policy suited to the needs and tastes of the tribes. Moreover, the French had not tried to beguile the Indians into
selling their lands, but had been content simply to proclaim
the King of France sovereign over the whole west. Except
at Detroit and in the Mississippi Valley, they had made no
serious effort to colonize beyond Montreal, a policy that
suited the Indians who could barter their furs for fire-arms,
blankets and brandy, and at the same time retain their
rights in the land. Since each tribe considered itself a nation, sovereign within its own territory, Indian etiquette
required strict regard for frontiers. The French fort, for
instance, at Michilimackinac, between Lake Huron and
Lake Michigan, lay partly in the territory of the Chippewas
and partly in that of the Ottawas, and members of either
tribe who visited the fort were careful not to encamp a
yard beyond their own limits. Civilized communities find
it difficult to understand a land system with no recorded

surveys. For the natives, however, oral tradition sufficed, and always they insisted that tribal claims to territory should be respected.

While the British proclamation, after the fall of Montreal, that trade should be unfettered seemed to involve the free competition from which the Indians should benefit, it let loose on the savages a horde of traders some, at least, of whom were ready to cheat them, to debauch their women, and to claim ownership of their lands. In a field hitherto open only to the French, the baser sort of trader was now free to act on the principle that it was no crime to defraud an Indian; that drugged rum was a great ally of trade; that with drunken Indians the scales might register at will one pound for three, or three for one; and that to get a debauched chief's reckless surrender of tribal rights to the land created a valid title. Many a savage was thus robbed and when, in the sober morning, he complained, he might receive hard words and be unable to get on credit the things vital to his life as a hunter and trapper. Though Washington said that the frontiersman thought it no crime to kill an Indian, this was not the French point of view. The priests at the French mission were so likely to report to the governor at Quebec any acts of lawlessness that the traders had been rather the nervous, conciliatory friends of the Indians than their masters. "The English treat us with much disrespect," said a chief of the Senecas at Detroit, in July, 1761. "We are penned up like Hogs," said another Iroquois at Philadelphia, a few weeks later. In the play "Pontiach," published in 1766, and written in part at least by the very Major Rogers who took possession of Detroit, one speaker says that to kill an Indian is "no more murder than to crack a louse"; "perdition to their faithless sooty souls," says another; a group of officers go off to drink damnation to the Indians. "Let me hear no more of your damned hellish clamour," says Colonel Cocksure to Pontiac.

"The wound is very deep," Pontiac retorts. On the other hand, though scheming traders were hated, just and honest men like Alexander Henry and Jonathan Carver were esteemed. Within a year, however, after the British had raised their flag at Detroit the Indians had become so resentful against them that, when Henry appeared at Michilimackinac in 1761, an Indian told him that the English must be brave men and not afraid of death, since they dared to come, as he did, fearlessly among their enemies.

After 1761, alarm continued to spread among the Indians. The British were building new forts. Why? The French had gone; defence against them was not needed; the menace must be to the Indians themselves. Near some forts, British settlers were clearing away the forest, in order to till the soil, something that would ruin the hunting grounds. The most urgent grievance was that, while the Indians believed the forts to be stuffed with needed things, they received few presents. When their anxious enquiries reached Amherst he said that the English would do nothing for what he called "those wild beasts," until they redeemed their promise to deliver up English captives, whom they still held, and promised also to be tractable and loyal. Though the French had had quarrels with their Indian allies, they had never adopted this tone. Now that they were gone the Indians idealized them as models of fair dealing, while, by contrast, they thought the British not only arrogant but also cheats and villains.

Though, with reason, the Indians feared the increasing numbers of the English, some boastful savages professed to despise them as fighters. Five years before the fall of Montreal, when General Braddock had been defeated and killed on his march to the Ohio, it was the Indian allies of the French, among whom was Pontiac, that had wrought the worst havoc on that fatal day. Tales of the triumph were repeated by Indian camp-fires. In the war just ended, how-

ever, another tale had been told. Many of the western
Indians, who had served as far away as on the St. Lawrence, had seen France defeated; and now, instead of contempt for the British the fear spread that, not satisfied
with mastering the French, they would follow the tribes to
the farthest west and take their land. To strike quickly,
before British power had grown, seemed wise, and the
Indians had delusive hopes of aid from France. French
traders, still active farther west, told them that France
would quickly recover what was lost. When, in 1761, Spain
joined France in the war, these traders assured the Indians
that these two mighty powers would destroy the British
enemy. The King of France, they said, was on his way to
Canada, and would soon appear to drive back the nation,
really feeble, which was acting as a brutal oppressor.
Meanwhile Sir William Johnson spared no effort of conciliation. After the fall of Montreal he wrote instructions to the
officers at the western posts in the English colonies to cultivate good relations with the Indians. They were to be
guarded in their intercourse and not to permit rambling
abroad from the posts as this led to disputes and quarrels.
The interpreter at the posts should watch the traders, each
of whom must have a licence under seal from himself or
his deputy. Johnson sent a list of prices of goods, reckoned
in beaver skins, so as to ensure fair dealing.

By midsummer of 1761 signs of trouble so increased that
Amherst instructed Johnson to go at once to Detroit. "I
cannot be absent at present," Amherst said, and added
light-heartedly that "Sir William will settle all matters with
the upper Indians." All his skill was required to meet a
grave danger and Amherst's instructions made his task more
difficult. "Entire Destruction," wrote Amherst in his wooden
arrogance, would be the fate of any who ventured on evil
designs. He would not buy good behaviour by presents.
None would be given in the future, for presents only tended

to make loafers of the Indians. When they were obliged to work to get furs for barter they would have less time to plot mischief. In future they should have only small supplies of ammunition and be thus the more dependent. Johnson set out in July. When he reached Niagara and summoned the Indians to a conference, he found the Senecas, the most westerly of the Six Nations, highly excited. They had heard from French sources of British misdeeds; of cheating; of occupying Indian lands; above all of refusing to make presents and also of holding back needed goods for trade. A Chippewa chief told Johnson that he was in sore need of many things—a smith to repair his gun, a spear for fishing, an axe to save him from the labour of cutting down trees by slow fire. He put first in his needs a hat to protect him, as he said, from the hot sun; really, it may be, for purposes of ceremonial, since an Indian loved to appear on parade wearing a European hat and a blanket, and sometimes only a hat. Johnson spoke soft words; he played cards with a Frenchman whom he met and made him drunk in order to get from him in his cups information as to French intrigues with the Indians. When, after a toilsome journey, he landed near Detroit, he managed to secure horses to make an impressive entry on horseback.

His coming was a great event. Captain Campbell, the officer in command, gave a ball at which the dancing lasted nine hours while Johnson's ball in return lasted eleven hours. No doubt endurance was aided by the supply of wine that he had brought. He had three chief problems; to regulate trade with the Indians; to insist that soldiers and settlers alike should show respect and conciliation in dealing with them; and, hardest of all, to explain the reasons for ending the practice of giving presents. On September 9, 1761, Johnson held a conference with some thirteen hundred Indians and made a long friendly speech in the florid style of native eloquence. In one respect, at least, even his gift of tact failed. He had in reality brought a few presents, ammunition, blankets and so on, and these he gave to the Wyandots, the former Hurons. Since they were ancient allies of the French, Johnson thought it wise specially to conciliate them; but this gave offence to Pontiac, chief of the Ottawas, who was looking for presents for his own people, a much stronger tribe. Johnson's nephew, Guy, was with him as secretary and must have had a busy time at the conference for we have a full report of the speeches. Johnson extended his attentions to the French community and it is recorded that he made some French gentlemen and two priests drunk at dinner, all in the interests of peace and good-will. He returned home deeply anxious. A dark cloud was rising and soon the storm broke.

Johnson had taken with him to Detroit a young major, Henry Gladwin, destined to play a heroic part in the coming conflict. He and Pontiac were old foes for, in 1755, at the age of twenty-five, Gladwin had been wounded in the fight under Braddock with Pontiac's French allies. While at Detroit in 1761, he fell ill, and after Johnson's visit he returned to England. Duty called him, however, to serve again in America and at the end of August, 1762, he was at Detroit, now in command, with the veteran Captain Campbell under him. The crisis came only slowly. During the bleak winter of 1762–63 Gladwin watched both the French inhabitants, who still hoped that the country would be returned to France, and the Indians. He punished acts of lawlessness. A man and woman of the Pawnee tribe brutally murdered one Clapham, a trader from Detroit with whom they were serving, cut off his head and threw his body into a stream. Though the man escaped to the Illinois, Gladwin secured the woman, gave her a public trial and, when she was condemned to be hanged, carried out the execution in the most public manner as a warning to all offenders. Mutterings followed among the Indians who regarded this form of punishment as specially degrading.

While the Indians were servile in begging for tobacco, gunpowder and whisky, they were also arrogant and resented Gladwin's tone when he rebuked loiterers at the fort and called them dogs. They concealed their thoughts behind an impassive gravity but gloated secretly over the prospect of the day when the fort should be plundered and rivers of rum should flow. On April 20, 1763, Gladwin wrote to Amherst that a rising was imminent. What was known as the Bloody Belt was being circulated among the tribes, a call to each of them to attack the British. In the thick of the plotting, so Gladwin learned, were Johnson's special wards, the Six Nations, who were joining the Shawnees and the Delawares in efforts to arouse the western tribes. While Pontiac could have had but slight personal influence with the remote tribes, he was the chief organizer of the conspiracy. Though he could not himself read or write, he kept two secretaries, one to interpret letters received, the other to send out his plans and instructions. The plot was simplicity itself. On the same day and hour, at every British post, Indians bearing concealed arms were to gain admission as friends and then to carry out a ruthless massacre.

Gladwin had scarcely written his report when open strife broke out. On the morning of April 27, 1763, many Indians gathered on the bank of the little stream called Ecorces, some ten miles south of Detroit, on the west side of the wide river, remote enough from Detroit to escape close observation. Seated on the grass in a circle and wrapped in their blankets on the chill April day, Ojibways, Wyandots, Ottawas, and a few other tribes, debated the great plan to destroy the English. After a lighted pipe had passed in

silence from hand to hand, Pontiac, in savage garb, moved
to the middle of the circle and burst into a fiery speech.
The arrogant English, he said, neglected and despised the
Indians; the French would, however, soon return, and then
the English would be humbled as he, Pontiac, had already
helped to humble them in the time of Braddock. The
Maker of Heaven and Earth spoke by a special message
through him to the Indians, to call them back to their old
ways. Why did they suffer the intruder? Why had they
given up their simple life to copy the white men; bows and
arrows for guns; furs for blankets? Why had they drunk
the deadly fire-water? The time had come to fling away
such things and to wipe from the face of the earth the
English dogs dressed in red.

Though Pontiac was simple enough to believe that Gladwin knew nothing of the plot, the meeting of so many warriors could not really be secret. The romantic tradition that
Gladwin was informed by a beautiful girl of the danger
must, it seems, give way to another not less romantic that
the daughter of a French settler, who later married one of
Gladwin's officers named Sterling, told her lover of plans
discussed in the house of her father, an enemy of the British. Gladwin heard too that the Indians were buying from
the traders many files and were using them to cut short the
barrels of their muskets so as to carry them concealed under
their blankets. Suspicion of a crisis was stimulated on the
night of the 6th of May, when the sentinels at Detroit heard
the beat of drums and wild cries in the Wyandot village on
the opposite, the left, bank of the river. On the right bank
the Indians had recently made a camp above the fort with
the result that squaws, children, and half-naked warriors
wandered freely in the open spaces outside the palisades of
Detroit. They professed to be friendly and Pontiac sent
word to Gladwin that on the 7th he should come to the fort
with the rest of the nation to pay a formal visit of good will

and to meet him in a conference that should end suspicions and ensure peace. Accordingly early on this morning tall warriors followed by their squaws and all, on this spring day, wearing blankets, sauntered to the strand before the fort. Others came paddling across the river and at ten came Pontiac wrapped in a blanket of bright colours. When three hundred Indians entered the fort and idly strolled about, they found sentinels at their posts, the garrison of about six score on parade, and all the stores closed. Gladwin had taken precautions.

What followed reads like a scene from a play. When the conference began and forty or fifty chiefs filed solemnly past the armed guard into the council chamber, they found Gladwin and the officers awaiting them with pistols at their belts and swords at their sides. So stern was Gladwin's demeanour that the chiefs became uneasy and would hardly sit down on the skins spread on the floor. At last there in a long line they sat with the British opposite in a similar line. When Pontiac ventured to ask why, on the occasion of a visit to show friendliness and goodwill, the soldiers were on parade in a manner so unusual, Gladwin replied that it was for discipline and exercise. Following Indian custom, Pontiac had brought a belt of wampum and, by a refinement of treachery that had been revealed to Gladwin, the raising in his hand of this symbol of peace was to be the signal to the chiefs to draw their concealed weapons, slaughter Gladwin and his officers, and rush to open the gate to the crowd of Indians waiting there to join in the massacre. But just as Pontiac seemed about to make this gesture, Gladwin gave a slight signal with his hand, the British officers half drew their swords, and from the passage without came the clatter of arms and the swelling beat of the drums.

Clearly, as Pontiac now saw, Gladwin was ready to fight. He might indeed have seized the chiefs and held them as hostages. Six weeks later Amherst wrote that on such evidence of treachery Gladwin "ought to have put the Villain and every Indian in the Fort to death." Gladwin was, however, still uncertain of the extent of the plot. He was used to and hardly surprised at Indian duplicity, and he may well have doubted whether Pontiac had the influence to lead an extensive rising. Accordingly, while not hiding his suspicions, he spoke calmly. Though he would, he said, take ample revenge for any hostile act, he hoped for friendly relations and to show his good intentions he gave some trifling presents to his guests. In the end Pontiac led his Indians away, denying any evil intent. That afternoon, however, six hundred savages dragged to the fort an old woman whom they accused of having told Gladwin lies about a plot. His insistence that not she but one of themselves had warned him proved of no avail; they carried her back across the river and according to one report Pontiac himself clubbed her to death.

Next day, Sunday, Pontiac and a few chiefs again paddled across the river to the fort. Though Gladwin rejected a proposal to smoke a pipe of peace, his tone was still conciliatory and Pontiac went off saying that next day he should bring his people to a council to clear up all disputes. Accordingly in the morning some four hundred Indians gathered on the strand before the fort, crowded up to the barred gates, and demanded entrance for a parley. To Gladwin's refusal to allow more than sixty chiefs to enter, Pontiac replied that all or none must be admitted. He went off in a rage and then massacre began. Some Indians ran to the house of an Englishwoman outside the fort, killed and scalped her and her two sons and followed this with the massacre of any whom they could seize. Among the victims was Sir Robert Davers, fifth Baronet, an educated Englishman of large estate, whose hope to secure grants of wild lands and love of travel and adventure, it seems, had brought him to America. He had been at De-

troit for at least a year and this Sunday was on Lake St.
Clair with a small party. The Indians murdered him, boiled
and ate his body, and killed also an officer with him, Captain Robertson, and half a dozen soldiers. An Indian made
a tobacco pouch of the skin of Robertson's arm.

Such was savage warfare; such were the risks not only
to men but also to women and children. The Indians now
closed in on Detroit and began the long siege that lasted for
more than a year. The fort itself was safe, so long as Gladwin had food and ammunition, for the Indians had no
stomach to attack its high palisades. Their camp was about
a mile and a half north of the fort, at the mouth of Parent's
Creek, and they kept up a desultory fire under cover of
neighbouring houses and barns. When Gladwin sent word
that he was willing to redress any grievances, Pontiac suggested that the veteran Captain Campbell, well-known as
friendly to the Indians, should go out to discuss terms.
Campbell soothed Gladwin's suspicions, secured his consent,
took with him Lieutenant George McDougall and, escorted
by four chiefs and some Canadians, walked out to Pontiac's
camp. On arrival he was attacked by excited savages, but
was rescued by Pontiac. In the conference that followed
Pontiac announced his impossible terms; the English must
lay down their arms, abandon the goods in the fort, and
leave the country under Indian escort, which meant treacherous massacre. He retained Campbell's party as prisoners.
In the end Campbell was brutally murdered and the savages
tore out his heart and ate it.

While a few Canadians who had some Indian blood in
their veins joined Pontiac, the more prudent saw little hope
of his success. There is a doubtful story that one settler
named Bâby, living on the opposite bank of the river, was
of great service in bringing provisions to Detroit under cover
of night. At one time famine was so imminent that Gladwin's officers began to think surrender inevitable. News

came in of the fall one after another of the British posts. Every horror of native savagery was inflicted along many miles of the frontier of the British colonies. Meanwhile Pontiac, though a savage in his methods, proved a resourceful leader. He had what Major Robert Rogers called "an air of majesty and princely grandeur," and his prestige held the tribes at Detroit together for a period unusually long in Indian warfare. He watched every movement of his enemy. When one of the two armed schooners, the *Gladwin,* sailed down the river to secure aid and lay becalmed at its mouth, suddenly many hostile canoes dashed out from the shore. In the bow of the foremost canoe the savages placed their prisoner, Captain Campbell, in order to prevent fire from the vessel. As he called out to take no thought of him, a breeze sprang up and the ship sailed away.

By the end of May rescue was on the way from Fort Niagara, but when the hundred men, in a score of whaleboats, incautiously landed at Point Pelée, just before entering the river, Wyandot Indians captured all but two of the boats and killed or made prisoners of some sixty men. Next day the watchers in Detroit saw many boats rowed by British sailors coming up the river near the opposite shore, but to the welcoming British cheer from the fort a war-whoop was the answering cry from far across the water. Though the rowers were British, they rowed under the compulsion of Indian captors. In the leading boat, carrying four soldiers and three Indians, a soldier suddenly stood up, as if to exchange places with the tired comrade at the oar, and so grappled with one of the Indians that the two locked together went overboard. The soldier perished but the Indian, according to one account, shook himself free and swam to shore. Then came an exciting chase. When the other two Indians leaped into the water the three soldiers in the boat rowed hard to cross the river to the armed schooner lying before Detroit. Indian canoes that put out in pursuit had nearly reached the distressed rowers when they came within range of the schooner's cannon which scattered them in panic. The other captured boats passed on to Pontiac's camp. Booty taken at Point Pelée included much liquor and now all day long Indians half drunk stayed in their camp to enjoy the slow torture to death of the soldiers. Some bodies were cooked and eaten; others, hacked and burned, came floating down the river past the fort.

Amherst, slow, contemptuous of the foe, unwilling to take precautions in advance, was at last aroused. On June 16, 1763, he wrote from New York that he was sending his aide-de-camp, Captain James Dalyell, to gather at Niagara all available forces, and proceed to Detroit. The Indians, said Amherst, would bring "Certain and Inevitable Ruin" on their whole race, if they caused further trouble. On the morning of the 29th of July there was a fog at Detroit. When it faded before a hot sun, the defenders found the river dotted with bateaux carrying Dalyell's force of nearly three hundred men. Hitherto Detroit had been on the defensive, but now when Dalyell, a high-spirited scion of an ancient house, urged an immediate attack, Gladwin yielded rather against his better judgment. At two o'clock in the morning of July 31, two hundred and fifty men, led by Dalyell, passed silently out into the darkness. They hoped to catch the Indians still asleep at their camp. Some treacherous settler had, however, revealed the plan and, as the head of the column crossed the rude bridge over Parent's creek ever since called the Bloody Run, a devastating fire came out of the darkness. When the British had fought their way back to the fort and counted their loss they found that of two hundred and fifty men sixty or seventy had been killed or wounded. Dalyell's body when recovered was found to have been horribly mangled.

Within a few weeks, every post west of Niagara, in the region of the Great Lakes, except Detroit, posts distant from each other by hundreds of miles, had fallen. Though the reality was bad enough, rumour made it worse. At Fort Pitt, on the upper waters of the Ohio, false news came in on June 1 that not one of the English in Detroit was left alive. The Indians were true to their code that in war every means is justifiable. At each post they professed friendship until they could strike. On May 16, at Fort Sandusky, on the south shore of Lake Erie, the officer in command, Ensign Paully, was told that seven Indians, some of them well known to him, desired an interview. When he received them cordially in his quarters and pipes were lighted and a talk began, an Indian at the doorway gave a signal. In a few minutes, after a hurried scramble, Paully was led forth a captive, while the bodies of his garrison lay strewn on the parade ground. At Fort Miami, farther west on the Maumee River, Ensign Holmes was in command. He was invited to visit and prescribe for a squaw lying ill in a cabin a few hundred yards from the fort and was shot dead on the way.

We have a dramatic account of events at Michilimackinac to which, after the open quarrel with Gladwin, Pontiac sent orders to destroy the British garrison. June 4, the birthday of George III, was celebrated as a holiday. The spring trade in furs, after the trapping of the winter, was active, and many Indians had come to the fort. When two Indian tribes, the Sacs and the Chippewas, asked permission to celebrate the holiday at the fort by a match in the native game of lacrosse, Major Etherington, the British officer in command, had no misgivings. Though warned by Alexander Henry, then trading at the fort, of the danger of treachery, he merely jested at Henry's timidity. The match took place outside the gates on an open plain where the rival teams had been practising daily. Most of the garrison went out to watch the game, but at the same time, within the fort, loitered many squaws, closely wrapped in blankets on this warm day in June. Several times the ball was sent flying over the palisades but was thrown back to the players. Meanwhile the rival sides kept edging up closer to the gate and when, once more, the ball went into the fort, the mass of Indians, a struggling shouting crowd, rushed after it. The squaws inside threw open their blankets, the players snatched tomahawks and knives, and within a few minutes one officer and fifteen men lay dead and scalped in the fort, while the unarmed spectators of the match had been made prisoners.

Henry had not gone out to the game but had remained in the fort writing letters to send by a canoe leaving for Montreal. Suddenly he was horrified by seeing from a window the wild scene of Indians cutting down and scalping British soldiers. Since inhabitants of French origin were not molested and safety seemed to lie among them, Henry dashed into the house next door of a well-known Canadian trader, named Langlade. "At my entrance," he says, "I found the whole family at the windows gazing at the scene of blood before them." When he asked for a refuge, Langlade turned his back with a shrug of the shoulders and said "What would you have me do?" An Indian slave woman showed more pity. Beckoning Henry to follow her, she led him to the garret, locked him in, and took away the key. He was able to look down upon the square through an aperture and saw, as he says, "in shape the foulest and most terrible, the ferocious triumph of barbarous conquerors. The dead were scalped and mangled, the dying were writhing and shrieking under the unsatiated knife and tomahawk; and, from the bodies of some ripped open, their butchers were drinking the blood scooped up in the hollow of joined hands, and quaffed amid shouts of rage and victory."

When the savages went to Langlade's house and asked if he was not harbouring an Englishman, he told them to search for themselves, and led them to the garret, the most likely place of concealment. Hearing their approach Henry crept behind some vessels of birch bark. Four Indians, carrying tomahawks and smeared with blood, examined the room, but it was dark and Henry lay still, though he feared that the throbbing of his heart should betray him. All the time the savages were telling Langlade about the murders and scalping. In the end they went away and again the door was locked. Major Etherington and a number of other soldiers had been seized and stripped of their red coats and, by concealing their character as soldiers, this may have saved them. That night the Indians had a wild debauch with the liquor seized in the fort. Henry did not escape capture. Next day the wife of Langlade, fearing savage reprisals, insisted that her husband should deliver him up. When the door of the garret was opened, a huge Indian, well-known to Henry, seized him by the collar and raised a knife as if to plunge it into his breast. He paused and then dropped his arm and said, "I won't kill you." He had lost a brother and now he declared that Henry should take his brother's place. Henry survived to tell the most vivid of all the tales of Pontiac's conspiracy. He continued in the fur trade and penetrated to the western prairies. He visited England and also France, where he received marked attention from the unfortunate queen, Marie Antoinette. A much respected citizen, he died at Montreal in 1824, more than sixty years after his stirring adventure at Michili-mackinac.

The Indians so wasted a long frontier and so tortured men and women alike, that every tree, wrote Colonel Bouquet, became an Indian for the terrified people. A passer-by, struck by the unwonted silence in a frontier schoolhouse in Pennsylvania, entered to find the teacher scalped and dead, with a Bible in his hand, and strewn about the room the horribly mangled bodies of his nine pupils. These things stirred so blind a fury of resentment that a band of fanatics in Pennsylvania pledged themselves to imitate Joshua of old and exterminate the native race, in order that God's chosen people might inherit the land: "Thou shalt smite them and utterly destroy them, thou shalt make no covenant with them nor show mercy unto them." Enraged men attacked even friendly Indians and killed without mercy men, women, and children, some of whom, as they died, protested love for the English. Avenging bands threatened even Philadelphia, because pacifist Quakers talked as if the white man's injustice lay at the root of the trouble. The menace created an enduring horror of Indian methods in war. When, a dozen years later, these colonies were at war with the mother country they were embittered by the report that she was employing against them the very tribes who had taken part in Pontiac's war. Pontiac's conspiracy produced, indeed, a startling effect on opinion during the American Revolution.

Amherst and some of his officers, even after long experience in America, had not learned to adjust themselves to the conditions of Indian warfare. Because they despised the frontier method of fighting from cover hundreds of brave soldiers were sacrificed needlessly. The man who won final success, Colonel Bouquet, was less rigid in his ways. In the summer of 1763, while Gladwin was defending Detroit, Bouquet was leading an army overland, from Pennsylvania, across the Allegheny Mountains to Fort Pitt. On the afternoon of August 5, when he had made a march of seventeen miles to a spot called Bushy Run, the camping place for the night, about twenty-five miles from Fort Pitt, Indians in ambush attacked his weary column in front and rear. The spot was near the scene of Braddock's defeat. By nightfall Bouquet had lost sixty men. In the great heat his force was suffering from lack of water. All night long the forest was hideous with savage war-whoops and at daybreak the Indians renewed the attack. When Bouquet feigned retreat and they came out into the open to pursue him his concealed men closed in and used the bayonet. On August 10, having lost eight officers and a hundred and fifteen men, he marched into Fort Pitt. He notes with pride one superior trait of the regular soldier. While no one of them would so much as touch an Indian corpse, the Rangers and the pack-horse drivers scalped enemies not yet dead, and mangled the bodies. When this rescue of Fort Pitt had broken the back of the conspiracy, the British race had asserted for good the mastery of the continent westward to the Mississippi.

At Detroit, meanwhile, the approach of winter had caused Pontiac's allies to scatter to the hunting grounds. When, on October 12, Gladwin agreed to a truce with some of the Ojibways, Pontiac, with his tribe, the Ottawas, still held aloof. By the end of October, however, he was assured from French sources that peace had come and he then sent to Gladwin a naïve letter, taken down in French by a Canadian. "My brother," it ran, "I have accepted the word which my father [the King of France] has sent me, to make peace, and all our young men have buried their hatchets." He had forgotten, he said, the evil things of the past and would come for a parley at Gladwin's pleasure. Gladwin replied that the message would be sent to the commander-in-chief, and that if Pontiac was in earnest all might be well. The baffled plotter, still really bent on war, went off to the Illinois country hoping for French aid. Gladwin wrote to Amherst that Sir William Johnson should be used to make peace; adding that, if further punishment for Indian barbarities was intended, there was one simple method; the free sale of rum would cause the Indians to destroy themselves; fire and sword would be less effective.

From the first Amherst was bent on hard terms. He had told his officers to take no prisoners and to put to death every Indian found in arms. He would, he said, trust no one of the race; they were more nearly allied to the brute than to the human creation. Meanwhile Johnson was trying softer methods. In September, 1763, at the very time when delegates of the Six Nations were at Detroit urging the western tribes to destroy the British before they had a firm grip on the country, Johnson had held a conference with the parent tribes at German Flats in their own country. One tribe, the Senecas, still held aloof but the three hundred and forty chiefs who were present declared that the trouble was chiefly due to French intrigue. While they complained that the British were occupying too many posts and seemed haughty and suspicious, they protested their loyalty. Since the Senecas continued hostile, Amherst ordered that the tribe should be destroyed. "No male Seneca capable of bearing arms will," he said, "be spared. The women and children will be taken prisoners and afterwards distributed among the other tribes. The Seneca nation, as an organized tribe, must disappear." He could have done this with his army now numbering sixteen thousand men, while the Senecas could muster barely fifteen hundred warriors. When they sued abjectly for peace, Amherst required the surrender for execution of nineteen of the ringleaders. He intended to hang them all and would hardly listen to Sir William Johnson's objections. Forthwith he hanged two Senecas, a mode of punishment more dreadful to them than burning at the stake; to kill a warrior with a rope, they said, keeps a man from showing his courage by singing his death song. Eight of the other leaders died in prison. When, three years later, Pontiac agreed to pledge fealty to George III the rest were released.

Since Amherst's great fame as the conqueror of Canada was in danger of being tarnished by the war with the Indians he was anxious to go home and late in 1763 he handed over the command to his former comrade, General Gage, and returned to England. Gage was much less of a martinet. In

January, 1764, he wrote in high glee to Johnson that he had had an extraordinary piece of good news: France was to cede Louisiana to Spain by which "we shall get rid of a Most troublesome Neighbour." In truth, however, he found one even more troublesome, since not only did Spain have an adjacent base in Mexico and her other colonies but she had Castilian arrogance in using her authority. Meanwhile Johnson, busy in his tasks of conciliation, revived the policy of making presents on a small scale to the Indians. During the winter of 1763, he sent messages far and wide inviting the tribes that wished peace to meet him at Niagara early in July, 1764.

Alexander Henry tells us of the reception at Sault-Ste.-Marie of the summons to the Ojibways who had led in the massacre at Michilimackinac and were now in nervous dread of vengeance. When a canoe arrived from Niagara with British envoys they were heard with anxious attention. The Six Nations, they announced, were allied with the English. Unless the Ojibways would go to Niagara to make peace they should be destroyed. When the startled savages consulted their medicine man, he increased their alarm. He told them that in a vision he had seen the great river at Montreal covered with boats filled with soldiers, in number like the leaves of the trees, coming to make war on the enemies of the British. Sir William Johnson would, however, be the friend and protector of the Indians. He would, said the spirit to the Ojibways, fill their canoes with presents; with blankets, kettles, guns, powder and shot, and with barrels of rum such as the stoutest Indian would not be able to lift. At this there were shouts to go to meet the great man. This was not the note of some other tribes. The haughty Delawares and Shawnees answered Johnson's invitation with what Gage called an "insolent audacious message," which they compelled a prisoner to write, that they despised the English as old women but out of pity would consider terms of peace. This for the time, however, they proved unwilling to make. Pontiac, too, would not come. He was still in arms before Detroit.

The assembly at Niagara in July, 1764, was on a grand scale. From as far south as Georgia and Alabama, from Montreal in the east, from the old Huron country in the north, from lands beyond the Mississippi, the Indians came in swarthy hordes. Even the Sioux from the distant prairies were invited but excused themselves on account of the long journey. Johnson brought together probably the greatest gathering in Indian annals. To soothe, feed, and keep the peace among two thousand warriors required all his patience and tact. Some of the Indians were still restless and treachery was not impossible. Accordingly, while during a month he sat for long hours in formal conclave in the council room of Fort Niagara, his military guards kept alert watch. To confer with so great a company at one time would have been useless; he met each tribe separately and used, as he admits, the old method, *divide et impera,* of making his foes suspicious of each other. In truth they were now at the mercy of the British with whom alone the ten thousand hunters in the north country could exchange their furs for the means to live. Johnson assured them of fair treatment and drew up a list of prices for blankets, for clothes, for arm bands, brooches and crosses of silver, and for at least one item not so innocent. They might buy a gallon of rum for a single beaver skin.

The Senecas had learned their lesson and now so courted peace that they made the great concession to the British king of a strip of land four miles wide on each side of the Niagara River from its mouth on Lake Ontario to its source in Lake Erie. They even insisted on giving to Johnson himself a large island in the river. In this way they paid what was not an unfair penalty for the ambushes that had caused heavy loss to British troops when proceeding by

this route to Detroit. Johnson's skill really ended a barbarous war in which not fewer than two thousand people
had been massacred and hundreds of families had been
made homeless. Success was, however, not yet complete.
Pontiac remained defiant at Detroit, still under siege.
Gladwin, while waiting for rescue, was able to report to
Gage that all the Indians there except Pontiac and his
Ottawas were anxious for peace. Gladwin's long endurance
at last triumphed. On August 26, 1764, well on in the
second year of the siege, loud shouts of seeming welcome
and the clattering of musket fire from the Wyandot village
on the east bank reached the fort. Bateaux laden with soldiers were coming up the river. Colonel Bradstreet, who now
arrived, had set out from Albany many weeks earlier. He
had met with many reverses, but now he made rescue complete. With him were two or three hundred Canadians who,
having experienced mild British rule under General Murray, could reassure the French settlers at Detroit; while
Canadian Indians in his force could dispel the tales of
British infamy that Gage was sure had been sent from
Canada to the west when he was himself governor of Montreal. Within a few weeks Gladwin was on his way to
New York, his campaign days ended. With a great show
of capitals, General Gage praised his Prudence, Firmness,
and Intrepidity. Ten years later, we hear of him making
a brief appearance at the court of George III. He was
happy, he wrote to General Gage in 1774, with a good wife,
two children and the rural pleasures of a small paternal
estate. He died in 1791, with the rank of major-general
and lies in Wingerworth churchyard.

Colonel John Bradstreet who took over the command at
Detroit had a considerable military reputation won in colonial wars. His early years had been spent in Nova Scotia
where in 1744 he was captured by the French and held a
prisoner at Louisbourg until exchanged at Boston for a

French officer. Since he knew the weakness of the French stronghold, he led in urging what proved to be the most brilliant exploit of the colonists in arms. Bradstreet always claimed that had he been a native of Massachusetts he would have had the chief command in the successful siege of Louisbourg that gave Sir William Pepperell his fame in colonial annals. In this, as in other phases of his career, Bradstreet was driven by eager ambition. On his way to Detroit he went beyond his authority by agreeing to peace with the insolent Delawares and Shawnees who went on, none the less, with savage murders and scalpings during that autumn, until Colonel Bouquet enforced a real peace.

At Detroit Bradstreet summoned the Indians to a great council. They seemed ready, he wrote to Gage, to comply with all his demands. They would restore prisoners and even hand over Pontiac himself who for the rest of his life should be controlled by the British. After this meeting on September 7 Bradstreet informed Gage that the Indians in this solemn council gave him "strong Assurances of Repentance for past Conduct and Promises of better Behaviour for the future." While it is true that their interest now lay in peace with the British, who commanded the sources of supplies, something was lacking to Bradstreet's facile success. Outrages continued in the Illinois country. Pontiac, so far from being handed over as a prisoner, went off to lead the remoter tribes into war. At last however, he gave up in a lost cause. In 1766 he travelled from the Illinois country to meet Sir William Johnson at Oswego at the east end of Lake Ontario, a journey of nearly a thousand miles. Here he, with a few of his own Ottawas, yielded to the victor. He shook hands with Johnson, embraced and kissed him, and smoked the pipe of peace. To Johnson, surrounded by a great company of Iroquois, he said that he had been a true ally to the French king and now, speaking not only for himself but also for the western Indians, he would be true to his new friends. Whether in his heart he was still dissembling, who shall say? A few days later, in a canoe laden with presents, he was on his way back to the hunting ground of the far west. On great occasions he still wore the uniform given to him by Montcalm. In 1769 he wore it at the fort, on the spot where now stands the city of St. Louis. One day, after drinking deeply in the little French settlement of Cahokia, he was followed into the forest and killed by an Indian assassin, incited, it is said, by an English trader.

The conspiracy of Pontiac was the protest of the backwoods against intruding civilization. From Nova Scotia to the Mississippi ran the mutterings of the old against the inroads of the new. While some, though not all, of the British leaders showed lack of sympathetic insight in their contact with the Indians, Sir William Johnson, by his conciliatory ways, made them such fast friends to Britain that, in two later wars, most of them stood with her against her revolted colonies. The tribes, for their part, no matter how petty they might be, had an arrogance as exacting as that of the British intruders. In time, when the British felt secure in their strength, the finer traits of their character asserted themselves. With the Indians as enduring allies and, in truth, wards, the British remained their friendly and loyal protectors. The rising under Pontiac had a marked effect on colonial policy in London. It seemed to show danger, not only from the natives, but also from French designs to recover Canada and from the Spanish, to whom France had ceded Louisiana. To meet this the British ministry decided to keep a standing army in the colonies and to tax them to pay at least a part of the cost—a policy that led to the American Revolution.

In 1761, before the peace, Massachusetts and Virginia on the sea coast were already in a state of irritation in

regard to British policy and soon after peace was signed we
find this spirit on the western frontier. The Proclamation
of 1763 aimed at strict control by the commander-in-chief
in America of trade with the Indian tribes and of attempts
to secure their lands. While the traders had the grievance
that the Indian rising destroyed their business, the settlers
on the frontier had the double grievance of brutal massacres
by the Indians and of denial of the right to expand into
the fertile regions bordering on the Ohio and the Mississippi.
No doubt with the consent of Gage, the commander-in-chief,
Sir William Johnson took the direct course of sending to
London, to put the needs of the situation, his tried agent
George Croghan, whom we have already seen at Detroit.
In April, 1764, Croghan reported that he was sick of London; that the squabbling ministers neglected public affairs
for private aims; that while some might be honest, probably all alike were rogues. They were indifferent about the
Indian war and even jealous that Johnson should have so
much power. The absurd pomp of their mode of life and
their pride made him regard them as slaves deserving of
pity though, perhaps, as he added, they hardly deserved
even pity; at any rate a little farm in America offered a
better life than the frothy excitements of London. Clearly
the rough frontiersman had found doors closed to his
urgency about Indian affairs. At the same time the British
fur traders were sending to the Board of Trade urgent appeals for relief. After French power had fallen they had
been encouraged, they said, to sell goods to the Indians and
thus to disarm the suspicion that the British were trying to
starve them. The result was that during the rising many
traders had been barbarously murdered while others
had gone bankrupt and were in distress. Clearly there was
a wide gulf between the thought of London and that of the
colonial frontier. The ministers of the young George III,
for the most part great nobles, absorbed in the rivalries
of politics and in the parade of life in a great capital, had

little understanding of the pioneer mind. Each side was beginning to feel distrust of the other. Already colonial grievances were many and when, as Croghan reported in 1764, ministers were talking of passing in London a bill that should lay a heavy internal tax on the colonies for the support of an army of which they felt no need, materials were gathering for an explosion.

Strong personal interests lay behind this plan to keep up an army. The end of the war had brought an era of speculation in land. While hitherto France had barred free access to the west and the north, now this field was open and it seemed boundless. Rival interests were acute and the Board of Trade in London was besieged by applicants for lands. The Duke of York secured a grant of gold and silver mines in Nova Scotia. On production up to ten thousand pounds he was to have a royalty of ten per cent, on the increase up to twenty thousand, twenty per cent, and a higher rate for anything more. Naval officers, military officers who had served in America, merchants with interests there, members of Parliament, all made claims for huge grants. Lord Adam Gordon, a Scottish member, secured twenty thousand acres in Florida and was also interested in a land company exploiting the Illinois country. In the end the Board of Trade laid down the principle that grants to individuals should not exceed twenty thousand acres, which seems a fairly liberal measure.

The history of an island, now a part of Canada, illustrates this hunger for land in America. The French Isle Saint Jean, lying near the entrance to the Gulf of St. Lawrence, became in 1763 British territory and later was named Prince Edward Island, after a British prince, the father of Queen Victoria. It consists of rather more than two thousand square miles of land, mostly fertile, and it supports to-day about a hundred thousand people. Its few French inhabitants had been deported during the war and

at the peace it lay an almost virgin field for the land-grabber. In 1763, when the Earl of Egmont was first Lord of
the Admiralty, he was charmed by the possibilities of this
beautiful island. Why not make it the home of a revived
feudalism, plant settlers there under feudal landowners
and show the world the advantages of a type of society in
truth already dead? It is not recorded that Egmont or any
of his nine children, on whose behalf, as he said, he acted,
or any one of his fellow applicants, had the remotest idea
of going to live on the feudal island. He asked for a grant
of some two million acres. When Egmont failed, Admirals
Saunders and Knowles, who had served with Wolfe at
Quebec, joined others in asking for the island. In the end,
in the year 1767, on a single day, it was divided among
sixty-six owners each of whom received a township of about
twenty thousand acres. The list of the new owners reads
like a rôle of military and naval leaders with others added.
Twenty-four of the sixty-six either were or had been members of Parliament. Saunders, Rodney, Keppel and Palmer,
naval officers, and George Townshend, James Murray and
Guy Carleton, army officers, were among the favoured; and
a system of absentee landowners was fastened on the island
that hampered its growth for a hundred years. There was
nothing corrupt in the grants; the new owners would, it
was hoped, and even required, bring in settlers, provide
churches, roads, mills and wharves in good feudal style.
Probably, however, none of them intended to copy earlier
lords of the soil in Europe and to live among their people;
while no doubt all hoped for the type of incomes from the
actual occupants that enabled landowners in England to
keep up the great mansions to-day so heavy a burden on
their descendants. General Amherst thought himself badly
treated when, for his services as conqueror of Canada, he
received a grant of the extensive lands of the Jesuits but was
baulked by effective protests against the unseemly plan.

CHAPTER V

By the time of the conquest of Canada most of the English colonies were old political societies. Like Canada and Australia at the present time, they had become sensitive and restless as to any attitude of superiority in Great Britain. They stretched for a thousand miles along the Atlantic seaboard and varied in both resources and type. New England, with a severe climate and an unwilling soil, looked to fisheries, to manufactures, to trade, as much as to land, for means of wealth. While in these northern colonies the white man performed his own labour; in Virginia and other colonies in the south the planters required the labour of negro slaves. In religion there were contrasts as sharp. The New England colonies had been founded or at least had been ruled chiefly by men austere in their mode of life, intense in religious conviction, and weighted with a sense of their duty to God that did not, however, interfere with keen worldly wisdom in trade. They hated the Church of England because it had persecuted the Puritans, but they were themselves not averse from persecuting those who opposed their views. Virginia was of another type. So far were its founders from a quarrel with the Church of England that they made it the state church and showed in their social habits little of Puritan brooding over the designs of Providence and the duty of man. We find even the grave Washington agreeing that his gardener should be allowed at the sacred season of Christmas four dollars "with which he may be drunk for four days and four nights" and that he should have two dollars for a similar purpose at Easter and at Whitsuntide. Another depressed class besides the negro had gone to the colonies. One of the things resented there was what Franklin called "the most cruel insult that was perhaps ever offered by one people to another,"—the sending of criminals to ease the pressure on English prisons.

A sedate and dignified social life had grown up in the English colonies. After the Restoration in England in 1660 emigration had been, on the whole, light. It was the social conceptions of the earlier period of James I and Charles I that had been transplanted to America. There was much deference for birth and the social grading was well marked. In the year of the Declaration of Independence we hear the complaint in Philadelphia that a poor man has rarely the chance of even speaking to a gentleman, except on the eve of an election, when the aristocratic chill gives way to an affected warmth in order to secure votes. At Harvard College students were ranked according to "dignity of family." In New England people were seated even in church in accordance with their social position. In the remote frontier village of Deerfield the question of social precedence in church was so acute that a town-meeting had to decide that a front seat in the gallery had dignity equal to that of the second row in the body of the meeting-house. In other colonies, especially in New York and Virginia, landowners had social dignity due to their great estates. Rich men in America lived in fine mansions, in luxury like that of the well-to-do class in England. William Byrd of Westover, in Virginia, had a hundred and eighty thousand acres of land, a fine mansion and a notable library. John Adams speaks of "elegant country seats" that he passed on his journey from Boston to Philadelphia in 1774, and of the high state of the "nobles of Pennsylvania," who feasted on ten thousand delicacies and drank madeira, claret and burgundy. The paintings and sculptures in Philadelphia caused him to regret that hitherto he had given no study to these things. George Washington delighted in a certain magnificence of dress, in silver buckles, scarlet cloth adorned by gold lace, and ruffled shirts; "whatever goods you send me," he wrote to his London agent, "let them be fashionable." At the same time he complained that his clothes fitted him badly, which is not strange seeing that the tailor lived three thousand miles away. When he and other delegates attended the Continental Congress in Philadelphia in 1774 there was much dining out in ceremonious style. John Dickenson carried his guests from the city to his fine country house in a coach drawn by four white horses. Colonial hospitality was generous and tolerant.

No doubt, to the European trained in the stateliness of royal courts or of great country houses with scores of liveried servants, American society so lacked finished elegance that tactless visitors adopted the tone of the Imperial Roman to the outer barbarian, assumed airs of patronage, and derided colonial opinions and manners. American luxury lacked the stability of an older society. Though writers on Virginia describe the ease and dignity of the mode of life, the spreading lawns, the notable horses and coaches, the silver plate and fine furniture, the excellent wines and the many black servants, the planters were often heavily in debt and their houses so out of repair as to have leaking roofs, broken windows and an air of neglect and shabbiness. While in the world of fashion New York was so backward as sometimes to adopt modes already fallen into disuse in England, it is also true that in a slowly moving age a seaport like New York was quicker in following fashion than many an English county. John Adams admitted that his countrymen "lacked the exterior and superficial accomplishments of gentlemen" and were now pert and vain and now so awkward and bashful as to excite ridicule and disgust. This was due "to the little intercourse we have with strangers, and to our inexperience in the world." None the less were the colonial leaders proud, self-reliant, conscious of their dignity.

The well-recognized tendency of an isolated people is to despise other societies of which they are ignorant. John Adams thought that natural advantages made the colonists superior to all the world, and that they would create an empire able to defy Europe. Boston was its exalted centre. He derided the manners of the neighbouring colony of New York and thought Philadelphia defective in culture. It was, he said, inferior to Boston: "the morals of our people are much better; their manners are more polite and agreeable; they use purer English; our language is better, our taste is better, our persons are handsomer; our spirit is greater, our laws are wiser, our religion is superior, our education is better." Though this contrast seems exhaustive, Philadelphia, for its part, looked out upon the world with a high sense of superiority. A visitor in July, 1778, noted the "most unbearable conceit" of its people who believed that no other land in all the world surpassed theirs in beauty, wealth and prosperity, while, adds the critic, it is as yet "hardly in the bud." Burke noted that the colonists were keen students of the law. Intelligence was widely diffused. By 1704 Boston had a newspaper; by 1750, there were as many as thirty-seven in the colonies. It is probable that, in proportion to numbers, ten men read and thought about politics in Massachusetts to one in England. Some colonial leaders were well versed in the classics. John Adams read Homer, Virgil, and Horace and both he and his wife Abigail could quote Shakespeare, Milton, Dryden and other poets. Chatham said that, well versed as he was in the literature of politics, he had read nothing to surpass the force, wisdom and reasoning power of the men who met in the first Continental Congress.

Circumstances had indeed forced the colonies to consider questions not yet ripe for decision in England. They were coming face to face with democracy, the working of which still puzzles modern nations. The need to expand the right to vote was more clearly understood in the colonies than in England. While considerable English towns, like Manchester, Sheffield and Birmingham, had still no representatives in Parliament, similar communities in America would not have tolerated this inequality. Though it is probable that before the Revolution began not more than one quarter of the male adults in the colonies had the vote, which was given only to freeholders, this condition was changing rapidly. As population pressed into the interior of New England, each town claimed the right to send two members to the legislature and usually they were hostile to the aristocracy and to the vested interests of the older communities. On religious questions, too, opinion was advanced. After 1700 the authority of the clergy declined and with it church-going. Though Virginia had a state church, many Virginians were battling, with eventual success, to get rid of it. There was probably hardly a colonist who doubted that he was a citizen of a community completely self-governing whenever it might choose to take a stand, or that his liberties were secure and beyond challenge.

In all the colonies we find a growth that now we well understand. The Virginian landowner thought himself an English gentleman; but he was not; he was an American gentleman and though he loved country life, lived off the land, hunted and, if he could, kept a racing stable like his model in England, his outlook was not that of his English ancestors. The climate with its sweltering summer heat, the food and drink, the habits of his household, were all different. Black slaves waited upon him and, together with white bondservants hardly more than slaves, toiled on his estate. Near him was the primeval forest through which rough pioneers were hewing their way westward in daily peril from the native tribes. Nothing in England corresponded to the aspect of nature in America; mighty rivers swollen by floods; the Great Lakes, tempest-tossed like ocean itself; cataracts such as Niagara. Outlook and even physique changed in the colonies. Masters noted that within a month servants whom they took to America had grown restive and sometimes insolent. Society in London would hardly understand colonial conditions in which leaders who had hewn down trees and built their houses with their own hands claimed social equality with the highest. Colonel Barré had amused his friends in London by telling them of an incident in the recent war. An officer sent to a fort summoned the barber to shave him and urged haste since he had important business with the commanding officer. "Sir," said the barber, "you need not lose your time, you may as well disclose your business now, for I am the commanding officer." We may imagine the laughter aroused by the story in an English country house.

It was possible to identify an American by the pitch of his voice, by his accent, even by his features and stature. Boswell records that a London shopman said to the Earl of Marchmont, "I suppose, Sir, you are an American." "Why so?" said the Earl. "Because, Sir," was the reply, "you speak neither English nor Scotch, but something different from both which 1 conclude is the language of America." Already there were Americanisms in speech like those that modern English satire tends to exaggerate. Many of the colonists, by some estimated as quite two-fifths, were, in truth, not of English, but of German, French and other foreign blood, so that England was not the land of their fathers. While London might deride the colonial type as alien and crude and might describe Americans as "Yahoos," the colonists, for their part, were hardly less insistent on differences from English custom. They jeered at the superior air of the English travellers. They knew nothing of the pensions, the sinecures, the lucrative posts in church and state that due subservience to those in power might secure in England. Peerages and titles of honour rarely, if ever, went to them from a grateful monarch. Every man among them earned his pay. George Washington knew and cared little about his English descent and John Adams, by origin purely English, said that no relation of his for whom he cared a farthing had set foot in England for a hundred and fifty years and that he was purely American. To him, indeed, this meant already the alienation from Europe that to-day all the world recognizes.

After the cession of Canada to Britain, Choiseul, the French Foreign Minister, had said that at last the English were caught, for the American colonies would soon be in revolt. By that time most of the leaders in the colonies were American-born. Attachment to England was traditional and sentimental. Such ties continue indefinitely, however, until some shock breaks them, and then, as happened in America, opinion is likely to fly quickly to the opposite extreme. The colonies looked to England as the source of supply for things both mental and material. The volumes on the table of colonial drawing-rooms came chiefly from England. As a matter of course George Washington of Virginia ordered yearly in England extensive supplies for his great plantation. Yet, in spite of England's deeper culture, it is still true that in the colonies a greater proportion than in England of the masses could read and write. We are apt to forget that most of those in the London mobs that clamoured for Wilkes and Lord George Gordon had never learned to read. On the other hand even remote frontiers in the colonies had mission schools that saved them from the degraded ignorance to be found in Ireland. The spirit was abroad that enabled Benjamin

Franklin to found in Philadelphia a society for mutual improvement that ultimately became a great university. The new world, unchecked by traditions, changed more rapidly than the old world. Before the Revolution progress was being made in manufactures. Ship-building had long been important. There were many paper mills and a considerable manufacture of glass, pottery, furniture, small arms and even of cannon. The colonies were more capable of supplying their own needs than was realized in England.

The Englishman of the ruling caste in the mother country was a member of an ancient society. His class had long dominated and lived on the labour of the masses, to whom time had brought only a slow advance towards political power. Though there were new men enriched by trade, the magnificence of the great mansions was due chiefly to the profits of agriculture, while the labourers whose toil had won this wealth were still little more than inarticulate serfs. The Duchess of Buckingham was insulted in the time of Wesley when told that her heart was as sinful as that of these common wretches. Those who ruled had two chief interests; one centred in the great mansions with their treasures of art, in the parks, the gardens, the sports, often in the learned ease, of the country; the other in the play of politics that decided questions of war and peace, tariffs, taxes, and public order, and offered rich rewards to many of the players.

The age valued the trappings of rank and spent great sums on ceremony; George III paid seven thousand pounds for the hire of jewels for his coronation and Horace Walpole says that his mother paid three hundred and fifty guineas for the use of a scaffolding from which to view the procession. Great nobles ruined themselves to build vast country houses that should be more magnificent than those of rivals. They had a passion for gardens and on them spent great sums. They collected pictures, statuary, china, glass, tapestries, and showed their treasures with pride like that of a modern owner in his stable or his prize cattle. Visiting in 1763 Drayton, inherited later by Lord George Germain who directed the war with the colonies, Walpole writes glowingly of the embattled castle wall, the great entrance gate leading to a sumptuous court, the towers, the turrets, the vast dining-hall, the chapel, the portraits, the old china, the rich furniture, "not a rag in it under forty, fifty or a thousand years old." To see these things, to be able to enjoy them, above all, to own them—all this might be the finest thing in life to the great of that time and the interest was absorbing. Since precedence gave importance there was rivalry for the king's gifts of lord lieutenantcies in the counties, for peerages and other honours. So dominant were "the Great" that their patronage was needed by an aspiring author. Dr. Johnson had waited in vain in the anterooms of the Earl of Chesterfield to solicit his patronage and at last was repulsed from his door. He had his revenge when, seven years later, with his own fame secure, he told the Earl that a patron is "one who looks with unconcern on a man struggling for life in the water and, when he has reached ground, encumbers him with help," a retort that aided the decline of the habit of seeking the patronage of an eminent name.

While in some great country houses libraries gave the opportunity for the study that might make leaders familiar with the best ancient and modern thought, rural monotony caused inferior spirits to seek relief in play at loo, that might last the better part of the night, and in other feverish gambling. The magnate of the time ruled the countryside; usually he had the right to name the rector or vicar of the parish, who was flattered at being asked to his table. The great man neglected not only a pleasure but a duty if he failed to attend the races in his neighbourhood. Compared with modern urgency due to the rapidity of communications that gives instant notice of events to all the world, the life was leisurely. Great landowners, even though heads of departments of state, went off to the country for such long periods that, if a crisis arose in London, no one of them might be within reach. Though roads were improving they still had soft surfaces that made possible ruts sometimes three or four feet deep. It was such evils that later caused John McAdam (1756–1836) to invent the method now so well known of covering roads with a thin layer of fine stone pressed by use into a compact surface. When roads were bad, when the horse was the means of rapid travel and there was no telegraph, two days might elapse before a minister living within sixty miles of London might receive a message and return to act upon it. The Duke of Richmond, when urged by Burke to hurry to London, replies that he has invited a large party to spend a month with him in fox-hunting and that, though willing to do his duty, he does not wish to stir from the place until after Christmas. The great country house would contain a fragment of London society, a charmed circle that rather ignored the country squires. Those in it might arrive when they liked and stay as long as they liked, weeks running at times into months, something that explains the vastness of the mansions.

Prize-fighting and cock-fighting, not yet frowned upon by polite society, appealed to sporting tastes. The fox caused vigorous exercise to hunters in rides across country. Coke of Norfolk, Whig magnate, friend of Fox, admirer of Washington and opponent of the policy of George III, thought the day in the open season lost that did not bring its shooting of the game birds on his great estate. The Squire Westerns who spent the day in sport sat down early to dinner. Eating and especially drinking were on a formidable scale. Dr. Johnson's statement is well known that "all the decent people in Lichfield got drunk every night and

were not the worse thought of," a state of opinion that as
he implied was changing. At Houghton in 1743 abstemious
Horace Walpole, visiting the electors who sent him to
Parliament, thought the consumption of beef, ale and
wine "stupefying." "I here every day see men who are
mountains of roast beef, and only seem just roughly hewn
out into the outlines of human form, like the giant rock
at Pratolino! I shudder when I see them brandish their
knives in act to carve, and look on them as savages that
devour one another. I should not stare at all more than I
do, if yonder Alderman at the lower end of the table was
to stick his fork into his neighbour's jolly cheek and cut
out a brave slice of brown and fat. Why? I'll swear I see
no difference between a country gentleman and a sirloin;
whenever the first laughs or the latter is cut, there runs
out just the same stream of gravy!"

Gentlemen who joined the ladies after dinner, often
more than half tipsy, showed the coarse manners that go
with this condition. Some even of those who moved in
the refined circle of Horace Walpole were not ashamed to
take a morbid interest in executions at Tyburn where a
merry, jeering crowd thronged the neighbouring streets.
"Execution Day" was regarded by many as giving the enjoyment of a public holiday. When taste seemed to be
changing for the better, Dr. Johnson deplored that "Tyburn
itself is not safe from the fury of innovation." Sir Joshua
Reynolds and Dr. Johnson defended the practice of attending the executions. It is not easy to understand the
distortion of outlook that led James Boswell, biographer
of Johnson, to ride in the cart with the murderer Hickman
when he was carried to execution at Tyburn. Colonel
Luttrell, who took in Parliament the seat to which Wilkes
had been elected, was in such danger of being killed in the
street that for months he feared to venture from his lodg-
ings. Dr. Johnson, attacked by four men, fought them off

with bull-dog courage until the watch arrived. On Lord Mayor's Day it was thought good fun to pelt foreigners with dead cats and dogs. To inspire fear was, so the age thought, the guarantee of obedience and order. Children, said Dr. Johnson, can be governed only by fear. Accordingly, flogging was deemed the necessary ally of education and the white hands and bodies of little boys, gently reared, were beaten until stained with blood. Offending women naked to the waist were flogged through the streets. A master was likely to beat an apprentice as a warning to do better.

Such phases of life in England stood in barbarous contrast with the refinements of Lord Chesterfield in the same age. Sights then familiar in the streets of London could now perhaps be found only in some backward city in China. Heaps of rubbish and festering excrement made a stench that would cause nausea to our more sensitive nerves. When Dr. Johnson, who knew London's streets, said that the full tide of human existence was at Charing Cross and that a man who is tired of London is tired of life, he must have held in suspense some of the pity of his nature. No doubt the streets of London were lively but he could not fail to see swarms of pallid and scrofulous people, who came out of the crowded courts where pigs rooted in the rubbish and where there was scant provision for drainage or decency. Brutal fights were a chief diversion in these courts on a Saturday night. The basement of tenements without floors or windows were the only homes of many occupants, filthy and diseased. As he returned late at night from dining with joyous friends at a tavern he may well have noticed deserted and homeless children lying asleep on the thresholds of closed doors.

A magistrate told Dr. Johnson that more than a score of people died weekly in London of starvation. The waste of life was terrible and one-eighth of the mortality was due to drunkenness. Deaths were so much more numerous than

births in London that but for recruits from the country
the population would have declined. London was indeed
preserved by the physical and moral health of those who
came from the more wholesome atmosphere of the villages,
a saving influence now, as it was then, in the life of great
cities. The devout Cowper complains of the "oaths and
blasphemies" of the time. When truculent Thurlow, the
Lord Chancellor, whom Burke called "a great and learned
magistrate," met a deputation of dissenters urging the removal of their disabilities, he is said to have replied, though
it seems hardly credible; "Damme, gentlemen, I'm against
you. I'm for the established church, not that I care a
damn for the Established Church or any other but because
it is established and if you get your damned Church established I'll be for it too." This illustrates the blind clinging
to the existing order, the resentment at the prospect of
change that made Thurlow defend slavery, refuse to listen
to complaints of misrule in Ireland, and insist on the right
to coerce America.

The advantage of London was in the alertness of mind
that the contacts of the city promote. The tavern, the
alehouse and the club were centres of debates on many
subjects and their wit was apt to be associated with gross
habits. Francis Place, a radical reformer in the days of the
younger Pitt, records that in his youth thirty members of
a club met weekly at his father's tavern and debated keenly
public questions but also drank so deeply that by midnight or later all were intoxicated. Dr. Johnson showed
wisdom in his practice, after drinking at a tavern, of slink-
ing away home before becoming too maudlin. At Almack's
where the Prince of Wales was often present there were
crude scenes; gamblers with ten thousand pounds on the
table turned their coats inside out for luck; wore masks
to conceal their emotions and might play on through the
night until the afternoon of the next day. Among them

might be Charles Fox losing many thousands of pounds at a sitting. He would receive his disciples in bed, unkempt, unwashed, wearing a foul night gown open on his dark skin and shaggy breast.

Manners in the House of Commons were far from stately. Though it was an aristocratic body in which sat the leaders of society on familiar terms with each other, they cracked nuts, ate oranges and stretched themselves out on the benches, all the more at home since the presence of strangers was forbidden until, after a long struggle, this rule was abolished in 1777. We are astonished at the licence of speech and action in this cultivated assembly. Burke threw a heavy book of naval estimates at the treasury bench. He described the ministry as consisting of "His Majesty's man-servant, his maid-servant, his ox and his ass." "The noble lord who spoke last," he once said in deriding North's portly form, "after extending his right leg a full yard before him, rolling his flaming eyes, and moving his ponderous frame, has at last opened his mouth." Fox declared North's char-acter to be such that he should deem it unsafe to be alone in a room with him, yet they called each other by their Chris-tian names, belonged to the same social class and in the end united to form a ministry. In the Commons Fox was de-scribed as a rake and a gambler. In the Lords Chatham called a fellow peer a rake while the peer called Chatham a dolt. Burke was said to be insane, having talked himself into madness. When forgetful for a moment of his own pedigree, the Duke of Richmond, who was descended with a bar sinister from Charles II, taunted Thurlow in the House of Lords with his low birth, Thurlow retorted that the duke owed his seat in that assembly to "an accident of an accident" and a newspaper described him as "the ille-gitimate spawn of the most vicious and profligate of the Stuarts."

We need hardly wonder that members so frank about

each other should describe distant colonists as turbulent
ruffians, scoundrels and cowards. North's good nature and
wit made him all but impervio ⌐ to insult. When a dull
speaker charged him with be ⌐g asleep in his seat, as was
indeed his wont, he retorted ⌐at he wished to Heaven he
was. To a member who also rebuked him for falling asleep
when accused of crimes that deserved the scaffold, he replied that even a condemned criminal was not denied a
night's rest before execution. None the less was there often
a high level of debate in Parliament for the members were
speaking to their equals in education without an eye on
absent and often ignorant electors. They were critical of
style and intolerant of harsh voices and a vulgar accent.
We may well envy the hearers of Fox, compared with whose
oratory, so Horace Walpole said, that of Cicero was puerile.
A speech of his, showing acute thought and wide reading,
held for five hours the absorbed attention of the House,
though, as Porson said, while Pitt conceived his sentences
before he uttered them, Fox "throws himself into the middle of his and leaves it to God Almighty to get him out
again." Pitt, faltering in a Latin quotation, was helped
out by Fox, a better scholar. When Burke made a false
quantity North, seemingly asleep, murmured a correc-
tion.

The chief leaders in England in the crisis of the American
Revolution were not corrupt. Pitt, Shelburne, Grenville and
the devout Dartmouth, who was secretary for the colonies
at the most critical period, were as strict in their daily life
as was even the Puritan John Adams of Massachusetts.
In private virtues, George Washington is equalled by a succession of prime ministers in England. The life of the Duke
of Newcastle, the kind and fussy dealer in government
patronage, was as respectable as that of Abraham Lincoln
himself, an equally troubled trustee of gifts from the state.

Newcastle spent in public affairs a large fortune and took nothing for himself; he was a devout churchman, beloved by and generous to his tenants, kindly, hospitable and without malice for his opponents. His successor as prime minister, the Earl of Bute, though derided by Lord Shelburne, was described by a friend as "a man whose goodness, politeness and attention were never wanting to those who lived with him." Himself a learned man he spent much of his great wealth in support of art and letters. The next prime minister, Grenville, was as austere as Pitt; and we have Burke's word for it that Rockingham, who followed him, headed a ministry that was not even suspected of corruption, and so urged economy as to be thought cheeseparing. His successor, the Duke of Grafton, though for a time lax in his private life and denounced by "Junius" with brutal abandon, never used his office to secure places and pensions for his friends. In later years he deplored his earlier slackness, wrote on religion, and printed and circulated at his own cost Griesbach's edition of the New Testament. His successor, Lord North, Prime Minister during the American Revolution, is described by Burke as witty, amiable, "and with a mind most perfectly disinterested."

Probably no other age has produced such a variety of great leaders. Chatham and Burke in politics, Wesley in religion, Reynolds in painting, Handel in music, Johnson in literature, Adam Smith in economic thought, Hunter in surgery, Blackstone and Mansfield in law are only the most famous of those who shared in movements that have profoundly influenced society to our own time. In spite of the coarse manners of the many and the aristocratic disdain of the few, the age learned a deep pity for prisoners and captives, for the sick, the insane, and the poor, and began measures of healing that we have only expanded. Its taste was more refined than that of the early period of Victoria.

Georgian houses, Georgian furniture, Georgian designs in glass and silver-ware may be compared to their advantage with what was in favour a century after George III began to reign. There is little in the imitative and formal Georgian music as banal as was much of the crudely emotional music so popular in the time of Victoria.

The age of George III repels us by its rigour of class distinctions, the scorn in high circles for the lower grades of society, whose labours made possible the ease and dignity of those above them. Few will doubt the kind-heartedness of George III, but to him the hard lot of the masses seemed a part of an inevitable order that must be accepted as enduring. His granddaughter, Victoria, had a similar outlook. She declared that she had rather abdicate than accept democracy. It was a duty to be kind to the poor, to visit them in their cottages and admire their endurance and content, but the foundations that involved their poverty must not even be threatened. While industry and trade might be all very well there was no place for their representatives in the ruling circle at the top. The merchant is rarely found in the chronicle of high political life under George III. He is hardly mentioned in the many volumes of Horace Walpole devoted to the gossip and rivalry of a small circle that meant to him what had significance in the world. In his set and even in that of Dr. Johnson what was colonial finds little place. Johnson could, as he said, love all mankind except an American. Benjamin Franklin, the most famous colonist of the time, a close friend of the liberal Lord Shelburne, hardly appears in either Johnson's or Walpole's circle. That a great novelist of a later period should write about the Virginians would have been almost incredible to Walpole. The colonies were outer planets deriving what light they had from the central sun. To this day an Englishman will think he is paying an American a high compliment when he tells him that his speech and

manners are not those of his own country but are such that
he might be mistaken for an Englishmen.

It is perhaps true that every nation believes itself superior
to every other, the Chinese to the Japanese and all the rest
of the world, the Poles to the Germans. The Swedes, a
minor nation in Europe, are certain of their superiority,
while the Frenchman is so sure of his that he is silent about
what needs no proof. The Englishman of the eighteenth
century travelled more than the citizen of any other country and was convinced that nowhere else could be found a
world equal to his own. It is indeed true that England was
then the freest country in the world with tolerance greater
than that of her own colonies who, when conflict came, sent
many to death for their political opinions. Voltaire said
of the English that "they are, I swear by God Himself, the
first nation in Europe" and added that if there was a
resurrection of the dead he prayed that he might be re-born
in England. Though the Englishman might go to Paris
for social polish, and travel in Italy to see, and often to buy,
pictures and statuary, it was then and it is still true that
he would deem himself half insulted if taken for a Frenchman, a German, or an Italian, or above all for a colonist. Dr.
Johnson, whose own manners were not without reproach,
said; "The French are an indelicate people; they will spit
upon any place"; at the house of a great French lady the
footman "took the sugar in his fingers and threw it into my
coffee," so that he "tasted Tom's fingers." In our own time
both the English and their American cousins of the same
breed go through the world, tolerant of other peoples, but
convinced of their own superiority. In the eighteenth century this was left to the Englishman alone, since to the
outer world the colonist had an inferior standing. Goethe
said a little later that Englishmen who visited him at
Weimar behaved as though they were lords and the whole
world belonged to them. They questioned him in bad Ger-

man as if he were their tutor. The Englishman of the time was taught the insular faith that all things in England were superior to what might be similar in any other part of the world; the English merchant was the most trustworthy, the manufacturer the most skilful, the physician or lawyer the best trained; no other nation could produce a rival to the English sailor in skill and courage. Private soldiers were wont to say that the subjects of Louis XV were slaves and that one Englishman was equal to three and sometimes even to five Frenchmen.

Though there was a real public opinion in England, government was carried on by the landed class. Usually it was peers or sons or relatives of peers who made up the cabinets of the time. Edmund Burke, the greatest mind devoted to politics in the time of George III, agreed that his rank was not high enough for him to aspire to be a cabinet minister and this outlook so endured that near the middle of the following century Lord Melbourne told Benjamin Disraeli, who confessed that he wished to be prime minister, to abandon this wild fancy, since ancient lineage, rank and wealth were indispensable for the post. George III said that no one of the trading class was fit to be a peer. Colonists were not in the charmed ruling circle. Sons of good American families, sent to England to be educated, found that to be a colonist was to be branded as inferior. To show in politics "the amicable and conciliatory virtues of lenity, moderation and tenderness to the colonies," was regarded, Burke said, as a sort of treason; efforts to stem this current proved "vain and frivolous."

In military circles the conviction was deeply rooted that as soldiers the colonists were poltroons and cowards, in no way fitted to rank with English soldiers unless, like the natives in other backward countries, trained by British officers. The military caste believed that if war should come with the colonies five thousand British soldiers would be enough to awe them into subjection and to march in triumph from one end of their borders to the other. When Washington, who, as a Virginian officer, had served with British regulars, was Commander-in-Chief of the revolutionary armies, British generals sent official communications to him as "Mr. Washington" and denied him the military rank of General that he held from the Congress at Philadelphia. Washington knew how to meet a slight; "This letter is directed to a planter of the State of Virginia. I shall have it delivered to him after the end of the war; till that time it shall not be opened." For a long time a colonial colonel was ranked with, but junior to, a British captain. It was deemed a great concession and it made Pitt popular in the colonies when in 1757 the military standing of colonial troops was recognized, though still all colonial officers ranked as juniors to those of the same grade in the British army. During the Seven Years' War colonial officers, serving with British in Canada, had been snubbed because ignorant of some of the traditions of English military and social life. Hitherto many of these American officers, leaders in their own society, had never known a superior. It was new and humiliating to be spurned and often laughed at as boors.

The people of England had only a slight sense of brotherhood with those of the same origin in the colonies. Few villagers in rural England stirred beyond their own parishes; even those living only a score of miles distant were spoken of as foreigners; while those who had moved across the sea seemed to have gone into a desolate, unknown and alien world. Otis, of Massachusetts, said with truth that in England "we are little more known than the savages of California," something that is almost equally true to-day of the state of knowledge in the United States regarding Canada. For the great majority of Englishmen the political tie between the mother country and the colonies related, on the one hand, to responsibility for their defence and, on the other, to the supreme authority of the king and Parliament in all their affairs. For the first the colonies themselves were keen when they needed help; the second they tended to deny when demands touched their pockets. The colonies had their own point of view, their own traditions. Englishmen had founded the colony of Massachusetts Bay during a period of bitter strife between the Parliament and a king who claimed on the scaffold, in the last hour of his life, that the people had no right to any share in government; "that is nothing pertaining to them." In consequence early colonists in Massachusetts, who had gone into hard exile to escape this tyranny, remembered in their public prayers not the "king" but the "civil magistrate" and not the "kingdom" but the "Parliament" of Heaven. They elected their own governors; they took no oath of allegiance; they refused to administer justice in the king's name. This, however, had been changed in the liberal days of William and Mary, when, though Connecticut and Rhode Island retained their old powers, Massachusetts was tactfully persuaded to accept kingly authority and to have the governor named by the crown with the power to disallow acts of the legislature.

Few in London had the insight to picture the state of mind, after the Seven Years' War, of leaders such as George Washington in Virginia, John Adams in Massachusetts, and Thomas Jefferson, a Virginian youth of twenty when the peace was signed in 1763, but already a man of vigorous mind and of varied interests. These men, each of whom became President of the United States, were in thought and character the equals of the leaders in London and were pondering questions soon to lead to flaming differences. Washington, a great landowner and a keen speculator in western lands, was watching jealously the plan in London

to remove from the control of Virginia the territory reaching to the discharge of the Ohio in the Mississippi. Adams,
already aroused in Massachusetts by checks on colonial
trade newly enforced by Great Britain, was ardent in support of the view that, no matter what Parliament might
claim, it had no right of interference in a colony. Just at
this time, too, in Virginia, young Jefferson, already expert
in science and mathematics, in languages, in out-door sports
and the country gentleman's knowledge of horses, was
supporting the opinion, widely popular, that the legislature
of Virginia was a sovereign body and that no authority in
England might disallow its acts. It is safe to say that practically no one in England accepted this view. Some years
after the treaty of peace in 1763, even Pitt, so enlightened
in some ways, declared that "We may bind their trade,
confine their manufactures, and exercise every power whatever—except that of taking their money out of their pockets
without their consent." Though Burke held that Britain
ought not to tax the colonies, he believed that Parliament
should be supreme over them, an opinion that held in law,
until renounced in respect of the self-governing Dominions
in the year 1931.

In the early days of the conflict with the colonies the
average Englishman was indifferent, since he did not believe
that their protests were to be taken seriously. Though he
did not doubt his ultimate control of them in all matters,
at first he eased their annoyance at the Stamp Act by the
pacific gesture of repealing it. He had not, however, changed
his mind. Thus, when again in the next year he taxed them,
he was angry at their stiff resistance, sent troops to cow
them into obedience, and in the end tried to coerce them by
war. Ever since that time a similar tone is found in the
higher circles of English society during every crisis of
change. The spokesman of the ruling class that in 1832
denied to the great mass of the people the right to vote

declared that the existing system of a narrow franchise
and rotten boroughs was so perfect that, if destroyed, it
would be best to replace it by an exact copy. When more
than ninety per cent. of the Irish people tried to throw
off an alien state church, they seemed to staid circles in
England to be the enemies of both religion and order. When
later an English party adopted the Irish demand for self-
government, society closed its doors to the hardy supporters
of a plan so outrageous. In the commercial world it was
long almost a truism that the English manufacturer would
not readily change to meet varying conditions in other parts
of the world. What he offered was good. Why should not
the buyer accept it? Probably he would desire the favour
of a long credit; let him take what the honest English
producer knew was best. Though Burke condemned what
he called the English "extreme pride and self-complacency,"
with perhaps smoother forms of expression it endures still in
some circles in England.

While Dr. Johnson's sulphurous utterances about the
colonies are not to be taken too literally, since often he was
merely trying to overwhelm an opponent in argument,
they reveal the gulf in thought between what was English
and what was colonial. The Americans, he said, "ought to
be thankful for anything we allow them, short of hanging."
"Why," he asked, "do we hear yelps for liberty from drivers
of negroes?" On the other hand, we find in the English
the admirable toleration in respect of opinion that helped
to correct this arrogance and that the colonists lacked.
During the American revolution when Fox and Burke spoke
their minds in attacks on the repressive policy of the ministry, when the great Whig, Coke of Norfolk, toasted in
public George Washington instead of the king, no effort
was made to check this freedom. By contrast the colonies
were so bitterly intolerant that any one who spoke a word
for the old loyalties might meet with the brutal violence

of a coating of tar and feathers, followed by confiscation of his property and enforced exile or even death. Unlike what happened with deplorable frequency in the colonies, no one in England was executed or killed for his opinions on the issue. Since there the fullest liberty of opinion was not questioned, free discussion produced, at last, a great effect. By reason, if also by disaster, the nation was so persuaded to correct its mistakes that to-day George Washington ranks as a champion of British liberty and a statue in his honour adorns Trafalgar Square in London.

Most of the colonies had, indeed, a narrow insular spirit. They had been planted by private effort, and each was chiefly absorbed in its own little world. Contact even with the other colonies was slight. In days when the voyage across the Atlantic and back might occupy from four to six months, and when the poverty of struggling pioneers made travel impossible, the colonists inevitably lost touch with Europe. Since they were citizens of a small state rather than of a world empire, in any clash of interests they would be certain to hold to what was for local benefit in each colony. They had, however, much in common. From all of them members of the well-to-do class had been sent to colleges in England where they shared a common colonial status. Harvard and Yale drew students from other colonies. Moreover similar conditions of life created a similar outlook. The influence of religion was unifying when "The Great Awakening" in religion, led by George Whitefield, swept through all the colonies. It is, however, true that they lived remote from each other with but slight personal contacts. The mail from Philadelphia to Boston usually occupied two weeks though the distance by land could be covered in a week. Roads were so bad that travel was chiefly on horseback and every important house had its horse-block for mounting. The wider rivers, still unbridged, were crossed by ferries, the lesser ones often by fords, dan-

gerous in time of flood. The interest of the colonies varied
with their position and their dangers. Massachusetts, Connecticut and New York, with frontiers harassed by the
French, had been zealous for the conquest of Canada. During the war they had raised more than two-thirds of the
armies of the colonies although they had only one-third of
the total population. Since the colonies farther south along
the sea-board were secure in the protection of the British
fleet, they took a slow and grudging share in the war. Even
Virginia and Pennsylvania, menaced, not from the sea but
on their rear from the French and the Indians in the Ohio
country, gave inadequate response to urgent appeals. The
most striking outcome of the American Revolution is, however, that in contrast with the colonies of Spain, the English colonies stood together to make in the end one nation
with the vast resources of half a continent.

Pitt had shown tact in dealing with the colonies. Of the
fifty thousand men needed to conquer Canada one-half
should, he thought, be raised in America. When he had
asked each colony to aid in proportion to its wealth and
population, each had manœuvred to lay the burden as far
as possible on the mother country. While he provided the
needed arms and asked them only to pay and clothe their
men, he did more than he promised; in the year 1759
Parliament voted two hundred thousand pounds to relieve
colonial finances. In spite of this no colony raised more
than its allotted number of soldiers and most fell far short.
While in England unemployment caused men to enlist and
endure the harsh discipline of the army, in the colonies
there was not this pressure. Pioneers busily creating their
own homes were reluctant to enlist. In consequence more
than one colonial leader, including George Washington
himself, declared that the least reputable elements in the
community made up a large part of the colonial levies.

In contrast with England the colonies, though rich in

the promise of undeveloped resources, were poor in realized wealth. If, in England, Horace Walpole thought that an income of less than twenty thousand pounds a year involved poverty, in America the governor of Connecticut had two hundred pounds a year and even this was uncertain since the colony claimed that it was too poor to pay so large a sum. The governor who had five hundred pounds a year was thought to be well paid; the head of a college had about two hundred; and a New England judge was paid only a hundred and twenty pounds, increased by a few uncertain fees. The government of Connecticut spent only four thousand pounds a year, a tax of about fifteen cents a head of the population. Stephen Hopkins, Governor of Rhode Island, said that the colony had never had at one time as much money as would be required to pay the annual amount of some fourteen thousand pounds involved in a tax of three pence a gallon on its imports of molasses. Thus, while to the Englishman the taxes levied in America seemed small, to the frugal colonist a few hundred pounds was so large a sum that he watched taxation closely and felt resentment at any added burden. When Pennsylvania had voted ten thousand pounds for military aid during the late war, the legislators thought themselves generous and were apt to be resentful at further calls. Amherst's slow deliberation in closing in on Canada is partly excused by his need to wait until the colonial levies should join him. After 1760 when, though French power in America had fallen, the war continued elsewhere, the colonies, relieved from the peril at their own doors, not only gave no further aid that mattered but objected to restrictions on their trade with enemy ports in the West Indies.

CHAPTER VI

THE BRITISH POLITICAL SYSTEM UNDER GEORGE III

REVOLUTION had menaced the first half of the eighteenth century in England. Under the foreign kings, George I and George II, there had been two risings in the interests of the Stuarts and the danger had made the Whigs, whose power had brought in the House of Hanover, seem the enduring support of the monarchy. Later, however, under the Englishman, George III, all danger had passed. Former Jacobites appeared at court, ready now for favours from even the House of Hanover. No longer could the Whigs pose as the sole props of a Protestant nation against the dangers of a Roman Catholic dynasty; a king secure on his throne was supported by all his subjects. Politics have the unchanging rule that change is inevitable. The Whigs were only part of the nation. Their power had been due to a crisis in regard to the succession to the throne that was long since past; change to another system was by this time due and George III became its minister.

The kingship, however weak it had been and indeed still remains in direct power, has usually commanded influence and authority with the nation. We need only remember the rapturous return to kingship that had followed the break of a dozen years after the execution of Charles I. No doubt its prestige with the nation had declined under two foreign and unsympathetic German rulers. Though George III revived it, after him it was weakened by the vicious licence of one and the folly of the other of his two reigning sons. Then a queen of another character renewed its prestige

and secured such real authority that, as under her grandfather, George III, not a member of the cabinet, not an
admiral, nor a general nor a bishop but must come under
her scrutiny before he secured his post. The majesty of
kingship still so commands awe as to cause many to wonder that the king is, after all, like other people in that he
has the human need to eat, sleep, dress and take exercise.

So true is this that even during the reigns of the two first
Georges mutterings were heard that the Whigs had degraded kingship. George II had had, however, real authority, especially in the army. His dislike of Guy Carleton had
kept that capable engineer from serving with Wolfe at
Louisbourg in 1758: on the other hand the limitation on
the king's veto is perhaps seen in Wolfe's securing Carleton
to go with him to Quebec in the next year. The checks on
the royal power endured into the early days of George III.
George Grenville, when head of the ministry in 1763–65,
demanded that no one but himself might presume to speak
to the king on public business and that, to ensure this,
George must not allow Grenville's predecessor, the Earl
of Bute, even to live in London where he might influence
the king. When it was urged at the time that the king
should be treated with respect, Rigby, using the blasphemy
that suited his character, said "By God, he shall not have
power to make a footman." The Duke of Bedford, leaving
town for a time, hands the king a paper complaining that
the royal manner has been cold, and declaring that he will
retire if, when he comes back, the king is not more cordial
to him and his friends and does not frown on those whom
they dislike.

When George III was a youth there was much talk of a
book, "The Patriot King," by the discredited statesman,
Bolingbroke, who has this link with Canada that he was the
author of the fatuous expedition of Sir Hovenden Walker
to the St. Lawrence in 1711. Party, said Bolingbroke, had

become obsolete. Its fruit was faction that had little regard for the real welfare of the nation. So held together by corruption was it that it had been able to encroach on the king's authority. He had the right to govern as well as to reign and as the protector and servant of all his people to refuse the dictation of any party. When, in 1760, nine years after the death of Bolingbroke, young George III, at the age of twenty-two, came to the throne, he was resolved to bring into operation Bolingbroke's outline of what a king should be, the enemy of faction, the leader of all his people, secure in his right to direct their affairs and watchful for their well-being. In due course he would end a system subversive of the royal dignity. Though hardly more than a boy in years he had even then a supreme confidence in himself and in his own high aim to be the friend and protector of all his subjects. Later he overruled decisions of the war office and he would not allow the fleet to sail from Portsmouth until he had himself inspected its equipment. Should war come with France he declared that he would lead his army in person, a task that had required the astounding genius of Marlborough.

Unhappily, as the event proved, George III lacked the generous imagination, the "large and liberal views in the management of great affairs" that alone are adequate, as Burke said, to wise rule. It is unjust to denounce him as the evil-minded tyrant described in the American Declaration of Independence. He was not a fool nor a bad man, but only an ignorant, obstinate and unwise one. We know the results of his policy and lament the unwisdom in regard to the colonies that, in truth, he shared with most of his contemporaries in England. In defence of what he thought a sacred cause, he was the servant of his own conscience. It told him to preserve unimpaired, as in the sight of God, all that, in Milton's phrase, had brought "this Britanick Empire to a glorious and enviable height." A great man

knows when to yield, but this art of conciliation obstinate
and small-minded George III learned only when it was too
late. While he loved his people and desired their happiness,
he believed it to be safe only in the hands of the guardian,
by right of birth, of their long traditions.

In contrast with some other rulers of the time, the British might count themselves happy in their king. Frederick
the Great of Prussia was, indeed, by ability and industry,
a giant among monarchs; but across the channel in France
a ruler by divine right spent his days in indolent pleasures,
comforted by the hope that a vicious system might last
his time. Though it did, it was followed soon after, as he
feared, by revolution. Compared with Louis XV, George III
was the model of a good king. There was such lack even
of vivacity at his court that his sons had to find diversion
elsewhere and did it with gusto. George's private life was
blameless. In personal habits he was rigidly temperate. He
practised a watchful economy even in regard to the use
of candles, sugar and soap, was content with a dinner of
mutton and turnips washed down by barley water and
with a supper of bread and butter or perhaps only of gruel.
When a stout uncle lamented to him that corpulence was
in the royal blood George told him that abstemious habits
were the cure. In all weathers he kept his windows open
and he took active exercise, sometimes in the saddle from
early morning to evening, sometimes in strenuous walks
across country, perhaps over ploughed fields. Those with
whom he was in personal contact liked him as kindly and
in small things considerate. He was so religious that he
would listen to interminable sermons and rebuke flattery
from the pulpit by saying that he came not to hear himself
but God praised. "I can scarcely conceive," said Benjamin
Franklin in 1768, "a king of better disposition or more exemplary virtues or more truly desirous of promoting the
welfare of all his subjects." He had gracious manners and

in Dr. Johnson's eyes was "the finest gentleman he had ever seen." So gracious was he with plain, homely people that cottagers near Windsor were not unlikely to have the king drop in for a chat over the kitchen fire about pigs and poultry and, if he saw something lacking, to find a five pound note left unobserved on the kitchen table. The queen, calling on Mrs. Garrick, found her peeling onions and joined in the task. George III was a keen farmer and even published articles on agriculture under an assumed name. Though he thought a great part of Shakespeare "Sad stuff, What? What?" he was, as far as defective education permitted, the sympathetic patron of art and letters, with some wit and some insight into values.

We need not read into the commonplace mind of George III any deep ponderings on the nature of the state or the philosophy of government. He knew, it had been drilled into his mind from childhood, that the office of king had a great reserve of authority, no matter what pressure bullying Whig ministers might sometimes apply, and he prepared himself for his chosen rôle with obstinate persistence. As king, George III considered himself a being apart, above self-seeking, desiring only the nation's good. When he gave audience to grave and elderly statesmen, he expected them to stand, though the interview might last for hours. Pitt, perhaps to relieve his gouty legs, did business with the king on his knees. To Pitt any word from the king is due to "infinite condescension" and in his letters he is always like Disraeli at a later time throwing himself at Majesty's feet. On one point the king and Pitt, the greatest leader of the age, were in agreement, for both disliked rule by party that was faction; but, while Pitt had been intent on rule in obedience to the public opinion of the nation, George, the guardian of the nation's good, would hold his ministers to his own policy. During the early years of his reign, when still only a youth, he dismissed half a score of ministers, each of them more capable than himself. It was his indomitable will that after 1770 held the pliant North, head of the ministry, to the impossible task of coercing the colonies to obedience. George never faltered in courage. When warned of plots to assassinate him, he would mount his horse and ride along the road named in the anonymous letter, attended only by an equerry and a footman. "I only hope," he said, "that whoever will attempt it will not do it in a barbarous or brutal manner."

It is unhappily true that to the indignant subjects of George III in America, whom he tried to conquer, the king so became the symbol of a ruthless tyranny that in the minds of many in the republic monarchy still has this quality. But George III, whose lack of imagination, linked with an iron consistency in a wrong course, did much harm, at least achieved this good that he broke up rule by faction and gave the nation the unity under the king that has expanded into the modern union of monarchy with democracy supported by the majority in the nation. It is possible that this type of rule may itself change or disappear as did rule by Whig groups, since rule by majority often involves the flaming resentment of the minority and causes deep cleavage in national life. Whig rule by groups had some measure of efficiency. It is by men rather than by a system that good government is assured and the record of modern democracy is not so uniform in merit as to entitle it to sneer at the politics of the age of George III. If under him the English colonies were lost, under him also two powerful rulers of France, Louis XV and Napoleon, were beaten in war and the chief parts of the present British Empire were secured.

No subject laboured with more tireless industry than George III. After he had defeated Whig faction he aimed to direct all the affairs of government. He seems to have kept no private secretary. We have many hundreds of letters written by himself at nearly all hours of the day or night and noting the exact minute of the writing. Though he was not vain, he kept always in mind "My Glory," linked with "the interest of My Dominions." Liberty would avoid licence only when in subordination to the king. He was a stranger to distrust of himself. If he thought that he was competent to direct every branch of the public service, appointments in church and state, in the army and the navy, he did not spare himself in his stupendous task. He read vast masses of correspondence and passed a final opinion on a head of a college or a professor with the same certainty that he named a minister or a general. He kept before him elaborate lists of bishops and deans with the incomes attached to these offices and to many other positions in regard to which his choice had authority. His eye is always on aged or ailing prelates and when one dies his successor is told at once of his appointment to the post. The following notes to Lord North are types of many: "The Bishop of Exeter has received no benefit by Bath water, and is now removed to Bristol, but with little hope of recovery." Accordingly there will soon be a desirable post to fill. Of a lay official the king writes: "I have just heard that Mr. Worseley, the Surveyor-General of the Board of Works, can scarcely outlive the day. I give you this notice, as it will make a very pretty House of Commons employment."

The king knew the record of most of the officers in the army. It is hard to imagine a modern ruler preparing with his own hand, in seventeen parallel columns, as George did, the names of the commanders and other details of thirty-six ships. He copied in duplicate long state papers. He considered appeals for pardon and, since crime menaced public order, he did not lean to clemency. Riot in remote Boston made him furiously resolute to restore there "order and obedience" for was he not its ruler? When the trouble began he was anxious to hear what he could of Sam Adams, Hancock and others of the discontented. He checked over the names in the divisions in Parliament and, it may be added, marked for his displeasure the members who opposed his wishes. Since he must have active support he is glad to learn that Colonel Burgoyne and Lieutenant Harcourt were not absent from a division; otherwise both would have lost their posts. It was the whip of a tyranny that only high courage and conviction dared to face. The king's resentments were so acute that when opposed he was sullen and vindictive. General Conway was one of the fine spirits of the time, a member of Parliament, and in the end a Field Marshal. He was not to be bullied and in 1763 voted against Grenville, then Prime Minister, for what he thought arbitrary acts directed against Wilkes. The young king was furious; already Wilkes had become his chief bugbear and he forced Grenville to dismiss Conway from his military command and his civil posts. George spent vast sums in buying support for the group in Parliament called "the King's Friends." He even canvassed a shopkeeper at Windsor for his vote by saying of the candidate whom he disliked "No Keppel, No Keppel" and adding that the queen needed a new gown. Lord Brougham has called him the slave of deep-rooted selfishness in all that related to the kingly office, without pity for any one who might challenge his power. Because the last and perhaps the noblest phase of Chatham's career centred in opposition to the coercion of the colonies, the king called him a "trumpet of sedition" and was so malevolent as to wish his death. When this came in 1778 George said that the nation's sorrow was offensive to himself personally. While his decisions on policy ranged over the whole British world in three continents his labours left him ignorant. At one time he thought the Ganges the western boundary of the English colonies in America.

The cabinet which now has about a score of members, most of them in the House of Commons, consisted then of seven or eight, nearly all in the House of Lords. The cabinet was an aristocratic body. The Commoners who might sit in it were of the same social class as the peers and almost certain to be related to some noble family. Formerly the king had presided at its meetings but under the foreign king George I, who could not follow the English of the discussions, this practice was discontinued and it has never been resumed. The cabinet might, however, meet only at the summons of the king and it must report to him its decisions which were carried out in his name and by his consent. It happened sometimes that not more than three members were present at a meeting of the cabinet. They might assemble not in the official residence in Downing Street but at the London house of one or the other magnate and dine together with perhaps a score of liveried servants waiting on them. There are ancestral portraits on the walls and rich plate on the table. When the servants have left the stately room the ministers settle the affairs of the country and indeed feel themselves to be the country. They are courteous to each other; "Your Grace"; "My Lord." No minutes are kept. They reach "a gentleman's agreement." To speak of these dignified men as associates in corruption is to miss the spirit of the time. How else could government then be carried on? Ministers must have support and to hold it must have gifts to bestow. What government of our time grants favours to its enemies while denying them to its friends? Is not government in France carried on by powerful groups to this day and is it done any better there in our time than it was done in England by these fine Whig gentlemen of great estate in the time of George III? Could a wide electorate have done better at the time? Most of the voters would have been unable to read or write and their vision would not have reached beyond their parishes. After all, it was under this system that Britain had won resounding victory over both France and Spain.

In spite of a narrow franchise Parliament expressed in some real sense the public opinion of England. Though the many boroughs, each with two members in the House of Commons, had few voters, each of the forty counties of England also sending two members had, on the average, about four thousand. In the larger counties, when rival interests were acute, an election might cause a great land-owner to spend a hundred thousand pounds. Since there was only one polling place, voters in a large riding might have to travel many miles. The poll was open usually for more than a week and neither the moral code nor, it seems, the law, forbade the champions of one side from taking possession of the poll and using force to keep opponents from voting. We have the instructions of a candidate at Rochester to his agents in 1768, during the second election of the reign of George III. In that ancient city on the Medway near London, the candidate ordered that, as the election drew near, stout fellows in his interest should collect voters in private houses, supply them for days with food and especially drink, and keep them from going out. When the poll was opened, the more doubtful men, in groups of twelve or fourteen, were to be made sober for the time and to be guided to the polling place by half a dozen active workers. Another half dozen were to take possession of the barrier at the polling place and to permit only friendly voters to enter. The vote was open and numbers were declared from hour to hour since it was desirable always to show a lead in the poll in order to attract those who wished to be on the winning side. Meanwhile parties patrolled the town to gather in drunken stragglers and to get them sober enough to vote. Towards the close of the poll no expense that seemed necessary was to be spared. The poll closed if an hour elapsed without the recording of a vote.

The House of Commons had 558 members of whom 69 came from Scotland and Wales; 80 English members sat for the counties; 4 sat for the universities; and the other 405 for what were, or had been, towns; some, populous centres such as the city of London, Westminster, and Bristol; others, on a scale descending to the most scandalous rotten borough of the time, Old Sarum, where the landowner, a member of the Pitt family, named the two members representing no one but himself. Nine-tenths of the members of Parliament were from a society that lived as if it was rich. Even the austere morality of Burke did not exclude the aping of the rich in his mode of life. When earning only a few hundred pounds a year, he borrowed money to buy an estate at Beaconsfield that cost £20,000, lived there at the rate of £2500 a year over and above his expenses in London, and drove a carriage drawn by four black horses in the best style of the landed magnate. The scale of his borrowings was such that Rockingham forgave him a debt of £30,000. Since the income from land of a family went to the eldest son who inherited the family estates, the younger sons must be provided for in some other way. They scorned trade and thus could look to no career in the expanding commercial life of the country. To become a successful lawyer meant such hard toil and natural capacity that the great posts in law of the time were won usually by humbler men disciplined from youth to work. The physician had a low social standing. The church was better, and the "good thing" of a bishopric went often to the scion of a great house. The other chief field of employment for a gentleman was under the government, especially in the fighting services. Failing other resources his class thought they had the right to maintenance by the state.

In the early days of George III parties did not stand

opposed on great public questions. Of these the electors knew little; they were, however, alert to local needs and saw wisdom in standing well with both sides. Accordingly counties and boroughs alike often accepted an agreement that one seat should go to a so-called Tory, the other to a Whig. Since the vital struggle for the Tory or the Whig was to get a nomination, as against rival interests, what usually decided the issue was the influence of some powerful family or group behind a candidate, combined with an assurance on his part that he could and would secure from the government posts, contracts, honours, that his constituents might claim. So effective was the bargaining for a nomination that, in fact, most members were returned to Parliament without going to the poll. A bargain saved expense. In the election of 1761, when the Parliament was chosen that planted the seeds of the American Revolution, there were contests in only forty-eight of the three hundred and fifteen constituencies.

During an election a candidate must pay court to the electors. When Horace Walpole, whose appreciation of social niceties was as acute as Lord Chesterfield's, stood for Parliament in 1761, he had to address boisterous crowds, ride in Lynn at the head of a procession of two thousand people, ask the inn-keeper for his support, compliment misses who played to him on the harpischord, admire the bad paintings owned by prosperous aldermen, and spend hours at feasts where the speeches, the songs, the conversation, the fumes of tobacco irritated his refined nerves. The wife of a candidate in 1754 describes what was expected of her. Rough people thronged her house and made it like a pigsty with the stench of tobacco and with the drink supplied freely at table. Her best floors were spoiled by the hob-nailed boots of trampling farmers. She had to receive and to be gracious at meals to a dozen rough boors, to entertain their wives and to drive their children with her in her carriage. She might not patronize a grocer or a butcher if he was of the opposing party. She was even expected to win favour by kissing the voters. The member who failed in such complaisance might be defeated by an aspiring merchant, or a rival landowner. Behind all was a government that must have a majority. Thus a member, so far from having leisurely security, was always under pressure either to support a ministry or to turn it out. The member himself, if he retired to give place to one more popular, might expect a sinecure or a pension, and he could get little without making urgent demands. Since a seat in Parliament gave a place in the great world, the holder with the needed rank or ability might command much influence. Inevitably while some members desired only to serve their country, others expected to get benefit from a system that offered rewards and favours. There is deep truth in what Soame Jenyns, a member of the House of Commons at this time, said, that a Parliament of men whose one thought was of the public interest never did and never could exist.

Means of being informed on great questions were scanty. The horse brought news only slowly from remoter places and the few newspapers were read by a limited circle. Meetings for the discussion of public affairs were hardly known; Burke said in 1766 that the ministry of Rockingham, just driven from office, "was the first which proposed and encouraged public meetings." Travel was so costly that only the well-to-do went far beyond their own district. The debates in Parliament were those of a meeting of gentlemen with no eye of the public upon them; it was a crime to publish what was said. Strangers admitted to the House of Commons were not allowed to carry in with them any scrap of paper, lest they should take notes. An artist sitting in the gallery was so struck by the appearance of Charles James Fox in his maiden speech that, since he might not have with him paper, he tore off a piece of his shirt and made a drawing greatly valued by Fox's friends.

The people, ill-informed, often showed their suspicions in brutal violence. While we are familiar with the wrecking of houses, the tarring and feathering, the riotous throwing of cargoes of tea into the sea that marked discontent in New England, we may forget similar scenes in the motherland. Nothing in America equalled the devastation of the Gordon Riots in London in 1780. If the London mob was aroused on any question, leading statesmen on their way to Parliament might be in danger of their lives. When John, Duke of Bedford, a man of vast wealth who exercised a princely charity, displeased the mob at Honiton he was hunted out of the town with a pack of bull-dogs. At Exeter, when it was known that he was seated in the cathedral, a riotous mob burst in to seize him. We have in the journals of that amazing man, John Wesley, all but incredible instances of the fury of the mobs. They attacked Wesley's followers because they prayed from morning to night and thus, so the mob said, pretended to be better than other people: they have *convarted* my wife, said one old man; she had been a scold and now was "as quiet as a lamb." A mob surrounded a house in which Wesley was a guest and dragged him before a justice of the peace, shouting "Knock his brains out," "Kill him at once." He says that he did not cease to speak to them, that he felt no pain or weariness, and in the end did not come off badly since he lost only one flap of his waist-coat and a little skin from one of his hands.

The times were tolerant of abuses that shock us. The conception of what is moral in politics changes from age to age. There is a wide gulf between what to the citizen of the eighteenth century was blameless and what the present generation, versed in the working of democratic institutions, has learned to think evil. In the eighteenth cen-

tury the law did not forbid a borough to regard its choice
of a member of Parliament as a saleable asset. The average
price was about two thousand pounds and men of high
character and position paid this openly. Tewkesbury required of its two candidates in 1761 that each should give
fifteen hundred pounds to aid in improving its roads. Oxford pointed out that it had a debt of some five thousand
pounds and made it a condition of election that its two
members should pay this debt. There was incessant bargaining for the support that should keep ministers in
power. While the Whig leaders were not corrupt men, they
had to carry on public affairs with the methods of the time
and to meet the needs of those who gave them support.
Many who sat in Parliament coveted some office or other
favour from government and their leaders must aid them.
Some sinecures were really pensions. It is to be hoped that
the House of Commons laughed when told by Burke in
1782 that one of its members held the office of turnspit in
the royal kitchen. The leader who found this refuge for
a needy fellow-legislator must have been hard pressed. A
salary as turnspit was, however, as good as any other when
no duties were expected.

No doubt such a system fostered a type of hanger-on
who, by clever intrigue, took advantage of the many openings for abuses. Sir John Rigby is an example of the worst.
"The profligacy of his principles," said Lord Charlemont at
the time, "would have scandalized the court of Tiberius."
In 1763, when Bute was seeking a majority to ensure peace
with France, Rigby had urged Fox to make a clean sweep
of the Whigs, and was himself a bluff, shameless, and treacherous claimant for place. In the end, he built up a fortune of half a million pounds. Grenville described him
as an illiterate coward who went off to a post in Ireland
to escape being hanged. While Rigby represents the evils
of a system capable of abuse, it was itself the expression of

forces in politics still by no means dead. Jobbery is the
easy vice of all governments. It is only great abuses that
even to our day revolt men's consciences. Titles, payments
for legal services, appointments still go by party favour in
most countries. In this respect England herself is in large
measure reformed, though peerages and judgeships remain
often the rewards of party. France and the United States
still give their great offices to friends of those in power.

It is amusing now to see what the moral standards of
the eighteenth century permitted. A certain John Twells
was "domestic apothecary" to the Duke of Newcastle. He
had given seventeen years "constant attendance upon the
Duchess of Newcastle in all her illnesses," was constantly
with her, and had become to her "very necessary." As a
reward he had received from her husband, the prime minister, a sinecure in the customs that brought in some £530
a year, an amount larger than the salary of a colonial governor. He was, however, one of Fox's victims and when the
Duchess wrote to the immaculate Lord Hardwicke to tell
the sad story, Hardwicke declared that the dismissal was
"most cruel," low and ungentlemanly. Later, under Rockingham who, as Burke said, was never even suspected of
corruption, the post was restored to the happy Mr. Twells.
In modern times, by competitive examinations, by Civil
Service Commissions, and by the press and the public meetings that form opinion, we have eased the strain on a member of Parliament of urgent claims for favours, though still
they are burdensome. But the eighteenth century had not
these safeguards. Civil servants sat in the House of Commons, to make or unmake ministers, their paymasters. Contractors sat there and pushed claims for privileges. Seaports
elected admirals as members, since these could get posts
for their sailors and employments on the docks. Officers of
the army sat in Parliament, since in this way they could
command influence in military appointments. To the

thought of the time this was no more corrupt than is the present practise of governments to favour only their supporters. Politics are not conspicuous for breeding a delicate moral sense or freedom from the bias of interest or of party.

While the British political system was clearly too rigid for the expanding needs of an empire that was becoming world-wide, it is also unhappily true that the men in power were nearly all second-rate in talent and lacked the ability to read the needs of the age. Imagination, required hardly less in politics than in poetry, is a gift not freely bestowed on any people. Yet it was needed in an island state that, in a little more than a hundred years, had created a great Asiatic and a great American empire. Since eighteenth century England did not understand its nearest neighbour Ireland, it was not likely to grasp the significance of events three thousand miles across the ocean. Members of Parliament were chiefly occupied with claims of their constituents in regard to local and personal needs. When Burke was member for Bristol he was expected to look after many petty private affairs in London. Inevitably voters had only a misty consciousness of issues in America. Communities so new could not, it was thought, have either a past or a present to interest the world of Europe. It may, indeed, be doubted whether, in our own time, more than a few thousands of nearly fifty million people in the British Isles have ever read a history of either the United States or Canada, or have a doubt that nothing in either country can be equal to what may be found in their own land. Except in some crisis, debates in Parliament relating to the great dependency of India attract a mere handful of members. Naturally the British mind was and it still remains essentially European in outlook, though in these later years a slow realization of forces that involve the decline of Europe in world affairs is taking place. There was point to Franklin's jibes at English ignorance when he described the cod fishing on the Great Lakes and the wonderful spectacle of whales leaping up the Falls of Niagara. The average Englishman could hardly be persuaded that anything written in America was worth reading. We may doubt whether, until the crisis came, more than a few members of the House of Commons had ever seen a colony, or heard of colonial leaders, or read an American newspaper or pamphlet, of which, as Chatham and Burke well knew, many were of high quality. When the dispute began some went through many editions and they reveal in men of Washington's type surprise at new demands by Britain that seemed to break with the past; affection wounded at her indifference to their protests; sorrow changing to resentment and, in the end, to disdain and angry defiance.

The real England was the England of the landowners, great and small, rooted in the opinions and prejudices due to their long predominance. To most of them a colony was remote territory, peopled by the younger children of a parent who thought that they had fallen to an inferior mode of life but still claimed over them full authority. Some naval and military officers in Parliament had been in America, and one of them, Colonel Barré, warned the House of Commons of dangers. A nation, however, that had just humbled France and Spain, was quite sure of its right and power to rule its own colonies. Pocket boroughs and a narrow franchise do not therefore explain the attitude of Parliament. A wider franchise would have proved that, at least in the early stages of the war, George III and his ministers spoke the mind of England in the demands upon America. In the counties, where the owner of land worth as little as forty shillings a year had a vote and where sometimes there were eight or nine thousand voters, an election always showed that the opinion of this, the real

England, was for strong measures. It could hardly be otherwise, for the voters believed that Massachusetts, not less than Cornwall, was under the direct control of Parliament. They had no insight to realize the difference that Cornwall had members to speak for it in high places while Massachusetts was a remote outsider, with a quite separate system of government.

War is so great a solvent in politics that its intensity disturbs easy-going conventions. The war that had ended in 1763 had in reality created a dangerous temper on both sides of the Atlantic. Great Britain, flushed with victory, wished even to extend her control of the trade of the colonies, while they, for their part, intended to please themselves. It was soon clear that they would challenge subordination to the central authority. Since in London this was thought to be necessary to hold together the Empire, resentment deepened. The Bedford faction, in spite of its kindly leader, breathed fury against rebels and cowards in America denying obedience to their king. The Grenville faction made a fetish of legal right over the colonies, not knowing what was even then true that the law may permit what constitutional practice denies: George III had, for instance, the legal right to veto an act of Parliament but even his unbending courage would not have ventured so far. "Mankind," said Dr. Johnson, "are happier in a state of inequality and subordination" and he and most of his countrymen believed that this was as true of England in relation to the colonies as of the landed magnate in relation to the villagers on his estate. Since Johnson would have had a landlord turn out any tenant who would not vote as he directed, it was natural that when the colonies refused obedience he should breathe against them threatenings of fire and slaughter. To him, so Boswell reports, they were "Rascals, Robbers, Pirates," in denying subordination.

He would "burn and destroy them." He so roared that Boswell thought he might even be heard across the Atlantic. The outburst caused Miss Anne Seward, the poetess, who was present, to say that "we are always most violent against those whom we have most injured." Protests from the colonies caused merely derision in most high circles in England, derision followed by the attempt to conquer them into subordination, a policy rarely surpassed in folly in the annals of mankind.

This ruling class despised democracy. Even John Wesley, who may be described as the discoverer of the poor, said that "the greater share the people have in government, the less liberty, civil and religious, does a nation enjoy." Since the democracy of the colonies caused revolution, a fixed feature of British policy during the next three quarters of a century was to discourage colonial self-government. As late as in 1844 the Governor of Canada, Sir Charles Metcalfe, a man of fine character, who had ruled in India and Jamaica, told the Liberal leaders, Baldwin and Lafontaine, educated men of high integrity and deeply learned in Englist constitutional principles, that a Canadian ministry might not control even internal affairs. He would not be, he said, the ignominious tool of rebels and revolutionaries. The mother country must be supreme in Canada and he would have in office only those on whom he could rely in the hour of need; it was absurd that even with a majority in the legislature colonial leaders should regard themselves as heading a responsible ministry. Of all this the British ministry of the time approved. For his part in the bitter contest Metcalfe received from Queen Victoria a peerage as a mark of her approbation and both Gladstone and Macaulay wrote in high praise of his policy as "a model for his successors." Lord Stanley, the Colonial Secretary, scholar, orator, afterwards three times prime minister as the Earl of Derby, denounced the Canadian Liberal leaders as mischievous demagogues; the conflict was, he said, between rebels and honest men; it was better that Canada should be governed from London than to be ruled by persons so base. While George III said that the true interest and happiness of the colonies consisted in subordination to Great Britain, Mr. Asquith, the prime minister, said in 1911, a century and a half later, that Great Britain alone must decide the issues in foreign affairs that might involve Canada and other self-governing parts of the Empire in war.

We cannot doubt the sincerity of these convictions. They show the normal working of the political mind encased in the older tradition that meant blindness to forces involving change. Modern thought, impregnated with the conception of evolution, regards society as a living organism, containing within itself the seeds of both decay and growth. We have abundant reason to cease to think even of a supposed changeless east. We know now that incessantly man himself is altered in outlook by his environment and by ideas that reach his mind. This law, valid for every generation, was not grasped by the political mind of England in either the eighteenth or the early nineteenth century. No more in 1844 than in 1763 had those in power realized that the subordination of the infancy of a colony could not endure in even its early manhood. There is this excuse for the governing class in 1763 that social England had itself changed but little during the previous hundred years. The revolution that drove out the Stuarts had altered rather the forms of government than the lives of the people. The old gradation in society endured; to own land remained the chief source of political power; estates rather than diminishing tended to increase in size, and the small yeoman to disappear when the village common became the private property of the magnate of the adjoining park. The forces of change were, of course, working, but so slowly as hardly to attract attention. Consequently the land-

owner of the eighteenth century, who believed that his
own society was based on eternal foundations, was not
likely to understand uneasy forces far away across three
thousand miles of ocean. To him and also to the commercial class of the time the use of colonies lay in benefit to the mother country. She did her duty by giving them
protection from alien powers such as Spain and France and
she expected in return profit from their growth. They were
"our subjects," "our colonies," "our possessions," "our dominions," rasping phrases still used in England with no
thought of giving offence.

CHAPTER VII

THE CONTROL OF COLONIAL TRADE

THE American colonies were chiefly agricultural and trading communities, divided into two groups; the north with an extensive sea-going commerce; the agricultural south growing chiefly the tobacco and rice suited to the climate. The first definite restrictions on colonial trade had come when, after the execution of Charles I, the Protestant English republic found Holland, another Protestant republic, its chief rival in trade. Since the godly Puritans who, for the time, ruled England were not blind to worldly interests, they aimed at checking the carrying trade of Holland and also at excluding all foreign trade from the English colonies. Accordingly the English republic of Cromwell's time took drastic action not only to forbid the Dutch to carry to England foreign goods other than their own but also to deny to all foreign ships the right to enter colonial ports. The Navigation Act of 1651 provided that all goods carried to or from the colonies should be in ships built in England or in the colonies, owned, commanded and, to the extent of three-fourths of their crews, sailed by Englishmen or colonists.

It was the hope of the English to go farther and to ensure that nothing should be carried to England herself except in English ships, that no foreign ship should enter an English port, and that England should build up a great monopoly in the carrying trade. It was, however, too much to expect that France and Spain, for instance, should agree that only English ships should be allowed to carry goods

163

between England and France or Spain. Since this would mean that their own ships might not enter an English port, the retort was easy that in such a case no English ships should enter a French or Spanish port. The English aim at monopoly both ways overreached itself; it would have made trade impossible. Accordingly England yielded the point that France or Spain or any other foreign country might send ships to English ports. They must, however, carry only the products of the country to which the ship belonged. This liberty of direct trade with foreign ports was to be limited, however, to England. No foreign ship might enter a colonial port and no ship might sail from a colonial to a foreign port. Colonial cargoes intended for France or Spain must be landed in England, pay the dues charged there and then be carried to the foreign port in an English ship. Though these narrow and selfish restrictions may seem to our time almost incredible, they express the policy of the age in regard to colonial trade. France and Spain had similar rules. No foreign ship might sail to French Quebec, or to Spanish Havana. Why, it was thought, have colonies, if they did not fulfil what was supposed to be their chief purpose of bringing benefit to the parent country? Long after the English system was first enforced, Charles James Fox, Liberal statesman, and Adam Smith, free trader, both believed that from it came the commercial supremacy of Britain on the sea.

In the year 1660, which saw the return of Charles II amid frantic rejoicings, the English Parliament had found time to turn from pondering on the best means of revenge on the Puritans, who had executed a Stuart king, to add new restrictions on colonial trade. Accordingly it decreed that the colonies might sell only to England or to other colonies certain of their important products, now to be called "enumerated articles," such as sugar and tobacco. This was to relate to England alone. Until the Union in

1707 under one Parliament, Scotland was excluded from trade with the colonies. Ireland remained in even worse case. That unhappy island felt indeed then and long afterwards English domination in its most ruthless form. Though Ireland was a grazing country, she might not compete with English producers by exporting to England her beef or her cattle. When her flocks of sheep brought her wool into competition with the English producers, she was forbidden to export wool, raw or made into cloth, not merely to England but to any other part of the world. It did not matter that the ports of Ireland were the nearest to the English colonies in North America; she was not allowed to trade with them.

In 1696 when, after the upheaval of the English Revolution, William III was securely on the throne, the rather chaotic colonial system was reorganized by the creation of the new Board of Trade and Plantations. A survey of the long history of the Board arouses a certain admiration for the care with which it worked. It was an alert and efficient body within the range of its own opinions. Its eight members, including in the person of the Bishop of London a guardian of spiritual interests, drew up instructions to governors that from time to time were so elaborate as to outline a colonial paradise of good order, virtue, and above all of well-being in the interests of the trade of the mother country. The Board was always insistent on the subordination of the colonies. Its officials caused the disallowance of many acts of the colonial legislatures. As time passed the tendency was to tighten rather than to relax control. In making the Seven Years' War chiefly a struggle for colonies, Pitt led England into her first great naval and military effort in the colonial field. While hitherto colonies had been regarded as a source of profit, now they had become also one of expense, and the Board of Trade, facing a new situation, was naturally desirous of tapping revenues to redress the balance. The result was that restrictions grew more severe just at the moment when the colonial mind was bent on new liberties. The governors sent out from England must, it was said, be obeyed.

Meanwhile another spirit was already evident in the colonies. The Swedish traveller, Peter Kalm, notes that as early as in 1748 he had heard there the opinion that within fifty years they must become an independent nation. This period, as we know, was shortened by the renewed insistence in England on the enduring subordination of the colonies, the deepest among many causes of the American Revolution. When restrictions had been first imposed the young communities in America had made slight objection. In the system were advantages as well as drawbacks. Though the prohibition to engage in certain manufactures seemed an outrage on their liberty, in practice it brought no great hardship. Production in England, with her large markets and central position, was so cheap that the colonies could not compete in a free field. Cases of seeming hardship could, however, be cited. When, after the conquest of Canada, Britain had a monopoly of the fur trade, furs were added to the list of enumerated articles that might be sent only to England. To entrench this monopoly each colony was forbidden to make hats of the fur of the beaver for export either to Britain or to another colony. Yet this manufacture was natural to communities that had at hand great fur-bearing regions.

On the other hand, the colonies received valuable favours. If they might send their tobacco and sugar and tar only to England, she in turn might receive these from no other source, even though smokers should protest that they did not like the tobacco of Virginia. When farmers planted tobacco, the Privy Council rebuked them for their insolence in thus contemning the "princely pleasure" of the king.

Troops of horses were sent to trample down the crops in some twenty counties and rewards were offered to the informer against any one importing foreign tobacco. Growers of sugar in the British West Indies had a monopoly that cost the consumer in England many millions of pounds. To encourage production in the colonies Britain paid a preference on naval stores, hemp and timber, since she feared that, in time of war, supplies for the fleet from foreign sources might be cut off. Because she needed whale oil for lighting purposes she gave, to encourage the whale fishery, a preference on whale oil, an important product of colonial seafaring life. It was the source of great wealth. Almost to this day a million barrels, worth five times as many pounds, have been taken annually in the seas south of the Falkland Islands. Though England forbade certain manufactures in iron, she encouraged the production in the colonies of bar and pig iron. Even the exclusion of foreign ships from the colonies aided their ships as carriers and so encouraged the use of their abundant timber in shipbuilding as to cause protests from rivals in England. As commerce expanded, colonial ships, little heeding the law, sailed away to half the world. So complex was the system that the authorities in Britain feared the effect of change to meet individual complaints.

The long strip of communities from Maine to Georgia had varied products. Since those of the northern colonies were not unlike those of England, she had less need for them than for half-tropical products. The colonies in the north had, however, to get from England large supplies for their expanding life and, in order to meet the balance of trade against them, they must find markets elsewhere. The British West Indies satisfied part of their needs. Though to-day they have sunk into relative insignificance, in the eighteenth century their trade was highly developed.

In 1763 the annual exports of the West Indies to England equalled three times the six hundred thousand pounds in value of all that she took from the continent of North America. After Guadeloupe was seized in 1761 it sent to England products worth all those from the American colonies. Since, in the same period, England took from Canada a beggarly value of fourteen thousand pounds, chiefly in furs, we can understand the view urged at the time that in the hour of victory over France, Britain had better keep Guadeloupe and let Canada go. The West Indies, including the French colonies, had such things as sugar, coffee and indigo that the New England colonies needed; and in return for these, the colonies sent fresh meat, grain and dried fish to the West Indies and paid its debts in England by what surplus it could make in its shrewd commerce.

Trade will filter through any openings that it can find and will enlarge its channels by the pressure of its own volume. As time passed, the colonies paid so little heed to the prohibition to sell tobacco, sugar and other "enumerated articles" to foreign nations that they traded wherever they liked and sold what they could. There was no regular British patrol of the seas to stop and examine their outgoing ships or to keep them from smuggling foreign cargoes into their own ports. Such illegal trade disturbed few consciences. Even so great a writer in that age as Adam Smith excused the smuggler, on the ground that restrictive laws violated natural justice and "made that a crime which nature never intended to be so." In any case offences against the Custom House usually sit lightly on men's consciences and in most colonial ports officials had blind eyes for infractions of the law. The French West Indian Islands were near. Since they and remoter countries needed what the English colonies had to sell, it did not much matter whether the colonies sold to them the "enumerated articles" that, by law, might be sent only to England, or anything

else in demand. Madeira had sugar and wine; Spain and
Portugal had wine, fruit and oil; the colonies in their turn
had for sale things lacking in these countries; and trade
resulted. Tea was much used in the colonies. A writer
of the time says that there was hardly a hut twelve feet
square that lacked the apparatus for tea-drinking and he
added that "this vice" could never be rooted out. In England the tax on tea was a shilling a pound and the same
tax applied to the colonies. Untaxed tea from the eastern
possessions of Holland, of which Ceylon was then a part,
could, however, be had, and those smuggling it in could
reap a rich harvest. Smuggling was not difficult. Along a
thousand miles of seaboard, with many inlets, the small
ships of the time could slip up even shallow rivers.
Many Virginian landowners had their own docks from
which vessels of fewer than twenty tons sailed across the
ocean.

In England itself to smuggle was almost a national habit.
Smugglers were so powerful that at night armed bands
would escort along the highway to the place of storage the
goods landed at some lonely haven. Servants in the great
country houses were often in league with the smugglers
and sometimes on the sea-coast near London farmers could
not get needed labour since the more active men earned better pay in the smuggling bands. Honest wine merchants
who paid the legal duty could be undersold and half ruined.
Rum that paid duty was not profitable at less than nine
shillings a gallon but many consumers bought it at five and
knew that it and cheap tobacco and tea were due to
smuggling. Even in the later days when the younger Pitt
was reforming England, a committee of the House of Commons reported that the loss to the revenue by smuggling
amounted to ten million pounds a year. It was estimated
that on land and sea forty thousand persons were engaged
in it and they employed a large fleet. Pitt himself said that

duties were paid on only about one-third of the thirteen million pounds of tea brought annually to England.

It was duties imposed on sugar and its product molasses which caused the first acute strain between England and the colonies that ended in revolution. Within two years after Columbus reached America, the Spanish had made such wealth from sugar that Philip II is said to have built from the profits the vast Escorial Palace near Madrid. When, in time, the English had rich sugar plantations in the West Indies, naturally the owners desired the trade with England and the other colonies for themselves, to the exclusion of rivals in the Spanish and French West Indies. This sugar interest was so powerful that in 1733, during the era of prolonged peace under Walpole, Parliament passed the Molasses Act. It applied to the colonies and imposed an absurdly high duty on foreign molasses of sixpence a gallon, leaving free that from British sources. In New England the demand was great for sugar chiefly to make rum, and only from the cane sugar of the West Indies could the best rum be made. New England had a great trade in rum. It sold rum to the Indians in exchange for furs; rum to fishermen of Newfoundland in exchange for fish; rum to traders across the ocean in Africa who paid for it with black and sweating human cargoes for whom there was a ready sale in the southern colonies and in the West Indies. The colonies were themselves heavy consumers of rum. In the back townships nearly every farm-house retailed rum in any desired quantity and paid for no licence, with drinking and debauchery as the result. There were sixty distilleries in Massachusetts and forty in Rhode Island. Since the British West Indies did not produce enough sugar for the rum needed in Rhode Island alone, imports must come from the French West Indies. In any case molasses was cheaper there than in the British islands. The result was that the tax of sixpence a gallon imposed in 1733 caused resentment so acute that, from the first, smuggling made the tax almost inoperative.

A grievance in the colonies related to currency. Since the balance of trade was in favour of England, the colonies had to meet with sound money what was not covered by exports. Naturally this drained away their gold and silver currency and tended to cause them to issue paper money. Virginia, for instance, made its paper pound legal tender at its face value and the time came when the Virginia debtor asked his English creditor also to accept this currency at par. Naturally the Englishman called this robbery, for the Virginian pound was at a discount of twenty-five per cent or more. In our own time France has done what Virginia tried to do, paid its debts in money worth, in the case of France, only twenty per cent of its face value. In the end when Parliament forbade the colonies to issue paper money, colonial discontent, so said both John Adams and Benjamin Franklin, was such as to make this prohibition one of the chief causes of friction.

The sea-going commerce of the colonies was protected by the British fleet and defence was needed; pirates still haunted the West Indian islands and adjacent coasts. Colonial trade was so extensive that two hundred vessels were engaged in carrying tobacco alone. Since both France and Spain forbade foreign trade with their colonies, their coast-guards sometimes seized in a high-handed manner ships of the English colonies and claims for redress were more effective when backed by the sea-power of the mother country. She had her own grievance against colonial ships for, during the war ending in 1763, some of them had helped the French by carrying to them supplies. The colonies were not alone guilty; ships from England, Ireland and Scotland did the same thing; but the colonies were the chief offenders and enemy privateers were able to keep at sea and even the French army in Canada was able to prolong the war because supplied in this way. Since in time of war this trade aided France, the French governors of the West Indies violated their own laws in order to give licences to British ships to trade to their ports. The methods of the traders were baffling. Sometimes a ship would get clearing papers for Jamaica and then land its cargo at a French port or at neutral ports used by the French after they had lost both Canada and Guadeloupe. One device was to send a colonial ship under a flag of truce to a French port on the plea of an exchange of prisoners. She would land a few prisoners and with them a cargo for the French, paid for in currency, or in sugar and coffee. While some of the colonial governors refused passes for such flags of truce, and Fauquier, the lieutenant-governor of Virginia, rejected an offer of four hundred guineas for one, Denny, the governor of Pennsylvania, sold them openly for twenty pounds or less and in the end issued, at a price, blank passes on which the holder might insert the name of the ship of his choice. Rhode Island, New York, and Pennsylvania were the most deeply implicated in this commerce, but it affected all the colonies.

Holland was neutral throughout the Seven Years' War and Spain until nearly its close and both nations claimed for their trade the privileges of neutrals. When the Dutch island of St. Eustatius became a source of supply for the French, Britain decided that, since the French would not let foreign ships trade with their colonies in time of peace, they might not do so in time of war. From this came what is known as The Rule of 1756 under which the British seized Dutch vessels trading with the French colonies. When, in spite of strained relations with Holland, this checked the trade, neutral Spain became the chief offender. She divided with France the great island of Haiti. On its north shore, near the frontier of the French portion, she had the desolate village of Monte Christi. Though, hitherto, Spain had permitted at Monte Christi no foreign trade, during the war she proclaimed it a free port, and thus made a mere collection of huts a thriving seaport. Agents of colonial firms went to live there to trade and to devise the best means of eluding seizure by the British fleet.

As time passed the mother country became more insistent in restricting trade and the colonies more assertive of their freedom. When, as sometimes happened, a British man-of-war seized a colonial ship on its way to or from a port in, perhaps, the French West Indies with which trade was illegal, the incident was likely to arouse fiery protest in the colony to which the ship belonged. We may imagine its vigour if we picture the state of mind to-day in Australia or Canada if, by an act of the British Parliament, they might not send a trading ship to Europe or to the United States. Privileged trade was linked with privileged industry. If, as the *Boston Gazette* said bitterly in 1765, the colonies made a button or a horse-shoe or a nail, some one in England would be sure to raise a howl that rascally Americans were cheating and robbing their protecting mother. There had been few real grievances in the raw communities of early days, but when the colonists had fine cities equal to almost any in England, except London, restraints on their freedom caused irritation. Yet still, for three quarters of a century after the American Revolution, British traders pressed the old privileges in what was left of the colonial empire. Though experience teaches, it undermines only slowly the narrowness of privilege. As late as in 1858 the Sheffield manufacturers urged that, since cutlery made in Canada injured their trade, it should be prohibited. By that time Canada met such claims with ironical defiance.

CHAPTER VIII

THE TAXING OF THE COLONIES

GEORGE GRENVILLE who became prime minister in 1763 had been educated at Eton and Oxford in the narrow social code of the landed class of the time. He had a strictly legal mind, and while obstinate in his opinions he supported them, it must be said, with ability, industry and integrity and scorned what Burke called "the low pimping politics of a court." George III complained that after Grenville had bored him for two hours of pompous talk he would look at his watch to see whether he might not go on for another two hours. Grenville said that his reason for taking office in 1763 was "to preserve the constitution of my country." He was to be its saviour and he knew so exactly what was needed to preserve it that he gave advice to the king in a manner so overbearing that George said he was ordered rather than advised what to do. He added that he had rather have an interview with the Devil. When, in 1757, in the midst of the late war, Benjamin Franklin visited England for the first time, Grenville, then Treasurer of the Navy, received him with great cordiality, but startled him by saying, "You Americans have wrong ideas of the nature of your Constitution." He added that the king is "the Legislator of the Colonies and that the king's instructions to colonial governors were laws which must be obeyed and must not be interfered with by any legislature in the colonies." "I told his Worship," says Franklin blandly, "this was new doctrine to me," and he stated his own belief "that our laws were to be made by our Assemblies." In this

Grenville assured him he was mistaken; since the colonies received protection they were in turn to give obedience. When later he repeated this opinion and asked for the date of the emancipation of the colonies, he was met by Pitt's demand for the date when they had been enslaved.

Grenville's self-appointed task of saving the constitution made him an ardent reformer. Since war had brought its Nemesis of debt, now new taxes must be imposed. Laws neglected must be enforced, especially those against smuggling. Abuses must be corrected and of these there was an abundant crop. There were hundreds of offices for which the chief effort made by the holder was to draw the salary. Some rewards of office stagger us. When Henry Fox, Bute's chief agent in driving Whigs from office, was Paymaster of the Forces, he made a profit of about two hundred and fifty thousand pounds from the interest allowed by the bank on the large balance at the credit of the Paymaster and from other perquisites. This type of evil was too strongly entrenched even for Grenville's zeal and was ended only by the younger Pitt many years later when he had attained a unique mastery in the state.

The eager reformer, conscious of high aims, is apt to forget obstacles due to self-interest or custom. Perhaps all mankind are agreed on at least one thing, the dislike of taxation. "To tax and to please" is given to men, said Burke, "no more than to love and be wise." When, in March, 1763, Grenville, then in Bute's ministry, supported the tax on cider, as unpopular in the cider counties as was later the Stamp Act in America, a scene in the House of Commons illustrates both the difficulties and the manners of the time. Grenville deplored the lavish cost of Pitt's war effort. Since new taxes were necessary, he asked the House to show where they must be laid. When he repeated the question in a monotonous tone, Pitt, his brother-in-law, who sat opposite, mimicked aloud his words, hummed an old song, "Gentle Shepherd, show me where" and then answered the speech with a bitter attack. When Grenville again stood up in a fury to protest that gentlemen should not be treated with such contempt, Pitt stalked out, only turning as he reached the door to make a sneering bow.

If stability required increased taxes in England, it required also, so Grenville thought, increased revenues from the colonies. The public debt was largely due to the successful effort to drive the French from North America, an effort from which it was the colonies that chiefly benefitted since it had removed an enemy from their gates. A commander-in-chief sent out by Pitt had directed this war, and it was chiefly British regiments that had carried on its sieges and fought its battles. Now, though victory had been won, danger was not past. France and Spain were planning revenge and the native tribes were restless. Accordingly, an army was still necessary. Canada, with an alien French population, must have its garrisons, as must also the many scattered British posts on more than half a continent. What more fitting than that the colonies should bear a part and in the end the whole of the cost of their security?

While the reasoning seemed sound enough, the plan for a standing army in America was more acceptable in London than in Boston. The colonist might well say: "We could look after ourselves when we had to face the proud France of Louis XIV; we even planned ourselves to conquer Canada. Now France has abandoned this field and yet you tell us that the danger is greater than ever and that we must accept new and heavy taxes in order to meet it." For dangers to the British Empire in other parts of the world the colonies felt no responsibility, while danger to themselves from any European power they now believed to be remote. Each colony was acutely interested in its own rather petty finance and with easy-going abandon was willing to take the chance of being able to meet any future crisis as it should arise. North America was not in that world of national suspicions which is Europe; it knew little of the parrying from month to month of the hostile designs of Britain's rivals. On the other hand the ministry in London saw the reality of danger, soon to be proved by the eagerness of both France and Spain to humble Britain by joining her revolted colonies in war.

In England no less a person than Horace Walpole now received a shock from Grenville's reforming zeal. When Grenville found that collectors of customs, supposed to be on duty in America, were living comfortably in England, he soon ordered them to their posts and Walpole was startled to learn that Mr. Grosvenor Bedford, who served him as a clerk, was to lose his other office as Collector of Customs at the port of Philadelphia. "If the least fault can be laid to his charge," wrote Walpole to Grenville on September 7, 1763, "I do not desire to have him protected. If there cannot, I am too well persuaded, Sir, of your justice not to be sure you will be pleased to protect him." We may wonder what possible fault could be found with Mr. Bedford's one task of drawing his salary. He had been appointed twenty-five years earlier by Walpole's father and since then had, it seems, lived in London with no remote idea of doing the work required at Philadelphia. No doubt, however, his deputy there winked at the prevailing smuggling and played into the hands of the easy-going governor Denny who encouraged it.

Grenville had now in his mind three features of colonial policy: the existing restrictions on colonial trade must be enforced; a standing army must be kept in America; and taxes must be imposed on the colonies to pay for this army. He could hardly have found three lines of policy more likely to cause irritation. The colonies had never had a standing army in time of peace and, like Britons in the home-land, they viewed it with suspicion and dislike. As to taxation, while they were accustomed to the regulation of their external trade by Great Britain, to submit to direct taxation by her was another matter. In the colonies trade was depressed after the war and the local burden of taxation was already resented in terms of such protest as to cause deep social cleavage. To add to this by a tax imposed from far across the sea was intolerable to the colonial mind. Grenville was, however, inexorable. When warned of the danger he replied that, though taxes are always disagreeable, they are also inevitable. To a merchant member of Parliament who urged caution, he said that nothing would alter his fixed decision. Meanwhile in the colonies the noisy agitator became active with a note so strident and defiant that Grenville was sure it came from only a few vulgar demagogues. His narrow, obstinate mind was closed to any realization that grave and quiet men, with a deep affection for the motherland, were stern in their resolve never to be taxed by the British Parliament. Benjamin Franklin, the one man in America who had a wide European reputation, expressed what was really in their minds. When, a little later, he was examined before the House of Commons and was asked whether the people of America would submit to pay taxes imposed by the British Parliament he replied: "No, never, unless compelled by force of arms"; and force of arms was exactly what distorted arrogance in England planned, if necessary, to use.

There were men in the House of Commons who knew America. Admiral Saunders, George Townshend, Simon Fraser, William Howe and Isaac Barré, all members of the House, had been with Wolfe at Quebec and ought to have learned something of the state of opinion in the colonies. Edward Cornwallis, another member, had founded Halifax and put Nova Scotia on its feet as an English colony. John Stanwix had served in America and was remembered in New York in the name of a fort. These soldiers or sailors

were, however, often absent on duty and in any case the
military habit of mind tended to place them on the side
of authority. One of them, William Howe, was destined
to be in command later when war actually began and his
reluctance to press the issue to extremes shows that he had
learned something. No doubt, however, military judgment
was for coercion and was convinced that conquest would be
easy against raw colonial levies. There was little independence of opinion. Gibbon, the historian, who sat in the
House of Commons during the war, never once uttered a
word against the fatuous policy of coercion. Thirteen
members of the House elected in 1761 had been born in
the West Indies to which Grenville's policy also applied
but no one of them used his colonial experience to speak
on the issue. Under the lead of an obstinate minister, England drifted into a conflict that was to affect profoundly
every phase of her life, her finance and her industry, her
place as a naval power, her relations with her European
neighbours. Above all it was to bring embittered separation
from her children overseas.

In March, 1764, Grenville explained his plan of taxation
to a House of Commons only too ready to think it, as he
said, "just and necessary" that a revenue should be raised
in America. He relied on two kinds of taxes for the required three hundred and fifty thousand pounds, a sum so
staggering to colonies with revenues of only a few thousand
pounds that, so Franklin declared, there was not enough
gold and silver in all of them to pay the tax for a single
year. Grenville's first move was by the Revenue Act to
tax such things as foreign sugar, coffee, wine, silk and calico,
going to the colonies. To lessen the temptation to smuggling he reduced the tax on foreign molasses from sixpence
to threepence a gallon and was soon able to prove that a
low tax brought in a revenue while a higher one simply
stopped legitimate trade. Another type of tax was to be

imposed by a Stamp Act, which he outlined. It was amusingly elaborate. Some two score of the fifty-five clauses reiterate the phrase that on "every skin or piece of vellum or parchment or piece of paper" used for a variety of purposes, there must be a stamp. The person so fortunate as to secure a public post must pay six pounds for stamps on his commission; on a set of dice ten shillings must be paid; on a pack of cards one shilling. The Act was devised to catch a wide range of interests. Even the small newspaper must have its halfpenny stamp; a small pamphlet must pay a penny, a large one the prohibitive price of a shilling; broadsides sold in the streets, advertisements and calenders must have stamps. Lawyers must have a stamp on their licence to practise and had to pay as much as two pounds for the stamp required on some legal papers; merchants must put stamps on their bills of lading and insurance companies on their policies. Without a stamp on the needed papers no vessel might sail, no court might be opened, no debt paid and no marriage of an eager couple celebrated. Even a college diploma must have a stamp to ensure its validity to the happy receiver. While England had long been familiar with this form of taxation, a favourite because an inexpensive means of collecting revenue, hitherto the colonies had not known a vexing system that laid trammels on business and touched both the great and the petty interests of every community, while the burden was imposed by a legislature far away in which no one represented the people thus taxed. The nature of the tax increased the grievance. A small annoyance constantly repeated is worse than a heavy one borne once for all and then half forgotten. The man who read a stamped newspaper or a stamped pamphlet would have a daily sting.

While the Revenue Act should go into force at once, Grenville made the concession that the Stamp Act should be postponed for a year. If meanwhile the colonies would agree to raise the needed taxes in some other way, this would please him. He was showing for them, he said, in a tone of authority itself irritating to these sensitive communities, a "real regard and kindliness." Taxed, however, they should be, whether by themselves or by the British Parliament, the council of the nation that represented the whole empire. He invited them to endorse his proposals and thus to create the precedent that they must be consulted before being taxed, something that they themselves had never doubted. Pitt gave the warning that, when in office, he had resisted a tempting proposal to "burn his fingers with an American Stamp Act." Burke said that to hold the proposal over for a year only gave time for discontent in America to fester and come to a head. Nothing, however, could shake Grenville in his resolve.

Grenville, brooding over a tragic policy, was aided by Charles Townshend, a member of the small circle of ruling families in England, and married to a daughter of the Duke of Argyle. While still in the twenties he had made a considerable reputation for rather mordant wit that might amuse a dinner table and for a dangerous gift of mimicry combined with a hearty and rather loud-voiced manner. Horace Walpole calls him "a man of incomparable parts" but also of such rashness and levity of spirit as always to make him a danger to his own friends. His brother, George Townshend, one of Wolfe's brigadiers at Quebec, showed the family gift of caricature by handing about drawings of Wolfe so malicious that Wolfe said, "If we live this shall be enquired into; but we must first beat the enemy." Since Charles Townshend, in spite of his love of popularity, sometimes showed contempt for his own colleagues and flouted their opinions, he was not likely to respect those of leaders in America, whom he regarded as of an inferior breed. To him what freedom they possessed was the gift of an indulgent parent and their discontent meant ingratitude and malignity. Twenty regiments, he said, were needed as a standing army to be kept chiefly in Canada and at western posts; to get the system started Britain would pay the cost for a year; but after that she must tax the colonies to meet it.

Townshend had liberal qualities of mind, for he condemned the high-handed prosecution of Wilkes, inspired by the king; but he could not be depended upon to take any consistent course. During the debate, in March, 1765, when the Stamp Act was finally passed, Townshend, though not at the time in office, dazzled the house, as Burke said, by pictures of the great revenues to be derived from America. Since, he declared, they were "planted by our care," "nourished by our indulgence" and "protected by our arms," it was craven of them to refuse to accept what their parent demanded. In truth the colonies had been founded by private effort, and not by indulgence or foresighted care or promised protection from the mother country, but rather by their own desire for a freer air than that of England. Accordingly, Townshend's misreading of history was attacked by a well-known member, Colonel Barré, who had fought under Wolfe at Quebec and was at his side when he died. Barré burst into oft-quoted invective that made even Townshend quail: "They planted by your care! No, your oppression planted them in America. They fled from your tyranny . . . They nourished by your indulgence! They grew up by your neglect of them . . . They protected by your arms! They have nobly taken up arms in your defence." They had been left unaided, he added, until they had become important and then office-mongers had sent out men "to spy out their liberties, to misrepresent their actions and to prey upon these sons of liberty." Barré's phrase "Sons of Liberty" was taken up quickly in America and became the title by which the discontented colonists loved best to call themselves.

In spite of such warnings the Stamp Act aroused little opposition and was passed readily by a bored House. Long after, when the American question dwarfed all others, Burke said that he had sat in the gallery during the debate and had never heard one more languid. Two or three spoke against the Act but with reserve. The House divided only once in its whole progress and no more than forty voted against it. In the Lords there was no protest and, as far as he could remember, neither debate nor division. "There scarcely ever was less opposition to a bill of consequence." Though, in the retrospect, Burke forgot that in some quarters the Act aroused alarm, on the whole England was indifferent. We are indeed astounded at the attitude of the ministry. Grenville had the fixed idea that when Britain gave orders the colonies must obey. Without doubt some of the colonies, if asked rather than ordered to pay, would have responded. If, however, others would not respond, the new burdens would have been unequal, a condition that now exists in the British Empire.

In the colonies a flood of pamphlets, some of them ably written, had attacked the Revenue Act. When it was followed by the Stamp Act resistance was most marked in the colonies peculiarly English. Though steeped in English traditions, the legislature of Virginia declared that, since the people in the colonies had the rights of Englishmen, it was no more fitting that the British Parliament should tax them than that they should tax the people of England. Though other colonies sounded the same note England remained indifferent. We should hardly gather from the most prolific annalist of the time, Horace Walpole, that the Stamp Act, which he barely mentions, was anything more than a parochial affair, a blunder possibly but of no great consequence. On the other hand grave George Washington of Virginia saw now a reversal of the century-long principles under which England had been linked with the colonies and a menacing change to tyranny and oppression; other crushing burdens, he said, would follow if the right to tax was once admitted. Newspapers poured forth vehement protests. All the colonies flamed up in anger.

Since, during some years, Boston had been nursing grievances, especially in regard to checks on smuggling, it now became the scene of greatest violence against the Stamp Act. Police were as yet unknown and disorder could be suppressed only by calling out the military, so slow a process that a mob was likely to get out of hand before control could be effected. Restless spirits in Boston had watched with resentment the building of a house that was to be used as a Stamp Office. It belonged to the appointed collector, Andrew Oliver, secretary of the province, and later lieutenant-governor. On August 15, 1765, two and a half months before the Stamp Act was to come into force, mutterings and protests led to sudden violence. The mob hanged rude effigies of Grenville, of Bute, supposed to be a malignant adviser of the king, and of Oliver, on a huge elm, from that time called Liberty Tree by these "Sons of Liberty," and then demolished the new Stamp Office. They forced Oliver to give a pledge that he would not act as stamp collector and, when darkness fell, they sacked his residence. After this, drunk with plundered liquor, they went on the hunt for the Lieutenant-Governor, Thomas Hutchinson, an opponent of the Stamp Act but, as Chief Justice, certain to uphold the law. They sacked his house, the finest in Boston, broke up his furniture, burned books and papers that he, a learned historian, had been collecting for thirty years, and even destroyed trees in his garden. Having searched in vain for Hutchinson to murder him, they carried off his clothing. When, next day, with high courage, he took his seat on the bench, he apologized for his dress; he had, he said, no other garments than those he wore and all his family were in a similar condition.

Some days later a mob at Newport, Rhode Island, paraded in a cart through the streets an effigy of Grenville with a halter round his neck, hung it on gallows near the town hall and in the evening cut it down and burned it under the gallows, in the presence of thousands. Huske, a citizen of Newport who had written in defence of Grenville, was also burned in effigy. His house was sacked, he himself was injured, and he fled for refuge to the man-of-war *Signet,* which carried him to England. Johnson, the stamp collector, was forced to resign his office and thus obey the will of "our Sovereign Lord the people." Later, when the Act had come into force, the Boston mob compelled Oliver to stand under the tree on which his effigy had been hung and to swear that he would do nothing to enforce the new law. It shows the crude violence of Boston that, when Oliver died in 1774, a jeering mob followed his body to the place of burial, gave three cheers as it was lowered into the grave, shouted huzzas as the mourning family left the graveyard and on the same evening exhibited in a window of one of the public offices a gallows, a rope and a coffin, suggestive of the fate that he had deserved.

Resentment against the Stamp Act was so widespread that the protesting colonies took common action. Following a suggestion by Otis on October 7, 1765, nearly a month before the Act was to take effect, twenty-eight delegates met in New York in what is known as the Stamp Act Congress. Now, for the first time, the colonies were in such complete agreement that they joined in an able "Declaration of Rights and Liberties." The colonists, they said, had the rights of Englishmen and could not be taxed without their consent. The British Parliament had no authority to take money belonging to Britons overseas who sent no members to that assembly. In this sense they sent to the King, to the Lords, and to the Commons, petitions written in a dignified style, which belied opinion in England that the protesting colonists were a rabble of ignorant backwoodsmen; in truth, some of the signers were the equals in constitutional learning of the best in the mother country.

In order to be ready to apply the Act, when it should come into force on November 1, 1765, the British Government sent the needed supplies of stamps and stamped paper to the appointed selling agents. They formed rather bulky packages. The senders had not, however, measured the intensity of resistance. On the momentous first of November the citizen of Boston found black lines on the columns of his newspaper and in the place of the required stamp bearing the royal crown a grinning death's head. The pulpits had proclaimed the day one of fasting and mourning and through the air came the tolling of church bells as for the dead. Merchants closed their shops. Hawkers sold in the streets copies of the Stamp Act labelled "The folly of England and the ruin of America." "Sons of Liberty" marched in funereal processions with emblems of sorrow. Flags floated at half mast from vessels in port, while mobs made bonfires of boxes of stamps and stamped paper. New York paraded effigies of the governor and of the Devil and burned them.

From its beginning Puritan New England had gone to extremes in both religion and politics. To the first settlers, fresh from the England of the Gunpowder Plot, the Roman Church was antichrist with death the due to any priest who should appear in Boston. The Church of England, ruled by prelates, was so hated for the tyranny of Laud, that during the whole colonial period no bishop was tolerated in any of the English colonies. When, about the time of the Stamp Act, efforts were made in New England and elsewhere to secure a bishop for the Church of England, since only a bishop could ordain deacons and priests and administer the rite of confirmation, the movement aroused violent protest. Jonathan Boucher, a Maryland rector and at one time a personal friend of George Washington, found, on going to take up a new post not only that the doors of the church were locked against him but that a parishioner had gathered eight cart-loads of stones with which to drive him away. In other matters relating to religion we find excess. The teaching of the devout Jonathan Edwards, who died only a few years before the passage of the Stamp Act, shocks us by its extravagance. He ranks with the greatest, with Augustine, and Calvin and Berkeley, in the realm of theology and philosophy and is perhaps the most subtle and original thinker whom America produced. He spent much time, he says, in meditating on "the sweet glory" and the "purity and love" of God as shown in the blue sky, the shifting clouds, the sun, moon and stars. Yet he pictured God as merciless in vengeance, hating and despising the unrepentant, as trampling upon them in his wrath until their blood stained his garments, and as torturing them over the pit of Hell before tossing them as men toss a loathsome insect into a torment of fire in which "millions and millions of ages" should be but a beginning of endless suffering.

When we see this extravagance in the educated we can the better understand the excesses of the multitude. During one of the preaching tours of George Whitefield, who died in 1773, a certain Farmer Cole suddenly hears that Whitefield is going to preach twelve miles away at Middletown, in Connecticut. He calls to his wife and they set out on horseback at a gallop as if flying for their lives. The news has spread over the country and as they near the main highway they hear on it a noise like rumbling thunder and see clouds of dust like a fog, due to a multitude in a steady stream, their horses dripping with sweat and nostrils lathered. Cole and his wife force their way into the hurrying mass, all of them too intent even to speak to each other. At

Middletown they find already gathered thousands of people who have heard the news; ferry boats cross the Connecticut River in furious haste and the opposite bank is black with waiting people.

We find in England extremes in religion and politics that parallel those in America. While the upper classes tried to maintain a cold aloofness from what they thought vulgar in both religion and politics, in each of these worlds excess ran riot among the masses. John Wesley describes amazing scenes at Everton near Cambridge in that May of 1759 when Wolfe was leading to Quebec a force that was to change the destiny of North America. The church in the village was crowded, a multitude even peering in at the windows. The fervour of the preacher, Mr. Berridge, led many to burst into cries of agony, "some shrieking, some roaring aloud." "Almost all the cries were like those of human creatures dying in bitter agony" and "just sinking into hell." Great numbers wept without any noise; others fell down as dead; still others struggled "as in the pangs of death." A stranger well-dressed suddenly fell on his knees "wringing his hands and roaring like a bull." Cries of despair were followed by radiant faces, happy smiles, shouts of joy: "He has forgiven all my sins; I am in Heaven"; "Oh, how He loves me." When a neighbouring duke accompanied by a lady looked in with disapproval upon this scene, "they seemed disposed," says Wesley, "to make a disturbance but were restrained, and in a short time quietly retired."

There was similar intensity in politics. For a long time in many of the colonies mobs had visited anger upon their victims in a dramatic manner. A favourite method of showing displeasure was to hang a rude effigy of the offender on a high scaffold, side by side with one of the Devil, and then, in the presence of a crowd, to burn the figures or hack them to pieces. Sometimes the image was whipped to express the punishment desired for the offender. Tar and feathers were used for a cruel form of torture. The victim, stripped naked, was rolled first in tar and then in feathers that stuck to the tar. Then he was likely to be paraded through the town on the bare back of a bony horse with his face to the tail and after this to be warned to leave and never to return. In 1768, at Boston, an elderly man of humble rank, indiscreet no doubt in speech, was stripped naked on a bitterly cold night, with such violence that his arm was dislocated; he was tarred and feathered and then dragged in a cart to a scaffold amid a mob which beat him with such violence as to knock him again and again out of the cart. They put a rope round his neck and, on penalty of his being hanged, ordered him to curse the king and the governor. "The doctors say it is impossible this poor creature can live," says the loyalist narrator, Mary Hulton, who no doubt makes the description as lurid as possible.

Why this violence? The answer is that while due to fury at taxation by England it came in part too from antagonism between conservatives and radicals, between aristocrats and plebeians. Political instincts divide themselves naturally into two types; those clinging to the old, those hoping to shape something new. In every colony was a governor, usually from England, with the point of view of the ruling class in England, and himself something of an aristocrat, possessing social influence, linked in some colonies with real political power. He kept up a certain state and his little court was the centre of rigorous social distinctions shown especially in New England. The officials were of his circle and inevitably there was some kind of gulf between this society and the masses of the people. The Stamp Act provided an excuse for embittering the cleavage already existing. Clearly, so radicals urged, the policy adopted in England was due to the malign influence of the local oligarchy. The chief officials moved in this circle and they were often

allied by inter-marriage. In New York the De Lanceys
and the Livingstones might be social rivals, but they formed
an exclusive set as against radical democracy. In nearly
every colony a violent radical press assailed the ruling
circle. The colonies varied, however, in the extent of their
radical tendencies. In the trading communities of Massachusetts and other New England colonies, the social conflict between classes was bitter. The radicals were the more
aggressive and in the end were triumphant. New York and
Pennsylvania were, on the other hand, stronger in conservative feeling and loyalty to the king. In Virginia, proud
then as it still is of being the oldest colony, it was not
radicals but a society largely of landowners that challenged
from the first the claims of the British Parliament to tax
them and thus to break with the old traditions of their
liberty.

The social cleavage in the colonies is shown in the tone
of those who opposed the rioters. With scorn and contempt
aristocratic Boston denounced them as an inferior breed,—
tailors, shoemakers, wigmakers, innkeepers, retailers.
Smugglers are not included—their business was respectable
—but we are amused to find the lawyers classed among the
ill-bred promoters of anarchy. When John Adams courted
Abigail Smith, her family objected to the marriage on the
ground, first, that Adams was the son of a small farmer
and, secondly, that he was a lawyer. During the first hundred years in New England the profession of law was hardly
known; until the year 1712 the chief justice of Massachusetts was invariably a layman and not until 1754 was
a lawyer made chief justice in New Hampshire. The lawyer's calling was thought to be hardly honest. In 1730
Rhode Island denied lawyers the right to sit in the legislature, while Connecticut classed them with drunkards and
other disreputable persons as a danger to society. Jonathan
Boucher says that in Philadelphia many lawyers were

"wholly illiterate." Accordingly we find lawyers in New
York described in 1765–66 as "Hornets and Firebrands of
the Constitution," "the Planners and Incendiaries of the
present rupture" and profiting in fees from it. Like the
frontiersmen they were new and aggressive factors in politics. So too were the printers, usually also publishers.
Strife helped their business by creating a demand for
pamphlets and news-sheets.

England had political as well as religious violence equal
to that in the colonies. In this same period the Gordon
Riots in London threatened its destruction. Like America,
England was enduring the birth pangs of democracy. After
a long exile in France, John Wilkes, outlawed for the "false,
scandalous and seditious libel" of 1763, returned to England in 1768 to ask for a pardon, made possible, he hoped,
by the soothing effect of time. There was, however, no forgiveness in the king's sullen, brooding temper. Incipient
democracy, no less brooding over its own rights, was so unwise as to make the reprobate Wilkes its hero and the
electors of Middlesex sent him to the House of Commons.
When George III declared that he must be expelled from
the House, this was done with "unanimity and vigour."
Three times elected, three times he was expelled. The
fourth time, when Middlesex gave him a majority of about
four to one against his opponent, Colonel Luttrell, the
House had the folly to declare that Luttrell, no less a reprobate than Wilkes, had been elected. These events caused
disorders during many months. Partisans of Wilkes blocked
Piccadilly, smashed coaches, forced their occupants to
huzza for Wilkes, and at night broke every window in
houses in certain streets not illuminated in his honour. In
May Wilkes, in prison as an outlaw, was released by a violent mob which then escorted him to the Parliament House.
When the fire of the defending soldiers killed a young man,

the mob carried the dead body with them in a parade through the streets. After dark four or five more persons were killed. The mob surrounded the house of the Duke of Northumberland, demanded beer for themselves, and forced the Duke and the Duchess to drink to the health of Wilkes. A year later disorders as great were renewed. The mob shut the gates at Temple Bar, barricaded neighbouring streets with overturned carts and coaches, then rushed to St. James's Palace, smashed the carriages of persons going to the king's court, dragged out their occupants by neck and heels and pelted them with mud.

The American radicals, indeed, shaped themselves on the English model. We find in New York in 1769 a certain MacDougall, clearly of Scottish ancestry, hailed as "The Wilkes of America." When charged with libel and sent to jail for attacks on the Tories of the De Lancey social type he, like Wilkes, made the prison a base for vigorous propaganda. Friends in large numbers went to visit him to be inspired by his principles. With singular maladjustment to the situation in America, they adopted Wilkes's famous No. 45 of the "North Briton" as a slogan in New York: forty-five ladies took breakfast with MacDougall; forty-five gentlemen dined and forty-five shop-keepers supped with him; his friends supplied him with forty-five pounds of beef, forty-five bottles of Madeira and of ale, and forty-five candles to illuminate the feast. Maryland sent him forty-five hogsheads of tobacco. The Assembly of South Carolina soared into higher numbers and voted fifteen hundred pounds to aid in paying his debts. Austere John Adams joined in a public letter to the dissolute Wilkes that described him as an "Illustrious Patriot." Wilkes and America, it was said, must stand or fall together.

There is this difference between England and the colonies that in England the lawbreaker was quickly checked. In populous centres he was soon suppressed by the military and in the villages he had to face a bench of magistrates consisting chiefly of landowners insistent on the rights of property. These restraints were so much weaker in the colonies that New York and Boston were scenes of repeated and often unpunished outrage. As the outlying towns had multiplied they had sent to the legislature men used to social equality and to untrammeled freedom. The frontiersman was an individualist, a law to himself. He hunted and fished where he liked. When the British government made reserves of tall timber for masts for the Royal Navy he was likely still to cut down trees as he pleased and to resent any effort to check this licence. Whatever his land produced must be his property. The outlook of the frontier community was narrow. Books and newspapers were few; roads were often mere trails through the forest; the life was isolated and, inevitably, the members sent to the assembly by such a community carried with them its spirit. It was a perennial method in some of the assemblies to try to coerce the royal governor by the power of the purse. Since they paid his salary he was to this extent their servant, and they were likely to deny him his pay until he should do their will. The judge who gave an unpopular verdict might have his small salary reduced or held back. If a new assembly did not like some commitment of its predecessor it might show no scruple in repudiating the obligation. Measures referred to England by a governor and there disallowed might yet be enforced in the colony in tacit assertion of its independence.

Any menace to his liberty maddened the colonial radical. Even authority exercised at a distance no greater than that to the provincial capital might have with him little weight, and when he was told that, by a mandate from distant England, he was to be taxed first for stamps and then perhaps for many other things, he felt a fury of resentment. When, in consequence, more and more men of this type were sent to the legislatures, these became strongholds of the extreme passions expressed in the frantic cry of "Liberty or Death," that ran through the colonies. In New England this heat was directed hardly less against the well-to-do elements than against the distant mother country. While stamps and tea made good ammunition for social discontent, they were not its first causes.

CHAPTER IX

TEA

IT might have eased the passions of the rioters in Boston in August, 1765, had they known that the minister chiefly responsible for the Stamp Act had fallen from power. George III so resented the bearing of Grenville that at last, on July 10, 1765, as Horace Walpole put it, he sent Grenville and his colleagues "to the Devil," in the hope that proved vain of gaining public favour by bringing Pitt into office. Unhappily Pitt held back. Had his now been the master mind the tragedy of the American Revolution might have been averted. Even as it was, the new men who came in were, as Walpole claimed, better then their predecessors. Their head, the Marquis of Rockingham, though lacking in insight, was a man of liberal opinions, of pleasant manners, and fine integrity. The ministry was composed chiefly of young men, drawn from the great landed families. Burke, Rockingham's private secretary, was now brought by him into Parliament and he describes in glowing terms the virtues of his almost inarticulate leader.

Naturally the news of violence in America caused anger in England. Such acts, it seemed, could come only from those dregs of the populace that in London itself caused riots, resisted by all decent people. The permanent officials who, in all governments, are likely to be on the side of authority, were for coercing this rabble, mad in its violence, and not averse from murder. Those in England who made excuses for them were, Grenville declared, equally guilty. "The seditious spirit of the colonies," he said in

195

the Commons, "owed its birth to the factions in this House." Steady firmness, he added, would have crushed its beginnings. Now soldiers should be sent to enforce obedience. "Severity," said Dr. Johnson, "is the way to govern men." "America must fear you before she can love you," Lord North said later. On the other hand, Shelburne, the one best informed about the colonies, condemned the Stamp Act, while its most powerful assailant was Pitt, still the oracle of the nation. In a fiery outburst he declared that if the colonists had not resisted the attempt to tax them they would be three million people dead to all feeling of liberty and fit only to be slaves.

Soon England was forced to recognize the gravity of the crisis. We realize the resolve and the bitterness of the colonial merchants when we find them entering into rigorous agreements to cancel orders already given in England, to send no new orders, even to refuse to sell English goods already on hand, and to practise a further and easy self-denial by refusing to pay debts in England while the Act was in force. From Boston General Gage warned Conway, now in charge of the colonies, that the opposition was serious and that no goods need be sent out from England unless the Stamp Act was repealed. Rockingham declared that ten thousand men were out of work in England because of the Stamp Act. In consequence manufacturers and merchants took alarm and they found a spokesman in Sir George Savile, one of the most respected members of the House of Commons. A great landowner, a man of penetrating judgment, he was so free from self-seeking that always he refused office with its rewards while at the same time spending his life in public service. There were not a few members of Parliament of equal patriotism and they soon realized that the Act could not be enforced. It seems that in most of the colonies the tax was rarely collected. Governor Murray so enforced it at Quebec that for opposing it the *Quebec Gazette* had for a time to suspend publication. Some merchants of Canada wrote collectively to London merchants that the Act was full of fatal effects and "more dreadful than the icy charms of our inhospitable winter." At Halifax, in Nova Scotia, a military post well under control, a hostile mob burned boxes of stamp paper. There were, however, some traders in Canada, perhaps a majority, who came from Great Britain and did not feel the resentment of those colonial-born. After meeting a hot assailant of the Act Savile wrote to Rockingham: "Trade is hurt; pray remedy it; and a plague on you if you don't." While one aim of English trade was to discourage colonial manufactures this Act was having the reverse effect of forcing the colonies to make things for themselves.

Thus it came about that even Charles Townshend, quick to detect what was popular, soon proved ready to vote for repeal. The opinion prevailed in Parliament, however, that while the Act was unwise the British Parliament had full authority to bind the people of America "in all cases whatsoever." To this even Pitt agreed, while denying any warrant to impose taxes. He did not realize that the most active element in the colonies was determined not only to resist taxation but also to refuse to accept subordination as a final principle. One reason of the liberal cabinet of Rockingham for passing a Declaratory Act asserting subordination was that, with it affirmed, George III might be induced as an act of grace to abandon the unpopular Stamp Act. Accordingly, when the Act had been in force during fewer than five months, and in that time had been flouted in America, both Houses of Parliament voted for its complete repeal and on March 18, 1766, the king gave the royal assent. While in the Commons Grenville, still unbending, prophesied that this yielding would only lead to further insolence and defiance, Pitt treated Grenville's arguments with derision and declared that he had rather cut off his right hand than support the enforcing of the Act. In the Lords thirty-three peers, including some of the bishops, with eyes on possible favours from the Defender of the Faith, protested that the king had been humiliated and were ready for the chance, that came only too soon, to show their resentment. Since the colonies were able to pay, equity, they said, required an equal sharing of burdens and it would be folly to let them think otherwise.

The repeal of the Act brought to some circles in England and throughout America a sense of relief. So greatly had trade suffered that when Conway introduced the motion for repeal the lobbies of the House were crowded until far into the night with anxious people from both London and remoter parts of the country. After the motion had been accepted and the doors thrown open, Conway stood in view and "there arose," says Burke, "an involuntary burst of gratitude and transport. They jumped upon him as children on a long absent father. They clung about him as captives about their redeemer. All England, all America, joined in his applause." Burke added that he himself stood near and noticed Conway's emotion; "to use the expression of the Scriptures of the first martyr 'his face seemed as if it had been the face of an angel.' " In the grey of the early morning when the crowd dispersed a better day seemed to have dawned.

In the colonies the tensity of emotion at the relief found expression in bonfires, ringing of bells, processions and thanksgivings. William Smith, President of the College of Philadelphia, declared that, "after the dreadful state of suspense," he now saw "joy in every look," the clouds dispersing, the sun shining again: "I feel, I feel a sympathy unutterable and an exultation of soul never felt before." Addresses poured in upon George III, who now shared with Pitt a brief and incongruous popularity. New York held high festival with much flowing of beer and an ox roasted whole in the fields. When the Assembly voted a statue to George III mounted on a horse no one could then foresee that, a few years later, the lead of which it was made should be melted into bullets to be used against his soldiers. In Charleston still stands the statue reared to Pitt, less one arm carried away by British cannon during the coming war. Boston, in spite of some grumbling and suspicious elements, gave itself over to rejoicing. John Hancock, whose sprawling signature was destined a few years later to be the first on the Declaration of Independence, broached before his house a pipe of Madeira wine, free to all. At interminable banquets a full dozen of toasts showed the general gladness. Poets derided tyranny and praised George III, "the Restorer of Liberty." This joy was, however, not felt by a reconciled friend, but by the victor in a severe conflict, uttering the note of triumph. Suspicions once aroused are not easily removed. Fiery words and deeds in protest against the Stamp Act had violated the tradition of a good feeling that had endured for more than a century. The golden bowl was broken. While on the remote frontier the meanest settler had begun to suspect danger to his untrammeled freedom, in London there was indignation at mob rule in America. Tact was still needed on both sides. Nevertheless the repeal of the Stamp Act had done so much good that for the time the needlessly aggressive terms of the Declaratory Act did not seem greatly to matter. Since the repeal was itself an expression of regret, the implied apology was effective and the colonies had some right to assume that no effort would again be made to tax them. "I am bold to say," said Burke, "that so sudden a calm recovered after so violent a storm is without a parallel in history."

Meanwhile the ministry of Rockingham, accepted by George III only as a means of getting rid of Grenville, had been too good to last. Burke wrote a glowing account of this "Short Administration" which, as he states with exactitude, "lasted just one year and twenty days." It was, Burke says, not only guiltless but not even suspected of corruption; its members sold no offices; unlike the masterful Grenville, they treated the king "with decency and reverence"; they had carried out some great reforms; they were moderate in their foreign and wise in their commercial policy. It was, indeed, because of their virtues that the administration was short. Place-men and pensioners had attacked it and found an ally in the king. Rockingham, called to office by the king's command, quitted it, in Burke's phrase, at his "earnest request"; and his going brought on perhaps the worst period of government that the British Empire has ever known.

One member of the cabinet had always been its enemy. The Earl of Northington, Lord Chancellor from the time of Pitt's triumphs, reveals the barbaric side of the manners of the age. Port wine was the enemy of its best spirits. Later it killed the younger Pitt at forty-five. Northington, who declared that he had loved it all his life and despised claret, a weaker drink, indulged in drunken brawls in a company suited to his wit, his buffoonery, his lewd stories and his hard swearing. These vices did not keep austere George III from enjoying his society and saying that there was no one on whom he more thoroughly relied. By what seems now an odd practice, the Court of Chancery sat in the evening and the king was so indulgent to Northington as to allow him to suspend twice in each week these evening sittings in order that he might linger over his port after dinner. Northington's coarse tone of invective in regard to the "rebels" in the colonies helped to fix the mind of the king on coercion. Every state must, Northington said, have a supreme authority and England would show the colonies where it lay; if they failed to obey she had only to withdraw her protection, "and then the little states Genoa or San Marino may soon overrun them." It was Northington's similar intolerance in regard to claims of the French in Canada that gave the final blow to Rockingham's ministry. The troubles of Governor Murray in trying to replace French law by English law led to a careful report to Rockingham's cabinet in April, 1766, by the Attorney General and the Solicitor General (Yorke and De Grey) favouring the wise concession to the Canadians of the French civil law, linked at the same time with the criminal law of England. Since a fit of gout, inevitable from his mode of life, kept Northington in his own house, the small cabinet met there and found him in a peevish temper. The proposal thus to relieve the Canadians was, he said, visionary and stupid. He would have none of it and he would take no further share in such a cabinet; "By God, they shall never meet again." This was on July 4, 1766, a date that may remind us of a Declaration exactly ten years later at Philadelphia. On Northington's advice George III promptly dismissed the ministry and British policy relapsed into reaction.

Though Pitt had supported the repeal of the Stamp Act, he had held aloof from Rockingham's ministry and thus did not share in its decline. The nation owed to him four glorious years of victory; no one could rival his fame; and now George III hoped to use a leader whom he really disliked. Pitt took office, but it was a changed Pitt, so ailing in mind and body that during many months he could not meet his colleagues. Party was to him odious and now when he chose the cabinet of which not he but the young Duke of Grafton was the nominal head he aimed to ignore party and to rule with the aid of the best men. In truth, however, he could not form the united ministry of all the talents that he desired, for party feeling ran still so deep that members of his ministry would not trust each other. In it were Whigs and Tories; "King's Friends" and men who wished for a republic; men at open enmity with each other and men professing treacherous friendships. The members, as Burke said, stared at the strange faces of colleagues and were obliged to ask "Sir, your name . . . You have the advantage of me . . . I beg a thousand pardons." The ministry was like "a tesselated pavement without cement . . . utterly unsafe to touch." It had some hopeful elements. Both Conway and Shelburne, the two Secretaries of State, were hostile to taxing the colonies, while Camden, the Lord Chancellor, had been even more strenuous than Pitt. Pitt now weakened his influence by becoming a peer. It was Pitt the commoner whom the nation had learned to trust and his removal to the chill atmosphere of the House of Lords as Earl of Chatham shattered for a time his popularity. The London mob burned in effigy "Will Cheat 'em Esquire, of Turnabout Hall." From this he could recover but the nation could never recover from what was involved in Pitt's absence from the House of Commons in those critical days. Whatever our belief in an ultimate wisdom directing human affairs, there are epochs in history when the fate of nations seems to be decided by mishap or folly. The mishap that now came was due to the incapacity of Chatham, through prolonged illness, to direct his ministry; the folly was that of narrow-minded men in a cabinet really headless.

At the outset, however, the omens seemed favourable. Chatham and also Shelburne, now in charge of the colonies, knew the temper of America. While Chatham's fervent eloquence had been one of the chief causes of the overthrow of the Stamp Act, the opinions of Shelburne were even more pronounced, for, unlike Chatham, he had opposed the declaration of Parliament that it had authority over the colonies in all cases whatsoever. His duties were many in a cabinet of only seven or eight members who had to divide among themselves the whole tasks of government. Then and still for years they were nearly all in the House of Lords. When the younger Pitt took office in 1783 his seven colleagues were all peers. It is both amusing and painful to realize how badly the government was organized at the period of the American Revolution. Shelburne, Secretary of State for the Southern Department, had charge of foreign relations in western Europe, including those, critical in nature, with France and Spain. He had charge, too, of India; of Ireland; and of the colonies.

History has been so unkind to a really eminent man that Disraeli called Shelburne one of its "suppressed characters." We have met him already in the affairs of Canada. Though suspicious of others and tactless in tone, he was able, upright and far-sighted; but, since he thanked God that he was independent of all parties and scorned faction, he was in that age not likely to be popular. George III, with the simple and honest conviction that every good man in the nation should support the wishes of his sovereign, thought Shelburne's aloofness the brand of selfish scheming and called him "the Jesuit of Berkeley Square," where Shelburne lived. He had served as a subaltern under Wolfe; at Minden in 1759 he had fought with distinction; he attained the full rank of general, and he was qualified to consider military problems relating to America. He was a prudent landowner who said that an income of five thousand pounds a year would sustain adequately a man of rank at a time when Horace Walpole thought twenty thousand hardly enough. His house was a centre of free discussion and long after, when he was the opponent of Benjamin Franklin in settling the frontiers of Canada, he reminded him of their earlier talks about hopes to increase the happiness of mankind. Like Pitt and like Pitt's antagonist, Lord Mansfield, Shelburne was a sincere Christian, who spent many evenings in reading theology, observed Sunday strictly and read aloud sermons to his family. At moments when even Burke wavered he held to liberal principles. He denounced the attempt to coerce the colonies by force of arms; he saw that the trading classes were destined to supplant the land-owners in political power; he was a free trader, a disciple of Adam Smith; and he favoured the parliamentary reform destined, sixty years later, to change the tenor of British politics. He urged, too, the relief from disabilities of Protestant Nonconformists and also of Catholics, in days when, because Parliament repealed a law under which a Roman Catholic priest might be sentenced to life imprisonment for giving the sacrament to a sick person, a fanatical London mob was so violent that twenty thousand troops were required to restore order.

In a troubled time the ministry lumbered on without guidance. Chatham's gout developed into the mysterious illness that withdrew him from public affairs during a long period. In his absence Shelburne was supposed to be his spokesman, but Shelburne could get from him no word of advice. On one occasion of urgency, when Shelburne set out to see Chatham at Hayes in the country, he was met on the way by a message that Chatham was too ill to receive him. Chatham's mind was in truth unbalanced and his mood such that he either would or could not do any business. "He sits," Thomas Whately wrote to George Grenville, "most part of the day leaning his head down upon his hands, which are rested on the table. Lady Chatham does not continue generally in the room; if he wants anything he knocks with his stick; he says little even to her if she comes in; and is so averse to speaking that he commonly intimates his desire to be left alone, by some signal rather than by an expression." This condition endured for months with the result that in the chief's absence there was no unity in the cabinet. The members quarreled in public and Shelburne more than any other member was denounced by his colleagues.

While there were many causes of difference, the most active enmity to Shelburne was due to resentment at his liberal views in regard to the colonies. However much the Grenville, the Bedford, and other factions might oppose each other, they were agreed on a stern policy for America. In the background was the king, resentful at opposition, glad of strife among the factions that should make him more completely the master, ready for any extreme policy that should teach the colonies a lesson in obedience. Across the Channel, Choiseul, Britain's persistent enemy, was watching for an opening to avenge France's recent defeat and hoping, as he said, that "the anarchy in England might last for ever."

After Pitt the most brilliant man in the ministry was Charles Townshend, Pitt's choice as Chancellor of the Exchequer. Each member went his own way, and the way of Townshend, in charge of the nation's finance, was to revive an issue that had seemed to be dead, and to reimpose taxes on the colonies. He showed contempt for Shelburne, on whom he knew the absent Chatham relied for reports. Burke, who opposed Townshend's policy, was yet dazzled by qualities that made him the delight and ornament of the House; "perhaps there never arose in this country a man of a more pointed and finished wit . . . of a more refined, exquisite and penetrating judgment." But Burke saw in this demigod the weak point, that infirmity of noble minds, "an immoderate passion for fame," and a love of popularity; "to please and conciliate was the passion of his life." He loved midnight revels with which nothing must interfere and so delighted, as was said of him, in "laughable bagatelles" as to take the colic of a lady's lapdog as seriously as he would the safety of a great nation.

Cynical Henry Fox, realizing his charm, his wit, his ability and zeal, yet said that his worst enemy was himself, since he could not be trusted for even half an hour. There must have been some insight in Townshend for he chose Adam Smith as tutor for his wards the young Duke of Buccleugh and his brother and paid him a salary of three hundred pounds a year with a promise of a pension for life of the same amount. The House of Commons then, as now, had an atmosphere of its own and this was so studied by Townshend that, as Burke said, he could hit the House "just between wind and water." He was truly the child of the House; he never thought, said or did anything but with a view to it, declared Burke in the Commons; "he every day adapted himself to your disposition, and adjusted himself before it as at a looking-glass."

This was a fatal temper in the House composed, for the most part, of men named by the great landowners and anxious to please a sovereign who had many gifts at his disposal. The word ran among the members that the king's dignity had been wounded by the prompt and total repeal of the Stamp Act; that concession had made the colonies so arrogant as to wish in the end to break away; in short that to ensure their obedience the plan to tax them should be resumed on broader lines; they should, moreover, be taxed for the general purposes of government, rather than merely to help pay for the troops that defended them. With this as his aim Townshend then took a fatal step. When Parliament met in January, 1767, he included in his budget the usual tax on the income from land of four shillings in the pound, a tax that touched the most sensitive nerve of men living chiefly from the land. Since they had looked for a reduction, now, by an organized attack, they secured in a full House a small majority to reduce the rate to three shillings. It shows their outlook that they told Townshend to find the other shilling in America, a lighthearted suggestion to raise an amount that would almost equal the total revenue of all the colonies.

Though the defeat of so vital a thing as its budget was a clear call to a ministry to resign, Townshend readily adjusted himself to the temper of the House. He too was convinced that kindness and indulgence were lost on the colonies and that if they would not pay willingly they must be coerced. Since the king and also the House had the same view, it did not much matter to Townshend what his few colleagues might think. To shock and defy them might even enhance his own position in Parliament. Accordingly, on January 26, 1767, he rose to say that the reduction of the land tax had involved the loss of half a million pounds of revenue, a large sum in those days, and that the colonies must now give relief by taking up their share of the burden of defence. He had, he said, approved of the Stamp Act and it did not seem to matter to him that this tax had been hotly denounced by his present leader, Chatham. Since the colonies must be taxed, he pledged himself to find a revenue in America nearly sufficient for what was required. New York, he said, was so opulent as to be arrogant and should be checked and kept in dependence. Townshend ought to have known something about opinion in America, for he had ties with the colonies. One brother had been killed at Ticonderoga and his elder brother George, who had succeeded to the command after the death of Wolfe before Quebec, could have told him much, though it might well have been in the same tone of scorn that Wolfe himself had shown for the colonial levies. The brothers moved in a circle that thought America a remote and inferior world. Their rich mother, separated from a vicious husband, was a gay lady in London society, whose conduct in the loose world of fashion fills many pages of the gossip of Horace Walpole. The interests and diversions of such persons of quality in town and in the country were absorbing. We may doubt whether Charles Townshend ever pictured to himself the outlook of a gentleman in Virginia or Massachusetts.

Walpole says that Townshend had been half drunk when he had made the promise to tax the colonies. Very likely he was. Then and for many years still leaders in Parliament appeared in society noisily or stupidly tipsy, their speech thickened by liquor, their gross manners in this condition accepted as a matter of course and not affecting their standing as gentlemen. While we may feel surprise that the declaration of a man half drunk should have been pursued to the ruin of a great empire, the explanation is that he said what most of the members of the House of Commons wished to hear. On the other hand he astounded his colleagues in the cabinet. While most of their small number sat in the House of Lords and did not hear him, those in the Commons had to listen in astonished silence to a momentous declaration about which they had not been consulted. The majority in the House for their part greeted the speech with delight. Grenville must have chuckled since this was, after all, his vindication for the Stamp Act. Burke says that "hear hims" on one side were "rebellowed from the other." Few saw the danger. Chatham, the one person with authority to apply the needed remedy of dismissing Townshend, could not be reached by any of the ministry and from him in this crisis came no word. Townshend himself, certain of royal sympathy and of support in the House, was contemptuous of cautious colleagues, such as Shelburne. Accordingly, by the caprice of a vain, rash man, anxious to win popularity from a selfish landed class, Britain was committed to a policy that in the long run meant war, defeat, and the deepest humiliation in her history. Though Townshend's policy involved coercion, even for such an extreme policy most members were ready. On November 6 of that year Grenville wrote to the Duke of

Bedford that the subordination of the colonies must be
insisted upon and authority must be asserted "over every
part of our dominions in every part of the world."

Walpole describes an impromptu speech of Townshend
in the Commons on May 8 as marked by torrents of wit,
beautiful metaphor and perfect finish, so linked, however,
with falsehoods, ridicule, buffoonery and vanity, as to be
painful to his friends. The speech, Walpole adds, was the
result of half a bottle of champagne poured on such genius
as to surpass Chatham in language, Burke in metaphor,
Grenville in presumption and Rigby in impudence. Five
days later Townshend brought in his promised bill to tax
the colonies. He now made his plunge boldly. The colonies
must pay duties on tea, glass, paper, painters' colours, and
some other things. This could have been effected by an
export duty levied in England but since Parliament claimed
the right to tax the colonies as it might choose these duties
were to be collected by British agents at colonial ports,
no matter what local resentment this might arouse. With
the exception of the levy on tea the duties were not important. Townshend could indeed tell the Americans that
the burden lay on the British manufacturer, by creating a
barrier to his market. Though Burke pointed out that no
one need really suffer from the taxes, he added that, while
John Hampden had been required to pay only twenty
shillings, he would not submit to what was a badge of
"perfect uncompensated slavery," with the consequence
that a king of England went to the scaffold. Townshend
did not long survive his disastrous triumph. On September 4, London had another sensation, when he died suddenly
at the age of forty-two, his power of resisting a neglected
fever weakened no doubt by his careless mode of life.

In regard to outbursts in America at the reversal of the
policy of conciliation, Lord North, who succeeded Townshend as Chancellor of the Exchequer, boasted that he

never paid attention to popular clamour. If his colleague, Shelburne, was restless, so much the worse for Shelburne. He had in truth more work than one man could do. The Duke of Grafton, the Prime Minister, said to him, "a horse, my lord, could not get through the business of your office properly." Accordingly the work was divided and Shelburne gave up the colonies. Grafton was less anxious to ease Shelburne than to get rid of him. He was the one man in the cabinet who opposed coercion and thus was a thorn in the side of his colleagues. At last, in October, 1768, Grafton asked Chatham to dismiss him. Chatham's answer was himself to resign as did also Shelburne a few days later.

The Earl of Hillsborough, Secretary for the Colonies, the new post now created, was ill-suited for a task that required judgment and tact. George III described him as the least man of business he ever knew. He was so arrogant as to make difficulties about even meeting Franklin to hear the case for the colonies. The vipers and rebels in the colonies, he said, had better learn to accept Britain's "sacred right" to rule them, otherwise he would grant them "nothing except what they might ask with a halter around their necks." They had been granted far too much liberty and now, he said, the minutes of their legislatures should be sent to him that he might know what they were about. "You are in danger," he said to Johnson, the Agent of Connecticut, "of being too much a separate and independent state and of having too little subordination to this country." This was the insistent demand—subordination, while at the same moment the denial of it by the colonies was expressed in Washington's scornful jeer at "our lordly masters" in London.

It was Hillsborough, apparently, who called forth the biting satire on the existing colonial system of Franklin's "Rules for reducing a great Empire to a small one." To achieve this purpose, says Franklin, tell the people of the province, your kinsmen, that they can never be the equals of those of the mother country. Punish them for their free opinions. Send them, as governors, prodigals and gamesters whose extortions will arouse anger. Flout their petitions with contempt as the acts of factious demagogues. Hang their leaders. No matter how heavily they may tax themselves, tell them that you are free to take their last shilling, and that it is treason to oppose your edicts. Refuse them the right to trade with other peoples, except by your leave, and if they break your rules have the offenders hanged, drawn and quartered. All this will work admirably and you will have no trouble about ruling a great empire.

CHAPTER X

WE can hardly wonder that in this crisis some of the people in the colonies began to realize what hitherto they had hardly suspected, that, while they had no great desire for separation from Great Britain, they had also no great desire for continued union except on their own terms. At Boston, Samuel Adams, a man of respectable station, who became the leader in the demand for independence, showed a superb talent for organization. Events had convinced him that Great Britain was so torn by internal feuds, so corrupt and bankrupt, that she had forfeited her place in the world and was held in contempt by other nations. Adams had the temper of a martyr; he was ready to die for his opinions which included hatred of popes, bishops and, in the end, of all kings, especially of George III. Parliament, he declared, had no power over the colonies and now political separation from Britain should be made complete. A Virginian prophet of liberty was equally urgent. In 1763, before there was any question of the Stamp Act, Patrick Henry had declared in a case before the courts that the king could not disallow acts of the Virginian legislature, which was supreme in its own affairs. Those were days of swelling oratory. Henry's appeals against Great Britain were grandiose and theatrical; eyes raised to heaven; arms extended; fervent words: "Almighty God, I know not what course others may take, but as for me, give me liberty or give me death." However wild the words they made Henry popular and fortified the resolve to resist taxation by the British Parliament.

A Virginian of another type, George Washington, reserved, but capable of strong passion, wrote on April 5, 1769, to his friend George Mason, that to "maintain the liberty which we have derived from our ancestors . . . no man should hesitate a moment to use arms in defence of so valuable a blessing." This should be the last resort, but it might prove inevitable. Washington felt, however, that the colonies had the means of victory without a fight. Since the British manufacturer had seen quickly the folly of the Stamp Act when its angry opponents in America refused either to buy his goods or to pay their debts while it remained in force, this pressure, Washington thought, should be renewed. Accordingly he and others now agreed not to use English goods until Townshend's taxes were "totally repealed." This would so starve England's trade as to make her realize the danger of her policy. At the same time, said prudent Washington, it would induce economy among landowners, in debt to England, but still spending money too freely. "Whenever my country calls on me," he said in 1768, "I am ready to take my musket on my shoulder."

Horace Walpole, surveying the outlook in June, 1768, found grounds for concern. No one was in control of the policy of the ministry. The king's mind was pre-occupied with the one obstinate aim of crushing Wilkes: "No Government, no police, London and Middlesex alike distracted, the Colonies in rebellion, Ireland to be so and France arrogant and on the point of being hostile." The universal cry in America was of danger to liberty. Long afterwards one of the volunteers who took part in the first fight of the Revolution at Lexington was asked for what he had fought. Had he been oppressed by the British Government? He had never noticed it. Was it because of the tax for stamps or on tea? He had never seen a stamp or drunk a cup of tea in his life. He had fought, he said, because "we had always governed ourselves" and "they didn't mean we should."

If Charles Townshend had created the new crisis in regard to taxation it was chiefly Hillsborough the secretary for the colonies who pushed it to the last extreme. In the colonies the summer of 1768 that followed Townshend's new taxes was one of terror, especially to those who checked the darling colonial vice of smuggling. "Sons of Liberty" went about at night howling like wild Indians, breaking windows and, when they could, maltreating persons connected with the customs. The zeal of Samuel Adams made Boston a chief centre of unrest, while far away in London Hillsborough, a handsome, opulent, and well-bred courtier, was bent on repressing the vulgar mob that defied the king, their indulgent ruler. Accordingly, on June 8, 1768, he ordered General Gage, in command at New York, to station permanently a regiment at Boston. The admiralty also sent a war-ship, the *Romney,* and as she lay in the harbour her Captain, in reply to protests, described Boston as "a blackguard town ruled by mobs" and added "By the Eternal God I will make their hearts ache." We may imagine the effect of this tone on fanatic Samuel Adams and on stately George Washington, owner of many thousand acres and served by many slaves.

Townshend's taxes were not only creating unrest in America; they were ruining the trade of the mother country with the colonies. Accordingly, when the cabinet met on May 1, 1769, Grafton, the Prime Minister, proposed that all the taxes should be abolished. Only one obstacle was pressed. The saving of face is an old form of human vanity; the right to tax the colonies had been claimed in such vigorous terms that now to draw back entirely would seem to be an admission of weakness. This led North to say that to assert this right, one tax, that on tea, should be retained. It would, he said, assert a principle that rather than abandon he would see America lie prostrate at his feet. When each minister was asked for his opinion and the vote was taken, a majority of one retained the tax on tea. The decisive vote was that of a new member of the cabinet, the Earl of Rochford, who held the post from which Shelburne had retired. Grafton said later that had Rochford voted with him as he had expected "the situation from America might have been avoided." With the tax retained he knew the danger and, by his urging, the cabinet agreed to send to America a conciliatory message. After all, except for the principle involved, it would in itself not greatly matter whether tea was taxed or not. Dutch tea was smuggled into the colonies and a patriot could easily avoid taxed tea. Austere John Adams at a social gathering in 1771 drank the green tea offered and hoped that it was smuggled Dutch tea though he was not sure.

The vote to continue the tax gave mischievous Hillsborough his opportunity. In truth patriotism in the United States should include as founders of the republic Charles Townshend and Hillsborough, since it was they who blocked reconciliation. In spite of the instruction of his colleagues to be conciliatory, Hillsborough hastily sent off to the colonial governors a circular couched in arrogant terms. While, he said, all taxes but that on tea were repealed, the government had no thought of yielding to misrepresentations of "enemies to the peace and prosperity of Great Britain." He hoped for the restoration of mutual confidence and affection; His Majesty's government had no plan to impose further taxes; at the same time, however, "the whole legislature" was resolved to accept nothing that should "derogate from the legislative authority of Great Britain over the colonies." Grafton charges Hillsborough with a lie in saying that this policy had unanimous approval.

Camden, too, accused him, in effect, of falsifying the minutes of the cabinet. The mischief was, however, done.

Exasperation on both sides now magnified every irritating incident. The presence of soldiers at Boston was so resented that they were warned not to venture out at night. On a February afternoon in 1770 soldiers were followed through the streets by a hostile crowd throwing sticks, stones and snow balls and shouting "Fire, Fire, why don't you fire?" The rioters were led by a negro and their clamour was bold because they thought the soldiers would not shoot without what the law required, the formal warning from a magistrate to the mob to disperse. When, however, one of the soldiers was clubbed to the ground, the exasperated men at last fired and killed three and wounded eight of the mob. Though conflicts between mobs and soldiers are not unusual in troubled times, colonial frenzy seized upon this unhappy collision and made the "bloody tragedy" the occasion for an annual appeal for vengeance against the brutal mother country that had bespattered the stones of Boston with the brains of those whose children, left fatherless, appealed to Heaven for justice.

It might have seemed to help conciliation that in August, 1772, Hillsborough resigned his post, and was succeeded by the Earl of Dartmouth, who had served as President of the Board of Trade in Rockingham's ministry and was well versed in colonial affairs. Franklin thought him "a truly good man," friendly to conciliation, though, as Franklin added, his strength was not equal to his wishes. And now when tea was related to the one remaining grievance, the ministry, with blind disregard of danger, chose to make tea a cause of renewed unrest. Since the East India Company had on hand a surplus of tea, the ministry came to its aid by an effort to enlarge its market in the colonies. While England must still pay a duty of a shilling a pound, the colonies were to pay only threepence. This, it was hoped, would end the smuggling of Dutch tea and enable the Company to get rid of its great surplus. Tea might henceforth be landed at only four colonial ports and the colonies would be happy in having cheap tea with no prick of conscience that it had been smuggled. To supply an expected demand, the East India Company planned for itself a monopoly of the sale of tea in the colonies, something that would put the former importers of tea out of business. In consequence, wrath among traders and among smugglers: among traders like John Hancock of Boston just when the low duty on tea promised larger sales; among smugglers because a low duty meant less smuggling.

The East India Company loaded its tea-ships and sent them across the sea to colonial ports. While they lay at Boston the same type of mob that had flouted the Stamp Act was now equally ready to prevent the landing of tea on which duty was paid. It happened that at a public meeting of protest a listener in the gallery who indulged himself in the freak of dressing as a Mohawk Indian illustrated this character by a sudden war-whoop. This suggested a well-known method of inspiring terror and accordingly on the night of December 16, 1773, some scores of men, wrapped in blankets to resemble Indians, forced their way on board the three tea ships lying at Griffin's wharf and spilt into the water the contents of three hundred and forty-three chests, valued at some eighteen thousand pounds. The "Mohawks" marched away through the streets to the tune of fife and drum. Next morning, in full view of British men-of-war, not a quarter of a mile away, the ruined tea that lay like hay washed upon the shore was stirred by men in boats to make sure that the salt water should make it entirely useless. Samuel Adams wrote with his own hand the notice to the Committee of Correspondence in the other colonies that, while the tea was destroyed, the vessels themselves, property lawfully owned, were in no way injured, a moderation proving, so he said, that the "pure and upright principles" of liberty had been vindicated by high-minded patriots. At New York, too, a captain who managed to land eighteen chests, had the unpleasant experience of seeing them go up in flames on the shore. In other places the hunting of the importers of taxed tea became a popular sport and tea itself more than ever the symbol of what was vile.

This destruction of tea touched a sensitive nerve in the English system. Then, even more than in our later time, the rights of property were held to be sacred, and yet Boston had destroyed costly property in a ruthless manner. This alarmed many in Boston itself. Gray, the Treasurer of Massachusetts, declared with fine fervour that God would punish the rioters with the tortures of fire and brimstone. In Benjamin Franklin's well-balanced judgment speedy reparation should be made for the outrage. In England Property raised a great clamour and asked, if this was allowed to pass unpunished, what next? Chatham, himself again, and the better self of his fine nature, condemned what had been done, as did also liberal Colonel Barré. Lord North thought that four or five men-of-war might bring Boston to time; while obscure Mr. Van, a member of Parliament, would destroy Boston, that "den of locusts." Burke urged moderation; Boston, he said, was only a symbol of wider unrest among free men; but his was a voice crying in the wilderness. Each side had a case; to one, with tea the symbol of tyranny, its destruction was a sacred act in the name of liberty; to the other this violence meant anarchy that, if unchecked, would ruin the British Empire. The temper of the time permitted no middle way.

The British ministry laid a heavy hand on Boston. After angry debates, that run to more than a thousand pages in the reports, Parliament passed, in March, 1774, what is known as the Boston Port Bill closing the port to commerce until the city should pay the East India Company the value of the tea destroyed. The bill killed the sea-going trade of Boston and made a desert of its docks and wharves. A further bill, which the colonies called the Murder Act, showed distrust as to the fairness of juries in the colony by the provision that the trial of persons charged with breaking the law in checking riots might be transferred to Great Britain or to another colony. By the further Regulating Act which gave wider powers to the governor, the council of the colony, hitherto elected, was to be named by him; he could remove judges and other high officials and prohibit the holding of town-meetings. To enforce this rigour General Gage, the British commander-in-chief in America, was made governor; his troops were to be quartered upon the inhabitants; and he was ordered to arrest the leading malcontents and to send them to England for trial. After this there was to be no going back. "Impudent rebellion" on the one hand was met on the other by charges of "Byzantine tyranny." When starvation threatened Boston, a wave of sympathy caused Virginia to set apart the first day of June, 1774, when the Boston Port Bill was to go into effect, as a day of fasting, humiliation and prayer. South Carolina sent rice, Virginia sent wheat, Pennsylvania sent flour to relieve Boston. Israel Putnam of Connecticut himself drove to Boston a flock of sheep. Sympathizers in Quebec sent one thousand bushels of wheat and Montreal sent money.

The ugly word rebellion was now the common charge against Massachusetts. Dr. Samuel Johnson surpassed himself in contempt for the colonial point of view. The legislature of a colony was, he said, only the vestry of a larger parish. It would now be easy to teach the rebellious ingrates a lesson; all Americans were cowards and the planters especially "a race of mortals who, I suppose, no other man wished to resemble." He could love all mankind except an American; if Britain did what the Americans deserved she would raze their towns and let them enjoy their forests. An American wrote from Bristol in July, 1774, that the tone in England was "horrid, cruel and detestable;" the people of Boston were denounced as "thieves, pirates, and rebels." For this, not to be outdone, the writer called the English "knaves, scoundrels and spiritual slaves"; "they are totally indifferent about liberty and lost to any sense of honour or virtue;" "formerly I loved the country and people, but now both appear odious to me." The historian Gibbon said that even the angel Gabriel could not make the House of Commons listen to pleas favourable to America. Soldiers and civilians alike were certain that a single campaign would suffice to bring the colonies to reason. There need be no anxiety as to the result. It would, indeed, be only a minor affair.

By this time young Charles Fox, who had hitherto spared no excess of invective against the colonial and other liberal causes for which Chatham and Burke stood, had awakened to find that he possessed a conscience. The most brilliant debater of his time, he was now saying things about public policy that aroused George III. "That young man," wrote the king to North, in August 1774, "has so thoroughly cast off every principle of common honour and honesty that he must become as contemptible as he is odious." Accordingly Fox was summarily dismissed from a minor post. Henceforth it was he, perhaps more than any other leader, who so applied liberal principles to colonial affairs as to make the conflict a party struggle between Whig and Tory. During the next thirty years he was a thorn in the side of George III. Another conscience than Fox's was now being stirred; the devout Dartmouth had misgivings as to the use of force for which as colonial secretary he was officially responsible. Shelburne, meeting him at a friend's house, found him anxious; his principles were, he said, being violated by the king's policy; but he was determined "to cover America" from the present storm even to the extreme step of repealing the Act coercing Boston. We may smile at the prospects of Dartmouth's weak will forcing obstinate George III to turn from a course on which he was bent.

CHAPTER XI

CANADA A STRONGHOLD AGAINST DEMOCRACY

It is to the credit of Rockingham's ministry that when General Murray was recalled from Quebec they had looked round to find the best man for a difficult task in Canada and had found him in a sterling officer, a friend of Wolfe, Guy Carleton. Naturally the choice was made by General Conway, then in charge of the colonies and himself, like Carleton, an old campaigner in Europe. He chose Carleton for his merit—for his knowledge of the country, his integrity, and his capacity. The decision proved to be momentous for Canada. At first as lieutenant-governor, and after 1768 as governor, Carleton shaped the system that made Canada a stronghold of both British and French tradition; he defended Canada and saved it as a British state when the English colonies themselves broke away. In the end he gathered at New York and guided to new homes the loyalists whom the young republic drove out; and he was governor-general when, after thirty years of well-meaning despotism, Canada received the measure of control by its own people that has expanded into the democracy of today.

In modern times the capable Irishman, with an inadequate sphere in his own country, has played an important part in the wider affairs of the British Empire. Posterity has given for the conquest of Canada a wider fame to the Irishman, Wolfe, than to his superior officer, the Englishman, Amherst. In the troubled years of the American Revolution the man most deeply read in the secret of governing a great empire was the Irishman, Burke. In that period, too, the Irishman, Shelburne, saw farther in colonial affairs than his English colleagues. Carleton was an Irishman, born of the sturdy stock that had made Ulster its home, ruled it with intense Protestant conviction, and sent to serve elsewhere in the same spirit many of its sons, honest, austere, and not rarely, when abroad, free from the narrowness that marked, too often, their mastery at home.

Guy Carleton, born in 1724, was a member of an ancient landed family, one of whom had the title of Lord Dorchester that Carleton was destined to revive. A junior branch went to Ireland in the troubled days when England broke with the old church and established in Ireland a Protestant supremacy over a Catholic people. The Carletons were a military family and to it, as was fitting for such a type, were born more sons than daughters. Guy had nine sons and himself was one of four brothers all of whom became soldiers. Inevitably they served abroad and, in spite of the habit of command, they learned what the soldier has to learn in the motley of an army, to tolerate differences of type so long as all conform to the supreme need of discipline. Carleton was free from religious intolerance in regard to the people in Canada of an alien faith whom he ruled. He had, however, a touch of the dourness of Ulster. He was strict, distant and reserved in manner, rather arrogant in temper, a man almost without intimates, though happily one of them was Wolfe who, with the instinct of genius, saw the merit that lay behind a cold demeanour.

Carleton's family was poor and proud. When he was fifteen his father died. In due course, the sons scattered, two of them to hold for the greater part of their active lives high office in what is now Canada, one at Quebec, the other as governor of New Brunswick from 1784 until 1817. For Guy Carleton, a poor man without powerful friends, promotion lagged. He had experiences sufficiently varied. He served on the continent in the war that gave Silesia to

Frederick of Prussia but ended in 1748 for Britain in the fruitless peace of Aix-la-Chapelle. In this war Carleton saw and formed an adverse opinion of the soldiers from Hanover, beloved of George II, its Elector. Disparaging remarks that he made then or later caused George to note his name and threatened to ruin his career. It was during these campaigns that he and Wolfe became friends. Wolfe was certainly and so also probably was Carleton in the fight at Culloden that ended Stuart hopes to regain the crown and earned from resentful Scots for Carleton's chief, the Duke of Cumberland, the title of Butcher.

Carleton was still only a lieutenant at thirty, while his friend Wolfe was a lieutenant-colonel at twenty-three. In the Seven Years' War Carleton, serving with Cumberland in Germany, shared in the defeat and humiliation of that unloved son of George II, who was forced in September, 1757, to agree at Klosterzeven to disband his army and returned to England, a defeated, broken man. Fiery little George II associated Carleton with his own disgraced son and angrily refused assent when, in 1758, Wolfe, given command of a brigade for the attack on Louisbourg, asked to have Carleton as his chief of staff. When, late in the year, Wolfe came back victorious, he said that Carleton's skill as an engineer might not only have brought quickly the fall of Louisbourg but might have enabled him to go on in the same summer and batter down the walls of Quebec. Next time, he was resolved, Carleton should go with him and this he again urged when named to do in 1759 what, with Carleton's help, he might have done in 1758. Though the king twice struck out Carleton's name, both Pitt and Wolfe were insistent and Carleton shared in the conquest of the country where most of his later life was to be spent. On a September day in 1759, he was one of the group of officers, in disguise to avoid attracting attention, who stood with Wolfe on the south shore opposite Quebec and examined

through their field glasses the high cliffs, in order to discover
some trace of a path up the steep ascent. They found it and
on the momentous early morning of the 13th Carleton went
with Wolfe up the cliff to the fight in which Wolfe died and
Carleton himself was badly wounded. His recovery was
slow, but in 1761 he was serving in France, and in 1762 in
Cuba, where again he was badly wounded, not once, but
twice. In this campaign he had as fellow officer a neighbour
from Ireland, Richard Montgomery, who was, like Wolfe,
to perish before Quebec, but in arms against the king, to the
undying scorn of Carleton in command against him. Though
Carleton became brigadier-general, his prospects, when the
war was over, were not good until, in 1766, perhaps to his
surprise, he was sent to replace at Quebec Murray, a former
companion-in-arms. The contrast between them is striking;
Murray, impetuous, given to scornful and rash words;
Carleton, cautious, reserved, meeting antagonism usually
with silence, but capable of high-handed use of authority
and of brooding resentment. Both were honest patriots,
friends of the oppressed; both also were soldiers with the
limited outlook of the officers' mess.

Murray's vehemence had produced its effect in England.
Evils attacked by him were now corrected; the useless
officials whom he had pilloried were recalled; and competent men were being sent to rule in Canada. Of William
Hey, the new chief-justice, we know little beyond the
record of his official career in Canada. When he returned
finally to England in 1775 he had already, in his absence,
been elected to the House of Commons for Sandwich, and
must therefore have been a man of standing. Though a
wise, careful and sound lawyer, probably he lacked aggressive character. This could not be said of Francis Masères,
the new attorney-general, who went with Hey to Canada.
A Huguenot by descent, Masères never overcame the bitterness against the old church due to the persecution of his

ancestors. He was a scholar who knew Homer by heart and loved Horace and Milton. He was also a learned mathematician, and an historian. While his voluminous works touch many subjects, his chief interest was in the law. He is described by Bentham as "one of the most honest lawyers England ever saw." He spent the greater part of his long life in the Temple in London, a conspicuous figure in his later years. Charles Lamb, living "a pistol shot" distant in the Temple, describes him as wearing the three-cornered hat, the wig, and the ruffles of the time of George III. "He keeps three footmen and two maids," said Lamb, "I have neither maid nor laundress." It is not clear why he, a man of means, should have chosen what, with his tastes, must have been exile in Canada. No doubt one reason for offering him the post was that, unlike his predecessor, he knew thoroughly French law and the French language.

Carleton sailed to New York in 1766 and had the opportunity to learn from General Gage his view of the effect on colonial opinion of the Stamp Act and its repeal. A month after landing Carleton reached Quebec by way of Lake Champlain, a route destined ten years later to test his powers against the colonies in arms. On September 22, 1766, he joined Hey and Masères already at Quebec after a voyage lasting nearly three months. They were young men: Hey thirty-three years old, Masères thirty-five. Even "grave Carleton" now forty-two must have felt a thrill to be master of a fortress that during many baffling weeks he had assailed. The place charmed Masères. He thought Canada more beautiful than England. Soon, however, he grew weary of the long winter and the difficulty, when the ground was covered with snow, of getting exercise by walking or riding. "There are no downs to ride upon," he wrote, "no pleasant green lanes, no parks or forests or gentlemen's seats to go to see, or gentlemen to visit at them, but the whole is a strip of cultivated country of perhaps three miles deep along the banks of the river St. Lawrence . . . in which every bit of wood is cut down, so that there are neither hedges nor trees left . . . and what is worse than all there are few agreeable people to converse with."

While, no doubt, Quebec lacked the amenities of an English county, it afforded a useful sphere of work. Strife was still acute between the old and the new subjects and between the military caste and the civilians. Since business was bad bankrupt traders so looked for relief to a benevolent government that Carleton scornfully says every indigent Protestant butcher or inn-keeper expected to be provided for by being made a justice of the peace. When we call up the picture of the English squire in that age who was likely to hold the unpaid but dignified office of justice of the peace and to administer the law with a mixture of prejudice, ignorance and common sense, we do not at first see how a man could gain a living in Canada from such a post. Greed is, however, ingenious and managed to find some petty plunder. Owing to a gross abuse, justices of the peace in Canada could exact heavy fees, and some used their power to oppress the helpless people. The legal tricks of an old society, "all the chicanery of Westminister Hall," says Carleton, were exaggerated in Canada. A favourite device was to summon a man to appear in two different courts on the same day and to condemn him by default in the one where he failed to appear. Tricky creditors seized lands for small debts and sold them before the French debtor, ignorant alike of the law and of the language in which proceedings were taken, could realize what was happening. Some families were thus reduced to beggary. Canadians, a people naturally litigious, were induced to bring suits for sums so trifling that the fees might be ten-fold the amount in dispute. Imprisonment for debt, unknown to French law, filled the jails with unhappy debtors for

small sums who were sometimes required to pay fees for
their keep amounting to more than their debts. Against
these evils leading Canadians addressed in 1770 a touch-
ing appeal to George III for the restoration of their laws
and customs. They declared that, in spite of the sympathy
of "a generous, wise and disinterested Governor," they had
to spend more than the value of their possessions to maintain their rights, and that these humiliations made life
unbearable and seemed to brand them as "a reprobate
nation."

If, in these days of disorder, recently conquered Canada
and India were alike in abuses, they were also different,
for the plunder in Canada was inevitably petty compared
with that of the stored treasures of the east. In both scenes
the sense of justice of the British rulers soon corrected
abuses. Carleton himself showed austere rectitude. From
the governor downward, officials, already receiving salaries,
charged fees for attending meetings of council and for
signing official papers and legal documents. There was a
published list of three hundred and fifty occasions for fees.
The clerks and the court crier, even the jailer, exacted them.
To Carleton, however, this system had an appearance of
sordid meanness and he decided for himself to end it and to
take no fees. It was staggering to the age that any one
should refuse a fee that the law permitted. Murray, in England, watching Canadian affairs, and still nominal governor,
protested that Carleton's act was a reflection on his own
practice. It is, indeed, not easy to see how a chief justice
with six hundred pounds a year and an attorney-general
with one hundred and fifty pounds could maintain the
dignity of their offices without other sources of revenue.

Carleton had scorn equal to Murray's for the trading
classes and also contempt for the lowly origin of some of
his council. He had been in Quebec only a few weeks when,
following Murray's recent example, he called together not

all but only a few members. To the unsummoned members this naturally seemed arbitrary but, when they suggested that the omission was due to accident, Carleton replied that his action was deliberate and that, except for formal business, he would summon as many or as few members as he liked. He said, with a great display of capital letters, that he would consult "men of good Sense, Truth, Candor and Impartial Justice; persons who prefer their duty to the King and the Tranquillity of His Subjects, to unjustifiable Attachments, Party Zeal, and to all selfish mercenary views." When a certain Captain Cuthbert, with a grievance, made a swaggering threat that he had powerful friends who would bring the governor to time, Carleton's comment was "I laugh and make no answer." The all-pervading Irishman was at Quebec to take a hand in agitation. John McCord had kept a small ale-house in the north of Ireland, and had made money at Quebec by selling spirits to the soldiers. Business had, however, fallen off and now, says Carleton, in a delightful phrase, "He has commenced Patriot" and become an agitator. An elected legislature had no lure for Carleton. Surely, he urged, Canada did not need a copy of the refractory bodies in the colonies whose insolent doings had been described to him by military friends. He was ready, as he said, to give just and firm government; it was troublesome enough to have the existing nominated council, which he considered rather a body to be consulted than one with authority of its own; to be obliged in addition to appeal to an ignorant electorate would be intolerable.

Carleton had been in Canada only a few months when, on February 15, 1767, he sent to General Gage at New York, his opinion as to the best way to meet the danger of what was to prove the American Revolution. By force, if necessary, the colonies must learn to obey. Quebec and New York were, Carleton thought, the keys to the situation, and each place, together with the line connecting them, should be strongly fortified. To build a needed citadel at Quebec would cost about £68,000. Montreal had only a flimsy wall. Of eighteen thousand Canadians capable of bearing arms, nine thousand had fought in earlier campaigns and were of better calibre than French regulars. Clearly to conquer the colonies into obedience was in the mind of the ruling world from the earliest days of the dispute. To Carleton, a soldier, no other course seemed possible, nor, one may add, did it to Lincoln a century later. Neither trouble nor expense, urged Carleton, should be spared to root out faction or to show strength to curb or overawe those who, though they ought to feel bound by the ties of loyal subjects and honest men, "might not be ready to do their Duty." By holding New York and Quebec it would be possible to separate New England from the other colonies. It shows Carleton's military foresight that he urged Gage to make impregnable the fort at Ticonderoga, guarding the route from Canada to New York. It was the first place to fall when war broke out.

In addition to military Carleton had difficult civil problems to solve. In the chaotic situation at Quebec appeals were made now to French and now to English law, as each seemed to favour self-interest. The Canadian seigneur was quite willing to have English law when it freed him from the French rule that permitted him to take only a low rental from the habitant. It was another matter when an elder son claimed, under English law, to be the sole heir to the father's estate and his brothers and sisters protested their right, under French law, to equal shares. This French law that gave inherited land in equal portions to sons and daughters had the defect that it tended to undue subdivision. To correct this a further rule had provided that each farmer must have enough land—about fifty acres—to support a family. In order to have so much, the heir to a small farm must buy out the other heirs. When Canada came under British rule some of the heirs kept their few acres, built on them little huts and lived a squalid existence. In vain did the seigneur urge them to clear and live upon new tracts of his abundant land, one purpose in making the rule. They replied that, under English law, every man had the right to build a house and live on his own land, and idleness, drunkenness, and vice were, says Masères, the outcome.

In the summer of 1767 Shelburne now secretary and brooding over the problem, asked Carleton for "every light that can be procured." He hoped it might be possible to set up a wise combination of French and English law that should be fair to both races. So anxious was he for exact information that in 1767 he sent to Canada his own private Secretary, Maurice Morgann, a man of experience and enlightened views. Morgann is on record as having so prevailed in a discussion with Dr. Johnson that next day Johnson made the admission, for him difficult, "You were in the right." It shows the ingenuity of Morgann's mind that he wrote a defence of the character of Falstaff, a defence still valued by Shakesperean scholars. Long after his visit to Quebec he was Carleton's secretary at New York helping to shepherd the banished loyalists to their new homes. While at Quebec he had every possible aid. The two capable lawyers, Hey and Masères, and Carleton himself, drew up elaborate reports, as did also Morgann and some of the best lawyers in England. Then in 1768 came the disastrous change in England when Chatham and Shelburne retired and the arrogant, rash and tactless Hillsborough became secretary for the colonies.

As soon as Hillsborough assumed office he showed for the Canadians a liberality lacking in his attitude towards his own countrymen in the English colonies. He assured Carleton that neither he nor his colleagues had ever thought of applying to the Canadians any other than the French law of property to which they were accustomed. This concession by Hillsborough to the French was opposed by Masères. He objected to preserving the whole body of French law. Before going to Canada he had printed the opinion that the Canadians were so "violently bigotted" that they looked upon their Protestant neighbours with an "eye of detestation." It would, he claimed, be illegal and void by English law to let the Canadians have a Catholic bishop. It might not indeed be impossible to make them Protestant, a vain imagining as we know. Masères thought that in secular affairs they were ready to conform to English customs; they disliked the archaic feudalism that France herself was soon to overturn and, vexed by what Masères called "the insolent and capricious rule of their superiors," the seigneurs, they were longing, he thought, for the freer system to be found under English law. The truth is that they were not longing for anything except to be left alone. So little of racial hatred did they show that some of them preferred English seigneurs to those of their own race.

The legal practice of Masères brought him into contact with the fanaticism of the Protestant trading element at Quebec whose prejudices fitted in with his own. Like them he distrusted what he called "the unhappy principles" of the "Roman superstition." How, he asked, could a governor command the respect of a people who thought him a heretic, the enemy of God, certain of eternal damnation? Masères had a belief, truly Prussian, in the capacity of government to organize even the souls of a people. By a painless process Protestant clergy might, he thought, gradually displace the priests. If, for instance, on a vacancy in a parish, it was found that a quarter of the people, or a minimum of twenty persons, wished to have a Protestant minister, such a minister should receive his fair proportion of the tithe. The chapel of the Récollets, at Montreal, and that of the Ursulines at Quebec had been borrowed for Protestant services, and Protestants, he thought, should have the right to use all the Canadian parish churches, from which, except during Catholic worship, images, crucifixes, etc. should be removed. The state should appoint the clergy and, to forestall intrigue from France, only clergy trained in Canada should be received. Parish priests should be allowed to marry. Under penalty, they must not try to keep their people from reading the Bible. While the priests should retain their former right to the tithe, no one should have more than four hundred pounds a year. If monks, friars, and nuns wished to leave their religious houses to return to the world, or to marry, they should be free to do so. The governor should regulate and, if need be, prohibit the carrying of the host through the streets. When three-fourths of the people of a parish were Protestant the whole tithe should go to the Protestant minister. In 1767 Masères wrote that if, from the first, vigorous measures had been taken to recommend the Protestant faith, half the Canadians would have turned to it.

While always this hope of Masères had little basis, in any case the British Government was fatuous in its efforts to make Canada Protestant. When General Murray asked for Protestant clergymen of liberal opinions and exemplary lives, a few Swiss pastors were sent out to preach in French to people warned by their priests not to go near them. There were military chaplains with the regiments and one of them, John Brooke, chaplain at Quebec, was titular rector. His wife, a literary lady, relieved the ennui of a garrison town by writing the first Canadian novel, "The History of Emily Montague." There was no French bishop. Canada, now a British colony, had come under the jurisdiction of the Bishop of London who, Brooke urged, was entitled to the property of the French bishop, including the episcopal palace at Quebec. But since the Bishop of London did not reside in Canada, clearly the rector on the spot at Quebec, Brooke himself and his successors, should enjoy this fine property. After the surrender of Montreal in 1760, the Reverend John Ogilvy from Albany formed there a congregation and claimed that the estates of the religious orders should be used as an endowment for the Church of England. The property of the orders was extensive. One of them, the Sulpicians, is still rich in land in Montreal and the Jesuits and the Récollets had valuable estates. Elsewhere in Canada similar claims were made. The rectors at Quebec, Montreal and Three Rivers, the three important towns, asked for the tithes, lands and powers of the former Roman Catholic curès.

These hopes were bound to fail; the Roman Catholic Church retained, in the end, all of its former rights and all property except that of the Jesuits and the Récollets. Carleton showed little zeal for creating Protestant parishes, since he was convinced that few English would live in the country and that it would remain French and Catholic. At first, thinking the wind favourable, one or two priests turned Protestant, but they added nothing to the spiritual wealth of the Church of England. One of them, Pierre Roubaud, a former Jesuit missionary to the Abenakis, became a spy and was employed in the British secret service. He turned out to be a forger and generally so disreputable that Carleton denounced him as a liar with no spark of honour or honesty. One Veyssière, a renegade priest appointed to Three Rivers, is described in an official report as "a most dissolute character." The rector, Guerry, appointed to the important parish of Sorel, drew a stipend of two hundred pounds a year. Though he visited Canada, he went back to England when the disturbances began that led to the American Revolution and, during ten years, drew his stipend but did not set foot in the country or even provide a substitute to discharge his duties. A patron in England, Lord

Plymouth, said that the rector of Sorel was so pleasant a neighbour that he could not bear to part with him. In the end he exchanged his good thing in Canada for what he thought a better one in England.

Meanwhile the ominous shadow of revolution is falling. In 1768, when given the full rank of governor, Carleton received the elaborate instructions usual to the holders of such an office. He was to copy the precedents of Nova Scotia and was also to allow no trade and no manufactures prejudicial to Great Britain. While commands of this kind were mere routine, he was told to keep a watchful eye on events in the English colonies. Already some colonial assemblies were flouting the governors, adjourning without his leave, and doing things "very detrimental to our Prerogative." It was an evil that during the late war the French had sometimes captured British merchant ships and from the letters that they carried had secured information about British plans. Accordingly Carleton was now to warn merchants, planters and others to be cautious in time of war as to what they should write. His own letters were to be kept by masters of ships in a weighted box, to be sunk when there was danger. Such precautions in time of peace show a nervous temper and justified Carleton's fears.

On June 10, 1769, when the Board of Trade made an elaborate report on the policy for Canada, Hillsborough sent it to Carleton with the strict injunction to keep it secret. He feared agitation in England over its liberal concessions. His own wish was that Carleton should rule as the despotic French governors had ruled. This would help to check the sweep of republican ideas in the English colonies and might, so Hillsborough hoped, sober them as they had been sobered in the past by the alien menace of France on their frontiers. Hillsborough would rank to-day as a perverse and arrogant little Englander. He did not wish

English settlers to go to Canada. There would be, he said later, danger to England in building up across the sea communities of her own people. Let the French and the Indians flourish in the whole vast region from the mouth of the St. Lawrence to the Mississippi. England had no call to induce her sons to weaken the home land by building up colonies overseas. Nor, in this, was he alone. In 1772, Wedderburn, soon to be lord chancellor, said, it was "not in the interest of Britain that many of her natives should settle there."

The report of 1769 went far in concessions, and shows a toleration unhappily not applied to Ireland. Eighty thousand brave and loyal subjects of French origin should, so it declared, have reasonable indulgence. They should have the French law of property, the basis of their family life; members of the Roman Church should be allowed to hold public office without taking the oath denying transubstantiation, compulsory in England; and if, what Hillsborough by no means desired, a legislature must be set up Catholic Canadians should have the right to be members. The Roman Church should have full liberty of worship and also oversight by a bishop, though no foreign jurisdiction such as that of the pope could be recognized. The bishop should have the title only of Superintendent, he must attend solely to spiritual duties and show none of the "outward Pomp of Parade" incident by tradition to the dignity of episcopacy. The religious communities of women should have no new recruits and thus would in time disappear, while the Jesuits, even then on the verge of dissolution in Europe, should be "entirely abolished" at once, as also the Récollets. The property of the orders should be confiscated with pensions during life for the existing members. However rigorous this policy may seem, it was liberal compared with anything to be found in Europe during the previous two hundred years, and it went so far beyond what the letter of British statutes permitted that it was liable to bitter attack.

Before this report was made, already, by informal consent of the British government, a Quebec canon of French origin, Mgr. Briand, had been consecrated secretly at Paris for the duty of a bishop in Canada. This concession to the French stands in contrast with the long persistent denial to the thirteen English colonies of a bishop of either the Roman or the Anglican Church. Though Mgr. Briand was to take no part in politics, he had full authority over his clergy and in the spiritual discipline of his own people. It soon came about that the alert suspicions of Masères detected in him the arrogant prelate. It is notable that Masères, of Huguenot descent, was more hostile to the Roman Church than was Carleton, the Protestant Ulsterman from Catholic Ireland. Perhaps one reason is that the Huguenots had been the persecuted while Ulster the persecutor could more readily forgive a creed that it had oppressed. The extreme views of Masères made him a thorn in Carleton's side. He was, so reserved Carleton said, indiscreet in speech and more conversant with books than with men. Accordingly when, in 1769, he desired a year's leave of absence and made it clear that he should not return, Carleton joyously granted the request. In an official despatch he ventured to hope that Masères might procure a post "where the fervour of his zeal can be of no essential Disadvantage to the King's service." And so, in 1769, Masères was gone. In London he remained during the next forty years the champion of the views of the English element at Quebec. He would have found a solution of the quarrel with the English colonies by creating a real Imperial Parliament in which the colonies should take their place.

It was not long before Carleton followed Masères to England with a policy clearly in his mind. From his first days in Canada he had been convinced that it must remain French and that in case of war with the colonies it should be the chief anchor of British power in America. He had been in the country only a few months when he wrote to Shelburne that "barring Catastrophe shocking to think of" the French would remain "unmovable to the end of time" in their hold on Canada. He was almost wholly right in respect of the Canada that he knew, but in due course the "catastrophe shocking to think of" came and loyalist exiles from the revolted colonies made the larger Canada prevailingly British in origin and in language. The land, Carleton urged, was poor and the severe climate would repel softer races. British settlers would avoid the long inhospitable winters and seek the sunnier British dominions farther south. Though some merchants, a few officers, a few soldiers and camp followers, with no better prospects elsewhere, had remained in Canada, they must, in so poor a land, practise strict frugality. Already some of the British had gone and the rest would go when they could. While the climate was healthful, only the French were inured to its severity. They are, says Carleton, a fruitful race; the land is already theirs; newcomers tend quickly to disappear. Linked with this opinion was Carleton's fantastic belief that eighteen thousand fighting men of French origin could be raised in Canada to subdue the colonies. Accordingly every means should be used to conciliate them.

It is remarkable that Carleton had foreseen in 1768 military dangers that took form ten years later. France looking for revenge on Britain, would hope, he had then said, that the restless colonies would "push matters to extremities . . . in their independent notions" and would join them in war. In such a case those eighteen thousand Canadian soldiers of Carleton's imagining, unless won by a kindly policy, might be a danger and not a help. There were many officers in France who had served in Canada, knew the country and had influence with the people, and Carleton believed that the King of France was maintaining them as a special reserve for use in this possible war. The tribes of the west were still attached to France. Above all, should the colonies revolt, the antagonisms of former days would disappear; France would seem no longer to the English colonies an enemy but "an ally, a friend, and a Protector of their independency." To counteract this, French Canada, by indulgence maintained different in spirit from the disloyal English colonies, must be made the bulwark of British power, "the principal scene where the fate of America may be determined." Quebec and New York as ports might be "essentially necessary to the British interests on this continent," while the British fleet would be needed to subdue the French in any adventure on the sea. Carleton's prophecy was exactly fulfilled in many respects. The disastrous struggle took place as he had feared; France declared war; Quebec and New York were the strongholds of the British cause; the British fleet made New York a secure haven for loyalists driven from their former homes and in 1776 it saved Quebec from the invading colonial army. If Carleton's hope was fantastic that an army from French Canada might coerce Boston into obedience to the British crown, it is still true that his deeper policy prevailed in Canada. Though passionate idealism for democracy ran from Boston to the far south, on the way north it was checked at the frontier of Canada by another idealism, that of ingrained respect for existing authority. It was an inheritance derived less from loyalty to George III than from monarchical France and Catholic Rome.

CHAPTER XII

THE PLANNING OF A VASTER CANADA

WHEN, in 1770, Carleton returned to England there were ominous signs of change. The cry of "Wilkes and Liberty" in London was not far removed from the cry of "Liberty or Death" in America. It is amusing to find France and England each welcoming uneasy elements in the other country. In 1774, Wilkes, outlawed in England, was received with favour at the court of Louis XV because he was a thorn in the side of the British king and, not many years later, Marie Antoinette received at Versailles in the same spirit "our dear republicans" from the revolted colonies whose principles were to bring her to the scaffold. On England's part Tory Dr. Johnson's friend Boswell escorted to London from France Jean Jacques Rousseau to find asylum in a country freer than his own. London lionized the morbid dreamer; George III granted him a pension, little suspecting that, within a few years, thrones should be wrecked by Rousseau's teaching that mankind, born free, is everywhere in chains, and that the people have the right at will to change their rulers. Rousseau landed in England on January 13, 1766. The next day, for the first time, Edmund Burke took his seat in Parliament, an omen of a new spirit in that assembly. Though Burke was destined to make a frenzied fight against changes largely due to Rousseau, he was one of the chief forces to challenge his own monarch and to make revolution in America seem inevitable.

In the church as well as in the state the unyielding temper of those who ruled was met by secession. John Wesley's teaching in religion, like that of Wilkes in politics, appealed to existing discontent. Had bishops and clergy met Wesley in a spirit of understanding and conciliation, his zeal would have warmed the chilly atmosphere of the establishment and dispelled its fear of enthusiasm. When past seventy he thought preaching to a great crowd at five o'clock in the morning "the most healthy exercise in the world" and said that he had never known lowness of spirits or lost a night's sleep. The church should have found a place for such zeal. As it was, Wesley's followers formed a government of their own and, in the end, about one half of the English people broke with the national church, a parallel in religion to what happened in the state. No more than Washington had Wesley any desire for disruption. His conservative mind so reverenced primitive usage that in his early ministry he always practised immersion of infants in baptism and excluded dissenters from communion in the Church of England. Authority would not, however, forgive him for such innovations as preaching in the open air, linked with fervent appeals to ignorant crowds. That was enthusiasm and enthusiasm was unwelcome in high circles.

The time had come for an Act of Parliament to determine the vexing questions relating to Canada. Had this been done quickly on Carleton's return, when the repeal of all of Townshend's taxes but that on tea had brought a short period of quiet, the situation might have been eased. The colonies were watching England's policy for Canada as an omen of what they might expect for themselves. Decision was, however, held back, and came in the end after a succession of jarring incidents that embittered passions on both sides. In Canada, too, delay made matters worse. The French, recovering from the panic and depression of the conquest, urged their grievances with bolder demands for their own system of law. The seigneur, M. de Lotbinière, whom they sent to London, even claimed that

French should be the only official language in Canada. On the other hand, the English merchants were growing more and more nervous. They were doing, perhaps, three-fourths of the business in Canada, and yet they did not know whether it was under French or under English law that the debts owing to them could be collected. Carleton, who knew his own mind, had expected prompt action in London. Time, however, slipped away. Owing to the slow methods of Parliament, only about one question of importance was dealt with in a year. The year 1770–71 was occupied by a struggle with Wilkes and with the city of London to keep the public from having reports of the debates in the House of Commons; 1772 was chiefly devoted to a bill giving the king the right to grant or to withhold consent to the marriage of members of the royal family; and 1773 was spent in bringing India under the control of Parliament and thus, for the time, of the king.

During the delay there was much pondering about Canada in official circles. Probably Carleton, always at hand, was summoned often for counsel. Should the muddle about the laws of Canada be ended by giving it a coherent system, whether French or English? The problem of Canada included the destiny of the great region spreading far west to the Mississippi river. On both sides of its mighty flood lay what frontiersmen and more remote speculators in land pictured as a new Garden of Eden with a rich soil, varied and beautiful forests, and open prairies where roamed great herds of buffaloes. France had claimed and in part occupied it. Traders and soldiers had come up from New Orleans at the mouth of the Mississippi, the capital of the French colony of Louisiana, founded posts on that river and its tributaries, gathered some small French communities and carried on trade and also devoted missionary work among the natives. The white flag with the *fleurs-de-lis* of France had floated over Fort Chartres, in time to be all but washed away by the rushing waters of the Mississippi; over adjacent posts, Cahokia and Kaskaskia; over Vincennes on the Wabash River, a tributary of the Ohio; and over Fort Duquesne on the upper waters of the Ohio. In 1763 France had yielded all claim to this great region east of the Mississippi and it was now British territory; over its forts and over former French villages floated the British flag and authority in London had to create a policy for governing it.

Successive ministries had pondered the problem. General Conway was, it seems, the author of a report to George III in 1766 which stated that the warlike tribes of the region, though they had been soothed into a treaty by Sir William Johnson in 1764, were again restless. He feared an outbreak. While the Indians wished for trade with the British they wished also to be left to themselves in their own lands. Every colony except Pennsylvania had ill-treated them. The best thing now to do, says the report, is to keep the white man, with his corrupting ways, from entering the country of the Indians. General Murray at Quebec had already urged that the French in the west should be removed to his neighbourhood, a mild copy of the unhappy fate of the Acadians ten years earlier. Weak posts scattered among the Indians would tend rather to provoke than to prevent war. The needs of trade could be best met by a few trading posts on the frontier of the British settlements. No matter how distant some tribes might be from these posts, they were natural rovers and time was of little moment to them when hunting was out of season.

During the years after this report was made General Gage, in command at New York, had frequent alarms as to the danger of war with the tribes. They had so little sense of the obligations of a treaty that a quarrel with a drunken white trader might lead to a massacre. Only at great expense could military posts be maintained in the west. The route by way of the Great Lakes was long and difficult. Even more so was that by way of the Ohio with its turbulent waters and its forest-clad banks, the home of warlike savage tribes. There was still another route to the Ohio country. The British might by treaty use the Mississippi. Spain, however, entrenched at its mouth, made this difficult and, in any case, the route was really impossible since four months were needed to battle with the river's shoals, its floods and currents, to reach the mouth of the Ohio. Little wonder that this problem caused perplexity in London. While, on the one hand, traders and settlers were pressing into a land of promise and demanding rights and protection, on the other, caution urged that to give them a title would stir into war the Indian tribes, as indeed it did at intervals during the next half century. Hillsborough, secretary for the colonies, was for shutting out settlers, withdrawing existing settlers and soldiers and leaving the farther west to its owners the Indians. Since the drift of thought on the question was against him, he resigned in 1772. The Earl of Dartmouth took his place and this careful, kindly, devout but ineffective man had to provide for the government of Canada and of the wild region in the west, tasks that might have baffled even the genius and tact of Pitt.

During a dozen years the problem of Canada had been debated and Dartmouth had reams of reports and advice. At last, on May 2, 1774, he introduced in the House of Lords the bill known by the short title of the Quebec Act. Since Dartmouth was a peer, it was, perhaps, fitting that the Act should be introduced in the Lords, though it was rather the function of that house to revise than to originate important measures. The Act was planned on broad lines. It accepted finally for Canada the principle, soon to be confirmed by a famous judgment of Lord Mansfield, that the laws of a conquered country continue in force until they are altered by the conqueror, something that in England could be done only by Act of Parliament. Since Governor Murray's laws made by ordinance after the conquest had not received the needed sanction of Parliament they were not really valid and French law was the law of Canada. There was to be one change; the milder English criminal law was to replace the barbarous French law, though the English law was itself harsh enough. For the rest, no change; the seigneurs were to retain their estates, in some cases vast, and their feudal rights over their tenants; and the Roman Church was to have all its former privileges. Not only were France and Rome to be entrenched in Canada; its frontiers were to extend to the Mississippi as far south as to the Ohio. Naturally the English colonies resented this at once and vehemently. Their traders and settlers were already scattered over the region. Virginia and Pennsylvania in particular claimed millions of its acres for themselves. Such obstacles showed that an arm in the north at Quebec could not in the conditions of the time reach out to the Mississippi. An enemy, Spain, was also on guard at its mouth.

In spite of this there was ground in history for linking this region with Quebec. It was from Quebec that had gone the pioneers in the west, Marquette and Jolliet, La Salle, La Vérendrye and other French explorers to face hardships and dangers that to-day astound us. There were French settlements scattered at points of vantage from the Great Lakes to the mouth of the Mississippi. It is true that their existence was all but ignored in England. More than once proposals had been made to deport these few French to the older Canada and thus leave the region the more completely to the Indian tribes and to wild creatures, the bears and the beavers. The French, for their part, were attached to the settlements that they had created and were alarmed at the prospect of a harsh fate like that of the Acadians. Ruthless Hillsborough would have abandoned the villages and carried off the inhabitants to they knew not where, but now Dartmouth seemed to link mercy with efficiency when he decided to leave them where they were, to bring them under the rule of the governor at Quebec, and thus to continue the traditions of the French régime. The fur-traders of Canada were all for such a plan; it gave them, as against rivals in the English colonies, an advantage in exploiting the rich fur-bearing country extending from the Ohio to the far north and the farther west. While the region was to be placed under the British military governor at Quebec, it was also provided that the new frontiers were not to affect the existing boundaries of any of the English colonies or to make void any of their rights. The Province of Quebec, thus created, extended from the mouth of the St. Lawrence to the Mississippi River and included the present states of Michigan, Illinois, Indiana, Ohio, Wisconsin, and part of Minnesota.

In the east on the Atlantic coast, as in the west, there were rival interests in regard to frontiers. During the French régime, British fishermen had been excluded, as far as the French could exclude them, from the coasts of Canada. After the cession, however, all these coasts became, as they still remain, British and to make them secure for the training of British seamen, Labrador was confirmed to the fishing interest of Newfoundland, to the dismay of the Canadians of that day, and to the enduring loss of Canada, deprived of this frontage on the North Atlantic.

The Act denied self-government to the people of this great Province of Quebec. For the present, it was inexpedient to call an Assembly and indeed it is hard to imagine an elected legislature possible. If, as in England, only Protestants might vote, there would be the farce of a few hundred obscure newcomers as the sole electors; if the

French too might vote, clearly they had as yet no stable footing in a British state. Accordingly, instead of an assembly the governor was to have a council named by the ministry in London and consisting of not more than twenty-three members or of fewer than seventeen, resident in Canada, with no restrictions as to religious beliefs. They might make laws, but these were to be subject to approval or disallowance in London, a provision that, though fallen into disuse, stood until 1931 in the constitution of federal Canada with its ten million people. This council might levy rates for local purposes but it might not impose other taxes, a right reserved to Parliament. Though this reservation was perhaps natural, since Canada had no elected legislature, it provided fuel to the protests of the watchful English colonies about taxation. Canada, said Josiah Quincy of Massachusetts, was to be under rule "as absolute as that of an Asiatic despot." "Unhappy people," said the Congress that met in October, 1774; they are "not only injured but insulted"; they are allowed to gather stones to build roads but liable to have their property, honestly acquired, seized by an insolent minister in London who delights to flout liberty.

This angry tone characterizes all the colonies in regard to the Quebec Act. To coerce Boston in March, 1774, by a measure that destroyed its sea-going trade and, a few weeks later, to follow this by a bill setting up a military despotism in the north formed to suspicious minds a wanton menace. Though Great Britain had just defeated France, it seemed that the colonies were to have still a restless French and Catholic neighbour with the new feature that he was now protected in his privileges by British power. A British general was to rule at Quebec under those institutions of France that Burke described as meaning slavery. French law was to be enforced from the Atlantic seaboard to the banks of the Mississippi; French priests with the special protection of a British ruler were to teach the religion that, under Louis XIV, eldest son of the church, had destroyed or exiled thousands of Protestants, many of whom had found refuge in the English colonies.

Among others in the English colonies, young and capable Alexander Hamilton, only seventeen years of age, but already a leader, worked himself into a fury of suspicion. The Act, he said, gave full liberty to the Roman Catholic Church to subjugate the souls of men; in time the Inquisition would be burning Protestants at the stake in Boston; French despotism at Quebec would spread all over the English colonies, even to England herself; a corrupt Parliament was engaged in a plot to destroy liberty; droves of emigrants from Roman Catholic countries would be brought in to overrun the colonies and Protestants would be shut out. Hamilton, as we know, was fighting phantoms, but his outbursts reveal the temper of the time. He wrote his two pamphlets after a visit to Boston where he had seen dismay and anger at the closing of the port. Not only in America but also in England objections were urged. To set up French law was to invite patriots in England to ask why English law was not good enough for a British state. To tolerate and also to endow the Roman Church was to arouse fierce prejudices illustrated six years later in the Gordon Riots that threatened to destroy London.

The ministry, aware of dangers, delayed the bill until, as the Lord Mayor of London complained, most lords and commoners had gone off to their estates in the country for the rural delights of an English spring. The public would hear little, for debates in Parliament were still secret. Even behind the closed doors of Parliament secrecy marked the proceedings. As if by design, methods were pursued well fitted to arouse suspicion in the colonies. The ministry permitted none of the many reports on which the bill was based to be laid on the table. Though it was usual to admit members of the Commons to debates in the Lords, on this occasion the privilege was denied. When the bill reached the Commons secrecy continued. Demands for reports on Canada were so persistently refused that one member, Thomas Howard, afterwards Earl of Suffolk, denounced what he called the "dark scheme to introduce slavery and oppression into the colonies." Colonel Barré saw "concealed mischief in the Bill" and added "I smelt this out from the beginning." Burke said that, owing to the lack of information, the House of Commons did not know what it was doing.

The Act was received in the Lords without debate or opposition until it came back for the approval of changes made in the Commons. That body, on the other hand, so debated it that, as one speaker said, the flood of words so washed away members to the serenity of the country as to leave a bare quorum. Some of those who spoke or gave evidence had first knowledge of Canada. Among them Sir Charles Saunders, the admiral who shared with Wolfe the glory of taking Quebec, agreed that the fisheries should go, not to Canada, to be linked with a French population, but to Newfoundland, to be nursed as a school for the training of British seamen. General Murray who, during the debate, haunted the precincts of the House, was not called, probably because he was likely to be an adverse critic of some of the provisions. Carleton himself when examined gave dry and reserved answers to questioning so severe that at one time he had to retire exhausted to take a rest. His dominating thought was to keep Canada in what he called "a proper and desirable subordination."

The king's Advocate-General, Marriott, had given, as he admitted, two years to the problem of Canada, but when examined he was, as Barré complained, "mounted very high and pranced and pranced," would give no information or divulge anything said in his elaborate report to the ministry. When asked whether the Canadians would prefer English to French law, he said "I never was in Canada"; nor had he any opinion on French law, since "I never was in France." In truth he had already published a work on the laws suitable for the Province of Quebec. When finally Barré, in despair of extracting anything, asked him what he thought of the King of Prussia's religion the solemn answer was that it might be gleaned from that monarch's writings. Clearly the ministry was either afraid or ashamed to reveal the purpose involved in the Act.

The two members of the Commons who knew most about the system proposed were Thurlow, the attorney-general, and Wedderburn, the solicitor-general, both of whom had reported on Canada. Their acute intellects were obsessed by the need of meeting danger from the colonies. "No one," said Charles Fox, "could be as wise as Thurlow looked." We may admire him for this, at least, that his profane tongue did not spare even George III. When, on one occasion, he carried some bills to the king for the royal assent, he told him that, since it was all damned nonsense for him to try to understand them, he had better sign at once. Thurlow was bent, if need be, on coercing the colonies to obedience. "Sedition and treason, like tobacco and potatoes," were, he said elsewhere, "the peculiar growth of the American soil." On purely legal matters, such, for instance, as the best system for Canada, he had a free mind and it was in the debate on the Quebec Act that he gained the reputation that, in due course, made him lord chancellor. If, he said, English law would make the Canadians happy, give it to them; if they wished for French law, let them have it. To impose an alien law upon conquered French people would be cruel tyranny. If English people went to live in Canada, they must well know that they could not carry with them their own laws, but must obey those found there. The Canadians had by treaty the right to their property and this involved the protection of the laws under which this property had been created.

Wedderburn, the solicitor-general, once the ally of the liberal Whigs, had now gone over to the court. When the news had come recently of the "Boston Tea Party," he had said that if Britain still held out to the colonies the olive branch with one hand, she should grasp the sword with the other. To live magnificently was an obsession of the time and where better than in subservience to the king could the means be found? On the day when Wedderburn became solicitor-general he went out and bought a service of plate costing eight thousand pounds. He too could assert liberal opinions about Canada. The very Turks, he said, left the people of conquered regions in possession of their own laws. If traders went for gain to Canada, probably they did not intend to stay and in any case must accept what they found there. The guarantee to adherents of the Roman Church, under the treaty of 1763, of the free exercise of their religion, carried with it not only toleration for the priests but provision for their support. Their clergy should be confirmed in their benefices. They should collect the tithe and have a bishop. The crown should, however, appoint to benefices; the resort in ecclesiastical cases should be to the civil courts. Wedderburn's general counsel was to make British supremacy secure in Canada, but to leave the country to the native Canadians. A liberal policy would strengthen, not weaken, British control. In a fine phrase he said "there is no instance of any state that has been overturned by toleration."

The Commons spent the better part of nine days in the debates. Lord North was suave, reasonable, always correct in tone, apologizing readily for any seeming brusqueness,

willing to concede that the future might reveal the need
of vital changes. He knew that he had a majority well in
hand. Facing North were Burke and Fox destined, seventeen years later, when revolution in America had become
a stern reality, to debate another bill about Canada needed
after that convulsion. Burke, already middle-aged, went
away when the debate was prolonged to late hours; but
Fox was just twenty-five and late hours did not matter to
him, since if not spent in debate they would be spent at
the gaming table. He was for wider liberty than the bill
allowed and had the courage to differ from others of its
opponents and to support the concessions to the Roman
Catholic Church, in whose teachings he found, he said,
nothing repugnant to political freedom. Burke said that
the thing to keep in mind was the well-being of the Canadians, who, by a dispensation of God, had come under
British rule. Give them liberty and they would be loyal
subjects of the king. He remarked later that the only part
of the colonial world to remain loyal was "Popish Canada."
But, English, not French, law should prevail in Canada.
"There is, Sir," he said, "as much reason to indulge an Englishman in favour of his prejudice for liberty as there is
to indulge a Frenchman in favour of his prejudice for slavery. The bill turns freedom itself into slavery . . . [since],
compared with the English government, that of France is
slavery. I would have English liberty carried into the
French colonies but I would not have French slavery carried into the English colonies."

Another opponent of the bill, regarded as well versed in
colonial affairs was a former governor of Florida, George
Johnstone, son of a Scottish baronet and, on his mother's
side, nephew of Murray, Carleton's predecessor in Canada.
He favoured the fullest liberty for Canada on the basis,
however, not of French but of British custom. Canada, he
said, should have an elected assembly; even if some as-

semblies in the colonies had proved tumultuous, this gave
no reason to condemn all assemblies; "the great maxim to
be learned from a history of our colonization is to let men
manage their own affairs"; they would do it better on the
spot than those at a distance could possibly do it for them.
This view Colonel Barré supported with fine assurance
that everything British was good. It could, he said, be no
grievance to any nation to bring it under the English constitution and laws. Burke's cousin, William Burke, said,
with broad inclusiveness, that the bill was the worst to be
conceived "since God made the world," and Thomas Howard, who wound up the debate, urged that some one should
kick the "abominable and detestable measure" out of the
doors.

These attacks did not really matter; North was sure of
his majority. When, on June 13, the vote was taken, fewer
than a hundred of the five hundred members were present
and the vote was fifty-six for the bill and a beggarly twenty
against it. When, on the same day, it went back to the
Lords from the Commons for approval of some minor
changes, Chatham, now a shadow of his former self, denounced it. He saw in it renewed elements of irritation
to the colonies. It denied, he said, both trial by jury (this,
however, only in civil affairs), and the right to a writ of
Habeas Corpus, the two guarantees of liberty. It was "a
most cruel, oppressive and odious measure, tearing up justice and every good principle by the roots"; inevitably it
would lose the hearts of all the Americans; it established
over a vast continent the Roman religion against which
Puritan New England had fought Canada for nearly a century. Turning to the row of bishops in lawn sleeves, Chatham asked them what they thought of it. Some of their
lordships slept placidly during the debate but, for once,
English prelates, unmoved by the appeal to their Protestantism, voted unanimously for the widest toleration of the

Roman Church. We may guess their answer to a similar question about Ireland.

Lord Lyttelton, defending the bill, admitted that it aimed to use Canada against New England, where riotous colonists were resisting the power and preëminence of Great Britain, were showing the fierce fanatic spirit of the Roundheads of old, and were trying to destroy the royal authority in order to set up an independent republic. Not freedom but power was their aim. The bill would check this and make it certain, he added, that the loyal inhabitants of Canada would help to bring them to their senses. Outside of Parliament there was a war of pamphlets. Lyttelton addressed an open letter to Chatham rebuking his statement that Canada was enslaved by the bill. Is it slavery, he asked, to govern a country by law and not by royal proclamation? A writer on the other side denounced George III as "the worst of princes" determined to be a tyrant. The bill, he said, was "abominable in the face of the Lord and under His heavy wrath"; "the Devil himself" would not have devised "more infernal clauses and provisions" for setting up "slavery so bloody" that only, so the irony ran, "the most *pious* and *best* of princes could have conceived it." One wonders whether these phrases fell under the eye of the monarch who had proscribed Wilkes during many years because he had said in milder terms that the king's ministers had put into his mouth a lie. Clearly opinion ran to violence in London as it did in Boston, and in both is evident a florid gift of invective.

The bill passed in the Lords by a vote of 26 to 7. It has a certain interest that Carleton's brother-in-law, the Earl of Effingham, regarded as a rather eccentric person, was one of the seven. When the day came for the royal assent, some wondered whether, though the power of veto had been long in abeyance, the representative of the royal line that ruled in England because it was Protestant, would accept the first wide measure of toleration for the Roman Church ever passed by Parliament, since Elizabeth was queen. The city of London so disliked both the faith and the system of law approved by the bill that, on June 22, when the royal assent was to be asked, the Lord Mayor, with the aldermen and a hundred and fifty of the common councillors, in all the panoply of office, went in procession to St. James's Palace. No doubt crowds watched the long line of the rulers of the city of London as the impressive parade wound through the streets; no doubt, too, when the crowd asked what it was all about the word ran that it was in protest against the designs of the Roman Catholic Church. The mayor and his supporters urged on George III opinions that he had no wish to hear. The Roman religion, "idolatrous and bloody," was being set up in Canada and no provision was made for the "true worship of Almighty God." Since the king reigned because he was a Protestant, to accept this bill was to violate his coronation oath; he had no power to erect any system not in harmony with the laws of England; the proposed despotic governing council was repugnant to those free principles under which alone His Majesty sat on his throne. We may imagine the emotions of George III as he listened to this harangue. He deigned no answer and the protesters backed out of his presence. Later in the day he was greeted by an angry mob with shouts of "No Popery" when he went down to Westminster and there not only gave formal assent to the Quebec Act but declared that it was based on justice and humanity and would make his Canadian subjects happy. The broad Atlantic made all the difference between Canada and Ireland. A tolerance that might be mischievous nearer home, did not, said Dr. Samuel Johnson, matter at Quebec.

The protests that followed the passing of the bill justified the effort of the ministry to discourage public discussion. Mascres sent to Quebec a vigorous attack: Canada

was handed over to despotism; English law was swept away;
Protestantism was so shelved that even the Roman Catholic bishop might sit in the governor's council and help to
make laws, something that no Roman Catholic might do
in England or in Ireland. At Quebec the English traders,
with emphatic tautology, declared their "unutterable, their
inexpressible" grief; they had lost the protection of those
English laws that alone had induced them to take risks
in Canada and were the admiration of the world. Their
property would be ruined. Trial by jury was gone. Since
they had no longer the guarantee of personal liberty furnished by the Habeas Corpus Act they might be thrown
into jail under a *lettre de cachet* and kept there for years
without trial as the king of France kept prisoners in the
Bastille. Canada was in effect handed back to France; in
vain had British soldiers died; and so on. Some even of the
Canadians were not pleased. While the seigneur and the
priest liked a bill that restored their former privileges, the
habitant had already learned, as Carleton complained, "the
American Spirit of Licentiousness and Independence," encouraged, as he added, by the turbulent English faction.
The Canadians were well aware that with the conquest had
come a new spirit and that seigneur and priest were no
longer backed by the despotic king of France. Chief Justice
Hey said, indeed, that the inhabitants had been pleased
and satisfied by the overthrow of the oppressive French
régime. We cannot interpret the inscrutable mind of a
class that could not read and had only vague if any knowledge of the change now made, but it is certain that some
Canadians expressed discontent at the return to the French
system.

Assuredly, in defying the clamour of the London mob,
British magnanimity went far when now it granted special
powers to the Roman Catholic Church in a British state.
Such powers to the church of the majority in Canada offer

favourable contrast with the wide privileges granted in
Ireland to the Protestant church of a minority of barely
one-twentieth of the population. The church in Quebec
became in effect an established church with powers to tax
its members going beyond any privileges of the state church
in England. Cavour's later conception of a free church
in a free state had not then reached the minds of even
enlightened statesmen. The tithe for religion was collected by law in England, Scotland and Ireland. Even Burke
did not object to the tithe in Canada; he did not see why
both Protestants and Roman Catholics should not so manage that no one should escape the tithe. The ungodly
should, he thought, not elude paying their share to support religion, on which the well-being of the state is based.

Though London might parade against the Quebec Act;
though the few English traders in Canada might denounce
it as treason to their interests; though the habitant might
protest that he was now again brought under bond to priest
and seigneur; not from these but from the English colonies
came the hottest protests. June had seen the passing of the
Act and in September came the first meeting of the Continental Congress. To minds already excited by the coercion
of Boston now came the new shock of special rights to a
church that most Protestants feared. This was one grievance; another was that a despotic soldier at Quebec should
rule the west. The Congress soon showed its temper. On
October 26, it appealed to the Canadians to turn against
the Act and to join the other colonies in a protest truly continental. The phantom of the Inquisition burning Protestants on Boston Common, conjured up by Alexander Hamilton, appealed also to an excited Congress which now
gravely protested that the king had no power to establish
the Inquisition. Such a warning to the ardent Protestant
George III is not without humour. Congress denounced
the governor and council at Quebec as despots, while their

masters, the infamous ministers in London, would halt at no attack on liberty. A countryman of the Canadians, Montesquieu, had, however, shown the way to check tyranny and they should heed his teaching. Nature had joined Canada with the other colonies and now all should stand together to support "transcendent freedom." Later, when Jefferson and Adams were framing one of the most important documents in human history, the Declaration of Independence, they devoted to denunciation of the Quebec Act some fiery paragraphs in which Washington, Franklin, and all the other leaders concurred. While fears in the colonies in regard to religious persecution were fantastic, the placing of the west under the governor at Quebec gave a solid basis for resentment. If there was anger in the Congress there was derision in the Ohio country where from the first the Quebec Act was flouted.

Though to the colonies the Act was a blundering provocation to rebellion, in other quarters it was considered a masterpiece of statesmanship that saved Canada to Britain. It had, in truth, something of both qualities. It held in sympathy with Britain the two most influential elements in Canadian life, the church and the landowner, and we may say this at least that it ended a long chaos in the laws of Canada. The seigneur was secure in his rights and the church in its privileges. The Act registered with some exactness the need of the moment in regard to Canada. Carleton believed and the Act expressed his belief that Canada would always remain French and he read the situation aright as to the Canada that he knew. It remains to this day vividly French with French law and the Catholic Church securely entrenched. When the effort was made later to endow the Church of England with similar privileges this was resented by dissenting Protestants. It may be that the dualism of race in Canada would have been softened by a uniform absence of privilege but it is also likely that voluntary support would have given the church its unique position in French Canada. No serious attempt has ever been made by the people to curtail its power while, on the other hand, they resented and at last abolished the secular feudal rights that the Quebec Act confirmed to the seigneur.

It was not the Act that kept the Canadians French and Catholic; what did this was the enduring devotion to their ancient culture, inherent in the French character, and this the presence or absence of formal law could affect but slightly. In this same period Spain, which received from France Louisiana and tried to impose upon it Spanish law and the Spanish tongue, was met by a rebellion ended only after the execution, with true Spanish ruthlessness, of five of the French leaders. But Louisiana did not become Spanish. Resentment at this severity so served to make the French in New Orleans more resolved to retain their French culture that their tenacity triumphed. When later, in 1803, the United States acquired the colony, the republic could indeed make English the only official language, but it found the old French law too deeply rooted in the habits of the people to be dislodged. To this day, while the criminal law is English, the succession to property and also family relations in Louisiana are based upon French law. A quarter in New Orleans still remains French, unabsorbed by the alien world that surrounds it. The Quebec Act had slight effect in inducing the Canadians to take up arms against the revolted colonies. For this Carleton himself is the best witness; when the war came they were, he soon found, indifferent to both sides and asked chiefly to be let alone. It is true that the priests thundered against those who joined the Americans, but the cause of the thunder lay rather in antagonism to the Protestant ideals of the English colonies than in gratitude for the clauses of a statute. It seems a strange paradox that had Canada not then been French, it might not to-day be British. The fire running through the English colonies was checked at the frontier by a wall of distrust and antagonism. No doubt sea-power helped to retain Canada by its control of the great waterway of the St. Lawrence as it retained Nova Scotia and Newfoundland on the open sea. It is true, however, that, though Britain's naval power held New York to the end of the war, at the peace she surrendered it to her sons who created the young republic. Quebec remained British because it was French.

CHAPTER XIII

CIVIL WAR

WHILE hitherto London, Boston and Quebec have been the centres of interest in our period, the scene now shifts to Philadelphia. The menace due to the coercion of Boston had brought to a head the need for action in common. Philadelphia lay midway between north and south and there in September, 1774, came together fifty-four delegates from the colonies. Their sense of unity is seen in the words of Patrick Henry, the President: "I am not a Virginian but an American." While they differed greatly in type they now declared that British oppression had made them one in spirit. Yet they knew little of each other. Roads were bad, rivers were often unbridged and means of communication were slow;—by sail along the coast, by horse on the roads. In consequence some members had to travel to the Congress for what seemed great distances. John Adams describes the long journey from Boston to Philadelphia. Never again, he thought, was he likely to travel so far. The occasion was memorable. He and his companions set out "with kind wishes and fervent prayers" of a large company gathered to see them off. This was on August 10 and they did not reach Philadelphia until the end of the month. Often, as they approached a town, they were met by gentlemen on horseback and in carriages and escorted to a banquet in their honour. At New Haven the bells rang and the people crowded to their doors "as if it was to see a Coronation." The delegates were told that they were going to "the greatest and most important assembly ever held in America."

In New York, where they were royally entertained at three o'clock in the afternoon at "the most splendid dinner I ever saw," they found a certain fear of the radicalism and levelling spirit of New England. New England, in turn, was critical. In spite of rich plate, silver coffee-pots, silver tea-pots, and fine linen, New York seemed to lack culture, and indeed to be rather vulgar. "I have not seen," says Adams, "one real gentleman, one well-bred man, since I came to town. . . . They talk very loud, very fast and all together. If they ask you a question, before you can utter three words of your answer, they will break out on you again and talk away." Adams went to see in New York the statue within an iron railing of George III "on horseback, very large, of solid lead gilded with gold, standing on a pedestal of marble, very high." Later it made good bullets, "leaden Majesty," with which to shoot the king's soldiers. Many of the houses were "elegant"; there were rich furnishings, fine linen and formidable bills of fare. Even some of the inns were "genteel." At Philadelphia two hundred carriages met the delegates in a stately procession.

The colonies were suspicious of each other. Virginia counted itself so superior to all the others that George Washington spoke of the Yankees of New England as "an exceedingly dirty and nasty people." Massachusetts, on the other hand, thought itself a light of the world. There were fears that Virginian soldiers, if sent to the north, might bring New England under the rule of racing and gambling sportsmen from Virginia, who led indolent lives on their great estates, were served by slave labour and felt scorn for "common people" who worked with their hands. Adams was indignant when Quakers in Philadelphia protested to him against the recent hanging of Quakers in Massachusetts. When, on Sunday, he listened to preaching "all day," he thought Philadelphia badly instructed in religion: "I hear no preachers here like ours in Boston." We gather from his diary a sense of the unity of the colonies on the great question of taxation, together with cleavage in lesser affairs. Every colony was represented except Georgia, the colony farthest south, founded only forty years earlier and still governed as a crown colony. Washington sat in the Congress, a planter sent by his native Virginia, a tall man with a fine figure, agreeable address, and powerful physique; "a good-looking genteel fellow," said a contemporary observer, with dignity of manner that made him always a striking personage in any assembly. As yet he was protesting his loyalty to the king and his unwillingness to break with England. His mind worked slowly. Handicapped by a defective education, he never read widely or wrote correctly. His pride was unbending. He was sensitive to criticism, resentful of slights and unyielding on a question of principle, such as that about taxation.

Tact and skill were necessary in managing the Congress. Since the members knew little of each other they had misunderstandings and prejudices that only personal intercourse would soften. Sometimes, however, intercourse had the opposite effect and so increased strife that they hurled abusive epithets at each other. For a time the unbending Adams would not speak to Dickenson and described him in contemptuous terms. Wild rumours flew about that George III had turned Roman Catholic and that revolution had begun in England. It was soon clear that radicals of defiant temper were in control. The delegates agreed that Great Britain must abandon wicked attempts "to enslave America" and must repeal the Boston Port Bill and other Acts of Parliament, including the Quebec Act. Pennsylvania and Virginia read into the Act a deliberate plan to cut them off from their natural field of expansion, while New England found chief offence in the toleration of the

Roman Church that had "dispersed Impiety, Bigotry, Persecution, Murder and Rebellion throughout every part of the world." This did not prevent an appeal to the Catholic Canadians. Differences of religion, the Congress urged, should not prevent coöperation in securing liberty that would raise all its children above "low-minded infirmities." The Quebec Act made the Canadians abject slaves to the whims of a minister in London. "Privileges and remuneration last no longer than his smiles. When he frowns, their feeble forms dissolve." From no quarter was there for Canada any hope of liberty, except by union with the English colonies, a great fellowship of free states.

The Congress made a "Declaration of Rights," and took steps to assert them. Unrest was spreading. In a convention, Suffolk County, Massachusetts, had declared that no obedience was due to any of the coercive acts; Massachusetts should set up a government in defiance of that in London. When Congress endorsed these "Suffolk Resolves," they had become of national import. We find already the ominous suggestion of an appeal for foreign aid. In spite of differences there was this unity, that probably no member really believed that Britain had the right to tax the colonies. While some, however, proposed to reason her into a change of mind, others intended to fight her if she did not abandon her claim. The members of the Congress united to form a "Continental Association" pledged, unless their demands were satisfied, to cease all imports from Britain after December 1, 1774, and to export to her nothing after September 10, 1775, a shrewd plan to keep their own markets a little longer while closing those of Britain at once. They agreed moreover to watch the traders, lest they should supply English goods, and to live simply and soberly without extravagance or dissipation. A lady who proposed to give a ball was rebuked by Washington, and a promoter of a horse race was forced to promise atonement for his enormity. Britain, by finding her great colonial trade ruined, was to feel the cogent pressure of finance. All who opposed the Continental Association were to be treated as "enemies of American liberty." Any one refusing to sign the required pledge regarding trade was likely to receive the attentions of a fanatical mob and a covering of tar and feathers. We shall never know what proportion of the colonists favoured the policy of the Association. It may be that its aggressive members silenced a less assertive majority. While John Adams declared that about one-third of the people of the colonies were loyal to Great Britain, others believed that many were forced into revolution by the active few.

It is certain that, as yet, comparatively few faced the prospect of a break with Britain. Before the Congress adjourned in October, with a plan to meet again in the following May, it issued an address to the king and people of Britain in terms of loyalty, linked, however, with a firm resolve not to yield on the points at issue. On the other side even kindly Dartmouth said that the members of the Continental Association were guilty of treason. The menace of the ruin of trade with the colonies and of armed resistance had stirred the obstinate courage of George III. He, the rightful sovereign over the colonies, to whom they owed obedience, was not to be coerced by loss of trade. "Sinister motives" and "dangerous designs" should not triumph. He would be indulgent to the colonies, children of their royal father. If they were good he would reward them, but if they were disobedient he would punish them; by all rules of justice Britain might, with a clear conscience, punish colonies guilty of rebellion. In April, 1775, before there was actual bloodshed, the king told North that "blows must decide whether they are to be subject to this country or independent." He had as lief, he said, fight the Bostonians as the French; the deluded Americans must have their

eyes opened, something one may add that in due course
came about though not in the sense that the king intended.
In the end he refused to receive the petitions of Congress.
They were, he said, impertinent.

It is probable that as yet public opinion was with the
king, since the average Englishman was likely to ask
whether England had founded and protected colonies only
to let them defy her at will. There were, however, other
voices. Wilkes said that coercion of the colonies was feloni-
ous and murderous. It would mean their independence;
they would become great and renowned on the solid foundation of liberty. The king might hold Boston by force but,
if he did, the city would be only a second Gibraltar with a
hostile country surrounding it. Chatham demanded that
the British troops should be withdrawn and a policy abandoned that was based on weakness linked with persistent,
ignorant and futile despotism. He knew that his opponents dreaded his invective and in January, 1775, wrote
to his wife; "Be of good cheer, noble love. 'Yes, I am proud,
I must be proud to see Men not afraid of God afraid of me.'"
Burke said that the king's government hurled nothing
but menace and defiance at America. We can imagine the
effect of this arrogance upon Washington, the owner of
thousands of broad acres, accustomed to military command
and to obedience from his many slaves, and rarely in all
his life in the presence of any one whom he regarded as
his superior.

By midsummer in 1774, we find armed strife certain unless one or the other side made a quick retreat. Boston had
become bitter. Its sea-going trade was gone. The charter
under which Massachusetts was governed had been in effect revoked and a British general was now governor and
prepared if necessary to use coercion. Opinion was so
aflame that many patriots were quietly arming and also,
across the sea, Great Britain was preparing to conquer her

own colonies. In retaliation for the colonial boycott, she forbade the colonies to trade with her or with the West Indies, their two most important markets, or to have any share in the Newfoundland fisheries from which New England drew its supplies. She declared the colonial ports in a state of blockade and by her command of the sea was able to ruin their sea-going commerce. Their answer was to declare that now their ports, hitherto closed to all but British ships, were open to the world. In England Franklin and Chatham met to discuss terms. Franklin would not, however, yield any right of Britain to tax the colonies or even to alter their constitutions, while Chatham, though in agreement with Franklin on the question of taxation, insisted that the colonies must make some perpetual grant of revenue to the king and also admit the right of Parliament to control their trade. Lord North invited Parliament to name the limit of conciliation and it did; Britain would not tax the colonies if they would tax themselves for defence and hand over the money to be spent by Great Britain.

By this time even Chatham's and Burke's opinion had become hateful to many in the colonies. One side or the other must give way completely. Boston was naturally the most inflamed since there the British soldier was in control. While John Adams was absent in 1774 and in 1775 at the Congress, his remarkable wife, Abigail Adams, remained in Boston and we see in her letters the growth of hatred against Great Britain. The preparations for coercion made her blood boil. As in later wars, rumours inflamed passions. Adams at Philadelphia heard that the British fleet was bombarding Boston, while his wife heard that it was planning to ravage the coasts of New England. Boston had real horrors, for to scarcity of food, due to the closing of the port, was added a plague that carried off many. To burning patriots, fire, sword, famine and pestilence seemed to be Britain's ruthless weapons of coercion. This coercion was real enough. There was a red-coat in Boston for every five of the inhabitants. Mrs. Adams thought that the citizens were even worse off than if closely confined in jail. To her the British seemed lost to all sense of honour, while their supporters, her Tory neighbours, were even more accursed; hungry tigers, traitors to their own race, they ought, she said, to be extirpated. The wanton and infamous motherland wished to make the Bostonians "abject slaves under the most cruel and despotic of tyrants"; "Blush, Americans that you derived your origin from such a race." No barbarity was beyond them; Mrs. Adams believed that they used poisoned bullets and later, after the fight at Bunker Hill, she believed that they cut off the head of Dr. Warren, a colonial leader, and carried it to General Gage, that he might gloat over it. When prayer was offered in church for reconciliation with Britain she could not join in it; "Let us separate; they are unworthy to be our brethren." This did not prevent her saying long afterwards when she knew England better that it is "the country of my greatest partiality." John Cleaveland, a preacher of Ipswich, in New England, called General Gage a "profane wicked monster of falsehood and perjury," an abandoned wretch, who "without quick repentance would have an aggravated damnation in hell." In rural districts the annual commemoration of the so-called Boston Massacre, with such symbols as bones, death-heads, and coffins, spread among the farmers the hatred of British tyranny that found expression in the frantic resolve to have "Liberty or Death."

It is an ominous fact that this intense passion had already spread before the first shot was fired at Lexington and two years before the Declaration of Independence. In these same early days the resolve in England was unshaken that Boston must pay the East India Company for the tea destroyed in 1773. This done, commerce would be allowed to return to that port; and meanwhile the people of Boston were merely suffering for their misconduct. The rights of the sovereign Parliament must be respected. Many who wrote to Dartmouth, the Colonial Secretary, urging action denounced the Americans as cowards and villains; England, they said, was too lenient; the pride and the ambition of "that damned rascal John Adams," were at the root of much of the trouble, but a peal of thunder was being prepared for the colonies that should shake even the mountains; the colonies must yield or be destroyed; their high language about becoming powerful states was ridiculous. Sir James Adolphus Oughton, commander-in-chief in Scotland, a man with colonial experience and described by Boswell as learned and of "a very sweet temper," wrote to Dartmouth on August 24, 1775, that England was at last aroused; the conflict was no accident; there was a deep plot; conciliation was pernicious; to treat with armed rebels showed only weakness; if these were sincere, "let them lay down their arms and implore pardon"; nothing but distress would, however, make them submit.

No moderate appeal from America had any chance of acceptance in high circles. British cruisers intercepted mails from America to such an extent that sometimes clerks in London spent twelve hours of the day in sorting the contents seized. The king himself with great industry read many of these letters and marked in his own hand the exact minute when he opened them. John Wesley, who knew America, assured Dartmouth that the colonies were "terribly united," a truth that did not keep him later from saying that they could not win because the hand of God was against rebellion. A statement, mild in tone, of the colonial point of view by Thomas Jefferson, dated from Monticello in Virginia, on August 25, 1775, is among Dartmouth's papers. Already, though only thirty-two, Jefferson wishes to retire from the public stage and never to hear again "of what passes in the world." The ministry, he says, is deceived by officials in America into thinking that only a small faction is aroused. He longs for reconciliation; he would rather be dependent on Great Britain than on any other nation; but he is convinced that the colonies demand only their just rights and if these are not conceded quickly they will seek foreign aid and have "an everlasting avulsion from Great Britain," a prophecy only too truly fulfilled. Joseph Reed, a respected lawyer of Philadelphia, who was later one of the founders of its great university, wrote repeatedly to Dartmouth pleading for better understanding of the colonies. He had been a student of law in London and was of a temper so moderate that he has been charged with disloyalty to the revolution. He insisted to Dartmouth that the colonies would never retreat from their demands. To this the answer was always that they must submit and ask for pardon. This done, they would be restored to favour on the king's terms; otherwise they were misguided rebels, to be coerced into obedience. This blindness about the colonial outlook was enduring. Three score years later, in 1838, Lord Durham, after a survey of British rule in Canada up to his time, wrote the bitter wish for his country that the experiment of governing colonies wisely should at least be tried.

In the summer of 1774, when Gage, holding his troops in Boston, sent out some officers in civilian dress to travel over the country roads and make what notes they could, they were so watched and suspected as spies that their lives were in danger. At the pleasant village of Concord, about a score of miles from Boston, where the officers knew that cannon, small arms and stores were being gathered, they talked with the leading lawyer, Daniel Bliss, who had warned his fellow townsmen of the mighty power of Britain to crush rebellion. "But your people will not fight," said one of the officers. The lawyer, destined himself to end his days as a loyalist exile in Nova Scotia, pointed out of the window to his brother, who happened to be passing in the street. "There," he said, "goes a man who will fight you in blood up to his knees." A militia officer who happened to be drilling his men under the windows of the tavern where the British officers were lodged was so sure of war that he counselled the men to wait for the British volley before they themselves fired. On September 1, 1774, when Gage seized three hundred barrels of gunpowder near Boston and the false rumour spread that six Americans had been killed, forty thousand men are said to have begun the march on Boston to take vengeance. A force sent by Gage to Salem to seize cannon stored there was obliged to retire. An officer at Boston reported in December, 1774, that the rebels stopped people on the highways and forced them to curse the king and the Parliament and to wish that the island of Great Britain might sink into the sea.

Gage, surrounded at Boston in a hostile country, spent a troubled winter. The colonists continued to gather arms. Since the blockade of Boston left many unemployed, hundreds of marksmen, lying sometimes half smothered in dung carts in order to conceal their arms, slipped out of the city to join in the drill of the gathering colonial forces. The people in the town watched every movement of the British troops and made it known to their friends by arranged signals from church steeples. In the spring of 1775, when Gage learned that the colonists were forming an arsenal at Concord, he planned a surprise attack with a strong force of a thousand men. Accordingly, on April 18, 1775, silently in the night many British regular soldiers gathered, one by one, secretly at the place appointed, for a night march in the hope of reaching Concord in the early morning of April 19. Many were watching Gage's movements and it had been noticed that boats had been brought

in from the war-ships in the harbour and lay at a convenient spot for moving a force across the bay above
Charlestown. In consequence when, soon after midnight,
the troops had reached the road to Concord church bells
and the firing of cannon aroused the country people. In
the dim light of early morning, as the force reached Lexington, some sixty rustic militia on the village green barred
the way. We do not know which side fired first. Lord
George Germain said later that the accidental firing of a
pistol caused the mischief. The British broke through the
obstacle, killing eight men, and the column moved on the
few miles to Concord. Here messengers had already so
raised the alarm that the stored cannon and ammunition
had been hastily buried in manure heaps or in ploughed
fields. When the soldiers arrived they rolled flour barrels
and threw powder into the pond, destroyed pork and beef,
burned tents and made a bonfire of gun carriages.

The tired soldiers, who had already covered twenty miles
during the night, had then to make the long march back
to Boston without any pause for rest. It proved a dreadful
experience and, marking as it did the first appeal to arms,
it had far-reaching consequences. Church bells and other
signals had summoned members of the militia, on the alert
after more than a year of agitation. They had weapons in
their own houses, they were skilled in the use of the musket,
and now from behind trees and rocks, from houses by the
road-side, hundreds of them fired on the soldiers. These
got out of hand, forced their way into houses from which
firing came, bayonetted the inmates, and set the houses on
fire. This only caused delay that increased the number of
the gathering enemy. Though Gage sent out a rescuing
force of fifteen hundred men under Lord Percy, the British
lost nearly three hundred men, of whom about a hundred
were killed, while the colonists had fewer than a hundred
casualties with thirty-nine killed. Many new graves marked

the bloody day of Lexington. The *Essex Gazette* of Salem, said that the cruelty and brutality of the British exceeded that of "the vilest Savages of the Wilderness," while a loyalist lady says that on the return from Concord the British "found two or three of their people lying in the Agonies of Death, scalped and their noses and ears cut off and Eyes gored out." Far away in England Dartmouth received the news with dismay linked with "the just indignation which every friend to government feels for the Insult offered to the Constitution and the rebellious resistance to the authority of Parliament." The obstinate courage of George III now insisted on obedience or war. The crisis had come. The Canadians turned loose on New England would soon, it was said, teach it reason. On the other hand the colonial militia men knew that now they were liable to the dread penalties of treason for firing on the armed forces of the king. They laid siege to Boston. Only the British fleet saved it then and, within a year, the British flag was hauled down, never to be restored.

The Second Continental Congress met at Philadelphia on May 10, 1775, when passions were hot over the affair at Lexington. On June 17 occurred an even more exciting event, the fight at Bunker Hill. When Gage found that, during the previous night, the colonial militia had occupied this height that commanded Boston, he decided that they must be at once dislodged. Lexington might have been thought an accident, a misunderstanding; Bunker Hill was a deliberate battle. The prevailing opinion among Gage's officers was that if it should come to blows the colonial soldier who could run fastest would count himself happiest. The British soldiers who charged on that hot afternoon in June up the low eminence carried a heavy kit for camping at the top and, thus burdened, they stumbled over land soft from recent ploughing and cumbered by high fences and stone walls. As the British toiled up the slope the colonial defenders waited until they could see the whites of the eyes of the advancing men and they were told to aim especially at the officers, easily known by their richer dress. When other ammunition failed the colonial militia loaded their muskets with old nails and angular pieces of iron. Behind the charging British were the smoke and roaring flames of the village of Charlestown which they had set on fire because of shots from the houses. In front were the well-defended colonial entrenchments. In a fury of emotion anxious people in Boston watched the fight from windows, house-tops and steeples. Abigail Adams, knowing that the attack was imminent, lay awake through the night and during the day that followed listened to the roar of cannon and of bursting shells that caused incessant rattling in the windows of the houses. Howe, who commanded the attack, said that he had never seen regular troops behave better than this colonial militia. Though the British occupied the hill, the slaughter, especially of British officers, was greater than old soldiers had seen even on the battlefields of Europe. Of three thousand British a thousand fell and the victors on that day ought to have learned that amateurs in war, ignorant of the niceties of professional military discipline and etiquette, had yet in some way learned how to fight. The British victory was in results a defeat. It did not end the siege of Boston that endured to the day of its surrender to Washington.

Meanwhile the Continental Congress was preparing for war by creating a Continental Army under a commander-in-chief. While Massachusetts had fiery zeal, there was fear that remoter colonies might hold back. Especially was it desirable to connect so distant and important a colony as Virginia with the struggle. Accordingly, on June 15, John Adams, from Massachusetts, rose and moved that the Congress should adopt as its own the army at Cambridge,

Massachusetts, holding General Gage in Boston, and that it should name a general. He added that he knew of one man supremely fit to fill the post—George Washington, from Virginia. Adams says that while he was speaking Washington was sitting near the door and that, as soon as he heard his name mentioned, he darted out of the room. John Hancock, of Massachusetts, who was in the chair, himself desired the post, and Adams noted the "mortification and resentment" in his face when the motion was made. Obviously, however, the fit man had been named and George Washington became the leader of the colonial armies.

Twenty years earlier Washington had taken part in Braddock's ill-starred attempt to drive the French from the Ohio Valley and had been disgusted by what he called the "dastardly behaviour" of some British regular troops. From that time the Virginian youth had been widely known as a soldier and now in the Congress he was the only member who appeared habitually in uniform. Though he served with zeal on the committees dealing with military matters, in tastes and habits he was like the better type of English squire—a country gentleman, loving rural life, well-to-do, methodical, intensely patriotic and self-reliant. His patriotism was wholly American. He had never been in England and had few family ties with the mother country. Boston and the West Indies were the farthest points to which he had travelled from home.

As soon as appointed Washington left Philadelphia for Boston and on the way learned of the bloody fight at Bunker Hill. Recruits were marching to Boston from distant points, from Virginia, Pennsylvania, and Maryland, as well as from nearer places in Connecticut and New Jersey. Along the country roads they tramped usually without uniform. Some carried tomahawks and scalping knives and wore leggings and mocassins in Indian style. They were

rough and angular and little used to discipline, more a
rabble than an army, but they were in deadly earnest. Now,
for more than a year, Boston had been under punishment
that involved acute suffering, and a furious passion was in
the hearts of these rough men. They had no means of considering which side was the more in the right, but they had
an intense belief that now they were fighting for freedom
to live. A symbol of their passion was abhorrence of tea.
To drink it was treason to liberty. Against the use of tea
they made solemn leagues and covenants. They swore
mighty oaths that they would neither "import it, nor buy
it, nor sell it, nor drink it nor have anything whatever to
do with it excepting to curse it." Even when famished
and fainting in the wilderness a patriot would scorn re-
freshment from a cup of tea, that "detestable plant, that
pestilential herb." No statesmen ever committed a more
foolish act that that of the rulers of Britain when they
aroused all this fury about tea. On the hats or breasts of
many of these warriors was roughly pinned the legend
"Liberty or Death." Philip Freneau interpreted their
thoughts:

> "To arms! to arms! and let the trusty sword
> Decide who best deserves the hangman's cord;
> Nor think the hills of Canada too bleak
> When desperate freedom is the prize you seek."

Washington's army was well fitted to arouse the contempt of the professional soldier who could not read the
deep purpose in the hearts of this ungainly array. Some
five months after Washington had taken command before
Boston, Benjamin Thompson, a loyalist in Boston who
later became famous as Count Rumford, described the
colonial besiegers to Lord George Germain. The men wore
the wretched clothing that each provided for himself. Unlike the British regiments they had no women to do the
washing and as they were not used to this work they let

their linen rot on their backs and were "as dirty a set of mortals as ever disgraced the name of soldier." The filthy mode of life and the lack of accustomed vegetable food produced malignant disorders. Soon many were heartily sick of the service and, when they could, went off to their homes carrying both their arms and their maladies, with the result that epidemics broke out in the villages. The military equipment was inevitably bad. There were few cannon. The men usually owned their own weapons. Discipline was difficult, since officers and men were often of similar stations in life and old neighbours. The colonies, unused to coöperation, were jealous and critical of each other. New Englanders thought Washington too severe to themselves, too partial to his Virginians, while men from the south complained, for their part, that the army had too large a proportion from New England. Virginian officers, gentlemen by birth and station, were shocked at the free manners of New England. One day at Cambridge, when men from Massachusetts were enjoying the sport of jeering at Virginians, passions so flamed up that riot and bloodshed were imminent. A thousand men were involved in the *mêlée* when Washington dashed in, seized a man by the throat with each hand, pressed back his victims through the crowd and awed all by his stern commands.

CHAPTER XIV

THE COLONIES INVADE CANADA

Boston and Quebec, the centres of rival interests in the early colonial era, remain opposed during the struggle of the American Revolution with this strange turn in their relations that the English colonies who attack Quebec are, in the end, allied with France, while the defenders of Quebec are the British rulers of a French population. Carleton, the governor of Canada, had been absent on leave during the four years preceding the passing of the Quebec Act but now, since the autumn of 1774, he is back at his post. During the fourteen years of British rule at Quebec the court of the governor had lacked a woman's grace but now this was to be changed for on his leisurely leave Carleton had found a wife. A romantic tradition is preserved in his family that he was a frequent guest at the house of the Earl of Effingham and had asked for the hand of one of his sisters. When the Lady Anne rejected him because she was in love with his nephew, whom she married, Carleton took a hint that the Lady Maria, a younger sister, might accept him. The marriage took place in 1772 and seems to have been happy enough, though the groom was nearing fifty and the bride in her teens. Lady Maria did her duty to her country in bearing Carleton two daughters and nine sons, six of whom, soldiers like their father, died on active service. Her brother, the Earl of Effingham, was a Whig who, in contrast with Carleton, resigned from the army rather than fight his colonial fellow-countrymen, and was so eccentric and perverse as to be the friend of Wilkes. Lady Maria

Carleton, who had been brought up at Versailles, understood and admired the ceremony of the church and the court in France in their great days. At Quebec she kept up impressive formality and knew how to receive with tact the sensitive French seigneurs and ecclesiastics. The Ursuline nuns expressed their delight at her attentions and prayed but, as they deplored, without success, for her conversion.

A scene in London shows how the heart of the capital was disturbed by the attitude to the colonies. It was in June, 1774, that official London had protested against the Quebec Act and now again on April 10, 1775, a few days before the fight at Lexington, the Lord Mayor, followed by a much liveried company, waited on George III in person at St. James's Palace, to petition him to dismiss the ministers responsible for the strife with the colonies. They added a renewed protest against despotism at Quebec. George III himself read an answer that was not conciliatory. He was, he said, astonished at the demands of the petitioners; he was resolved to continue the policy already begun. There was a dead silence and then, with low bows, the Lord Mayor and his company left the king's presence. Across the sea at Montreal there was a more vulgar protest. Under a canopy on the grand parade stood a statue of George III and during the night previous to the coming into force of the Act a mitre had been placed on his head, no doubt at a rakish angle to his face which had been painted black; around his neck was a rosary of potatoes and in his hand was a cross bearing the words *"Voilà le Pape du Canada et le sot Anglais"*—the Pope of Canada and the English fool. The outrage, declared the military, could not be due to the French Canadians for they would not deride the pope; one of those accursed traders from the English colonies must have done it. The bad feeling caused fights and riots. Clearly the traders would not give

Carleton strong support. When he offered them commissions in the forces to be raised, he had many refusals and the Quebec Act was given as the cause.

The Continental Congress, to justify its name, tried to include both Nova Scotia and Canada, and in both it failed. Nova Scotia was held partly by the military strength centred in the fortress at Halifax, but even more by the British command of the sea. Canada, on the other hand, could be reached by land. Accordingly, the Congress sent a confidential agent to Canada. This envoy, with the unromantic name of John Brown, had a terrible journey in winter by way of Lake Champlain. A man of education and of personal charm he was well received by the Montreal traders in March, 1775. Hostilities had not yet begun and Carleton, always deliberate, checked Brown so little that he circulated freely in both French and English the message of the Continental Congress urging revolt. He addressed at a coffee house a meeting of the leading British traders, some of whom pleaded that, in spite of their good wishes, they were helpless slaves under the tyrannical governor who had British soldiers and many French Canadians ready to coerce them. Brown believed that the heart of commercial Montreal was with him and he went away in chastened hopefulness that Canada would be on his side in the great struggle.

Active warfare, involving Canada, soon followed, Fort Ticonderoga, lying on a neck of land between Lake George and Lake Champlain, had been left weak, in spite of Carleton's urging that it was the key to Canada. When the fight at Lexington made war imminent, Benedict Arnold, a shrewd Connecticut trader of respectable ancestry but whom Carleton calls contemptuously a "horse jockey," hurried to Cambridge and secured leave from the local committee to seize Ticonderoga. Ethan Allen, a Vermont colonel of militia, was, however, ahead of him, and Arnold, denied

the chief command, joined Allen as a volunteer. At Ticonderoga the British garrison of fewer than fifty men had
heard little, if anything, of hostilities when, in the early
morning of May 10, three weeks after Lexington, Ethan
Allen, backed by two hundred and fifty men who had crept
up in the night, summoned the unsuspecting garrison. To
a half-dressed officer who appeared at the head of a stair
he cried out "You damned old rat, come down." When
asked in whose name he demanded the surrender he said,
according to his probably embroidered narrative written
many years later "In the name of the great Jehovah and
the Continental Congress." If surrender was not immediate no man, woman or child should, he said, remain alive.
Most of the garrison were made prisoners in their beds and
what Carleton feared came to pass at the outset of the
appeal to arms; the way to the heart of Canada was in
control of the rebellious colonies. From Ticonderoga it
was easy for Allen to go in boats down Lake Champlain to
the River Richelieu. Within ten days, he was actually at
St. John's, twenty miles from Montreal, demanding aid
from all "Lovers of Liberty." Panic spread through the
whole Canadian country-side. Allen soon went back to the
lake but already his venture had made it clear that the
Canadians would not stand together to resist invasion.

As Carleton had feared, war had now come and this
reality so obsessed his mind that his policy became purely
military. He had long believed that the security of Canada
lay in the power of the seigneurs and the clergy to lead
their people against any menace from their ancient enemies
in the English colonies. Accordingly, on June 9, 1775, a
few days before the bitter fighting at Bunker Hill, he proclaimed martial law and brought Canada under the despotic
rule of the soldier. Carleton found opinion among priests
and seigneurs wholly with the British. On May 22, 1775, the
Bishop of Quebec issued a *Mandement* full of grateful expres-

sions to George III for concessions to the French and urging
his people to be deaf to the lure of American invaders. In a
letter to one of the clergy the bishop met the sneer that he
had abandoned his own race and become an Englishman
by saying that, since he had taken the oath of allegiance
to George III, he was in effect English, bound to be such
by every sacred obligation. Canadians who joined the invaders were to be placed under the ban of the church.
The clergy might not perform the marriage ceremony for
a rebel. Those aiding the Americans were not to have the
sacraments, even in case of mortal illness, until they had
made public retraction and reparation. Those who died
unrepentant were not to be buried in holy ground except
by the bishop's special permission. Even then the body was
not to be carried into the church and the priest was to
say no prayer at the grave. No masses were to be sung for
rebels who died unrepentant. The bishop charged that
the rebel Canadians were drunken thieves and plunderers who betrayed, pillaged, and murdered their fellow
Canadians.

In spite of the bishop's stand Carleton hoped in vain
for support from the Canadian peasantry. In truth he over-
estimated the authority of both seigneurs and clergy. It
was not the seigneurs but the captains of militia, now
abolished, who had made military levies under the French
régime; to the seigneur it was an unaccustomed service. As
to the clergy, their people respected their spiritual authority, but felt free to act for themselves in matters secular.
A dozen years of British rule had wrought a change. During the last days of the old régime the taxation of the
habitant had been so crushing that often his all had been
taken. Now almost the sole tax was on imports and, as he
himself made nearly everything that he used, he had little
to pay. Under France he had been forced into military
service. In the time of Pontiac when a call had come for

recruits, some three hundred Canadians had been enlisted to fight side by side with British soldiers against the Indians, but even then some measure of compulsion had been necessary in the Canadian villages. Since that time, however, unbroken peace had reigned and the peasantry seemed happy in a new security based on Carleton's friendly and sympathetic rule. It became a common threat of a habitant who thought himself wronged to say "I will go and tell General Carleton." It happened that, as it seemed, by design, a habitant ran into and upset a carriage containing the General's brother. He was promptly chastised, and when he uttered the usual threat to tell the General, the irate officer retorted "Tell him, too, that his brother did it." The habitant loved his new security and seemed docile. He had great respect for the king's authority and if flattered a little and given explicit orders he might obey. But, as Colonel Caldwell wrote from Quebec to Lady Chatham on June 2, 1775, only a mandate from that high source would draw the habitants from their farms "where they enjoy the comforts of ease and affluence." They could, indeed, hardly be expected to grow hot for a cause so abhorrent even to Lady Chatham that she wished her son, Lord Pitt, then in the army at Quebec, to avoid taking any part in the conflict if this was consistent with his military duty.

Since Canada was exporting nearly half a million bushels of wheat annually the farmer was sharing in the prosperity from enlarged markets. He had this reason to be grateful to his new rulers and Carleton expected loyalty and obedience. Dartmouth wrote to Carleton in July, 1775, to raise a force of six thousand men, instead of the three thousand previously ordered, and sent needed clothing, accoutrements, and arms. But Carleton could not secure three hundred. The habitant was now no longer submissive to former leaders whom he had obeyed under the French régime; "we are now subjects of England and do not

look upon ourselves as Frenchmen," the habitants at
Terrebonne said, when the seigneur, La Corne, summoned
them to military service. They added that if they agreed
to serve it should not be under him but under a British
officer or even a common soldier. When Carleton ordered
that in each parish the militia should muster and that fifteen men out of each hundred should take up arms, he was
not obeyed. Often recruiting officers met with threatening
hostility in the parishes. In some districts the peasantry
declared their readiness to fight if Carleton would promise
that the Quebec Act should be repealed. That they had
been "wantonly and most cruelly" deprived of their liberty,
many peasants in all parts of the province proclaimed.
From one parish a threatening seigneur, who insisted on
the old service, was forced to take refuge in Montreal.
When, at Berthier, an important seigniory, the seigneur
tried to enforce the old French military system, the peasants
gathered round a wayside cross and made solemn oath not
to take up arms against the revolting colonists. They would
not fight, they said there and elsewhere, "to defend a pack
of rascally pensioners of the Crown." Even after the Americans were nearing Montreal, not a French Canadian had
enlisted. In September, 1775, Carleton spent a night with
a seigneur at Three Rivers. An armed man was on guard
before the door and when Carleton realized that this sentinel
was a Canadian he gave him a guinea. "Here," he said, "is
the first Canadian whom I have had the honour of finding
in arms."

No doubt in respect of secular affairs the seigneur was
still held in some awe in the parishes while in regard to
the hopes and fears of the unseen world the priest had a
strong hold. Even for the church, however, the habitant's
tongue was sharp. When the Bishop of Quebec issued his
pastoral letter promising indulgence for taking up arms
against the Americans and threatening those who refused

with excommunication, some rather ribald ballads were soon in circulation. Bishop Briand, it was said, aimed to be a new and greater St. Bernard, leading a crusade. If the Canadians would follow him cheerfully to Boston and have their throats cut, they might be certain of an eternal home in the realms of light. From all over the province came vigorous protests against the bishop's attitude and insinuations that, since he received two hundred pounds a year from the government, he was anxious to please his masters. It should be his sole office, they said, to ordain priests and to be an example to his people of mildness, moderation, and holy living. Agents in the interest of the revolted colonies had the skill to invoke the superstitions of the ignorant people, not to support but to oppose their spiritual leaders. In every parish they circulated terrifying rumours: Carleton was playing the harsh despot, building barracks by forced labour without pay, putting defaulters in prison, compelling the farmers' wives to weave cloth for his men, allowing drunken soldiers to insult them, and so on. By one tale he had been bribed to hand over Canada to the detested Spaniards. According to another a vast horde of men to aid the colonial cause was coming up the St. Lawrence. These invaders possessed charmed lives that made them bullet proof. It was added that in despair Carleton was working what havoc he could; the only chance of the habitants to escape being burned alive by him was to join the colonial side.

In consequence of this opposition Carleton soon realized that he had both over-estimated the influence of the priest and the seigneur, and underestimated the effect of what he called the poisoned hypocrisy and lies of the English colonists. The attitude of the Canadians so disgusted him that on September 21, 1775, he wrote to Lord Dartmouth regarding concessions to the French: "I have seen good cause to repent my having ever recommended

the Habeas Corpus Act and the English Criminal Laws."
The Canadian simply would not fight. "I think," he wrote,
"there is nothing to fear from them, while we are in a
state of prosperity, and nothing to hope for when in distress . . . The multitude is influenced only by hopes of
gain, or fear of punishment." At a later time Carleton
denied that he had ever placed much hope in the Canadians.
On May 29, 1777, he wrote from Quebec to Burgoyne; "If
government laid any great stress upon assistance from the
Canadians for carrying on the present war, it surely was
not upon information from me. . . . These people had
been governed with too loose a Rein for many years and
had imbibed too much the American spirit of Licentiousness and Independence administered by a numerous and
turbulent Faction to be suddenly restored to a proper and
desirable subordination." This was one way of explaining
a natural indifference on the part of the Canadians to what
was not their quarrel. Though they were ready to sell supplies and to furnish guides to the American invaders, they
would have been equally ready to supply a loyalist army.
Nor can they be blamed. Was it to be expected that they
should feel any affection for the cause of a nation, an age-
long enemy, that had mastered their land only a dozen
years earlier?

Meanwhile Canada loomed large in the plans of Washington. He feared its military possibilities. The British by
their command of the sea could make Quebec a great arsenal and from this base they could strike at the colony
of New York by way of Lake Champlain. To John Adams
as to Washington it was vital to secure Canada; "In the
Hands of our Enemies it would enable them to inflame all
the Indians upon the Continent." Accordingly, Canada
must be won and the leader chosen to do this was Philip
Schuyler, a great landowner who belonged to the old Dutch

aristocracy of New York. He had served as a colonial officer, had been present at the disastrous British defeat at Ticonderoga in 1758, and now was one of the four major-generals serving the Continental Congress. His second in command was Brigadier-General Richard Montgomery. Like Carleton, Montgomery was an Irishman, and it was an odd chance that brought into prominence as opposing leaders two men whose families had been neighbours in Ireland. Montgomery, the son of a member of Parliament, had served in the British army that conquered Canada and had been present at the capture of Montreal in 1760. Later he and Carleton had served together at Havana. After the war he had returned to England but, seeing no career in the British army, he settled in 1772 in the colony of New York where he married Miss Livingston, a member of one of its conspicuous families, keen on the colonial side. Montgomery was a Whig. He had known Burke and Fox in England and it was inevitable that he should take the Whig view and support the colonial cause. Yet, as he said, it was "sadly and reluctantly" that he served against Britain.

While it seems inconsistent with the enthusiasm for liberty that colonies rebelling against coercion should try to coerce Canada into joining them, they had a two-fold answer: one that the British would use Canada as a base; the other that they would come as liberators to the Canadians, held down by British power but longing to be free. On September 5 Schuyler with about fifteen hundred men was at Isle aux Noix where Lake Champlain discharges into the Richelieu River and there he issued in tolerable French an appeal to *"nos frères"* the Canadians. The ministry was, he said, preparing chains for them too and no differences of race or religion should keep them from joining in the fight for liberty. Nothing unwelcome to them was planned; as brothers they should all unite to repel the insults and outrages of a brutal tyranny. Soon after Schuyler issued this appeal, illness caused his absence from the army and Montgomery led the invasion of Canada. He offered the Canadians good pay and the hope of plunder and promised freedom from taxes that in truth few paid. By placards posted secretly on the doors of parish churches he promised to each man enlisting with the Americans two hundred acres of land in any American province and forty more for a wife and for each child. Some disbanded British soldiers were thus enticed into joining Montgomery and also a few Canadians, though for the most part these held aloof from military service. Six parishes on the Richelieu River, with fifteen hundred fighting men, renounced allegiance to George III but few, if any, joined the invader.

Ethan Allen who had taken Ticonderoga was a guerilla officer under Montgomery. Certain that rapid action similar to that of his former success would win Canada, he pushed on in advance of his leader in hope of the glory of taking Montreal. Part of the force was to cross the broad river above Montreal, part below the town, and the two forces were to meet before it, the plan followed by Amherst fifteen years earlier. Allen counted in vain, however, on the readiness of the Canadians to join him. They doubted his success and feared British vengeance for treason. Though the plan to cross the river above Montreal failed, below the city Allen was able to cross to the north shore with about a hundred and twenty men. His rashness had its due result; it was easy for Colonel Prescott, in command at Montreal, to capture him and his men. Prescott put him in irons as a traitor and later sent him to England for trial with the assurance that he would "grace a halter at Tyburn." It was, however, no part of British policy to practise this severity. In the end Allen was exchanged and he lived to publish a lurid account of his treatment that helped to inflame colonial opinion.

Meanwhile the invasion of the main army was making

startling progress. From Carleton down the Canadian leaders seem, on the one hand, to have doubted the reality of war and, on the other, whether, if the war was real, they could rely upon the support of the civilian population. The result was the paralysis of initiative. Montgomery's army was badly trained and badly equipped, the kind of rabble that disciplined soldiers might have cut to pieces. It had come down Lake Champlain from Ticonderoga for the most part in unwieldy open bateaux carrying perhaps a small square sail but rowed with heavy oars. Sixteen years earlier Amherst, advancing with a trained army by this route, was so dismayed by the defence in front of him that he paused at Crown Point to build a costly fort, with part of the ditch hewn out of the solid limestone rock. In the end, however, he had retired rather than face the French defences at the head of the Richelieu River that flows into the St. Lawrence below Montreal. The contrast in Montgomery's invasion does little credit to the defenders of Canada. He made a triumphant advance to St. Johns, a fort on the upper waters of the Richelieu where Colonel Preston, in command, had some six hundred trained men. In the river by the fort lay two schooners, one of them the "Royal Savage," a fighting vessel carrying twelve brass four and six pounders. Though she was not quite ready for service, the work of a few days could have equipped her and made her capable, so the colonial leaders later admitted, of destroying all their shipping on the lake and of forcing the soldiers, huddled in the open boats, to surrender. Preston, however, made no attack but shut himself up in the fort; the Americans captured the two schooners and, not pausing to molest St. Johns, swept on down the river to Chambly. This was a well-built stone fort with square bastions at each corner. Though the officer in command, Major Stopford, son of an English peer, had only a small garrison of eighty men he had stout walls, guns and ammunition enough at least to cause delay. Instead he made no effort to destroy his stores, and surrendered after a day and a half. His six tons of gunpowder and his cannon were precisely what Montgomery needed when he turned back up the river to St. Johns. Meanwhile to face the crisis Carleton was hurrying to Montreal from Quebec. Yet though Quebec was, at least for the time, safe, he feared to take with him any of its defenders and arrived at Montreal all but alone. There he found fewer than two hundred regular soldiers and he had no men to send to the aid of St. Johns or Chambly.

Montgomery describes the motley force with which he laid siege to a garrison of British regulars in St. Johns. There was, he says, little sense of discipline. Every man considered himself a general fit to command. Those from New York were the sweepings of the streets while the New Englanders, who made up most of the force, were the "worst stuff imaginable for soldiers," lazy, homesick, feigning sickness, though he could not find any seriously ill. Few had uniforms. An occasional officer had indeed a red coat or a cocked hat, from previous service in the British army, but most officers were distinguished only by a ribbon of a special colour. Hardly two men in the ranks were dressed alike, except those in the buckskin of the backwoods. They had this advantage that they were accustomed like the Indians to fight from cover and were well armed and skilful with musket and bayonet. They had also artillery, taken at Ticonderoga and Chambly, which soon caused discomfort in the fort. No help came from Carleton in Montreal; he had none to send. Soon the garrison was starving and Preston had to ask Montgomery for terms. In reply he praised the valour of the garrison but, when he added the insulting wish that it had been in a better cause, Preston replied that unless the words were withdrawn he should fight on and neither give nor take quarter. Montgomery withdrew the words and on November 3, with the honours of war, Preston's fine force marched out through lines of seeming ragamuffins, a bitter humiliation for British regular soldiers.

After victory at St. Johns the cry was "To Montreal" and the invaders moved on to the St. Lawrence, crossed it both above and below the city and from all sides closed in, exactly as the British under Amherst had done. The parishes received them as triumphant liberators. Carleton meanwhile had remained in Montreal, chafing and all but helpless. He had fewer than two hundred regular soldiers and he could depend on neither the English traders nor the Canadians. His Indians had deserted and the militia at Montreal refused to muster. When the Americans reached the outskirts and the inhabitants received them with joy, sadly enough Carleton realized that he must abandon the town and get away, if he could, with his little force. While passage to Quebec by land was barred, he had a few small ships with which to attempt it by the river. Accordingly, on November 10, a week after the fall of St. Johns, he marched his men to the wharf at Montreal, bade farewell to loyal inhabitants who had gathered, and set sail with a fair wind.

Though Carleton's military capacity was never tested in a pitched battle, he was skilful and obstinate in the crisis of defence that he now faced. The eleven small ships carrying about one hundred and thirty regular soldiers under Colonel Prescott had neared Sorel when some ran aground. Nature had turned against them in a strong wind from the east. Prescott seems then to have fallen an easy victim to the wiles of a colonial officer, Major Brown. As the ships lay off the shore Brown sent an officer to demand their surrender. To show that resistance was useless he offered to allow a British officer to survey his battery. When the officer landed Brown asked him to wait half an hour until the arrival from Chambly of some thirty-two pounders then only a half a mile away. He added that if his first battery should fail, he had a grand battery at the mouth of the Richelieu River with which he could infallibly sink all of Prescott's vessels. Though in fact he had no cannon mounted at either place, Prescott's envoy reported that defence was useless and eleven ships, so the invaders jeered, hauled down their flag to "a single gondola." Prescott's vessels were later useful for carrying the colonial army down to the siege of Quebec and his soldiers became prisoners of war.

Carleton, however, was not among the prisoners. When a resourceful Canadian, Captain Bouchette, offered to carry him in a row-boat down the river past danger, under cover of the damp, dark night of November 16–17, Carleton disguised himself as a peasant, dropped over the side of the ship and floated down stream in the boat with one officer, a sergeant and Bouchette himself as companions. At Berthier, the danger point, colonial bivouac fires blazed on both shores and threw their light far across the water. The refugees could hear the sentinel's shout "All's Well," and the barking of dogs, as the boat, with its occupants lying at the bottom, slipped past, looking like a log drifting in the swift current. It was paddled for miles by the hands of its prostrate occupants reaching over the sides. At Three Rivers Carleton thought he had passed the point of danger but, within a few hours after he had landed and had lain down for rest in the house of a Canadian gentleman, the Americans occupied the house. The tradition is preserved that Carleton, awakened hurriedly, rose in his peasant's dress and went out past the unsuspecting American guard at the door. Again he set out in the skiff. At the foot of the Richelieu rapid lay the armed brig, the *Fell*, and there he found safety. On November 19, nine days after leaving Montreal, he reached Quebec. Cannon boomed a welcome. Among the loyal there was, we are told, "unspeakable joy," and among "the abettors of Sedition and Rebellion, utter Dismay" because the trusted leader was now at the post of danger.

When on that November day Carleton was able to look out from the walls of Quebec to the Plains of Abraham where he had fought in Wolfe's last battle, the contrast in the scene might well have staggered even a sluggish imagination. Over Quebec now floated the British flag instead of the *fleurs-de-lis,* but out on the plains was a besieging army composed of men of English blood in arms against their king and bent on taking from him a prize that some of them had helped to win for him. Carleton's flight to Quebec was due to a colonial force closing in on Montreal, and now he found such a force before Quebec itself. Their leader was a brave and resourceful man, whose name yet carries with it the stigma of base and calculated treason. He was Benedict Arnold. His quick mind had planned and shared in the sudden taking in May of Ticonderoga where first in this civil war the British flag had been hauled down. In the following advance into Canada other leaders of higher military rank were given the command and Arnold turned to another plan. He would win the glory of taking the famous fortress of Quebec. Washington was almost obsessed by the idea that to have Canada was vital and now gave support and strict instructions for the expedition. He warned Arnold "as you value your own safety and honour" to treat the Canadians as friends and brothers and to respect their religion. He was to come not as a conqueror but as a deliverer.

Arnold was to go by a route well known but difficult. Southward into the Atlantic where now is the city of Portland, in Maine, flows the Kennebec River, while from near its source flows northward into the St. Lawrence a little above Quebec the Chaudière. They rise in the same rocky, swampy high lands and together form a route, up one river and down another from Quebec to the sea, a distance of nearly two hundred miles in direct line. On both rivers were rapids past which, however, Indians and hardy Frenchmen had carried their canoes during a hundred years. In the upper reaches the rivers forced their winding ways through a wild, barren region to-day traversed by railway lines but then uninhabited.

The Maine forest was gay with autumn tints when Arnold started up the Kennebec with about twelve hundred men to reach and, so he hoped, to surprise Quebec. We see that the eminent colonial families were not all on the king's side for many of the best names were on Arnold's roster. Young Aaron Burr from New Jersey, a youth of nineteen and grandson of the most famous colonial theologian, Jonathan Edwards, was destined to reach Quebec with Arnold, to become in time Vice-President of the United States and to inflict deadly injury on his country by killing in a duel Alexander Hamilton, perhaps its greatest statesman. Rough men from the frontier were there too, some of them so skilled that, while on the run, they could load their guns and hit a target seven inches in diameter at a distance of two hundred and fifty yards. In most of Arnold's men, young and eager, burned the spirit of the hymn of the Revolution:

> " 'Tis God that girds our armour on;
> And all our just designs fulfils;
> Through Him our feet can safely run
> And nimbly climb the steepest hills."

Many steep hills they had, in truth, to climb. They set out from the seaboard in ships to the head of navigation where now stands Augusta, the capital of Maine, then called Fort Western, and there took to their boats. Though September sunshine may well have aided a cheery sense of adventure, rains soon made the Kennebec River a turbulent flood. While the route had been tolerable for Indians and other earlier travellers who had light canoes, it was otherwise for Arnold's heavy bateaux. They had been built hastily, perhaps of green wood, often by unskilled hands. They leaked interminably and many were the curses of his men on "the villains" who had made them: "they are accessory to the death of our brethren who expired in the wilderness. May Heaven reward them according to their deeds." The men had to drag arms, kegs of powder and other stores, and also these heavy boats, over portages, through swamps and tangled woods, up and down hills, and often to wade in water up to the breast and, in the end, through snow. They had to pass bitterly cold nights in bogs where hardly a dry spot was to be found and arms and ammunition were ruined by the water.

By the time that they had reached the desolate high land on the other side of which the waters flowed northward to the St. Lawrence, provisions had so failed that the men ate even their own leather moccasins. Some starved to death and others were so broken by their hardships that Colonel Enos, Arnold's second in command, broke with his leader and turned back with some hundreds of dispirited men, nearly half the force. Though it looked like desertion, a later court martial found that conditions justified Enos's action. When, soon after this, Arnold left those with him free to save themselves, to turn back had become as dangerous as to advance. Arnold pressed on over the height of land to Lake Megantic in a region where he hoped for aid from Canadian frontiersmen but during thirty-one days he met no human being in that waste. The outlet of the lake, the Chaudière, was now, with autumn floods, a dangerous torrent. Leaving behind most of his men, including the weak and famished who made piteous protests that they should perish of cold and hunger, Arnold embarked on the rapid stream. At one swift stretch he dashed through foaming rapids and covered twenty miles in two hours; at another his boats swept over a waterfall and were upset. By the end of October, however, just when Montgomery was closing in on St. Johns, Arnold reached the Canadian settlements. At his urging the peasants went out with horses and brought to their cottages men found lying half dead in the snow and mire. A few Indians also helped. Rumours had spread of the coming of a great host and when Arnold's men appeared in their grey hunting suits, the Canadians mistook this clothing for linen (*toile*). As the report was repeated the word for linen was transformed into that for iron-plate (*tôle*) and ignorant peasants believed that a host of steel-clad warriors was advancing on Quebec. The army, numbering only about seven hundred, straggled in a long line down the east bank of the Chaudière, all of them ragged, some barefoot, some broken invalids.

On the 9th of November, the day before Carleton abandoned Montreal, Arnold reached the banks of the St. Lawrence and saw through the mist of a snow storm the dim heights of Quebec lying far across the great river. Only some five hundred of his men were fit for duty. His approach was known to Cramahé, in command at Quebec, who had an adequate supply of arms and at least twelve hundred loyal men. We may wonder that he did not destroy Arnold's weary force, ill-armed and ill-fed, as they straggled to the strand of the St. Lawrence. It appears, however, that he, like Carleton himself and the other officers facing Montgomery's advance on Montreal, was too uncertain of support to be aggressive. In Quebec itself Cramahé was not sure of the attitude of the Canadians or of the traders from the colonies and feared to go out lest he might find the gates closed to his return. As the crisis approached some citizens had withdrawn to the Island of Orleans and to other places in the surrounding country, where, prepared to shout for the side that might prove victorious, they awaited events. Cramahé removed what boats he had to the north shore, in the hope that Arnold would not be able to cross the dangerous river, swept by autumn winds and tidal currents.

Though two war-ships lay in the line of the crossing, on the dark night of November 14, Arnold reached the north shore in light bark canoes, paddled in some cases by friendly Indians. Sixteen years earlier Wolfe, moving too by night, had landed an army at the place henceforth to be known as Wolfe's Cove and at dawn had stood in brave array on the Heights of Abraham. Now Arnold landed at the same spot and in the morning he, too, mustered his army on those heights. Unlike Wolfe's it was shabby, ill-clothed and ill-armed. Most of the men had lost even their bayonets; they had little ammunition and no artillery. Yet such was the hardihood of Arnold that in the name of the united colonies he sent messengers to demand the instant surrender of the fortress of Quebec. Early in December the false report reached and cheered the Congress that Quebec had surrendered.

The Canadians had helped Arnold willingly; the trading class, many of them from the English colonies, were, he thought, so on his side that only a feeble garrison kept them from welcoming him as a deliverer. So much was he already, in his imagination, the master of Quebec that he threatened to lay a heavy hand on any one who should injure its inhabitants in person or in property. Naturally there was derision among the defenders of Quebec at such bluster from what they called a rebel band of plunderers thinking only of loot. No reply was sent to Arnold's florid messages. No meeting under a flag of truce was allowed; a group whom he sent to St. John's gate for a parley was fired on. The besiegers were outlaws with no title to the courtesies of war.

Though the habitants were ready to sell supplies to both

sides they, unlike the priests and seigneurs, had little zeal
for either. From Arnold they feared robbery and from
Carleton rigour for treason. Meanwhile Arnold was growing uneasy. The grim silence of the fortress from which
came no reply to his demands was itself disturbing and it
fortified rumours that a sortie in force was secretly preparing. Since Montreal was now securely in the control of
the invaders and the great flood of the St. Lawrence sweeping down nearly two hundred miles from Montreal to Quebec was open to their use, Arnold decided to wait for the
aid of these jubilant victors. It soon came. Montgomery
gathered what ships he could, among them the little fleet
lost by Carleton, and moved down the river. Companies
sent by land were well received in the villages. Arnold met
his leader at a point above Quebec and on December 4 the
united force began the long siege of the fortress. As yet
Montgomery had barely twelve or thirteen hundred of his
own countrymen. In addition were several hundred Canadians on whom, however, he could place little reliance. He
had only a few cannon and he lacked ammunition and
stores. The winter cold was already devastating and sickness was spreading. When smallpox broke out some of his
men exposed themselves to it purposely to escape the
dangers of fighting.

In Quebec, meanwhile, Carleton mustered some eighteen
hundred men of all ranks. He had four hundred sailors
from merchant ships and especially from the two British
war-ships *Lizard* and *Hunter* that soon were frozen in by
ice many feet thick. He had about four hundred trained
soldiers and about a thousand untrained Canadian militia
and civilians useful only for garrison duty. He knew that
time was on his side for Britain had command of the sea
and in the spring, could he hold out so long, succour would
come. On arrival he had warned the disloyal element to
withdraw and now he had to provide for a population in

all of about five thousand. While he had provisions enough, he lacked fuel and to secure it made occasional forays to near-by forests with success so scant that in many Quebec houses there was bitter cold during that winter. He repaired the walls and gates, posted his slender artillery, and waited, a policy suited to his patient character.

Quebec settled down to the fourth siege in its history. Montgomery extended his lines from Wolfe's Cove on the west to Beauport on the east and so had Quebec surrounded by land. He was, however, helpless to harass Quebec from the water. The great river with its raging tides, now flashing in the bright northern sunlight and now sullen under a cold wintry sky, was not friendly to the shivering force before Quebec. As the season advanced the frigid waters were dotted by floating blocks of ice and before the winter was over the frost made it a solid highway to the south shore. While the Canadians were ready to supply provisions to the invaders, this commerce lacked vitality since the inhabitants had little confidence in the paper promises to pay. Even amid the urgency of want we find patriotism denying itself one offered comfort. Tea had become the symbol of British oppression. While it is true that the scruples about tea of even austere John Adams went only so far as to prefer smuggled tea to that which had paid the hated British duty, these humbler patriots refused to drink it. "No, Madam, it is the ruin of my country," said a fainting soldier, when offered a bowl of tea by a kindly woman. "Poor deluded devils," said the British.

We find on each side the exasperation that marks this and usually all civil war. To Carleton, Montgomery deserved hanging. The only message that he would receive from him was an appeal to the king's mercy. When, in some way, a message reached him, he ordered a drummer to seize it with a pair of tongs and throw it in the fire. Montgomery had to shoot his demands into Quebec tied to an arrow. Once an old woman brought a message that remained of course unanswered. It was the gossip of the mess table in Quebec that the colonial officers were low ruffians. Of captured officers, a major proved to have been a blacksmith; among the captains were a butcher, a shoemaker and an inn-keeper. "Yet they all pretend to be gentlemen," says an astonished officer. Carleton's scornful demeanour angered Montgomery to frenzy that seems out of line with his dignified character and his training as a British officer. At first he professed contempt for the British, based upon what had happened during his advance to Montreal, when most of the influential people had seemed to welcome him. He believed that in Carleton's force of supposed ragamuffins there were not more than sixty regular soldiers. When smallpox raged in the American camp Montgomery believed that captured blankets had been deliberately infected. He wished, he said, to save Carleton from destruction and offered him a safe conduct to Europe. Carleton, he thought, must have such a sense of shame and disgrace as to wish to die. Montgomery reproached him for cruelty to prisoners, for firing upon a flag of truce, for "illiberal abuse" and "villainous falsehoods" about the noble deliverers of the Canadians who had come to uproot tyranny and to give liberty and security to the down-trodden. His men, he said, were so incensed that he could hardly restrain them until he could get his batteries in position. He derided Carleton's folly in opposing troops "accustomed to Success," for whom the more danger, the more glory. If, before surrendering, Carleton should destroy stores, "By Heaven, there will be no mercy shown." With Quebec taken, "all is ours."

Before the besiegers, ill-lodged, sometimes ill-fed, suffering from intense cold, rose the proud mass of Quebec's defences glittering with snow and ice in the winter sunshine. Drifts in the town rose twenty feet high and so banked the first storeys of many houses as to permit the use of the windows of the second storey as doors. In the ditch before the walls snow now lay thirty feet deep, up to the muzzle of the guns. The ground was so hard frozen that Montgomery was unable to dig trenches; his "earthworks" were made of snow drenched with water and frozen into a solid mass. He wrote to Congress that he could batter the town into ruin when he pleased, but when the bombardment began on December 10 it proved so feeble that a contemptuous diarist in Quebec wrote that the rebel cannon killed one boy, wounded one soldier, and broke the leg of a turkey.

Montgomery was in a hurry. Congress believed that it had been only necessary for him to appear before Quebec to bring surrender. His reputation was at stake and, relying partly on discontent in the garrison and on civilian unrest, he decided to take the place by assault. Under existing rules of war a town taken by assault was subject to pillage and massacre. Montgomery did not threaten massacre but he told his men that they should have the plunder of Quebec; one hundredth part, to be sold at auction, was to be at his own disposal to reward those conspicuous for activity and courage. The terms of service of some of his men expired at the end of the year and as they intended to leave at once for home he planned his attack for the very last day of the year 1775. While a small force should feint a direct frontal attack on the walls of the upper town a larger one from the east under Arnold and another from the west under Montgomery would advance along the strand of the river, meet in the lower town and then push up the winding Mountain Street to the upper town.

The night of December 30 was wild with a blinding snow-storm. Quebec feared that it might conceal an attacking force and was specially alert. Deserters, it is said, had revealed the plan of attack. About four in the morning of December 31, when enemy signals were seen, the bells rang out in Quebec and drums beat an alarm. Arnold, advancing from the east, succeeded in destroying the barricade at the Sault-au-Matelôt, and reached the heart of the lower town where, however, he was checked with heavy loss. From the west Montgomery advanced along the edge of the St. Lawrence by the lower road from Wolfe's Cove. The night was so dark and the snow so blinding that the men stumbled over cakes of ice strewn on the shore by the tide. At the post, Près-de-ville, where Cape Diamond towered over the narrow road between the high cliff and the icy river, a guard of fifty defenders behind a barricade blocked the way. Suddenly, when the assailants, in a thick mass, were seen in the dim light to be near, the word "Fire!" rang out and four cannon and many muskets crashed into the advancing column. Montgomery and a dozen others in the lead fell dead; the rest turned and fled. Fresh snow continued to fall and when at daybreak a searching party went out they found a frozen hand protruding from the drift at the barrier. It was the hand of Montgomery. Arnold, too, had been defeated and wounded in desperate fighting. The Americans had some seven hundred and fifty casualties; many fought with the words, "Liberty or Death" pinned on white strips on their caps.

These events at the dawn of the momentous year, 1776, caused among the enemies in England of the coercion of the colonies not delight at the British victory but regret that a brave officer had fallen in a noble cause. A public subscription was started for "our beloved American fellow-subjects," "inhumanly murdered by the king's troops," because they preferred death to slavery. We are told that in Parliament a former companion of Montgomery "shed abundance of tears" as he described their friendship. It was, it seems, at this time that Carleton's brother-in-law, the Earl of Effingham, resigned his commission rather than

serve against his fellow subjects. Burke and Chatham called
Montgomery a martyr in the cause of liberty. Even Lord
North admired him as a "brave, humane and generous
soldier," misled into becoming a rebel. To be a rebel, protested Charles Fox, was no certain mark of disgrace; all the
champions of liberty had been rebels. In the colonies sorrow for the dead leader inspired not despair but the resolu-
tion to win ultimate success. Washington wrote from Cambridge on January 27, 1776, that Quebec must be won; the
glorious work must be accomplished in the course of the
winter. Arnold, sufficiently recovered from his wounds to
take command, replied from before Quebec, perhaps with
truth, that half of the citizens of Quebec would open the
gates but for Carleton's strict discipline. He added that
Carleton could have little confidence "or he would not
suffer a blockade and every distress of a siege by 700 men."
When, in time, Arnold went away, he was succeeded by
General Wooster, a rough, arbitrary, illiterate man from
Connecticut. He failed to obey Washington's counsel and
denounced the Roman Church. Every one of its priests,
he said, preached damnation to all who would not arm
against the Americans. Montgomery's failure, he said, had
so revived Carleton's cruel resolve that he had hanged sixty
suspected Canadians on the ramparts of Quebec, without
giving them time even to pray for the mercy of God.

During the winter of 1775–76 naval and military circles in
England were getting ready to conquer to unwilling obedience many hundred thousands of English colonists, scattered for a thousand miles along the Atlantic sea-board.
It is hard now to imagine it possible that any one in authority in England could have believed that a problem of
taxation as between the mother country and her colonies
could be solved by an appeal to arms. To-day such a
method would excite only ridicule, and it is also true that

even a century and a half ago opinion on taxation, though not on the control of trade, was as advanced in the English colonies as now it is at Ottawa. In vain, however, did Burke, Chatham and other leaders denounce the policy favoured by the king. Young Charles James Fox was now their strenuous ally, having abandoned, so the king said, "every principle of common honour and honesty." The king and his ministers, bent on coercion, believed that a quick, heavy blow would solve the difficulty.

Accordingly there was activity at military arsenals; much hammering at navy yards in the building and repair of ships. The coercion was to be thorough. Three armies were to go out: one to Quebec in the north; one to the Carolinas in the south; the third to wrest New York from the colonial army. British policy had been stiffened when, soon after the beginning of open warfare in 1775, the kindly, the good Dartmouth, growing uneasy in his mind and unequal to tasks of war, had taken a minor post in the ministry and in November had handed over the office of Secretary for the Colonies to Lord George Germain. Even Dartmouth's mild temper had yielded to the ignorant cry that to use overpowering force was the only remedy to cure disobedience in the colonies and Germain adopted it with stark conviction. We shall hear much of Germain for, by an odd twist in the organization of the government, it was he, the colonial secretary, who directed the war that was to end in the greatest disaster in Britain's history. He was able, brave, in spite of his stigma of cowardice in one phase of his career, a strong, active man, and with these qualities an arrogant upholder of colonial subordination. When he faced the responsibilities he made one quick decision. It was that, with Boston besieged, Canada invaded, and the Congress defiant, Gage, the commander-in-chief in America, was "in a position of too great importance for his talents." Soon therefore Gage was gone and Sir William Howe took his place. We part from Gage with some regret. Perhaps, as his subordinate at Boston, Burgoyne, charged, he left too many things undone but he had been tactful and moderate—more so than Amherst—in dealing with the native tribes at the time of Pontiac's rising and he showed courtesy and restraint in the early days of the Revolution.

William Howe had fought with Wolfe at Louisbourg and won high praise from that exacting soldier; by some accounts it was he who led the twenty-four volunteers who dragged themselves up the steep cliff at Quebec in the early morning of Wolfe's last day, surprised the guard at the top, and made possible the victory that won Canada. Howe had been present at the surrender of Montreal in the next year and by that time had made a high reputation. In 1758 an elder brother, the third Lord Howe, had been sent by Pitt to America to stiffen his leader, the futile Abercrombie, in that year's campaign against French Canada. Near Ticonderoga, in a chance skirmish, this brilliant, loved young officer had been killed and Massachusetts had reared a monument to him in Westminster Abbey. William Howe sat for Nottingham in the House of Commons and when trouble became acute with the colonies he condemned sharply the policy of coercion and said he would take no command in America. In spite of these opinions, he was now, by a capricious fate, in command at Boston, while his brother, the fourth Lord Howe, soon arrived in America in command of a powerful fleet. To Horace Walpole the admiral was "undaunted as a rock and as silent." In spite of a harsh, ungracious manner, due to shyness, he was gentle and kindly, especially to the sailors, who adored him. Because of his grim dark features they called him "Black Dick" and there were never mutterings of discontent on any ship that he commanded. Though agents of coercion and ready to do their duty, the two brothers disliked this policy and were at heart more with Burke and Chatham than with the king and Germain. Both of them resigned their commands in 1778 and Lord Howe then declared that never again would he serve while North with his tortuous policy was in office. Not till 1782 when coercion had its disastrous ending did the brothers again serve. Lord Howe then relieved Gibraltar after a siege that had lasted three years and thus cancelled Spain's demand that there should be no peace to end the revolutionary war until that fortress was yielded to her.

After the victory at Quebec on the last day of 1775, the premature cry is heard in England that "the back of the rebellion is broken." Events at Boston in March, 1776, soon destroyed this complacence by bringing a striking success to the colonial cause. The British had found Boston not easy of defence. It was commanded on the north by Bunker Hill, which, but only with costly losses, the British had been able to hold in June, 1775. It was also commanded on the south by Dorchester Heights. As time passed the British position grew worse. The troops suffered much from cold and they had to destroy wooden houses for fuel. The force in tents on Bunker Hill suffered from frost, snow and biting winds. In respect of food the situation was not much better. While Boston was blockaded by land and the besiegers had abundant food, ill-fortune befell food coming by sea to the British. The West Indies, for some reason, furnished little, but from England copious supplies were sent: 5000 oxen, 14,000 fat sheep, a vast number of hogs, and, not least, 10,000 butts of strong beer. Many transports were employed but much of the live stock perished at sea in storms. When colonial vessels captured British supply ships at the very entrance of Boston harbour the army faced scarcity. It helped to relieve Washington's lack of guns that a British ship laden with cannon and ammunition fell to him. He had besides fifty heavy

British guns brought with the great labour from Ticonderoga.

On the morning of March 5 Howe was startled to find that by a movement in the night, so skilful and sudden that it seemed miraculous, Washington had occupied Dorchester Heights and dragged up guns that now commanded Boston. At first Howe was bent on re-taking the Heights as the British had re-taken Bunker Hill. He hesitated. It was winter. Snow lay on the hard-frozen ground. The colonial forces far out-numbered his. Moreover he still hoped that the colonies might be so impressed by Britain's power as soon to agree to peace. Accordingly, he decided to avoid bloodshed and to move to the safer base of Halifax. We may imagine the dismay of the loyalists at the sudden decision. If the army went they too must go. They had so derided the disloyal as a vile rabble deserving the scaffold and so fomented the coercion that had brought on the stricken city famine, cold, nakedness and disease that now, without the protection of the British army, none of them would be safe. For the most part they belonged to the staid elements in Boston society and now they must in haste abandon all,—land, houses, furniture, even pictures and wearing apparel—and hurry to waiting ships. These refugees numbered more than a thousand and when, on March 17, under a great array of spreading sails, the ships went out they carried soldiers and civilians numbering in all about five thousand. As they headed eastward to find both security and the chill of lingering winter in Nova Scotia, Washington's motley troops marched into a jubilant Boston. The great loyalist migration to what is now Canada was already under way. Washington had won his first personal success in the war. Soon, however, Howe had his measure of revenge. Before that summer ended the Howe brothers drove Washington's army from New York and made it the centre of British effort for the long duration of the war.

Meanwhile the Congress at Philadelphia was alarmed and discouraged about Canada. Reports were coming in of disease and famine in the army, of discipline relaxed, of the growing hostility of the Canadians, of the great need of money, good money, not paper promises. Accordingly Congress urged patriotism to lend its gold and silver and decided to send a tactful commission to Canada. Its most conspicuous member was Benjamin Franklin, now seventy years old but ready to risk his life on a long, hard, wintry journey, if by so going he might save the cause. A year earlier he had conferred in London with such foes of coercion as Chatham and Shelburne, but in vain, since, while they condemned the taxing of the colonies, they insisted on the enduring union that meant subordination. Though usually calm and bland, Franklin had been aroused to fury by the recent bloodshed and now to him the king and his ministers were murderers. The other two members were Samuel P. Chase, later a justice of the Supreme Court and at one time a possible president of the United States and, perhaps most suitable of all, Charles Carroll of Carrollton in Maryland, owner of a vast estate, a rich man reputed by John Adams to be worth possibly two hundred thousand pounds; a member of a Roman Catholic family hounded by Protestant intolerance from Ireland into exile in the English colonies, and now an ardent revolutionary, to whom in his daily talk England had already become "the enemy." It shows the wide culture of some of the colonists, despised by many in England as ignorant provincials, that Carroll had been educated in France, had studied law in both Paris and London, and had formed a vigorous literary style. He was now in his thirty-ninth year; when he died in 1832 he was the last survivor of those who had signed the Declaration of Independence. Though a Roman Catholic, he had found wealth and distinction in an English colony and he was well fitted by this experience and by his mastery of French to commend the colonial cause in Canada. With him went his cousin, a priest, John Carroll, later Archbishop of Baltimore, who could appeal to the clergy.

The commission had an arduous journey. Franklin, old and wearied with exposure and discomfort, has recorded little of the venture but Carroll kept a copious diary. They set out from New York to ascend the Hudson on a sloop on April 2. A raging storm split the mainsail of the ship and caused a long delay. They were still subjects of George III but as they went up the river Carroll and Chase landed at strategic points, examined the sites of so-called forts as yet only batteries, and planned to ensure the command of the river against British ships that might try to go up to Albany. At Albany General Schuyler showed hospitality at both his town house and his country seat; "he behaved with great civility; lives in pretty style; has two daughters (Betsy and Peggy) lively, agreeable, black-eyed girls. . . . The citizens chiefly speak Dutch, being mostly the descendants of Dutchmen." We get the impression of both opulence and dignity. Schuyler owned lands stretching for twenty-five miles on each side of the Hudson and his neighbour Livingstone had three hundred thousand acres. Such men were not of the rabble, derided by the loyalists in Boston, but aristocrats of the colonial world who had staked their all in the revolt and, should coercion win, would, as traitors, warring on their king, lose all, a fate that in the end overtook the loyalists who opposed them.

The commission moved on partly by boat, partly by waggon, over dreadful roads to Ticonderoga at the head of Lake George, the ruin called a fort that had been seized in the previous year by flamboyant Ethan Allen. On Lake Champlain ice caused both delay and discomfort. They landed at farm houses for meals and slept under awnings on the cabinless bateau in beds brought by wise foresight all the way from Philadelphia; once at least Chase and

Carroll slept under bushes on the shore. From Chambly the commission drove overland to Montreal in the two-wheeled calèches, the vehicles of the country. "I never travelled through worse roads or in worse carriages," Carroll says, and we may well wonder how the aged and ailing Franklin could bear the hardship.

When they reached Montreal on April 29, four weeks after leaving New York, ubiquitous Benedict Arnold received them cordially. They were welcomed by the firing of cannon and at head-quarters "a genteel company of ladies and gentlemen had assembled to welcome our arrival." The ladies were chiefly French. After tea came an elegant supper, the ladies sang, and at last the weary guests went to what seemed the finest house in Montreal—that of the opulent fur-trader, Thomas Walker, whose loss of an ear a dozen years earlier had thrown Canada into a ferment. The Canadian clergy held aloof. A priest who allowed John Carroll to celebrate mass was disciplined by the bishop, who forbade courtesies to the visitors. The day after arrival bland Franklin and his colleagues made and received visits and on the day following they sent a report to Congress.

The commission found the army broken and dispirited and the Canadians now acutely hostile. Though the two Carrolls were well fitted to reason with their fellow Catholics in Canada, centuries of distrust between French and English made persuasion difficult. Events had forced the Canadians to be realists. Colonial enthusiasm for "Liberty or Death" had not been allied with tact in meeting Canadian suspicions. The Continental army, sent by a body without money, had forced the habitants to accept in payment for supplies the continental dollar, a form of paper currency like that which the Canadians had known well in Montcalm's time and destined even to our own day to be proverbial for worthlessness. Some of the rabble in the colonial army had done worse. It was believed that, scattered in Canadian houses, were savings amounting in all to as much as a million pounds in gold and silver, and soldiers plundered Canadian farms in search for this and other booty. Even the clergy had not been spared outrage. When the leaders before Quebec learned that curés, instructed by the bishop, refused absolution to Canadians serving with the invaders, they not only put some priests under arrest but engaged a renegade priest to give to Catholics joining the colonial army the rites of the church forbidden by the bishop. Puritan officers had been heard to deride its ceremonies and to say they longed for the day in Canada when Satan should be bound and Antichrist overthrown. The Canadian clergy asked awkward questions. They were invited, they said, to turn against Britain, which had given them their own laws, respected their religion and protected their property. What then was the record of the colonies which they were to join? The Congress itself had publicly declared that their faith carried hypocrisy, murder and bloody revolt to all parts of the world and people of their creed were not even allowed to live in some of the colonies.

These objections were reinforced by the truth that the colonial army was in a shocking condition. It was ravaged by smallpox; half the men were ailing and there was almost no medical service. Discipline had broken down. The soldiers were without pay, there was no regular supply of food, and the Canadian farmers were so able to hide supplies that foraging yielded hardly more than a few half-starved cattle and a little flour. Sometimes farmers had to yield to demands at the point of the bayonet and half the orders in payment were likely to be dishonoured by the paymaster. In consequence the Canadians were growing so sullen and insolent that when Franklin's party had reached the south shore of the St. Lawrence the ferryman demanded cash—"hard money"—before he would carry them across to Montreal.

Meanwhile the colonial army held on before Quebec with the tenacity of the British race. Ever since the death of Montgomery it had been slowly reinforced. The inept Wooster had been removed and General Thomas, a brave and capable leader, had now nearly four thousand men under his command. In May, however, mobile sea power struck the blow that shattered the designs on Canada. The British fleet had made so early a start that in early spring the ships were battling with storms in the vast stretches of the Gulf of St. Lawrence and sometimes were surrounded by masses of floating ice that reached to the horizon and threatened to hold them in a chilly vice. By the beginning of May the ships were straggling past the scattered settlements of the south shore with their background of hill and forest. The wondering habitant must have noted the difference in type of these great ships of war from the traders that he knew; but though, even in that age, there was a primitive telegraph of signals that carried news swiftly, no word reached Quebec to tell Carleton that rescue was near.

In early May he had a dramatic alarm that turned, however, into comedy. In naval warfare, from at least the time of the Spanish Armada, to send a fire-ship to drift among the anchored wooden vessels of the enemy might cause panic and heavy loss, since the ships might not have time to move under sail before the floating furnace reached them. The French had menaced in this way the attacking fleet before Quebec in 1759 and this now the colonial leaders tried against Carleton. On May 3 watchers saw a ship come into full view past the Island of Orleans and head towards two war-ships and other vessels huddled together at what was called the *cul de sac* in the harbour. Hope that she was an advance ship of a rescuing fleet ended when suddenly a prodigious smoke broke out, her sails and rigging took fire, rockets flew into the air, cannon went off and shells burst. She was a fire-ship that the nervous crew had abandoned too soon. She came up in the wind while still safely distant from the moored ships and soon, a helpless mass, drifted away amid cheers and jeers from the ramparts.

At daybreak, on May 6, the watch in Quebec again saw a ship off Point Levi. When the cry went out "A ship! A ship!" men rushed from their houses half-dressed, a crowd gathered at the Grand Battery, and soon in full view were not one but three British war-ships, the *Surprise*, the *Iris*, and the *Martin*. When, to the joy of the inhabitants, boats filled with soldiers and marines pulled to shore, Carleton lost not a moment, for he knew that the arrival of the ships might spread panic among the besiegers. He called for volunteers and, at noon, nine hundred men marched out of Quebec and stretched a thin red line across the Plains of Abraham. Carleton was not mistaken. On seeing the war-ships the Americans had fled, leaving behind, in their haste, not only cannon and other heavy things but clothing, private papers, books, food, muskets and bayonets. Heaps of bread and pork lay by the roadside abandoned from laden carts as the pursuer came up. In this wild flight the army had become a disorderly rabble with a deadly fear that if Carleton could cut off retreat he would massacre them as outlawed rebels.

We may imagine the dismay of the commissioners of the Congress when, on May 10, this alarming news reached them at Montreal. It reinforced discouragement already acute. Disease was devastating the army and Franklin himself was so ill that on May 11, attended and cared for in his feeble state by the priest John Carroll, he set out for home. We find him in New York on May 27 and later in the year in Europe where with sage diplomacy he helped to attain the decisive result of bringing France into an active alliance with the colonial cause. Though the other commissioners remained for a time they feared that warships might sail up even to Montreal and had the further fear of a descent on Montreal from points higher up, by the route that Amherst had used for the final conquest of Canada. This fear was justified. The British hold on the upper St. Lawrence and the Great Lakes was secure. At a fort, Oswegatchie, on the site of the present city of Ogdensburg, in the state of New York, they had a small force. The commanding officer, Major Forster, with about fifty white soldiers and two hundred Indians, swept down the river, attacked the American outpost at The Cedars, on the north shore, a little above Montreal, and by May 20, ten days after the news had come of the relief of Quebec, he had some four hundred prisoners in his hands. Across the river on the island of Montreal Benedict Arnold had at Lachine a force of fifteen hundred men. Forster was so embarrassed by his many prisoners that he agreed to exchange them for the same number of British whom Arnold was to set free. When he had handed over his prisoners he retired to Oswegatchie. The British prisoners were, however, not released. Much to the wrath of Carleton, the Congress declared that some of Forster's prisoners had been abused and robbed, some murdered, and demanded that before the four hundred British were freed the offenders should be handed over for punishment and the stolen property restored.

With the retreat from Quebec followed so soon by these events above Montreal the two commissioners had an embarrassing task. While it was chiefly military, they were civilians with, however, so they declared, supreme authority over the army in Canada. Naturally there was friction when the commissioners undertook to be generals. They interfered with the orders of General Thomas and censured him when he failed to carry out their own. At the end of May, however, the commissioners, convinced of their own futility, left Canada and went home, leaving the army to fight a losing battle. Congress, still hoping, sent six new regiments to Canada and the chief American force gathered at Sorel, where advance into Canada or retreat up the Richelieu River to Lake Champlain seemed alike easy.

When General Thomas died of smallpox at Sorel on June 2, the command went to General Sullivan, a New England lawyer, turned soldier, a brave and competent leader, destined later to be the scourge of the Mohawk chief, Joseph Brant. The British pursuing force from Quebec had reached Three Rivers when Sullivan sent General Thompson with about two thousand men to attack it. He crossed the river at night from Sorel and, marching eastward along the north shore, lost his way, perhaps indeed was so purposely misled by a Canadian guide that disaster soon overtook him. In an attack on the town he was captured and the wonder is that his force was not annihilated. After this the one thought of the invaders was to get out of Canada with as little loss as possible. Though they were starving, the Canadians refused to sell food to them for worthless paper money and at last grew so definitely hostile that not a cart could be hired without payment in coin. The only vegetables to be had were a few peas, and meat was so lacking that one of the urgent appeals to Congress for help was "For God's sake send us pork." In bad weather the retreating army pressed up the Richelieu River to Lake Champlain with officers so ineffective and discipline so broken down that regiments slept at night without even posting guards. Though smallpox spread, medicine and nurses were lacking. One observer says "I did not look into a hut or a tent in which I did not find a dead or dying man." "It would make your heart bleed," says another, "to hear the moans and see the distress of the sick and dying." The dead were thrown into pits and the line of retreat was marked by many graves.

When the American forces reached Lake Champlain they were safe, for they had boats, some of them taken from the British in Montgomery's conquering advance, while Carleton had none for pursuit. The supply of boats was, however, so indifferent that some of the sick colonial soldiers, carried in leaky flat boats with no awnings, in intensely hot weather, lay for hours and even days in water. By the beginning of July, the wreck of an army reached Crown Point on Lake Champlain. Then, just at this time, the Continental Congress took the decisive step. On July 4, 1776, it made the Declaration of Independence by which the thirteen colonies became thirteen independent states, no longer with any tie to Great Britain and with, as yet, no organic union among themselves. The Declaration pictured George III as an arbitrary despot, who had been guilty not merely of some acts but of every act "which may define a tyrant" and was "unfit to be the ruler of a free people." He had inflicted "death, desolation and tyranny" on the colonies, ravaged their coasts, burnt their towns and destroyed human lives. Not least, he had by the Quebec Act established in Canada the absolute rule that menaced the liberty of all the colonies. Ever since this fiery indictment the title of king has remained to the great mass of the people of the United States the symbol of despotism, while their own country is the home of free men abhorring the title of "subjects" of a would-be tyrant.

Meanwhile day after day in the summer of 1776, British war-ships and transports arrived at Quebec. Tall masts marked the busy harbour; flags waved everywhere; martial music stirred the streets of the little capital as the arriving regiments marched to their quarters. Out on the Plains of

Abraham was the debris of the abandoned camp of the colonial army that had held on there for six wintry months. On June 1 Carleton received at Quebec amid rejoicings his second in command, General John Burgoyne, destined, in the next year, to meet with disaster that went far to ensure the final success of the colonial cause. "Gentleman Johnny Burgoyne" was a man of fashion and a wit whose play "The Heiress," praised by Horace Walpole as "a delicious comedy," was translated into half a dozen languages. At the age of twenty-one he had made a romantic elopement with the daughter of the Earl of Derby and, though the outraged father had declared that never again would he see his daughter, a reconciliation had come with the result that Burgoyne now had in his support the powerful Derby interest to aid his career as a soldier. Like William Howe, Burgoyne was a Whig, a member of Parliament and in his later years an active ally of Fox and Burke; like Howe, too, he loved pleasure and wine and women. Burgoyne had served with Gage at Boston, had seen the hot fight at Bunker Hill, and later had returned to England, critical of Gage's army, led by a man of indecisive character and top-heavy with too many generals and brigadiers, whose insolent tone to the restless colonists had aggravated the strife.

Burgoyne must have been gratified when, partly through his influence, Gage was recalled and he himself was sent to Canada as second in command to Carleton, who was to have a formidable army of seven British regiments of the line, four batteries of artillery, and seven German regiments. This appearance in the war of hired Germans stirred in the colonies enduring resentment. Since even the common man in England as well as Burke and Chatham did not like the job of fighting fellow Britons, George III had turned to German princes, his relatives, and had literally bought in Brunswick and Hesse these regiments ill suited by their training to the conditions in America. Europe was familiar with this use of foreign mercenaries: English, Scots, and Irish served in foreign armies; Swiss and Germans had been so employed for generations; and foreign legions still exist in our own time. German regiments had even been brought to serve in England until Pitt had sent them away during the Seven Years' War with the indignant protest that a nation relying on foreign defenders was not fit to be free. The use of these now caused Burke to denounce "the hireling sword" of "German boors and rascals" employed by the "liberal government of this free nation." Burgoyne's Germans were led by Baron von Riedesel, a competent officer. Most of them knew hardly a word of English or French. They wore the cumbrous German uniform of the time, with heavy sabres, huge head gear, and great boots coming up to the thighs, a strange equipment for warfare in America.

Carleton had foreseen that the lack of vessels would cripple him on Lake Champlain and had urged that needed parts should be sent out in the hold of the ships arriving from England in the spring of 1776. Had this been done, he could have followed quickly the retreating army up Lake Champlain, and might have recaptured Ticonderoga as easily as he recaptured Chambly and St. Johns. But the vessels had not been sent and, since the timbered shores of Lake Champlain were impassable for an army by land, Carleton had to pause to build vessels. One small vessel, the *Inflexible,* he took past the rapids on the Richelieu in sections, hauling the heavy timbers over the portages with infinite labour. But during the summer he advanced no farther than to Isle aux Noix. In command against him was now resourceful Benedict Arnold, occupied, like himself, in equipping a small fleet in order to meet the expected advance of the British.

Late autumn with heavy winds had come before Carle-

ton was ready. At last, on October 11, in a stiff little
naval battle on Lake Champlain, he defeated Arnold, who
managed, however, to slip away with most of his force.
When Carleton occupied Crown Point, Arnold had escaped
to Ticonderoga. Should Carleton go on to attack Ticonderoga? Since winter was at hand and the fort was in hostile
country, he thought it unsafe to try to hold so remote
an outpost. In this, as the event proved, he made a decision
that was to involve, for a time, a disastrous check in his
career. His victory had seemed all but complete. When
he withdrew his forces to the north of the lake, not an
American invader was left in Canada except those held
as prisoners of war. But to his critics it was disturbing
that, on the long stretch of Lake Champlain, there was no
British force and that the banner of the Revolution still
floated over Ticonderoga. Carleton's defect was over-
caution; certainly Burgoyne chafed at his inaction. But
Carleton knew that it would be easy to do what was, in fact,
achieved, to secure the lake in the spring and meanwhile
it seemed wise to keep the army near the base of supplies.
A final result had, in truth, been achieved. The attempt
to bring Canada into the American Union had failed disastrously and in it was involved the momentous outcome
that North America was not to be one vast republic. To
call the Congress at Philadelphia continental was henceforth a misnomer. In spite of this its members might glean
some comfort from their campaign. By keeping a small
British army occupied at Quebec they had weakened the
British elsewhere. They had forced Howe to abandon Boston. Moreover in this, their first campaign, the colonial
army had learned much about actual warfare. Except for
the panic flight from Quebec the men had, on the whole,
shown courage and resource, if also a provincial tactlessness
that embittered the Canadians.

CHAPTER XV

WHEN the failure of the attack on Canada was followed a little later in the summer by Howe's defeat of Washington and the capture from him of New York, many on the British side believed that final victory was near. There was gaiety of a stately kind in the Château St. Louis at Quebec. On the anniversary of Montgomery's final attack, Carleton gave a great dinner and his guests danced in the New Year of 1777, destined to see a reverse all but ruinous to the British cause. When the bishop celebrated an impressive mass in the cathedral, he required some accused sympathizers with the invaders to do public penance. In the following spring more British regiments arrived for the campaign of the coming summer. General James Murray, the former governor, had written from Minorca to Germain the facile opinion that the rebels were already beaten and would probably soon beg for peace; ten thousand Canadians would serve under Carleton if he were ready at the outset to hang renegades who held back; the native American was, Murray added, "an effeminate thing," quite unfit for war. This was little more than stupid gossip of the officers' mess. On the other hand rumours flew about that France had declared war and that a French fleet was likely soon to sail up the St. Lawrence; rumours, Carleton declared, that nearly every rebel Canadian and Indian in the country believed with pleasure.

Meanwhile in London his own prospects changed. Instead of friendly Dartmouth, an enemy was now in charge of the war in the person of Lord George Germain, the Secretary for the Colonies. Son of the Duke of Sussex and now a man of sixty, he was rich, arrogant, a sharer in the costly pleasures in town and country of fashionable society. On the other hand, he is described as one of the few men in Parliament of conspicuous ability; he was one of the best speakers in the Commons and he had a vigour of character that made him influential in the small cabinet of the time. Some even believed, though rather absurdly, that he was the author of the brilliant and bitter letters of "Junius." While his father was viceroy he had been a member of the Irish Parliament and for a time Secretary of War for Ireland. He had had an extensive military experience in campaigns on the continent, had fought with distinction at Fontenoy in 1745, and later had reached the high rank of Lieutenant-General. Disaster overtook his military career when at the battle of Minden in the year when Wolfe won Quebec he failed to obey the repeated orders of the commander of the allied army, Prince Ferdinand, to push his cavalry forward and attack the French horse that had been repulsed by the allied infantry. Though in the end the cavalry advanced, the opportunity was lost and the British soldiers raged at their leader's failure to win their share in the honours of a great victory. In consequence Sackville (he took the name Germain in 1770) was tried by court martial and dismissed from the army with every mark of ignominy. Military opinion was certainly not unanimous as to the justice of the verdict. When it had reached James Murray at Quebec in July, 1760, shortly before the fall of Montreal, he handed it round among his officers and then wrote Germain that "there is not an officer who does not blush that such a sentence should have been pronounced by a British court. A clear surprise, by the Eternal God."

George II, however, deprived Germain of posts worth some seven thousand pounds a year and caused an order of the day to be read to the British regiments stationed in all parts of the world that Germain was unfit to serve his sovereign in any military capacity whatever. Such a censure, the king said, was worse than death to a man with any sense of honour. No doubt the wrath of the explosive little king, counting himself a fighting soldier, was excessive; Germain, though of wayward and obstinate temper, was a brave man. His friend, Richard Cumberland, describes him in glowing terms as the Sir Roger de Coverley of his time, almost absurdly methodical in personal habits, kindly to the sick and the poor on his estate and watchful over the welfare of all. On Sunday, in gala dress, he led his whole household to church and was apt to approve passages in the sermon by calling out "Well done!" and to rebuke a discordant note in the choir by saying loudly "Out of time, Tom Baker." He was a model landowner. But, though he had ability, he was a bad official. He had the haughty air of a duke's son in an age that paid great deference to rank. He was bitter to the last against the colonies, spiteful to his opponents and a relentless place-hunter for his friends. He is said to have borne Carleton a grudge for giving evidence against him before the court-martial. More recently, too, Carleton had refused to make a place for one of Germain's protégés.

With Germain in England directing the war, Carleton had an implacable enemy as his superior, and his failure to take Ticonderoga provided an excuse for his undoing. He had been in fact too cautious; his long delays caused his warmest friends to chafe; clearly he was better at defence than attack. General von Riedesel wrote in September, 1776, "There is much talk but whether the work is pushed through with the same zeal is another matter." Resolute Colonel Christie persistently assailed Carleton in letters to Germain urging that he lost time by his indecision and idleness; that his discipline was slack; that by his carelessness stores were wasted; and that he was so silent and self-absorbed as to make it impossible to understand his designs. When, late in 1776, Burgoyne had carried to England Carleton's plan of campaign for the coming year, he told his own story of recent events with some complaint of Carleton's inactivity. The result was that in May, 1777, Carleton received a despatch from Germain declaring him guilty of neglect of duty in failing to take Ticonderoga in the previous autumn and telling him in some detail what he should have done. Now his command was restricted to Canada and Burgoyne was to lead the army in the advance to the Hudson. In hot resentment Carleton asked at once to be relieved of his post and wrote to Germain on May 20, 1777, a letter such as officials rarely send to superiors. Under courtesy of phrase itself rather stark he was really insulting. He derided Germain's military plans as those of an arm-chair strategist, three thousand miles away from the seat of war, where rapid and unexpected change was inevitable. When George III saw the letter he said that Carleton was "highly wrong" in writing with such asperity to a secretary of state but none the less he praised Carleton's defence of Quebec and the day came in 1782 when he was willing to let Germain go in order to secure the return to America of Carleton to end the long folly of the war and to wind up in final disaster the business of the British Empire in the English colonies.

When, in the spring of 1777, Burgoyne was again in Canada, intending to drive through to the heart of New York, Carleton gave him such loyal support that the relations of the two leaders were excellent. It was intended that Howe, in possession of New York, should send an army northward towards Albany to meet Burgoyne advancing southward and that the united forces should hold the line from Canada to New York. But everything on the British side miscarried. Burgoyne was so misled as to count on the armed support of the population of New York, exactly as Benedict Arnold and other colonial invaders of Canada had counted on the French. Moreover while he had been promised fifteen thousand men for his advance, he mustered only half as many. By Germain's order Carleton was to furnish a "sufficient body of Indians," dangerous and useless allies.

The London man of fashion, Burgoyne, was in truth, unequal to such a type of expedition. He made a leisurely progress southward according to the accepted rules. His advance up Lake Champlain was a military pageant. He easily re-took Crown Point and also Ticonderoga. George III knew the name Ticonderoga and when the news of its capture by Burgoyne reached him on August 22 he rushed into the Queen's room crying "I have beat them, beat all the Americans," whom, however, he hoped to retain still as his loving subjects. Horace Walpole rejoiced that Burgoyne had "kicked Ticonderoga into one of the lakes; I don't know which. I am no geographer." In truth, however, Burgoyne was heading for disaster. He knew little of the kind of warfare in which he was to be involved and of the people opposing him. "He is," said Charles Lee, one of Washington's generals, "as ignorant of the dispositions of the people of America as he is of those in the moon." He thought that the mass of them would welcome him and that in any case there was hardly a leader on the American side but could be bought.

Burgoyne's luxury of equipment astonishes our modern austerity in war. Thirty carts were needed to carry his personal supplies, which included two barrels of Madeira and two of rum. There were many women in the army. At that time every regiment had its quota of women to do the washing for the men and render other domestic services. They tended to be a degraded class but were often not without a measure of oversight by ladies who accompanied their husbands. It astonishes us that General von Riedesel had with him not only his wife but also his children and servants. Other officers had their wives. Burgoyne himself was not without female consolation. Gossip, aired in Parliament, said that in all there were two thousand women with Burgoyne's army; no doubt this is a gross exaggeration but the scandal had some basis. War was then a gentleman's game with its accompanying indulgences. We read of riotous parties during the advance at which the drinking and singing lasted all night. Burgoyne had too much of some things; too many cannon for a country almost without roads; but too little food for an army at times half starved. As he advanced into the colony of New York, to his surprise the population was persistently hostile. Stories of outrage by his Indians aroused colonial fury. His alien Germans caused resentment that justified what Chatham was saying in England that forty thousand German boors could never triumph in America; "You may ravage—you cannot conquer, it is impossible." Charles James Fox had told Burgoyne that he would come back to England a prisoner on parole and Fox proved to be a prophet. When Burgoyne pressed on to the Hudson the Americans retreated before him until he was across the river, far from his base. Then they so surrounded him that on October 17, 1777, he surrendered at Saratoga with his whole force.

The disaster to Burgoyne was perhaps in any case likely but it was made inevitable by a type of official fatuity that haunted much of Britain's effort in this deplorable civil war. At New York Howe had a powerful army, well equipped, well disciplined, while on the other hand Washington's forces before New York and at Philadelphia were ill equipped and not yet fitted to meet British regulars in the field. In addition to an excellent army Howe had a powerful fleet under his brother's command. What more natural than that, surveying the problem, the brothers,

holding New York securely, should think that to have also
the political capital, Philadelphia, might end the war
quickly? At Philadelphia sat the Continental Congress; at
Philadelphia strident colonial patriotism had submerged
moderate opinion; at Philadelphia had been made the
Declaration of Independence. Holding Philadelphia, Howe
thought he could pacify the south where loyalist sentiment
was strong. Accordingly he planned to strike in the summer of 1777 a final blow by occupying the rebel capital.
Though Washington hurried from New York to face Howe,
on September 26, 1777, Howe's army marched into Philadelphia while Washington retired to Valley Forge, twenty
miles away, in the hills, to spend a desolate winter, during
which nearly everything that an army requires was lacking.

It was not many days after Howe entered Philadelphia
that Burgoyne surrendered at Saratoga. He and Howe
were alike the victims of crude ignorance in England. Both
the king and Lord George Germain had expected Howe to
go early to Philadelphia and then turn back to sail up the
Hudson and meet Burgoyne, but this plan ignores the
urgency of time and space since distances forbade such a
double success in a few summer months. While Burgoyne
was ordered to go south, Howe had not received orders to
go north to meet him. In any case Howe seems to have been
given a large measure of discretion and, himself on the
spot, he was certain to think that he knew better what
to do than any one in far-away London. It matters little
now to find where the chief blame lay. The mischief was
done. Howe's victory at Philadelphia counted for so little
that the British abandoned it in the following summer.
On the other hand Burgoyne's failure ended the dream that
defeat before Quebec had ruined the colonial cause. The
disgrace of the failure rang through Europe which, as a
rule, took pleasure in Great Britain's disasters and de-

plored her successes. Frederick the Great, himself a despot, derided George III's plan to master his own people by shedding their blood. In truth Burgoyne's surrender had an effect so far-reaching as to involve the ruin of the British cause. While France had long been waiting for an opening to strike a blow at Britain, she had replied to the urging of the colonies to join them that they must first prove their capacity by a great success. Now they had won it.

Though on learning of the disaster to Burgoyne Howe sent in his resignation at once, being anxious, no doubt, to return to England in order to meet inevitable censure, he remained in winter quarters at Philadelphia. Before he went away in May his officers with whom he was popular gave in his honour a parting festival in the form of a mock tournament in which brave knights contended for the favour of Turkish damsels and fireworks said to Howe in flaming letters "Thy laurels shall never fade." The powder for these fire-works might better have been directed against Washington. During the winter his army at Valley Forge was losing daily from death and desertion while Howe had gaiety and dissipation for his officers and comfort for his men. Spring brought, however, the startling news of the declaration of war by France. Since it was not until after Trafalgar in 1805 that the British won final command of the sea, it seemed possible in 1778 that the French fleet might be the stronger in American waters. This so changed the outlook that the British decided to evacuate Philadelphia. Admiral Howe carried his fleet to security at New York and then in disgust with the ministry resigned and went home. General Clinton took command of the army and, not without losses on the march, reached New York, held by the British throughout the war. After this it dragged on with two things, however, certain; only final, irreparable defeat would bend the resolve of George III not to yield independence while, on the other hand, Washington and many with him would find refuge in the western wilderness rather than renew their allegiance to the king.

The Iroquois Indians, the Six Nations, living in the northern part of the colony of New York, were drawn inevitably into the struggle of the American Revolution. Since most of them took the British side, many were driven into exile as loyalists and by a romantic turn in their history found refuge in the Canada on which, while it was French, they had waged barbaric warfare during a century and a half. The great estate of Sir William Johnson, who had known best how to manage the Indians, lay, as we have seen, in the Mohawk valley in northern New York, near the villages of that tribe. Though he died in 1774, his influence was so enduring that all but the Oneidas of the Iroquois tribes fought on the British side. Had Johnson lived, his experience and tact might have softened the barbarity of the opposing sides in guerilla warfare of raids and massacre. Sir John, who succeeded to the baronetcy, lacked the capacity of his father. When the Revolution began he tried to remain on his estate, fortified his house, enlisted a bodyguard of five hundred men, and formed a military force of a hundred and fifty Highlanders who had settled near him. When, however, his neighbours joined in the rebellion and menaced him, he fled to Canada as did also his cousin Guy. Their great estates were confiscated. With them went the Mohawk chief Thayendanegea, better known as Joseph Brant. He had the tie with the Johnsons that his sister bore Sir William many children and after his death spoke of herself as his widow.

Brant is as near in type to the noble red man of fiction as we are likely to find in real life. He was a brave leader, at times savage in his methods but also at times chivalrous. He had been born when his people were on a hunting expedition to the remote banks of the Ohio and then, no doubt, was carried along forest pathways on his mother's back. Though he had not the rank of hereditary chief, the so-called Sachem who ruled in time of peace, he became an elected war chief. His grandfather was one of the Mohawk chiefs whom Peter Schuyler, a leader in the colony of New York, took to England at his own cost in 1710 in order to disarm Iroquois leanings to the French by letting the chiefs see with their own eyes the greatness of England. They created a sensation in London, were presented to Queen Anne, one as "Emperor of the Mohawks," the other three as "kings," and proved a stimulus to the effort to conquer Canada that failed so disastrously under Sir Hovenden Walker in the next year. When a youth of nineteen, Brant was sent by Sir William Johnson to a missionary school out of which grew the present Dartmouth College in New Hampshire that bears the name of the colonial secretary of the time. Brant soon learned to be at ease in a cultivated society. The Baroness von Riedesel who met him at dinner in Quebec says that "he conversed well" and "possessed polished manners . . . He was dressed partly as a military man and partly as an Indian. He had a manly, indulgent cast of countenance." To her he seemed "very gentle." Brant went to England late in 1775 and like his grandfather was for a time a somewhat barbaric lion in London society. He was tall, erect, a striking figure in his dress, half Indian and half military. The king granted him the rank of colonel. Boswell, keen in pursuit of other celebrities besides Dr. Johnson, took him up. Romney painted his portrait. Fox presented him with a snuff box. When he was received by George III he so counted himself a fellow ruler that he refused the homage of a subject in kissing the king's hand though he willingly bent over that of the queen. He promised that he would bring three thousand warriors to the loyalist side and by midsummer of 1776 was back among the Six Nations. It was perhaps his fame as a chief that led the outside world not only to laud him for what merits the Indians deserved but also to blame him for outrages in which he had no part. He would, however, have belied his Indian origin if scalping of the enemy and savage war-whoops and raids under cover of night had had no place in his methods. He denied, however, charges made in that era of furious hatreds that he killed women and children: "It is a shame to destroy those who are helpless. I have always been for saving and releasing." He failed sometimes to resist the craving of the Indian palate for fire-water and took part in wild debauch. He was none the less a sincere friend of the decorum of civilized life and of mission work among his people with, in his occasional relapse, perhaps less of moral obliquity than that of Dr. Johnson's hard-drinking friends at Lichfield.

The policy of Governor Haldimand at Quebec was to prevent a second invasion of Canada and so to harass the northern frontier as to weaken the enemy farther south. The wide tract held by the Iroquois in northern New York was a natural base from which to raid neighbours, and Fort Niagara, held by the British throughout the war and long after, was a secure haven in case of a reverse. Parties of so-called "Scouts" dashed out on colonial settlements from Iroquois lands and brought in scalps and prisoners. British officers, who commanded Indian allies, found their authority so flouted that, as one of them, Colonel St. Leger, said, it was harder in this ignoble warfare to restrain the Indians than to fight the enemy. This alliance with the Indians aroused such hate that to harassed people in New York and Pennsylvania every British officer became a savage and every British success a brutal massacre. Burke ridiculed in the House of Commons attempts to control the blood-lust of the Indians. "My gentle lions, my humane bears, my tender-hearted hyenas," he pictures an officer as saying,

"I exhort you as you are Christians . . . to take care not to hurt man, woman or child."

In July, 1778, Colonel John Butler, a loyalist from Connecticut who had settled near Johnson, led into the Wyoming Valley in Northern Pennsylvania about eleven hundred men of whom five or six hundred were Indians. The party burned a thousand dwelling houses, eight forts and some mills. Butler reported that his Indians, while injuring no women or children, gave no quarter to those in arms, an admission of brutalized warfare. This massacre marks the beginning of a series of savage forays that lasted for three years. The word went through all the colonies that Butler had allowed Brant to let loose his savages to slaughter women and children while, in fact, Brant was not present with Butler. In November of the same year, Brant joined Butler's nephew, Walter, who had been ejected from his estate and had barely escaped hanging for treason to the Revolution, in an attack on the settlement of Cherry Valley on a small branch of the Susquehanna. When the assailants crept up to the village in the dim light of an early morning of drizzling rain, the Indians who were in advance rushed in with wild war-whoops, set fire to the houses and slaughtered many of the helpless inhabitants. Naturally Brant, himself an Indian, and Butler, a rather rash and headstrong young leader, with injuries to avenge, were blamed for the outrage that in truth was beyond their control. A British officer, Captain MacDonnell, who was present, wrote that the massacre was the most tragical and barbarous in the war; but he adds that both Butler and Brant tried, at the risk of their lives, to restrain the Indians: "The reflection never represents itself to my view but when accompanyed with the greatest horrors; both sexes, young and old, Tomahawked, Speared and Scalped indiscriminately in the most inhuman and cruel manner . . . Out of a hundred and seventy scalps three-

332 CANADA AND THE AMERICAN REVOLUTION

fourths were those of Women and Children." Not only did
the Indians disgrace the British cause by their lust of car-
nage; they were all but useless as allies except to inspire
terror in enemy settlements. Burke declared that one
Indian cost as much as five regular soldiers; they ate vora-
ciously, wasted supplies, and were likely to desert in time of
danger. Major Nairne, in command for a time at Carleton
Island on the Upper St. Lawrence, had little use for them.
They made "almost unbearable greedy and importunate"
demands, especially for rum, and they resented the discipline
of the camp. When serving as scouts to detect possible
hostile raids, they raised false alarms at night, fired off
guns in the woods, and disturbed the rest of the soldiers.
"My men work hard in the day," Nairne told them, "and
I will have them to sleep sound at night." He would, he
said, fire on the Indians if they disturbed him further.

All the outrages in this ruthless civil war must not, however, be laid to the account of the Indians. Alike in the
southern colonies and in the north, savage passions flamed
out on both sides and so lacked restraint as to cause even
Brant to declare that some whites became "more savage
than the savages themselves." While the regular British
officers usually disliked the raids and left them to the
embittered loyalists and to the Indians, this was not always
the case. As late as in the autumn of 1781 Major Ross of
the 34th regiment described his ravaging of seven miles
of settlements near Schenectady, the burning of a hundred farms and of mills and grain, and the destruction of
live stock. While he says that he harmed no woman or
child we are not told what he did to the men.

The Six Nations paid a heavy penalty for these outrages. General John Sullivan had shown skill in rescuing
the colonial army that had fled from Canada after its
failure before Quebec in 1776 and early in 1779 he was
chosen to "chastise and humble the Six Nations." There

was no force on the British side in the colony of New
York that could resist his army of five thousand men, well
equipped and well led. In three weeks Sullivan burned
some forty Indian villages, destroyed orchards, devastated
the crops in fields and gardens, and then hunted down the
Indians like wild beasts. A fertile region in the early stages
of civilization was made an unpeopled wilderness. "General
Sullivan," wrote Washington, "has completed the entire
destruction of the country of the Six Nations, driven all
the inhabitants, men, women, and children, out of it." So
indeed he had. Barbaric war had met its Nemesis in barbaric devastation. But even though Sullivan had a large
army he did not dare to attack the British fort at Niagara.
Accordingly the British with Brant and his Indians were
able to continue from this base forays that resulted in further devastation and massacre. "No other hatred is so
bitter as that of near relations," said discerning Tacitus
long ago, and his other comment is true of this savage
warfare: "They make a solitude and call it peace."

While foreign wars and internal strife weakened Britain's possibility of victory she had an even more deadly
menace within her own ruling circle. The instrument that
had created her widespread empire, the navy, was in a
state of decay, and one chief root of the trouble was in the
Earl of Sandwich, First Lord of the Admiralty. He must
have had some merit for when he had held this post in
1748, a young man of thirty, he had supported Anson in
carrying out some stringent reforms. He was, however, a
man of evil character, the friend of Wilkes in his earlier
disreputable days, later his treacherous and malignant
enemy. George III said that Sandwich, in spite of his
vices, was a good man of business whom he found useful. He became First Lord again in 1771 and, with disastrous results, held the post during eleven years. It is per-

haps to his credit that he supported Captain Cook who
preserved his memory in the name of the Sandwich Islands.

None the less Sandwich well nigh ruined Britain's sea-
power. He was so blind a partisan as to fill the service
with men whose only merit was party zeal. With few exceptions, the best of the higher officers in the navy so
feared his treachery that they refused to serve under him.
In consequence Sandwich had to use what poorer material
he could find. The Admiral Arbuthnot who succeeded
Lord Howe in America was a blustering bully, whose ignorance of naval tactics was one of the chief causes of the
disaster at Yorktown. When Spain, seeing a chance to
recover Gibraltar, joined France, the summer of 1779 was
critical. With a powerful combined fleet they massed forty
thousand men at St. Malo and at Havre for the invasion
of England. As the united fleet put to sea the British
channel fleet scattered before it and the government in
London, with invasion imminent, ordered residents of
the south coast to remove inland their movables, their
cattle and other live stock. The danger seemed real when,
on the quiet of a Sunday morning, August 15, 1779, the
hostile fleet entered the bay at Falmouth and anchored
near the shore. The threatened capture of Plymouth did
not, however, follow for the incompetent French admiral
sailed away without firing a gun or landing a man. To
command against a supreme effort of France and Spain,
Sandwich had had the folly to commission Sir Charles
Hardy, an old admiral who had not been to sea for twenty
years. Other evils continued. Corrupt officials made great
gains by drawing high prices for bread and supplying a
cheap quality to the service. It was found that, for their
own profit, some officers kept pigs in naval store-houses
and fattened them on biscuits provided for the fleet. Others
carried off and sold supplies and equipment. Rotten hulks
unfit for service were sent to sea. The *Royal George*, lying

at Spithead, was in such a bad condition that her bottom
fell out. And this at a time when Britain was at war with
almost the whole world. Yet Walpole wrote in 1781 that
"the nation is more besotted and the ministry more popular than ever." Young William Pitt, destined as prime minister himself to wage the great war against Napoleon, was
fiercer even than Walpole. On February 21, 1781, he denounced a peer who, untaught by events, had called the
war a holy war. For his part, Pitt said, he was persuaded
that it was a most accursed, unnatural, and diabolical war,
conceived in injustice, nurtured in folly, and marked with
blood and devastation.

The years between 1778 and 1781 are perhaps the most
dismal in the whole history of the British Empire. In
America no colonial leaders would listen to terms of peace
that did not include independence, while in England this
even Chatham was not willing to yield. Yet he saw her
ruin imminent if she did not end the war. No one had
better right than he to say: "But yesterday England might
have stood against the world [she had done it under his
guidance], now none so poor to do her reverence." Other
leaders—Rockingham, Fox, the Duke of Richmond—were
all ready as early as in 1777 to accept independence in the
hope that, as against Bourbon France and Spain, a "true
British Family Compact" might unite in trading interests
and be strong to confront the world. The Whigs were even
ready, as Richmond said in the Lords, to give "full and
entire satisfaction" for injuries inflicted in the colonies.
George III, however, with a devout belief that God was
on his side, had told North on January 13, 1778, that no
one was "either bold or Mad enough" to treat on the basis
of independence. He had rather lose his crown than let
base men, among whom, by this time, was Chatham, to
force his hand. In April, 1778, Chatham died protesting

that the crown should not give up "its fairest inheritance" and by so much he reinforced the stubborn temper of George III. In vain had North, a liberal Whig at heart, begged to be allowed to resign. He had told the king in May, 1778, that "to prevent the ruin and disgrace of the country" he should retire. He felt unfit to remain in a cabinet where, he said, "I never could, nor can decide between different opinions." The king had no such difficulty; "no consideration in life shall make me stoop to opposition [to Fox and his allies] . . . I will rather risk my crown than do what I think personally disgraceful. The nation must stand by me or find another king." In vain during four years did North, in truth unequal to his responsibility, plead his lack of capacity. He was mastered by a stronger will. For him to go, so the king urged, would be an act of treachery. Accordingly he remained in office until 1782.

Meanwhile the nation itself was becoming ever more restless. In 1780, on Dunning's motion, the House of Commons voted that "the influence of the Crown has increased, is increasing, and ought to be diminished." Still, however, the king's will prevailed. To him the colonists were "Deluded People" who must soon ask for peace. He was, he hoped, not less forgiving than a Christian ought to be, but the time had not arrived to display this virtue either to the colonies or to the supporters in England of their claims. He had indeed some reason to hope that, as time passed, success was near. Benedict Arnold was a shrewd man and when, in September, 1780, though so trusted as to be in command at pivotal West Point on the Hudson, he sold himself to the British, he must have had some grounds for thinking that they would triumph. Even later and after the devastating British disaster at Yorktown, Luzerne, the French envoy at Philadelphia, was writing to his government that, while the people hated the English, they would like to be free to trade profitably in English goods which they preferred to all others; the government, he added, so lacked vigour that in a renewed campaign the British would not have to meet a strong defence. Thus George III's intuition that he must win seemed to have some excuse.

It was, however, profoundly mistaken. Arms could never bring the colonies to obedience. Britain was losing ground. The French were aggressive in the West Indies and captured more than one British island. John Paul Jones was working havoc with British shipping. In 1779 Spain declared war. In the next year Russia led in creating the armed neutrality of the north, ready to go to war against what seemed the arrogant use by Britain of her naval power. When at the end of 1780 war broke out with Holland, Britain had hardly a friend in all the world. Nor was she any happier within herself. She was not only at war with her own colonies; conquered Ireland, inspired by their example, was in a state of rebellion and had grievances to which theirs seem almost trifling.

Under a leader with the patience and the skill of Washington the Americans slowly gained ground and at last the powerful aid of France to the colonies proved decisive. By 1779 the chief fighting was in the south where Lord Cornwallis commanded the British forces. After three indecisive years, in 1781, by skilful manœuvring, the French and American land forces shut up the army of Cornwallis in Yorktown, in Virginia, on a narrow peninsula on Chesapeake Bay. A French fleet, arriving suddenly from the West Indies when a more powerful British fleet was far away at New York, gave a brief command of the sea to France. Since no rescue could come in time to save Cornwallis, on October 19, 1781, almost exactly four years after the capitulation of Burgoyne, he surrendered with his whole force. Two weeks later but before the news had arrived, George III wrote to North that, though the moment was anxious, "success must ensue." Truth, he said, is strong. France, sobered by disaster, will be sick of her duplicity. The tender royal heart was still ready to receive the penitent colonies. Great Britain, said the king, was fighting to decide whether she should be "a great Empire or the least dignified of European states." Though, when the bad news came of the disaster to Cornwallis, North, pacing wildly up and down the room, cried "Oh, God, it is all over," George III, conscious as he said of the rectitude of his intentions, faced the crisis with a courage admirable though futile. "If we despond," he said, "certain ruin comes" and he still hoped that measures "well conceived" might bring a favourable end to the war. That the colonies could win their independence he would not imagine.

Though in January, 1782, North told the king that peace must be made with America, it was only after many months of wrestling with his conscience that George yielded. Over and over again he said that he would never accept separation. When Conway carried in the House of Commons on February 28, 1782, a motion that it was expedient to end the war, the king still hoped that at least some of the American colonies might be induced to remain loyal and to separate from the rebels of the young republic. He would, he said, do what he could to save the Empire and would have the comfort of self-approbation at not letting himself be "a tool in the Destruction of the Honour of the Country." "I am sorry," he wrote on February 22, "it has been my lot to Reign in the most profligate age," when knavery, indolence and timidity made his own brave efforts unavailing. More than once he drafted his abdication. Since he could not save the nation he was, he said, "resolved forever to quit this island" and to retire to Hanover. By October he was comforting himself for the coming separation from America by saying that knavery was so rampant in the colonies that "it may not be in the end an evil that they become Aliens to this Empire." He was offering "the most fervent Prayers to Heaven" to enable him so to act "that Posterity may not lay the downfall of this once respectable Empire at my door." He did not wish to survive the coming ruin. May we not think that Abraham Lincoln would have had similar thoughts if he had been compelled to face the triumph of the South? He, not less than George III, thought rebellion treason.

CHAPTER XVI

THE CANADIAN SCENE

THE internal life of the whole British Empire was deeply affected by the American Revolution. Remotely it caused the founding of the present great Commonwealth of Australia, begun for the melancholy purpose of a penal settlement when the colonies in America ceased to be available. More immediately the Revolution so affected Ireland as to cause there a declaration of independence that aimed at making Ireland completely self-governing; and it profoundly affected Canada by sending to it exiled loyalists of British origin who spoke English and in time turned a Canada that had been wholly French into an expanding Canada where, beyond the fortress of French culture in Quebec, the English language and English law and political tradition should prevail.

In Ireland, though about nine-tenths of the people were Roman Catholics, no Roman Catholic might vote, or hold public office, or teach any child but his own. While the Parliament in England could legislate for Ireland, the Parliament of Ireland might only pass laws first approved in England (Poynings' Law). The best paid offices in Ireland went to strangers from England. Though no Roman Catholic might hold a commission, Catholic Ireland had to support an army of some fifteen thousand men. She paid many pensions forced on her by the king's ministry, often too ashamed of its nominees to venture to propose them in London. At the time when the Stamp Act was passed in 1765 these pensions had been increased, during

340

the previous two years, by about a hundred and fifty thousand pounds and the whole sum was far greater than any taxes Great Britain could raise in all the thirteen colonies. Moreover England imposed upon Ireland what was really direct taxation for she sent to Dublin money bills that its controlled Parliament did not dare to reject. It is amusing but also painful to find Charles James Fox, a generous champion of liberty, drawing a pension of £1700 a year from the taxation of Ireland and receiving £30,000 for renouncing further privileges.

Irish discontents had an important place not only in the American Revolution but also in the bitter antagonism to Great Britain that endured in the United States long after the Revolution. There had been extensive Irish emigration to the English colonies. In the three years preceding the outbreak of the war, as many as ten thousand Irish had gone out yearly, carrying with them fiery resentments against England that fitted easily into sympathy with restless colonial patriotism. This helps to explain the rather singular truth that, though the Congress at Philadelphia denounced the Roman Catholic Church, the members of this church supported the Revolution. In Ireland itself the early sympathy for the Revolution was checked for a time when the age-long enemy, France, joined the colonies and threatened to invade Ireland. Then forty thousand Irish volunteers enlisted against that alien nation. But when the danger passed the volunteers remained under arms to assert Ireland's rights. It is sometimes forgotten that the Declaration of Independence in America is inextricably linked with a similar declaration that soon followed in Ireland. Backed by the power to employ armed force in his support, Henry Grattan led in demanding a sovereign Parliament in Ireland as free as that of England. Out of this came on April 16, 1782, not long after the British disaster at Yorktown, a striking scene in Dublin, when armed volunteers lined the approaches to the Parliament House and Grattan passed through them to press his demands. Within a month his urgency had won in London as well as in Dublin. When the reactionary government of Lord North gave way to the régime of which Fox was an ornament, Parliament renounced all right to legislate for Ireland and declared her to be a free nation with her own Parliament in supreme authority, a policy that eight years earlier would have more than satisfied the demands of the colonies. While Washington had to fight in the field to create a nation, Grattan freed Ireland by what Sydney Smith called "his manly courage and all the splendour of his astonishing eloquence." He lies near Fox and Pitt in Westminster Abbey and his statue in the outer lobby of the House of Commons and that of Washington before the National Gallery in Trafalgar Square mark England's generous recognition of two rebellious sons who challenged her with success, though that of Grattan did not endure.

Owing to delays in the coming of his successor as governor, Sir Guy Carleton had been obliged to remain in Canada for a year after his resignation in the summer of 1777. It may be that the disaster to Burgoyne consoled him, since he might have met the same fate had he been in command. It was a fretful Carleton who ruled at Quebec. The time was dreary with plots, with fears of invasion, with domestic strife between English and French. Carleton so distrusted some of the score of members of his appointed council that when they insisted on his laying before them his instructions from the British government and on consulting them as a body, he replied tartly that he should consult whom he liked, refused to call them together, chose five of their number as his "Privy Council" and let the others grumble. He was instructed, so they

believed, to establish trial by jury and the safeguards of
Habeas Corpus, not incorporated in the Quebec Act, but
he would not do it with war at his door. It mattered
little to him what his detested superior in London, Lord
George Germain, might order. When the English traders
demanded with reason that, instead of the French they
should have the English commercial law to protect their
credits, and added that he had been instructed to grant it,
he refused to disturb the minds of the Canadian seigneurs
on whose support and that of the church he relied. All
this was arbitrary, but he would not budge and when the
Chief Justice, Hey's successor, Livius, demanded to see his
instructions, he promptly dismissed him from office in a
letter of three lines, giving no reasons. Even George III
would hardly have dared such summary action since, under
English law, a judge's independence was secure; but Carleton, a soldier, saving a country, holding on in Canada
against his own wishes, did what he considered his duty
and never offered a word of explanation.

Soon after Howe had gone home from New York Carleton sailed from Quebec and these two companions of Wolfe
did not serve again until Germain retired from office.
Carleton's successor was Frederick Haldimand, a Swiss
Protestant with a long record of service in the British
army. No one of the three governors of Canada during
nearly two score years after it became British was an Englishman. Murray gloried in being an "honest Scot," Carleton had the dour temper of Northern Ireland, and Haldimand was a Swiss. These men from lesser nations were
perhaps more adaptable in new conditions than was the
proud Englishman conscious of his nation's supremacy.
It is important to remember that they were dictators.
Haldimand always spoke English with a foreign accent and
was so unfamiliar with English tradition that when in
command at Three Rivers in 1762 he showed a naïve in-

terest in a document called *Magna Carta* to which some one appealed. During centuries Switzerland had sent many of its educated classes, lacking an adequate sphere at home, to serve in foreign armies. Haldimand was a citizen of the world. He had served in Piedmont lying across the Alps from Switzerland. He is said to have fought under Frederick II of Prussia and to have spoken of him as "my old master." After 1750 he had been Colonel of the Swiss guard at the Hague. At the outbreak of the Seven Years' War he and his Swiss friend, Henry Bouquet, joined the British army. It was Bouquet's skill in the Ohio region that ended the frontier war led by Pontiac. Meanwhile Haldimand had served in Canada. When the British took Montreal in 1760 it was he who received the surrender. Four years later he was in Florida in succession to his lamented friend Bouquet, watching the designs of the Spanish in Louisiana; trying to find some route by which British vessels could ascend the Mississippi without interference by the Spanish at New Orleans; dealing with restless native tribes and making vain plans to ensure a permanent hold on the country by the British. Then, in 1773, he took the place of the commander-in-chief, General Gage, on leave in England, and was at Boston and New York during the stormy period when mobs threw tea into Boston harbour and burned tea on the strand at New York. When Gage was recalled Haldimand was his natural successor, but since to have a foreigner in command was likely to offend the ticklish sensibilities of the aroused colonists, Haldimand was summoned to England, in order, so he was told, that he might give an account of conditions in the colonies. The day came when his foreign birth with French as his native tongue was an advantage and in the autumn of 1777 he was ordered to Canada to succeed Guy Carleton as governor.

Though Haldimand set out in October, 1777, he was

driven back by storms and he did not reach Quebec until June of the following year. Carleton, still at Quebec, welcomed him and the citizens presented a loyal address expressing their joy at the coming of "a gentleman of your conspicuous Abilitys and extensive knowledge." All of his military talents and skill, they added, would be required to check "depredations from the unhappy Spirit of Rebellion." So indeed they were. France was now in the war. The people of Canada were French and at Washington's side was the young Marquis de Lafayette, with two fervent passions; one, hatred of England, the other, love of an ideal liberty that soon when applied to despotic France was to make him a leader in events that overthrew the monarchy. France had, however, no serious desire to recover her lost colony. Haldimand himself said that nothing would cause greater dismay to the Canadians than the arrival of a French fleet. Uncertainty, however, remained to haunt his mind. The very ignorance of the Canadians made them susceptible to wild reports. When a French fleet set out for America in the summer of 1778, the rumour spread that it would soon appear in the St. Lawrence.

We may well imagine that the Canadian clergy, who in 1775 and 1776 had refused the sacraments to those who joined the heretic American invader, should have seen in a different light the appeal from Catholic France. At first, indeed, it seemed as if France wished to regain Canada. In December, 1778, the French Admiral d'Estaing issued from a war-ship lying in Boston harbour an appeal to the Canadians to turn from tyrant Britain and become again subjects of the king of France, the guardian of their French traditions, the protector of their faith. At the same time Lafayette, relying on the influence that French tact had gained among the Indian tribes, appealed to them to throw off the galling British yoke. By some subtle agency d'Estaing's appeal was posted on the doors of many village

churches. While most of the habitants who gathered there
on a Sunday morning could not themselves read, those who
could, we may be sure, explained its meaning. No doubt
this call to treason to Britain was quickly torn down but
its effect remained. Word went abroad that Lafayette was
coming; that a French fleet was coming; and, when Spain
declared war, that a Spanish fleet was in the St. Lawrence.
Haldimand himself believed that many of the priests hoped
for a return to Catholic France.

The kindly, anxious, elderly governor at Quebec reveals
himself in his own diaries and reflections. He resembled
Washington in character. Each of them practised self-
discipline and drew up guiding rules of conduct. Washington wrote out, apparently from French sources, an outline
of the perfect gentleman for his own guidance. When in
the presence of others he is always to remember what may
be pleasing to them; he is to defer to superiors; he is to
give reproof only in a sweet and mild temper, never in
anger; he must not laugh at his own wit nor indulge in
unkind gossip. Haldimand for his part makes the rule
"to be always polite and obliging but also to be always
watchful; . . . to ask time to consider things of any importance, but also to make it an inviolable rule to do whatever has been promised; not to become heated in conversation, rather to leave the room under any pretext, as was
the case with a bishop, who prayed in order to give time for
his blood to cool"; and so on. Haldimand's mode of life
was simple. But while he disliked ceremony he had something of the aloofness of the *grand seigneur* and he saw
little of the Canadians. He was housed in the governor's
residence at Quebec on ground where now stands a great
hotel overlooking the majestic river. Carleton seems to
have lacked an æsthetic sense; the house was bare as a bar-
rack until Haldimand refurnished it in the English style.
During his six years in Canada he created there a beautiful

garden, built a country house a few miles away at the Montmorency Falls, with the music of the cataract in his ears. He created the first public library in Canada, where, partly due to a long era of war, so many were backward that two ladies fond of reading were regarded, Haldimand said, as prodigies of erudition. He wished to see a free school in every parish, something that England herself did not achieve until nearly a century later. In these schools, so urged a governor whose own English was to him an alien tongue, the masters should speak English and he hoped in this way to educate the French into the English outlook. He tried to improve sanitation in Quebec where people used the streets as drains. We may imagine the shock to his soldierly, tidy mind when he saw wandering about in the streets not only horses but pigs that fed on the refuse thrown from houses. Perhaps, however, Quebec was not worse than the unclean London and Edinburgh of the time.

Haldimand's rule has the deadly monotony of a period of suspicion and repression. None the less was his work important. He was responsible for the security of the country. To this day the French Canadians, looking back on his rigour, denounce his rule as a leaden tyranny. Yet, though invasion threatened that counted on treason in Canada, he put in prison only nineteen suspects. No Habeas Corpus Act prevented his holding them without trial and we may admit that to be in prison in Canada at the time was in itself a severe punishment. The winter cold was bitter, the heating inadequate, the accommodation primitive, while the food often meant half starvation if the prisoner had himself no resources. A certain printer, Mesplet, a Frenchman, had practised his trade in Philadelphia and had translated into French and printed the appeal in 1774 by Congress to the Canadians. In 1776 during the American occupation, perhaps wishing to live among people of his own speech, he moved to Montreal, set up its first printing press, and remained after the flight from Canada of the invading army. So backward was Canada, in contrast with the English colonies, that this printing press seemed a dangerous innovation and Mesplet himself justified this suspicion by circulating scurrilous items against the government. Haldimand put him and his editor, one Jautard, in prison for a time and then banished them. Though Haldimand had power of life and death he executed no one for treason and in this was more merciful than Congress itself and also many of the states.

Haldimand's rule was that of an alert soldier. His Province of Quebec, spreading to the Mississippi, had military posts for which he was responsible. When he found that at some of them the officer in command might make a handsome income by scandalous overcharging for supplies, he decreed that all purchases must come under his eye at Quebec. He carried out an engineering task, the forerunner of a vast one in our own time. He had been in the army of Amherst in 1760 when turbulent rapids had cost many lives on the route down the St. Lawrence from Oswego to Montreal. To descend the river was dangerous and to ascend it was tedious. Heavy boats must be dragged past the rapids by men wading near the shore, with straining muscles, and sometimes for long hours in water to their waists. To ease this labour Haldimand employed military engineers and soldiers to build a narrow canal past each of the four lower rapids. The canals were only about six or seven feet in width but this sufficed for the bateaux of the time. To-day great ships pass through canals of which the first outline was made by Haldimand.

Feudalism, the feudalism retained by the Quebec Act, gave Haldimand the right to require the peasants without pay to build or repair highways, to help with their horses and carts to transport the effects of a regiment changing its quarters, and to discharge other burdensome services. While this *corvée* had hitherto been light, Haldimand made it heavy by building good roads. At great cost of labour he improved the highway between Quebec and Montreal and though the peasants grumbled the country was bene-fitted. Haldimand would not permit priests from France to enter Canada, something quite natural since France and Britain were at war. Though he had an inherited prejudice against the French monarchy, the persecutor of his Prot-estant ancestors, he had none against either the Catholic Canadian people or their church to which indeed he gave firm support in the exercise of its authority. The Canadians were, as he said, "the people of the country" and he urged on the ministry in London regard for them rather than for the English traders, here to-day and gone to-morrow. He declared, probably with truth, that had the demands of these traders for an Assembly chosen by themselves been adopted under Murray and Carleton, Canada would have joined the revolted colonies at the first opportunity. The Canadians had been given what he called the "sacred charter" of the Quebec Act. "These unfortunate people," he said, had suffered "too Much by Committees and Houses of Assemblies to have retained any prepossessions in favour of that Mode of Government."

Without doubt Haldimand's rule was stern and stiff. Spies and traitors were corresponding with the enemy and promising that most of the Canadians would welcome the invaders. He ruled his army in the rather brutal manner of the time. Military discipline was so rigorous that a soldier might receive five hundred lashes for firing off his musket without leave at a pigeon or a rabbit. There were a good many floggings and there was at least one hanging for theft, then, in tribute to the age's reverence for property, punishable by death. Haldimand would not permit of-ficers to marry without his consent and showed sometimes the confirmed bachelor's lack of sympathy with the emotions of the lover. The monotony of life at the posts led by way of relief to rash adventure and often to quarrels. In the governor's voluminous correspondence, which must have kept his secretaries busy, are warnings to officers about drinking and gambling, each of them a persistent vice of the age, sometimes involving ruin to the offender.

CHAPTER XVII

PEACE AND FRONTIERS

ROCKINGHAM's second ministry that took office in March, 1782, was not a happy family. In Europe peace was to be made with France, Spain and Holland. In Asia great territories were to be annexed. In North America the former colonies insisted on independence. Between Shelburne and Fox, the best debater in the cabinet, there was enduring distrust that involved refusal to coöperate and caused the retirement of Fox from office that, except for a brief interval, lasted for more than twenty years and also a little later that of Shelburne for the rest of his life. The office of secretary for the colonies, filled so disastrously by Germain, was now abolished. Shelburne at the Home Department was in charge of the colonies, while Fox was secretary for Foreign Affairs. This Whig ministry had the formidable task of dealing with two Declarations of Independence. That in regard to Ireland proved the easier since it had no foreign complications and the king's ministers were certain to retain a potent influence in ruling the country. Accordingly, in April, 1782, Parliament declared the Irish Parliament to be a sovereign legislature like that of Great Britain and under the same king. Following this, on June 30, Fox declared in the cabinet that the independence of the colonies must be recognized without conditions; they would accept nothing less. When Shelburne was not ready for a concession so sweeping, a nice question arose between the two ministers. Since the colonies must become a foreign nation, to treat with them, Fox claimed, fell to him

351

as foreign secretary; while Shelburne, on the other hand, claimed that, until a treaty recognizing their independence was signed, relations with them fell to him as in charge of the colonies.

The king, who was exercising still a real authority, favoured Shelburne. The dispute was ended by a new crisis that brought the retirement of Fox. On July 1, 1782, Rockingham died suddenly and Shelburne succeeded him as leader of the government. A youth of twenty-three, destined to great fame, William Pitt, became Chancellor of the Exchequer and a mediocre Whig politician Thomas Townshend, afterwards Lord Sydney, took Shelburne's place as the secretary in charge of the colonies. Fox's distrust of Shelburne was such that he now refused to be his colleague under any circumstances; he resigned and it was Shelburne who made the peace with the United States and settled the frontiers of Canada. In an earlier chapter we have seen him so interested in colonial questions as to send his secretary, Morgann, to Quebec to make enquiries. No one could doubt his care and industry. But though Disraeli described him as "the best and most accomplished minister of the eighteenth century," always he was thought to be secretive and insincere. Gainsborough, trying to paint him, threw down his pencil after two sittings and said "Damn it! I never could see through varnish." Shelburne's friend Bentham thought he was apt to build up a whole system on "the scrap of an idea." He was, no doubt, a doctrinaire holding fervently to the belief that if barriers to trade were removed national frontiers would lose much of their importance, an opinion that had some effect on the fixing of the frontiers of Canada. Though Shelburne had always opposed the effort to coerce the colonies he had also declared that he would never acknowledge their independence and in this was in sympathy with the resolve of the king. Accordingly, in Paris during

the summer and autumn of 1782, two separate negotiations
for peace were carried on, one with foreign nations, the
other with the colonies. At the head of that treating with
France and the northern powers was Alleyne Fitzherbert,
highly trained in the ways of diplomacy, while to treat
with the colonies was Richard Oswald, a merchant with
no experience in that world.

The American commissioners sent to Paris to negotiate
peace were the astute Franklin and with him John Adams,
John Jay and Henry Laurens. Franklin was the chief
spokesman. He always protested that he treasured no bitterness on account of the incident many years earlier, when
a future lord chancellor had called him a thief in the presence of members of the Privy Council, and when he had
been dismissed with ignominy from his employment as the
head of the colonial Post Office. It is true, however, that
he was now bent on severe terms of peace. Shelburne still
hoped for union under one king, with each Parliament
fully sovereign. This had just been conceded to Ireland
and Shelburne even yet realized so little the fiery hatred
of monarchy in the colonies as to think that they would
consent to have a king. Franklin, no doubt with courtesy,
said that the proposal was impracticable. Another proposal,
that the treaty should provide for perpetual free trade between Great Britain and the United States, had no better
fate. The colonies would accept nothing short of sovereign
rights that should leave them bound in no way to Great
Britain.

In a dissolution of partnership, said Franklin, the assets
are shared, and he claimed that the British Empire should
be divided between the two former partners. The United
States would be content with Canada, Nova Scotia, and a
half share in the Newfoundland fisheries. For Britain to
keep Canada would, he said, cost more than it was worth,
since it would involve constant friction with the United

States. It was perhaps by an oversight that Franklin did not mention the great territory of the Hudson's Bay Company in the north, though probably he intended it to be included in order to make the United States truly continental. He overlooked nothing elsewhere. He demanded Sable Island, near the coast of Nova Scotia, and asked also for Bermuda in order that England might not use it as a base for privateers. Damages should also be paid in money by the defeated side. Since Great Britain had waged a wanton war against the colonies, she should now frankly acknowledge her fault and as a mark of goodwill and regret for the past pay a sum that he thought might be about six hundred thousand pounds for devastation by herself and her Indian allies. It would be fitting also, he added, that Great Britain, but of course not the United States, should indemnify the loyalists for their confiscated estates. He quite realized that a proud nation might resent the humiliation of doing these things at the demand of her former colonies. If, however, she would act in this sense before such a demand was made it would show her generous temper. Large-minded conduct on the part of Britain, Franklin urged, would soften existing resentments in the United States against the tyrant nation that had waged unholy war on them during seven years, and it would make for pleasant relations in the future.

Franklin's claims, in themselves really extravagant, were urged with great tact and an assurance of the most benevolent intentions. They were based upon the conviction that Great Britain was utterly defeated and that France would stand with the United States in exacting hard terms. In truth, however, Great Britain was not defeated, except in her own colonies, and even there the year after Yorktown brought something like disillusion to the victors. Congress was penniless. The army, which for a long time had been paid in the paper continental dollar at its face value, though it was worth only two cents, was still unpaid and was mutinous. All the skill of Washington's master hand was needed to avert a crisis. Accordingly, while using the language of the conqueror to the British, Franklin had to go as a beggar to the French government to plead for the money needed in America to stave off disaster. A striking victory aided the British. In spite of corruption under Sandwich the navy had competent seamen. In April, 1782, the fleet under Rodney was in the West Indies looking for the French fleet under the Comte de Grasse, that in the previous autumn had cut off Cornwallis in Yorktown from rescue. Early on the morning of April 12, 1782, when off Dominica, Rodney's chief captain roused him from sleep with the news that "God had given him the enemy on the lee bow," a position that ensured him the advantage of the wind. His victory was complete. He carried the French admiral a prisoner to England and wrote in glee that "within two little years" he had made prisoners of one French, one Dutch, and two Spanish admirals. Power on the sea was doing its wonted work; France was cut off from sending further aid to America. Spain, too, was really defeated. She had declared that never, never, would she make peace without recovering Gibraltar, and in 1779 had begun a siege, one of the most memorable in history, that lasted for more than three years. By the summer of 1782, however, her supreme effort had failed when Richard, Lord Howe, who in 1778 had gone home from New York in disgust, ended the siege. Henceforth Gibraltar was safe and the British were stiffer than ever about terms of peace. They are never better fighters than in the desperation of adversity, and their enemies had soon to admit that they had gained only a limited victory.

France had gone into the war, less to secure the freedom of Britain's revolted colonies than to humble the enemy so completely victorious twenty years earlier. The young

Lafayette had, indeed, risked his life and fortune to secure in America an ideal human liberty. He was now back in Paris and our belief in his idealism is chastened when we find this "vain and insolent young man," as the acute and polished Alleyne Fitzherbert called him, flitting about the French court, hoping to be a member of a French mission to London in order that he might insult George III by wearing in his presence the uniform of an American general. With Britain humbled, France was ready for peace. She had no desire to see a strong United States to rival in time her own expected dominance in the world. Vergennes, her capable foreign minister, a thorough realist in politics, had no dreams like those of Lafayette about republican liberties. He was at work at four o'clock in the morning, toiled eleven hours a day, received no visits, and looked with industrious prudence into the prospects for the future. He desired no conquests but aimed at an equilibrium in Europe that should give France security. He would use Prussia and Russia to balance a hostile Britain and Austria. England he thought near ruin, with her upper classes profligate, her Parliament corrupt, Ireland in arms, and the masses savage and turbulent. She would, he hoped, dissolve like Poland and it was to the good that she should retain territory in North America that might involve her in conflict with the United States.

The attitude of Vergennes explains in part the later destiny of Canada. Though France wished to extend her influence in India and to secure the Newfoundland fisheries, she halted, as we have seen, before the prospect of recovering those "acres of snow," called Canada, so contemptuously dismissed by Voltaire a score of years earlier. While, so Vergennes said, Canada belonged rightfully to France, she would waive her claims. Great Britain should remain there, a menace to keep the United States dependent on France. It was not only Canada that French opinion would deny to the Americans. For similar reasons they ought not to have the great western region bordering on the Ohio. This might even go to England though it seemed better that it should go to Spain. The Mississippi should be a Spanish river, with no rights granted to the United States of navigation on the turbid waters that flowed to the Gulf of Mexico. France, dreaming, perhaps, that some day she might be Spain's heir, would indeed have been content that Spain should take the whole *hinterland* stretching northward from West Florida to the frontier of Canada and that the United States should not extend westward beyond the Allegheny Mountains. This surely would be territory enough for a young republic that owed its being to the powerful and despotic monarchy now counting itself the strongest in the world. Vergennes had no wish that the United States should become a commercial power, able to rival France, or so strong a democracy as to menace monarchy. He was endeavouring, said John Adams, "to make my countrymen meek and humble and I was labouring to make them proud; as Christians I wished them meek; as Statesmen I wished them proud; and I thought the pride and meekness very consistent."

Richard Oswald, the commissioner to treat with the colonies, son of a Scottish Presbyterian minister, was a man of strong character who had won striking success in the commercial world. As a youth he had left his native Thurston to join relatives in Glasgow, engaged in the West Indian and Virginian trade. They owned a privateer that preyed on enemy commerce when war broke out in Walpole's time, and a share of the prize money was the foundation of Oswald's fortune. He set up for himself in London, married a rich heiress, with property in the colonies, and bought a beautiful estate on the river Ayr in Burns's country where, during a hundred years, his family remained opulent. Clearly Richard Oswald had striking qualities. He was a friend of Adam Smith who introduced him to Shelburne; and he had come into contact with Franklin and other Americans. He read widely and so important had he become in trading circles that he had been made Commissary-General for the British army on the continent during the Seven Years' War. These successes belong to the world of business. In British political annals Oswald does not rank high. His mind was concerned not with national prestige nor triumphs in diplomacy, but with free trade that should override frontiers and unite the world in material prosperity. Franklin praised his "air of great simplicity and honesty" and urged Shelburne to make him the sole means of communication between himself and the British government. He persuaded Oswald that if Britain remained in North America there would be enduring friction with her former colonies and consequent loss on both sides. Her withdrawal would show wise magnanimity. Trade would be helped not hindered. It reveals something of the spirit of the age that Shelburne chose a man of the middle class to deal with colonists of the same type and Oswald was alone in the negotiations possibly because a colleague from the high circle of politics in London would have been unwilling to act under him. He lacked one equipment of a diplomatist for he knew no French but this defect was remedied when Shelburne sent to Paris, as secretary to Oswald, Caleb Whitefoord, also a Scot, a wine merchant, an intimate friend of Franklin, near whom he had lived in Craven Street, and a travelled man of the world.

Burke, remembering Pascal's phrase, *"diseur de bons mots, mauvais caractère,"* stopped short by saying that Whitefoord was nothing more than a witty *"diseur de bons mots."* He was, however, sensible and acute. He reports that he and Oswald "hired one of the best Hotels in Paris" and kept open house. France was feeling the glow of victory. One Frenchman boasted to Whitefoord that the French would soon have ten thousand regular troops in India, and offered a bet of one hundred louis that the English would be driven out of India within a year. Whitefoord, with confidence in England's effort "on our natural Element the Sea," retorted that it was unfortunate for the plans of France that in India she "did not possess a single foot of Land for her troops to stand on." When told that England's lost thirteen colonies would "form the greatest Empire in the world," he replied "Yes—and they will *all* speak English,—every one of them." No play of wit against the French could, however, move the Americans. They were adamant on the question of restoring loyalist property: "It is strange that you should insist on *our* rewarding People who have been plundering, burning, and cutting our throats. If you think them so very deserving, why don't you reward them yourselves? But it would be very hard to oblige us to do it even if you had conquered us; and you will please to recollect that you have not conquered us."

While Whitefoord toiled at his desk, copying confidential papers sometimes from seven in the morning until eleven at night, in those laborious days was settled in some measure the future of Canada. What should be her frontiers? Franklin was plausible but rarely, indeed never, generous. Jay, an acute lawyer, so rigid in opinion that he distrusted the French ministers because they were Roman Catholics, was resolved that no loose phrase should obscure the full demands of the United States. In a sense, however, he was friendly to Canada. He had been the American envoy to Spain, had learned something of the arrogant spirit of that country, ruler of the vast west beyond the Mississippi, eager to secure all east of it that lay beyond the Allegheny Mountains and intent to recover Florida that stretched along the whole southern frontier of the United States.

Better give content to Great Britain in the chill north so as to have a freer hand to check Spain farther south. Adams was suspicious both of Shelburne's sincerity and of the capacity of Franklin whom he regarded as an "unmoral atheist." Laurens had bitter memories of his treatment while a prisoner in the Tower. All four were naturally intent on forcing Britain to yield as much as possible. There was no one there to speak for Canada, the nation yet to be, that should some day include much of the North American continent. A discerning man might have made the Americans uneasy. It looked as if the friendly Whigs might soon be out and the Tories back again in an unyielding temper; and the argument could have been pressed that the Americans had better make peace while they could. Even Washington admitted the deadly apathy of the people in respect of further military effort. As early as in 1778, when France joined the colonies, a French agent in America had said that there was a hundred times more enthusiasm for the revolution in the coffee-houses of Paris than in all the colonies. Colonial life was based on trade and war was the enemy of trade.

Oswald, now seventy-seven years old, was no match for these astute negotiators. To him Britain had been defeated and now, in regard to territory in America, was at the mercy of her rebellious children. His back was stiffened for a time by the support of the capable Alleyne Fitzherbert but in the end an aged merchant, so little alert as to ignore the swift changes in Britain's position due to Rodney's and to Howe's great victories, was left alone to treat with the American commissioners, each of whom was his superior in insight and capacity. Franklin, a man of genius, of international fame, a member of nearly every learned society in Europe, had tact, wit, sarcasm and irony at his command. John Jay was a trained jurist, the chief author of the first constitution of the State of New York and so eminent as to become the first chief justice of the Supreme Court of the United States. John Adams had been associated with Thomas Jefferson in drawing up the Declaration of Independence. Later he became the second President of the United States and the founder of what is almost an Adams dynasty in the political life of the republic. Henry Laurens, the fourth commissioner, a man of marked ability, was a former president of the Continental Congress. While a prisoner for a year in the Tower of London, charged with treason, he had been denied access to his friends and even the use of writing materials. Oswald, an old friend, had gone bail for fifty thousand pounds to secure his release. Facing these determined and embittered men, Oswald is almost a comic figure. When he dined with the American commissioners, it ended in his agreeing with them. He did not guard his lips but, in simple candour, told Franklin that England's distress was such that her enemies might do what they pleased with her; they had the ball at their feet but he hoped would be moderate and magnanimous. He flattered Franklin by saying that the British ministers held him in high esteem. In return Franklin assured him that he had still an affection for "old England" and might be trusted to give her friendly counsel. Her threats would not impress him because "they who threatened are afraid." He hoped that between the republic and England an era of eternal good-will should now dawn. Since in Oswald's mind this good-will meant free trade, frontiers were not important.

Oswald was as ingenuous with John Adams, to whom he was a simple, voluble old man dazed in a world of political intrigue. "God, I understand it now," he said, when Adams explained to him why France no more than England desired American independence. On December 9, 1782, after terms of peace had been agreed upon, Adams assured him that England should be careful to remove from the American

mind all cause of fear of her. "Is it possible" said Oswald,
"that the people of America should be afraid of us or hate
us?" To this Adams replied that he was astonished at Oswald's talking as if ignorant of what had happened during
recent years; three million people in America hated and
dreaded England more than anything else in the world.
"What," said Oswald, "now that we are come to our senses?"
At this Adams said dryly that England's changed outlook
was not yet known in America and he proceeded to describe what would promote peace. He doubted its possibility if Canada and Nova Scotia remained British and in
this he assured Oswald many of the best minds in England agreed. In any case no standing army or regular
troops should be kept in Canada and the frontier should
not be fortified on either side. When Oswald asked "What
else?" Adams urged that England should promote the dignity and interest of the United States in every way consistent with her own position and should send out as minister "a clever fellow" who should understand America.
If England tried to cramp, clip, and weaken America as a
possible rival, her former colonies would become "the natural and perpetual ally of your natural and perpetual enemies."

Oswald flitted between London and Paris and naïvely expressed to Shelburne his sense of Franklin's moderation.
He was surprised that though Franklin asked for, he did
not insist upon, the cession of Canada. He himself thought
that "for the sake of future peace" Britain would do well
to yield Canada, Nova Scotia, Newfoundland and Florida,
and like France get out of North America altogether. He
added that she could not well resist such a demand. No
doubt all this was an echo of the talk that the receptive
Oswald had heard at Franklin's table. In truth, however,
the British ministry, supported in this by France, never
seriously thought of yielding Canada, though they were

uncertain about the frontiers. Britain had command of the sea. In the spring of 1782 she held the seaports of New York, Charleston and Savannah. She held Niagara, Detroit, Michilimackinac and other military posts commanding the Great Lakes. Two things, however, prejudiced the future frontiers of Canada: the British public was impatient to know that peace had been agreed upon with the colonies; and Oswald was a pliant negotiator. If Canada was to be retained he was quite willing to accept a frontier that ran north of all the Great Lakes to Lake Superior and would have put wholly within the United States the most populous part of the present Province of Ontario together with the entire coasts of Lakes Ontario, Erie, Huron and Michigan. In England it was said contemptuously of the venerable Oswald that he was only an additional American negotiator. He knew little about Canada; to him its frontiers meant only lines on a map and more or less on one side or the other was of little consequence. To the Americans on the other hand the securing of wide frontiers was a vital need of national life.

The American commissioners soon realized that their views of peace were not those of France, who wished neither Britain, nor Spain, nor the United States to be so powerful as to become future rivals. The French and the Americans were not happy together. While Vergennes said that the Americans had "all the presumption of ignorance," John Adams said bluntly that France had gained most from the war since the colonies had kept Britain occupied in America and thus enabled France to weaken her chief enemy in Europe. Accordingly, no gratitude was due to France from the United States. True, France had lent and spent money freely in America, but she had gained such advantages from the war that it would be fair for the United States to pay forty continental dollars that France held in loans for one gold dollar issued by the republic. By an amusing turn in history, France herself in the twentieth century paid her own debts with a currency worth one fifth of its former value while the United States demanded payment at full face value for money lent to France and other allies in Europe. Jay's contact with the French caused him to jump to the censorious conclusion that they were not a moral people. He and Vergennes could never agree.

Accordingly, each country treated separately with the British, and each was ignorant of the proposals of the others until agreement had been reached. The Americans and the British accepted a frontier better for Canada than that first accepted by Oswald, much worse than that of the Canada of the Quebec Act, which extended westward to the Mississippi and southward to the Ohio. The English colonies had always refused to acknowledge the validity of the Quebec Act. In 1777, as we have seen, George Rogers Clark, a Virginian colonel, of iron will and reckless courage, had been able, with only about two hundred men, to seize most of the British posts on or near the Ohio and the Mississippi. After this, possession meant much for the American claims. But the British were in control of the Great Lakes and this might have enabled a skilful and determined negotiator to secure at least some compensation in other respects for renouncing the claim to the region in which were to grow up Detroit, Chicago and other great American cities. Oswald accepted the present frontier of Canada that gives Lake Michigan wholly to the United States but divides the other lakes between the two countries.

There was little discussion. Probably at the time the Americans were themselves surprised that the British yielded so readily the priceless territory now constituting some half dozen states of the American Union, lying between the Great Lakes and the Ohio River. Vergennes said he could not understand Britain's so readily giving up a great region in which French and English rivalry had been the cause of the war that had led to the British conquest of Canada. It is pretty certain, however, that the political future of this region would, in any case, have been determined by the outlook of the incoming settlers, who were flocking in from Virginia and other colonies that had now become states in the Union. Though the whole great region north of the Ohio to the Mississippi had been annexed to the Province of Quebec in 1774 even then the only prospect that this settlement should endure lay in friendly immigration from the adjacent English colonies. The revolution made it unfriendly and it was patriots, chiefly of an extreme type, many of them rough frontiersmen, ready, too ready, with the gun, who occupied the Ohio region. The Revolution freed it from restrictions on settlement that the British government had imposed in 1763 in order to protect both the fur trade and the natives themselves from plundering traders and settlers. Accordingly, both before the war and after it had ended in 1783 settlers by thousands were making their way in lumbering caravans over the mountains from Virginia to the fertile lands bounded on the north by the Ohio. Others went by boat down the Ohio in such numbers that, in the single year 1788, 967 boats passed down the river carrying 18,370 persons with 7,986 horses and many cattle and sheep. Some of these filtered into the country north of the Ohio and so made it their own that no available British force could have finally dislodged them. Later, in 1812, these pioneers were so bent on having the whole north to the Arctic Ocean that they brought on war to secure it and it may be that it was in a real sense a British success that Canada then retained the frontiers of the treaty made in 1783.

After frontiers the chief questions at Paris related to the fisheries, to the loyalists, and to the payment by the

Americans of private debts to creditors in Great Britain. As to fisheries the colonies retained some of their former rights. "God Almighty," said John Adams, "made the banks of Newfoundland" and the right to fish "is ours as much as yours." The colonies, he added, had fought long against the French to retain this right. It was agreed that they might fish on the banks of Newfoundland and in the Gulf of St. Lawrence but they might not use the shore for drying purposes. No similar rights were, however, accorded to the British on any coast of the United States. On the other hand Great Britain was resolved that the United States, now a foreign country, should come under the restrictions of the Navigation Acts and be excluded from direct trade with the British West Indies, a heavy blow to the commerce of the republic. There was another thorny problem. Colonial debtors were claiming that the Revolution had cancelled the rights of their British creditors and, of course, they spoke much of the cruel losses in property in America caused by the British. Honest John Adams took, however, the high ground with his American colleagues that a private person should pay his debts, and that no political change should relieve him of such a liability. Accordingly, it was agreed that British creditors should have the right of recovery against debtors in America.

There remained only the hard problem of the loyalists. "Lord Shelburne," Oswald had announced, "will never give up the Loyalists." But on this question Franklin and his colleagues were firm. To them the loyalists were enemies worse than the English oppressor, traitors to liberty, murderers of their own people. It was loyalists who had devastated great tracts, burned towns and committed outrages,—loyalists and not the regular soldiers of the British army who took little part in and rather scorned this type of warfare. Accordingly sufferers from it were savage against any relief to loyalists. George Clinton, revolution-

ary Governor of New York and later Vice-President of the
United States, thought that no one, whether an avowed
loyalist or not, who had even remained in territory occupied by the British, should be conceded the right to vote in
the republic. He had, he said, "rather roast in hell to all
eternity than . . . show mercy to a damned Tory." Franklin fumed at the thought that the men who, as he claimed,
were chiefly responsible for the war and had brought ruin
to many colonial households should now recover their confiscated property and be received as good citizens. In the
end, when even France urged conciliation, Franklin fell
back on a plea of constitutional right. Since he represented
only the Congress of the United States and since each individual state and not Congress had seized loyalist property, he had no power to deal with the question. The
federal government would recommend to the states liberal
treatment of the loyalists, but it could do no more. This
meant, as both sides well understood, that little or no
mercy would be shown to them.

On November 30, 1782, preliminary articles of peace between Great Britain and the United States of America were
signed at Paris, by Oswald on the one side, and by Franklin
and his colleagues on the other. Later, George III did not
carry out his threat to abdicate but with a wry face agreed
to the inevitable. On December 5, at the opening of Parli-
ment a few days after the agreement on terms of peace, he
announced that he had assented to declare the American
colonies free and independent. "Did I lower my voice," he
asked, "when I came to that part of my speech?" France
and Spain were still haggling with Great Britain but they
reached agreements on January 20, 1783. Though France
had borne the chief burden, she secured little but the recovery of what territory she had lost during the war. She
handed back to Britain all but Tobago of her conquests in
the West Indies and later Britain recovered Tobago. Spain

fared better. Though George III had expressed willingness to give up Gibraltar to her for compensation elsewhere, British military and naval opinion opposed this and in consolation for Spain's failure to attain her chief aim in going to war, Britain had to return the vast territory of East and West Florida that she had taken from Spain twenty years earlier. Added to this, Spain had the whole of North America west of the Mississippi northward to the territory of the Hudson's Bay Company, so that her fertile areas in North America remained greater than those of either Great Britain or the United States. Minorca also Britain had lost to Spain after a long siege. By the later peace with Holland the most disastrous struggle in which Great Britain ever took part had come to an end. Considering the strength of her enemies she had not fared badly. She retained and soon vastly expanded her possessions in India. She kept her West Indian colonies. While she lost the colonies created by herself in North America, she retained there a great territory. The negotiations at Paris were prolonged and not until September 3, 1783, nearly two years after the surrender at Yorktown, were the treaties finally signed and given to the world.

CHAPTER XVIII

THE EXILED LOYALISTS

WE have seen Sir Guy Carleton as the successful defender of Canada and at the close of the war we find him at New York winding up the business of Great Britain. The disaster at Yorktown had discredited the British leaders and most of all the commander-in-chief, Sir Henry Clinton, whom with justice Cornwallis so blamed for too tardy support that his recall was certain. Who should succeed him and revive confidence? It was George III himself who gave the answer. It should be Sir Guy Carleton. There were difficulties to overcome. Lord George Germain was still directing the war; his quarrel with Carleton was well known and Carleton was firm in declining to serve under him. In spite of this, on December 13, 1781, George III told Germain that he thought Carleton should take Clinton's place. No doubt to select from all the high officers in the army the man whom he had in effect disgraced was a shock to Germain, but he assured the king that many—though he did not add himself—considered Carleton a good officer and that, should the king so wish, he would be happy to see him appointed though, in such a case, he should cease to be minister. The matter dragged, but on February 23, 1782, Carleton was appointed. A few days later North's ministry resigned. On quitting office Germain received the compensation of a peerage as Viscount Sackville while Carleton, we may suppose, was human enough to feel that the king's support confounded his former critic.

Carleton had before him not only the melancholy task of accepting Britain's final defeat but also the duty to protect and aid the many thousands of loyalists now to be driven into the exile that involved poverty and hardship. When, early in May, 1782, he arrived at New York as commander-in-chief, it was not yet settled that the break with the colonies must be complete. He had looked for compromise and reconciliation and when later he learned that independence was conceded, at once he tendered his resignation. He was, however, prevailed upon to remain. When Congress, still tinged with the bitterness of the long civil war, harassed him with urgent demands for rapid evacuation he declared that he should not budge from New York until every loyalist who sought his protection was rescued. Though ever since the spring of 1782 rumours of the terms of peace had brought to the loyalists the fear, fully justified, that their cause was lost, they still hoped that, whatever concessions Britain might make, they themselves should be restored to what they had given up. When, however, on March 25, 1783, authentic news of the terms of peace reached New York, their awakening was rude and bitter.

The story of the loyalists and their foes is one of exasperation and hatred. Long before the Revolution Whig and Tory had been opposed and when civil war came their antagonism was ferocious. Since a Whig was then already a Whig and a Tory a Tory and the Whigs were on the side of the Revolution, they were apt to assume that all Tories were on the side of the king. Many so-called Tories were not blind to mistakes on the British side. They objected to being taxed except through their own legislatures but they looked to lawful means to remove the grievance and condemned violence that disgraced Boston and other turbulent centres. Protests should be made by properly constituted authority; those who resorted to the methods of the mob should, so loyalists said, be met by contempt and derision. They were "vile insects," "the refuse and dregs of mankind," "hardy knaves and stupid fools," recruited from quacks, cobblers, barbers, obscure shopkeepers and pettifogging attorneys, upstarts, feeble and low-born, who thought that their puny efforts could intimidate an ancient empire. The colonial army, with its neglect of military etiquette and its lack at times even of uniforms, came in for stinging satire. At the head of a regiment might be a strutting General Convict or a vulgar Colonel Shoeblack. The men sent to Congress were keen to enrich themselves by gambling in public money. They made a great fuss about petty taxes for stamps or tea while they themselves, a body with no legal authority, taxed their own people by forcing them to accept worthless paper money. A rhyme declared that

> "When insects vile emerge to light,
> They take their short inglorious flight,
> Then sink again to native night,
> An emblem of the Congress."

The loyalists issued a counterblast by a parody of the Declaration of Independence. They too appealed to the "laws of nature and of nature's God," under which "all men are created equal" and are entitled to "life, liberty and the pursuit of happiness." They replied to the long list of grievances against George III in the original by charges of "licentious and despotic abuses" inflicted on themselves, of outrages by mobs, of fines, imprisonments and banishment, of "dreadful scenes of death and desolation." "A decent respect for the opinion of mankind" led them to put their case before the world. Finally, they said, we loyalists pledge "our lives, our fortunes, and our sacred honour" to remain loyal to our king.

The loyalists jeered at the hope of an alliance with

France, since contemptible rebels could not treat with that great nation; after the alliance was actually made, they anticipated the outcome ten years later, when the king of France should rule the colonies as a despot and when French nobles owning great tracts of land in America should live from the toil of serfs who had once been free British citizens. The Church of Rome would be established and the Old South Meeting House in Boston would be in process of becoming a Catholic cathedral. The satire described the recent edifying spectacle of Samuel Adams recanting his Protestant heresy, then going to mass, and in the end preparing to become a priest. By order of the new ruler five hundred youths of the best families were to be sent to France there to receive a careful education "in the Catholic faith and a due sense of subordination to the government."

The clergy of the Church of England, usually conservative, were from the first suspect in the colonies as Tories. Among them was Samuel Seabury who had to seek British protection at New York. He was born in Connecticut, graduated at Yale University, was ordained in London in 1743, and later became rector at Westchester in New York. In 1775 Seabury, who had a pungent literary style, attacked the "unlawful congresses and committees" that undertook to regulate the conduct of free men. The Congress at Philadelphia represented, he said, not the wisdom but the turbulence and the folly of the population. If one of these "committee gentlemen," so busy with the affairs of their neighbours, should come to his house and give himself airs, "I shall," he said, "show him the door, and if he does not soon take himself away, a good hickory cudgel shall teach him better manners." There is, he added, a great outcry about tea. England, forsooth, is oppressing the colonies, when a single bushel of flax seed would pay the tax on all the tea that any one person would use in more than thirty years. Moreover the very people who fought this tax as imposed by an outside assembly were trying to fasten on New York the authority of a factious congress that interfered with the commerce of every colony. Along this way, he said, lay disaster. Even if the colonies should break the tie with their king, they would soon be at war among themselves as to the kind of government to set up and more blood would be shed to establish the new commonwealth.

This loyalist doctrine taught by Seabury had not gone unpunished. When, on November 22, 1775, he was absent, teaching in his school, an armed mob had entered the rectory, pushed a bayonet against the breast of one of his daughters and threatened to kill her if she would not tell where her father might be found. Ruffianly elements in the mob pillaged the house and carried off everything of value. Seabury himself was seized at the school, put on his horse and, wholly without legal warrant, was taken across the frontier of New York into Connecticut. At New Haven he was received by an insulting crowd, thrown into jail and kept there during many weeks. Though he was allowed, in the end, to return home, his life was continually in danger and at one time he and others of his friends were obliged to lie hidden behind a chimney in a secret room of a country house where their food reached them through a trap door in the floor. Seabury's church was gutted, his rectory was used as barracks, and for thirty miles round the country was laid waste. Seabury himself escaped within the British lines. In spite of his fiery loyalism he had no personal ties with England. "I have no interest," he said, "but in America. I have not a relation out of it that I know of." After the Revolution he accepted the republic and he lived to become the first bishop of the Protestant Episcopal Church in the United States.

This persecution of loyalists began long before war broke out. When, as early as in November, 1774, John Chandler, a judge at Worcester, Massachusetts, refused to join in the popular agitation about tea, he was, under pain, as he said, "of ignominious Death," forced to leave "a beloved wife and sixteen children to the mercy of the Rebells," to abandon an extensive property that he never recovered, and to take refuge with the British forces in Boston. Each side matched the other in bitterness. The fury of Abigail Adams against the British, her shame that English blood ran in her veins, was equalled by a lady on the Tory side, Mrs. Higginson, who hoped for the day when Boston should so pay for its treason that she should drive through Whig blood to the hub of her chariot wheels. In March, 1776, Whigs in Boston, who declared that they had lived in dread of massacre by the loyalists, with Howe's military strength behind them, were naturally elated to find that he had decided to withdraw his army. On March 17 they saw their loyalist enemies hurrying to the departing ships "as if the very Devil was after them," in a long procession of carriages, carts, trucks and wheel-barrows, laden with their own goods and in some cases with loot gathered by lawless spirits, bold to plunder while the British army was still in control. With gladness in her heart Abigail Adams saw the ships sail away to Halifax, the largest fleet, as she believed, ever seen in America. Many officials who had carried on the government were now among the sorrowing exiles and many stately mansions were then abandoned by loyalist owners. They took with them the royal arms that had adorned the council chamber of the State House. The Lion and the Unicorn, wrote Edward Winslow humorously from Halifax in 1785, were "constant members of the council at Boston . . . ran away when the others did, have suffered, are of course Refugees and have a claim for residence at New Brunswick." They may still be seen in Trinity Church, St. John. Six days at sea, in some cases on uncovered decks in the biting March air, must have involved prolonged torment to the exiles, among whom were children and delicate women. The hunting out of loyalists continued. In 1778 an Act of the Legislature of Massachusetts banished a portentous number, who were forbidden to return on pain of death without benefit of clergy. Their names read like a list of the leading families. The property of these absentees was confiscated.

While it was in Massachusetts that the exile of loyalists on a great scale began, that colony was soon so entirely revolutionary in character that loyalism was silenced. On the other hand the continued British occupation of the city of New York gave its loyalists both standing and hope, with the result of prolonged and bitter strife. Though Virginia had its marked social distinctions, New York was the most aristocratic of all the colonies. The city itself was one of castes where already, long before the Revolution, Whig and Tory were in sharp conflict. While we are sometimes staggered by the vast holdings of land of some of the great families in England, we find similar conditions in New York. As late as in 1763 grants of a million acres each were made by the governor. The Van Rensselaers had estates some fifty miles long by forty wide and were like feudal lords to vassals already restless in their demand for free lands. Though, as a result of the Revolution, the Tory owners lost their estates, the Whigs kept theirs and this problem of dividing up the land remained acute, especially on the upper Hudson, long after the Revolution. Though the city of New York did not then rank in influence with Boston or Philadelphia, it was already a cosmopolitan seaport. When in 1776 the Howe brothers laid siege to it, John Jay and other leaders urged that it should be destroyed by Washington's retiring army rather than left in the hands of the hated loyalists. There was, of course, a mob element in New York of crude and turbulent dock labourers and artisans who raged against the king as a similar class raged in Boston. On the other hand a few influential families dominated social life and, during the seven long years of the war, those among them who were loyalists had the support of a powerful British army and fleet. These loyalists so intermarried as to form a kind of "family compact," that blocked the aspirations of democracy. Two-thirds of the property of New York belonged to the loyalists or to the crown. The most powerful religious body, the Church of England, was so entirely on the loyalist side that when the day of exile came the whole congregation of Trinity Church, the spire of which is now dwarfed by the higher towers of Wall Street, went into exile in Nova Scotia, headed by their venerable rector. The King's College that the revolution turned into Columbia University was controlled by Anglicans. Half of the population of one hundred and eighty thousand in the colony of New York remained loyalist to the end of the revolution and they furnished a third of the hundred thousand loyalists forced into exile.

The loyalists always held that at any time a free vote in the colony of New York would have given them a great majority. While this is probably true, they lacked the organizing skill of their opponents. The assailant is usually more urgent than the defendant. He has a grievance, he desires change, and is likely to be bolder and more clamorous than those who wish merely to preserve things as they are. The early zeal of Samuel Adams of Massachusetts in appealing to the passions of the multitude was copied in other colonies. In consequence, while it is probable that most of those concerned in summoning the Continental Congress had no intention of separating from Great Britain, radical elements so gained control from the outset that long before the Declaration of Independence they pursued the Tories as traitors and held themselves to be the only patriots. Because in New York the danger was greatest, New York was probably better organized to suppress loyalism than any other colony. The provincial Congress, which took over the functions of the deposed legislature, named a "committee to detect conspiracies" and each county and even each small community had a committee to watch the Tories. So complete was the organization that probably the point of view of every family in the whole colony was known to the varied agencies warring on enemies of the Revolution. The Declaration of Independence, based on the right of revolution, made the loyalists the traitors to the newly established system. It so ended the legality of the British administration of justice that an easy test of a loyalist's opinions was to require him to take an oath that renounced allegiance to George III. He was a traitor if he refused.

Except in the part of New York held by the British and, for a time, in the extreme southern colonies, Tories were hunted down with systematic rigour. To fail to join the militia to fight Britain became, for the able-bodied, evidence of treason. In order to make clear the identity of such black sheep, practically every colony passed a Test Act requiring each good citizen to carry on his person a certificate that he was free of the suspicion of loyalty to King George. To secure a certificate the holder must swear allegiance to the colony where he dwelt, renounce allegiance to the king and promise to support his state in its war upon him. Usually a date was named before which a person under suspicion must secure his certificate, and woe to the suspected man who failed in doing so. Since in some cases magistrates were paid a fee for each certificate, they were naturally zealous to make sure that any designated person should secure one. When a loyalist fled rather than abjure the king, his property was almost certain to be confiscated, some provision being usually reserved for the wife and children whom he might leave behind. If he remained at home and, while not active in politics, still refused the test, he was treated much as the Roman Catholic recusants had been treated in England in the days of James I. Suspected loyalists were not allowed to keep arms and had to give up motley collections of muskets, pistols, and swords. If a loyalist went away from home he might not stay at an inn unless he could produce a certificate of character. He was expected to illuminate his house for victories over the British. He had to pay special taxation. He might not hold a government office, nor act as guardian or executor, nor vote, nor serve on a jury, nor be a lawyer, nor a physician, nor a schoolmaster. He could not buy nor sell land, nor sue a debtor, nor seek legal redress if he considered himself injured. Even to drink tea was to become liable to outrage. A loyalist who named his dog "Tory" was reprimanded by a magistrate, since he seemed thus to imply that a Tory lived a dog's life, though, so it was declared, Tory treason brought only deserved justice.

Fussy committees watched a loyalist's every action and he was likely, at any time, to be hauled before a self-appointed tribunal and compelled to give an account of his words and deeds. Mounted local militia would sometimes scour a county in order to uncover Tories and might plunder mercilessly those whom they deemed guilty. The informer against a supposed offender received, in some cases, half the fine imposed and this sharpened zeal. To be an avowed loyalist meant in most of the colonies ultimate exile and meanwhile to be a social outcast, sent so completely to Coventry that even old friends would not greet him in the streets. Good Whigs would not sit in church with a Tory present. Sometimes public warning was given by name against Tories. The saying of a wit of the time was generally accepted by Whig partizans,—that "a Tory is a thing whose head is in England and its body in America and its neck ought to be stretched." Even the memorials of the dead were not spared. When the burial plot of Governor

Hutchinson at Copp's Hill in Boston was sold, the purchaser erased the names of the governor's family, graven in stone, and inserted those of his own choice, retaining, however, the governor's armorial bearings.

The loyalists were charged with inciting Indian savagery. While the colonies had themselves tried to make an alliance with the more aggressive Indian tribes and had failed, the British had succeeded. In consequence every massacre by Indians was said to be due to the Tories. Fictitious accounts of horrors in war are not the invention of modern journalism. Franklin, who had a sparkling gift of humour and satire, described with apparent gravity, intended by him to conceal a grim jest, a wholly imaginary barbarity. Since, so he wrote, it was known that George III took delight in seeing the scalps of his rebellious subjects, the Senecas, a tribe of the Iroquois, had made up bales of scalps to send to him. These when captured by the colonial forces were found, so the story went, to contain the scalps of 43 soldiers, 297 farmers, some of whom had been burned at the stake, 67 old people, 88 women, 193 boys, 211 girls and 29 infants. There were other bales that had not been captured but Franklin's exact figures were sufficiently large and were taken seriously by some people.

In days before the Revolution mob resentment had expressed itself even in England by covering its victim with tar and then rolling him in feathers. When, early in the struggle, a reckless shoemaker in Virginia shouted in the highway "Hurrah for King George," some colonial soldiers tied a rope round his waist and hauled him back and forth in the adjacent river until he was nearly drowned. Nevertheless, each time when he came to the surface he cheered for the king with what breath was left. While still giving half-smothered cries the man was plunged head first into a barrel of tar and was then rolled in the feathers of a bed taken from his own house. Similar scenes are found in nearly every colony. Though tarring and feathering was perhaps the most favoured punishment, it seemed appropriate to revolutionary justice to carry through jeering crowds a loyalist gagged and bound, astride a rail with sharp angles, or of an unsaddled horse, with his face to the tail and his coat turned inside out; to cause a hot Tory to sit long on a lump of ice and so be cooled; or to hoist these enemies of liberty upon a liberty pole and for a time keep them there with perhaps a dead animal hanging beside them. Patriots of the new school remembered the torments that their ancestors had suffered in the days of Laud and now copied them. It was a grim pleasantry to brand High Church Tories with the cross. Sometimes there was added whipping, a cropping of ears, and exposure in the pillory. Savage mobs expelled aged people from their houses, which might then be burned; sometimes they destroyed the mills of loyalists and maimed their cattle. Loyalists, carted from town to town, might have to pay a fine at each town. They might be compelled to pay for a guard to their houses, not always effective for its purpose, since some loyalists were murdered. To hang a loyalist in effigy before his own door, or to fire at his lighted windows was an evidence of patriotism.

From the first Washington was relentless to loyalists. It happened in New York, before the city fell to the British in 1776, that along the street, past the house in which Washington lodged, came a mob carrying on the shoulders of two stalwart men a loyalist astride the sharp edge of a rail and held in place by a man at each side. When later, in the provincial Congress of New York, Generals Putnam and Mifflin denounced this cruelty, Washington rebuked them; only an enemy to the cause of liberty would, he said, discourage such proceedings. To him all loyalists were cowards, traitors, the vilest of mankind, unfit to live. It could not have shocked Washington that in December, 1776, the

Provincial Congress of New York ordered the securing of all the pitch and tar "necessary for the public use and the public safety," a purpose that we may imagine. Even in the hour of victory he remained relentless. At the surrender of Cornwallis at Yorktown in 1781 he would grant no terms to loyalists who had fought on the British side. They were, he said, guilty of treason and deserved its penalties. By smuggling them away on a despatch ship sent to New York, Cornwallis saved them from the gallows. When in the next year the British evacuated Charleston twenty-four loyalists were hanged while the British fleet still lay in the harbour.

There were, of course, many loyalist spies and also many loyalist plots. In some states arrested offenders were treated mildly, but where loyalism was a real menace punishments were severe. In May, 1777, a court martial in the colony of New York sentenced fourteen loyalists to death and twelve were executed. Pennsylvania attainted four hundred and ninety persons for high treason and treason might involve death and the confiscation of property. After the British evacuated Philadelphia in 1778, a blind fury burst out against persons suspected of friendly relations with the recent victors. Two loyalist citizens, Roberts and Carlisle, men of standing, were tried for treason and sentenced to death. The wife of Roberts, leading her children, made on her knees an agonized appeal for mercy to the Continental Congress, but in vain. The two men, with halters round their necks, were marched behind a cart to the place of execution. Before dying Roberts declared that he suffered for no wrong-doing but only for devotion to his sovereign and he turned to his children, who were present at this scene, and urged them never to give up the principles for which he died. Though the severity to these two men caused such a reaction that a sympathetic crowd attended their funeral, the confiscations continued on an extensive scale. Samuel Adams, writing from Philadelphia in October of that year, expressed the fear that this zeal might slacken and urged increased efforts to stimulate it. Only corrupt men, he thought, would have any feeling of mercy for "Traitors who first conspired the Ruin of our Liberties," wretches "who basely forsook their country in her Distress." To suffer such men to return and enjoy their estates would be madness.

Inevitably loyalist retaliation showed similar bitterness. A policy of frightfulness, disliked by most British officers, was deliberately adopted by General Clinton, who succeeded Howe in 1778 as commander-in-chief. His father had been governor of the colony of New York and his own youth in the colony may have given him special sympathy with the loyalist refugees. From the secure base of New York he sent out many ravaging expeditions. One to the shores of Chesapeake Bay destroyed property valued at three hundred thousand pounds. Guerilla warfare made the country near New York, in Long Island, New Jersey and Connecticut a No-Man's Land where life was unsafe. The loyalists were the aggressors since the ruin was chiefly in country hostile to them, but each side had a share in the desolation. Loyalist raiders were called Cowboys while the other side were Skinners. The names seem to imply that their chief loot was cattle, for which both found a market in New York. In the southern colonies, where each party in turn gained the upper hand, the massacres and executions were a discredit to human nature. General Greene, perhaps the most capable of the leaders in Washington's army, wrote that "the Whigs seemed determined to extirpate the Tories and the Tories the Whigs," and that unless this could be stopped the country would be depopulated. The devastation of a whole country side in this savage warfare is described by the colonial general, William Moultrie, who defended Charleston in 1780, was taken prisoner by the victorious British, and later exchanged for General

Burgoyne. During a ride in 1783 of a hundred miles in a district of South Carolina, once rich and flourishing, he found only devastation. Houses had been destroyed and stock scattered. Included almost in the category of beasts were half-savage negro slaves who had run away. "The most dull, melancholy, dreary ride that any one could possibly take," wrote Moultrie. The destruction was so complete that signs of the life even of the squirrels and birds had disappeared. Only scavenging buzzards remained. Moultrie found the house on his own estate an empty skeleton. In much of the fighting in the south no quarter was given. The Congress troops hanged ten loyalist prisoners of position after the victory of King's Mountain, in October, 1780. Along the western frontier of the colonies there had been a long tradition of merciless strife and horrors familiar during Pontiac's war nearly a score of years earlier were now repeated on a larger scale.

On the sea coast there was similar destruction. Each side fitted out privateers and British commerce suffered heavily from American attacks. In international warfare it is easy to know the enemy for he has the brand of another nation. But in civil war the enemy may be a next-door neighbour professing friendship. If he is insincere the resultant fear and suspicion may inspire cruel deeds. Lord Dunmore, the Governor of Virginia, was forced, as early as in June, 1775, to take refuge on a British man-of-war which he then declared to be the seat of government. When the Virginia Assembly named a committee of safety to rule the colony, Dunmore ravaged towns on the coast, proclaimed martial law, and offered freedom to all slaves who should enlist on the British side. This stirred the Virginia slave-owners to frenzy. When, on January 1, 1776, Norfolk, the chief seaport in Virginia, was burned to ashes with a loss of four hundred thousand pounds, Dunmore was chiefly blamed for this devastation. Connecticut, lying so near the British in

New York, was specially harassed by the loyalists. They burned Fairfield and Norwalk and the ships in New Haven harbour and set on fire the town itself. Under cover of night loyalist parties dashed up the Hudson and into Connecticut, burning an occasional village, devastating farms and seizing cattle, sheep, poultry and grain.

The treatment of prisoners deepened bitterness on each side. Even at the best, to be in prison in that period was to suffer great hardships. Just at this time John Howard, while working for prison reform, found terrible conditions in the English prisons. He had, as Burke said, surveyed "the mansions of sorrow and pain" all over Europe and had found the prisons of England hardly better than the worst. Owing to bad sanitary conditions they were ravaged by gaol fever and smallpox. It was a British practice to confine prisoners in the hulks of old ships lying in harbour, and often these vessels became loathsome with disease. If the British treated their own people with such savagery, it is certain that they would not be gentle when they held as prisoners colonists whom they regarded as rebels and traitors. When Henry Laurens, a friend of Washington and one of the commissioners who negotiated the final treaty of peace, was a prisoner in the Tower of London for more than a year, he declared that his treatment amounted to slow murder.

At New York, a loyalist centre, the British held many prisoners whose sufferings on the prison ships seem now almost incredible. It is estimated with some care that in the "Old Jersey" ship, that lay in New York harbour, perished as many as eleven thousand American seamen, captured by the British. Thomas Andros, a youth from Connecticut, kept for a time in this rotting hulk, declared that the food, drink, air and treatment were all alike foul. The prisoners were crowded below decks at night and were always half starved. Dysentery, smallpox, and yellow fever raged and Andros saw no attempt at either medical or spiritual care for the sick. Some prisoners became deranged by suffering and there was a panic when a madman with a knife ran amok among the prisoners crowded in the dark hold. Philip Freneau, a poet who lived to write fiery patriotic verse about the war of 1812, was at one time a prisoner. Sir Walter Scott thought his lament for the American dead at Eutaw "as fine a thing as there is of the kind in the language";

> "They saw their injured country's woe,
> The flaming town, the wasted field,
> Then rushed to meet the insulting foe;
> They took the spear—but not the shield."

In 1780 Freneau, after his capture on a ship sailing to the West Indies, was confined in one of the hulks at New York. He describes how the prisoners were driven below at evening:

> "Three hundred wretches here denied all light,
> In crowded mansions pass the infernal night."

The cry came to them in the morning "Rebels, turn out your dead." When they went on deck the usual daily sight greeting them was a boat-load of dead bodies leaving the ship. We need not attach special malignity to this treatment. Brutality to the unfortunate is a characteristic of the time and some domestic prison ships in England were, in a measure, the "complete image and anticipation of Hell" that Andros found at New York.

Since the loyalists in New York had special reasons to be bitter against the Revolution, we hear reports of their bayonetting and hanging rebel prisoners for real or supposed misconduct, and exulting over the dead bodies. As we have seen, Colonel Ethan Allen, who had seized Ticonderoga in 1775, was made prisoner in the autumn of that year. When taken at Montreal he barely escaped being executed but instead was sent in irons to England with the promise that he should be hanged. He was a provoking person, for he himself exults in his "flood of language" that assailed his jailers. In the end he was carried back to New York. There, he says, he saw loyalists gloating over prisoners shivering with cold, pleading for food, and in their need sucking bones and chewing wooden chips. He saw, in churches used for the sick, the dead lying in filth among the living and no touch of humanity relieved the horror. While it is certain that Ethan Allen's gift of language caused him to exaggerate, he expressed the conviction of the time that the British treated the colonial prisoners with brutality. On the other hand loyalist prisoners were sometimes treated with equal rigour. Prisoners were so crowded in the jail at Reading that they could not lie nor even sit down. They had a daily allowance of ten ounces of bread and also ten of meat, this usually, however, so rotten as to be unfit for food. At East Granby, in Connecticut, there was an old worked-out copper mine reached by a ladder in a deep shaft and here, sixty feet under ground, loyalist prisoners were confined in darkness, damp and filth. In May, 1781, late at night when the hatches were removed to admit a visitor, the prisoners attacked the guard, and twenty-eight escaped. They must have had friends near who helped them, for only a few were re-captured.

On both sides language was vivid. When Samual Adams called the loyalists "puling pusillanimous cowards," Peter Oliver retorted that if he "wished to draw the picture of a devil" he should ask Adams to sit for him. Edward Winslow, the elder, a staid official of the law-courts at Plymouth, Massachusetts, says that for his loyalism in the early days of the strife he became "the butt of the licentious and . . . received every species of insult and abuse which the utmost rancour and malice could invent." To the frantic colonial patriot the British red coat became the symbol of a brutal tyranny, with the cowardice of the bully at its heart; pipe clay, perfect manual exercise and marching in reviews, all the pomp of the life of the British soldier could not conceal the truth that he was a slave unable to win in a fight with free men. Britain's sailors were pirates, her statesmen scoundrels. Even her bishops showed the cruelty of butchers, and all were ready to die for a smile from a tyrant king. The hot colonial poet, John Trumbull, described the breed:

"A dastard race who long have sold
Their souls and consciences for gold."

They were under a crowned ruffian. Since a king was at the head of the British system, kings became, as the colonial poet Freneau says, "the choicest curse that man e'er knew," and George III the incarnation of all villainy, a disgrace to human nature, a fiend in human guise. To-day we can afford to smile at the picture by Hugh Henry Breckenridge, a Scot turned colonial patriot, of the devout George III as the master of "such accomplished fraud, perfidy and murder, that every one heretofore mentioned is lost and disappears." George is worse than Cain. Fathers and mothers are to teach their children that the country which tolerated him should be execrated by mankind. The colonies were forever expecting that revolution in England would overthrow such a monster.

Even if all this is provincial, lacking in a sense of proportion and of humour, the passion was so real as to make reconciliation impossible except with the lapse of time. Newspapers spread tales of British barbarism; they were thundered from pulpits Sunday after Sunday until colonial civilians and soldiers alike were filled with loathing for a cause that to them meant degradation and slavery. Poems were written, dramas were played to illustrate the baseness of the British king and of all who still owned to him allegiance and bore "the all-disgracing name of Englishman." Even in Hell, one poet says, the most foul and ugly ghosts shall point to one object of special loathing and say "that was an Englishman." Such hate, once created, is apt to have an enduring tradition. A whole literature grew up to consecrate it. England herself was less embittered. She had no towns in flames, no countryside ravaged in civil strife. In England no one friendly to the rebel cause suffered loss of property, or death, or even violence. The tone in high circles was one of wounded pride at the presumption of colonists who dared to defy their lawful sovereign. Always in England leading men, among them Richmond, a Duke, Rockingham, a Marquis, Chatham, an Earl, Burke and Fox, eminent in the House of Commons, spoke out fiercely for the colonial side. Coke of Norfolk, a great landowner, toasted Washington instead of George III at a public banquet. While a statue of Washington adorns London, not, to my knowledge, has any British leader against or, it seems, even for the Revolution been so remembered in the United States. To the masses George III remains so disgraced that among them kingship has become a symbol of tyranny and England herself is branded with infamy.

Though Shelburne, the real author of the treaty of peace, had declared that he would never abandon the loyalists, there was little in the treaty to bring them comfort. The Congress of the United States had disclaimed any obligation to help them and had promised only to ask for mercy from the pitiless legislatures of the states. Even the appeal that Congress knew would not be heeded was grudging in its terms. For "real British subjects," that is, citizens of Great Britain, Congress would ask the restoration of confiscated property. For citizens living in areas occupied by the British, it would ask the same, if they had not borne arms against the United States. For all others there should be liberty for a year to go where they might wish and to do what they could to recover their property, but only on condition that the existing holder of confiscated lands should receive the *bona fide* price that he had paid. Congress promised that imprisoned loyalists should be freed. It promised too that there should be no future confiscations or vengeful legislation for action during the war.

These pledges were not, and perhaps could not be, fulfilled. In truth the conclusion of peace added to the oppression of the loyalists. While the war continued there was always uncertainty as to the outcome and some moderation was wise in view of the possible day of wrath when loyalism should have triumphed. The victorious peace ended such fears. Vigilance committees remained active. On March 17, 1783, the seventh anniversay of the evacuation by the British in 1776, Boston resolved that no loyalist should be allowed to return or to have "lot or portion with us" and it invited other towns to take similar action. The citizens of Worcester, Massachusetts, passed in public meeting on May 12, 1783, nearly two months after the terms of the treaty were known, a series of votes that it would be dangerous to the public safety to permit the return of "parricides" who had involved their country "in tumult, ruin and blood," and that no free and independent people would submit to the outrage of having among them such criminals. As to the restoration of their estates, this would be "unreasonable, cruel and unjust." Thousands of good citizens, "innocent, peacable and defenceless inhabitants of these states" had lost their property, and there had been no serious talk of restoration or compensation to them at the expense of loyalists. In flying, the loyalists had refused to protect their own property and had thus abandoned and forfeited it. We should not look too closely into this reproach for refusing to protect their property, since those who made the charge would probably have killed or im-

prisoned loyalists trying to stay on guard, but it was a
plea good enough to use against absent owners. Worcester,
like dozens of other towns, was quite resolved that no loyalists should be allowed to return.

A vigorous public opinion in nearly all the colonies
favoured a similar policy. Few even of the national leaders, including Washington himself, had a word for conciliation. Though John Adams believed that moderation
might now be politic, he had, none the less, the relentless
opinion that Tories "ought to be hanged." Religious leaders were sometimes foremost in calling for extreme measures.
"It is the command of God that in cursing we curse them,"
said the Reverend Nathaniel Whitaker, a leading pastor in
Salem, Massachusetts. Such vermin, it was said, ought not
to be allowed to remain among a free people. To spare
them would be to betray posterity. There were few to
protest that the state which drove out so virile an element
injured itself. Joseph Stansbury had been an ardent loyalist writer whose patriotism may be seen in his verse:

> "On cristal throne, uplifted high,
>   Imperial Britain sate;
> Her lofty forehead reached the sky,
>   Her awful word was fate."

When, however, peace was made, he proved ready to accept
the republic and in 1783 returned to Philadelphia. But to
alert patriotism a spirit so ardent could not be forgiven. A
letter thrown in at his door gave warning that he could
not live there, though it was added significantly he might
easily die there, and he had to fly. In the end he found a
refuge in New York where he remained obscure. A certain
Cavalier Jouet wrote to Carleton that while, during the
war, a prisoner on parole in Woodbridge, New Jersey, he
had received civility, but that a change came with the news
of peace. Then a threatening mob told him that all paroles
were ended, that he had been a traitor to his country and

should never again enjoy its benefits. He heard a militia
general ask what they intended to do with the "damned
rascal" and a local Justice called out "Hang him up, hang
him up." Aided by the intercession of the local clergyman
and of a man whom his family had befriended, he escaped
to New York. Samuel Jarvis from South Carolina described
his experience after the terms of peace were known. A mob
came to him at daybreak of May 22, 1783, and told him
that to save his life he must be thirty miles away by sun-
set. Already some of his neighbours had been ridden on a
rail or on the bare back of a horse with their face to the
tail, their coats turned inside out, and a wooden sword at
their sides—a spectacle that brought "great joy and satisfaction to the spectators."

This harsh treatment stiffened Carleton's resolve while
in command at New York to render to the loyalists the utmost possible service. It was his duty to urge the carrying-
out of the terms of peace. New York was securely in his
hands and in Europe Great Britain, triumphant on the
sea, had humbled her enemies. Her flag now floated unchallenged over Gibraltar; it floated too over the forts within
the territory of the United States that commanded its whole
northern frontier; even the French admiral who had had
the chief share in her humiliation at Yorktown was now
her prisoner. Naturally her temper was rising; she was
critical of the manner in which the republic was meeting
its obligations under the treaty of peace. Congress was doing nothing to protect the loyalists and was giving little aid
to British creditors whose claims on private debtors it had
recognized as valid. The belief was widespread in England
that the colonies could not hold together and might indeed
soon be at war among themselves. Their differences were
acute. Connecticut even imposed a tariff against New York.
In consequence the British government was resolved, even

when it should give up New York, to hold Niagara, Detroit and other western posts as hostages for justice and mercy. This was one motive; another related to the advantage to the fur-trade from control of the routes to the west. The British continued to hold the forts for so long a period after the war that this seemed likely to cause a new war; the last fort, Niagara, was not given up until thirteen years after Carleton went home.

In time some loyalists were pardoned by the state legislatures while others of the more obscure or moderate were merged in the population and became good republicans. The sterner loyalists would not, however, even accept pardon, granted, as they thought, by the sinner to the saint, and preferred exile. In any case, for the more conspicuous and determined there was no forgiveness and persecution endured. The federal government, even had it desired to give relief, could do little. It was so weak during the four or five years after the signing of the treaty that many, including George III, expected its collapse. It had almost no money and it commanded slight authority. Only when in 1787 a convention met to frame a constitution was it certain that the colonies could form a great union and not, as did later the Spanish colonies, divide into many nations. Unhappily for the loyalists it was in these days of paralysis of federal power that their fate was sealed. Not a single state repealed its laws respecting the confiscation of their property. Since, in many cases, this had gone as plunder to patriots enriched by such booty, these were sure to find golden reasons for an irreconcilable temper. The long war had brought into the army a class of officers who, Washington himself said, were "not fit to be shoe-blacks." Congress had deteriorated. In the first Congress were remarkable men but it is on record that Gouverneur Morris of Pennsylvania said to John Jay of New York: "What a lot of damned rascals we had in that second Congress," and that Jay replied "Yes, we had." When, half-heartedly, Congress recommended moderation most of the thirteen legislatures derided its appeals. The loyalists must go forth like Milton's primitive man from the garden:

"The world was all before them, where to seek
Their place of rest, and Providence their guide."

In July, 1782, the British evacuated Savannah. In December when the loyalists left Charleston they carried away with them even the church bells which, however, Carleton promptly returned. In spite of crowding and cold, those were happiest who could travel by sea. But even from distant Virginia loyalists travelled overland to New York, singly or in companies, sometimes in carts or carriages, often toilsomely on foot. Tories of the humbler sort, held still as prisoners, were sometimes chained together in bands of ten or twenty, and driven like cattle on rough roads for long and weary journeys of two or three hundred miles until they reached the British lines. For the most part, their possessions were only the few trifles that they could carry with them. Carleton received with sympathy and pity these "brave unfortunate people . . . many of them of the very first families," reduced, as he said, "to a condition that makes one's heart bleed." He housed some in tents or rough huts on vacant land in New York, others on the derelict farms of Long Island, and in Kings, Queens, and Suffolk counties. In the end he had about thirty thousand on his hands. Some, no doubt, were of the baser sort, but all shared a common misery, and for all it was necessary to find new homes.

The refugees at New York formed a motley collection. The many negroes were for Carleton a hard problem since it was not easy to determine whether they were persons with rights like those of other loyalists or, as slaves, property of which he had no right to deprive their American owners.

The many soldiers from Europe were to be sent home unless willing to remain in the new world and share a fortune similar to that of the loyalist exiles. The regiments of loyalists, their military tasks ended, were to be disbanded on reaching their grants of land. There were other and varied types; men and women, formerly well-to-do, now sometimes with young families facing a stern struggle to live they knew not where; men used to work with their hands, including some who could and would not; good characters and bad characters; hundreds of freed black men destined not greatly to thrive in that northern cold which has helped to save Canada from the colour problem of the United States.

A joint commission supervised the embarking of the exiles and of the British regiments and the harbour of New York was busy with the many ships brought together for the purpose. Almost daily in the summer of 1783 transports left New York, now with a German regiment for Europe, now with a British regiment setting out for England or Scotland or Ireland; now for the West Indies; now with families destined to find sympathy but also a cheerless outlook in Halifax and other places too thronged with their kind. Some six thousand embarked in May and the same number in June. Ward Chipman, destined later to hold high official position in the New Brunswick that had been part of Nova Scotia, wrote of his anxious watching at New York from day to day and of the prevailing bitter temper against any loyalists who might remain. By November came the final departure of the British that must be regarded as marking a momentous phase of human history.

During the seven years in which New York had been a British garrison town, it had been in some respects gay, since the many British officers were, for the most part, young and keen for enjoyments that often passed over into dissipation. There were dinners, dances, plays, gambling, chiefly in a game called *Pharaoh,* and horse-racing. Carleton entertained so elaborately as for one occasion to have to borrow one hundred and forty-two dozen pieces of china and glass. Eligible young men of good family, wellbred and with plenty of money, inspired loyalist mothers in New York with hopes for their daughters. Many visitors arrived, among them the royal prince destined some fifty years later to be King William IV; Rodney who made prisoner of the French Admiral de Grasse, the naval victor at Yorktown; and, most interesting of all, young Horatio Nelson in training finally to give Britain the command of the sea by his victory at Trafalgar, a quarter of a century later. Fashion paraded daily to see the mounting of the guard in the Mall at Trinity Church, the centre of a fervent loyalism based on religion. Business had been lively in New York. Officers spent their pay in good British coin; owners of houses secured high rents; and some contractors made fortunes in supplying not always honestly the needs of the army.

Towards the end prices rose until wood cost five pounds a cord and a pound of mutton or a quart of milk cost eighteen pence. When Baroness von Riedesel sends her cook with ten guineas to buy provisions, he returns to tell her that he must have more money since the ten guineas would buy only enough for a couple of days. The high prices were hard on the thousands of poor. By the summer of 1783 when, with the hope of victory ended, there was a feverish desire to get away, loyalists had to sell their property under adverse conditions. Their lands and houses brought low prices since the purchaser had to take risks as to the security of the title of loyalist property, liable to forfeiture for treason. New York had suffered most of American cities during the war. There had been two great fires in which hundreds of houses and Trinity Church itself had been destroyed. Its ghostly steeple still towered

over a burnt area which the occupying army had covered
with huts and tents. When returning citizens saw this
desolate nakedness and found that churches and public
buildings had been used for military purposes with the inevitable rough treatment and disgusting debris, their resentment was such that in 1784 the legislature of New York
not only deprived of civil rights all who had in any way
lent what was called comfort to the British forces but
also forbade loyalists to re-enter or repurchase their former
estates.

A sunny, cold autumn day, November 25, 1783, saw at
New York the final act that ended the long drama of the
American Revolution. From early morning crowds thronged
the streets. Most of the thousands of loyalists were already gone and it was chiefly triumphant patriots who now
watched this last parade of the vanquished. At one o'clock
a column of British troops met at a point arranged, north
of the town, an American column commanded by General
Knox, a former Boston bookseller, now Secretary for War,
chosen for this parade, it was said, because of his commanding figure. His troops, a lady observer remarked, "were
ill-clad and weather-beaten and made a forlorn appearance." Followed closely by the Americans, the British
marched down the Bowery, watched by people in holiday
array. At Wall Street the British column turned to Broad-
way and on to a wharf where they took boats at once for
the ships at Staten Island. Knox's column turned to the
left. A body of mounted civilians had gathered at Bowling
Green and Knox led them to meet Washington who rode in
from Harlem with an escort. Carleton was on parade but
he and Washington did not meet on that day of ceremony.
Chipman, who watched a scene so melancholy for one of
his opinions, said that Carleton looked unusually dejected.
New York had begun its amazing history as a republican
city. Chipman, still remaining there for two or three days,

met, he says, with no insult or molestation; the city was quiet but, with the true loyalist derision, he adds: "a more shabby, ungentlemanlike looking crew than the new Inhabitants are I never saw." He was received politely when he paid his respects to General Knox. Washington he saw and thought "a really good-looking genteel fellow." He adds that "scarce any of our friends or any man of respectability remains at New York." When he and other friends embarked for England, "I assure you" he wrote to his friend Winslow, "we make ourselves very cheerful." It is natural to feel relief when a period of strife has ended, but it was heroic for a penniless exile to be so cheerful as to say that, granted the companionship of his friends, he could be happy in a desert.

Both Carleton and Washington soon gave up their commands. On December 4, Washington said farewell to the officers with him in New York, kissed each of them, a French touch learned perhaps from Lafayette, and rode away to Philadelphia, where he ended his command; then he went on to Mount Vernon, hoping for the quiet and privacy in which, as he said, "I will move gently down the stream of life, until I sleep with my fathers." It was on November 29 that Carleton went aboard the British ship *Ceres* and sailed away from New York with his business in the United States wound up. He thought he was leaving America forever but within three years he was back again, as Lord Dorchester, to aid in shaping the future of Canada during a further half score of laborious years.

Carleton and Washington are symbols of Canada and the United States. They were alike in appearance, alike, too in outlook. Both were men of action rather than of deep thought, with talents that it is not unfair to describe as little more than mediocre but with the dominating quality of high and resolute character. It would have been a great day not merely for their two nations but for humanity if their political opinions and those of their countrymen could have been reconciled in a common citizenship based on freedom and unity. They were the final figures on the stage in a drama that has influenced the whole world and that in another century may show results even more astounding. We may doubt whether, aristocrats as both were at heart, they would have welcomed the rule of the multitude that time has brought in both nations with unexampled and perplexing fruits. Carleton had led in saving for Great Britain in the north a great territory, destined in time to show in America the contrast in government of a federal state, under the old British traditions, with a federal republic, creating its own system, making a new tradition and, during a century and a half, opening wide its doors, not indeed to Asia or to Africa, but to Europe, and inviting all classes, the fortunate and especially the distressed, to find new hope in the vast expanse of its territory and in the welcoming freedom of its institutions.

CHAPTER XIX

EXILE IN ENGLAND

THOUGH a majority of the loyalists found refuge in what is now Canada, about forty thousand scattered to other regions. Some went to the West Indies where Britain kept nearly all her former possessions, a tribute to her seapower. A goodly number of the more prominent thought that England herself would welcome patriots who had made such sacrifices. In the year 1775, long before the Declaration of Independence, an Anglican clergyman, Jonathan Boucher, a rector in Maryland, enjoying the intimate friendship of George Washington, was attacked because of his stout conviction: "As long as I live, yes, while I have my being, will I proclaim God save the King." Since he had knocked down a blacksmith insulting him for his opinions, no one could doubt his courage. When, on a day in 1775, two hundred armed men filled his church, Queen Anne's in St. George's County, and told him that he must not preach, he replied that to stop him they must take his life. He struggled toward the pulpit with a sermon in one hand and a pistol in the other, until one of his friends seized his arms and held him back, for twenty men had been ordered to fire on him should he enter the pulpit. As he was conducted from the church to his house, his enemies played "The Rogue's March" by way of added insult. In the end, with a pair of pistols lying on the pulpit cushion, he preached in his church the sermon that he had prepared. The opposing forces were, however, too strong for him and by the end of September, 1775, he was obliged to go to England, where he died as Vicar of Epsom.

A few loyalists prospered greatly in England. John Singleton Copley, a Boston artist, became a fashionable court painter. His more famous son, born in Boston in the year before the "Boston Tea-Party," became Lord Chancellor, as Lord Lyndhurst. Benjamin Thompson, another loyalist, had an astonishing career. In 1775 he was put in prison as a suspected loyalist and he was one of the exiles who sailed away from Boston to Nova Scotia in 1776. On going to England he served as under-secretary for the Colonies and was intimate with his chief, Lord George Germain. Later he had a military command in the southern colonies and on Long Island. At the close of the war he went again to England. All the time his active mind gave an austere devotion to science. He could speak French, German and Italian, as readily as English. His fellow exiles watched his career with pride. When still at loose ends in England, he told them that they should soon hear of his making a dash that should surprise them. Russia and Turkey were on the eve of a serious war and he was determined to have a hand in it on one side or the other. To his friend Chipman he became "one of the wonders of the age." George III knighted him and gave him leave to serve the Elector of Bavaria, and there he became minister of war. He turned a great area of waste land at Munich into a beautiful public park still known as the English Garden. He introduced the cultivation of the potato. The citizens put up a statue in his honour and the Elector conferred on him the title of Count Rumford, from the town in New Hampshire that is now Concord. Whig historians have delighted to deride Germain but it is to his credit that he befriended Thompson, who wrote to him from Munich in 1785 that he could be happy in his exile but for the loss of the society of "my best, my only friend." His titles, decorations literary and military, were due, he said, to Germain's friendship which had put him in such a position as to open the road to secure fortune. Rumford lived in Paris where he sat beside Napoleon in the Institute of France and he married the widow of the great chemist Lavoisier, a union that led to a bitter hate. He founded the Royal Institution in London and endowed a professorship of Physics in Harvard University, a sign that he treasured no animosity against the people who had sent him into exile. Indeed John Adams, when president, offered him high office as a military engineer in the service of the United States.

In spite of an occasional success, the loyalists in England were for the most part heart-sick exiles longing to return to the American scene where their tastes had been formed. Though imagination may deceive us about joys of the past, we like to recall days of buoyant youth, the school, the friends, the landscapes with the Psalmist's "green pastures" and "still waters," and when in an alien world we turn to them with longing regret. The heart of the exiles was not in England. There is little to encourage the view, sometimes lightly held, that England can build up other Englands remote from her shores. Surroundings and circumstances mould the daily thought and activities of people and shape their outlook. Time instead of lessening differences tends to increase them. Governor Hutchinson of Massachusetts had made heavy sacrifices to preserve the tie with England, but he wrote: "I had rather die in a little country house in New England than in the finest nobleman's mansion in Old England." He longs for apples from his native land; a few Newton pippins would, he writes, have an inspiring effect on "us Refugees." Benjamin Marston, another exile, wrote to Winslow from London in 1790 that though idle for two years he has good health and is "free from all humour, fretfulness and repining . . . Don't let misfortune depress your spirits. He who feeds the Moose and Caribou, the Wild Ducks and Geese, the Shad, Gaspereaux and Salmon takes care of you & me also . . . I don't say that to cultivate in you any liking to misfortune, no—fight, scratch, kick, bite, throw stones, do anything to her. I hate the very name of the Toad." In the next year he is longing for his native land: "O my country, when shall I revisit you and when shall I again behold your serene skies and bright suns." Since the rigid society about him had no place for one so forlorn and since "anything with something to Eat is infinitely before nothing and starving," he took in the next year a post on the west coast of Africa. "God in His Providence has at last opened me a door to escape out of England, the worst prison I was ever in." He died of the deadly African fever in the same year.

The loyalists were awed by many things in England. In January, 1776, Jonathan Sewell saw at court on the queen's birthday evidences of wealth "truly astonishing," "sufficient to have purchased our whole continent," but, he added, "unless a Gentleman can get his share of it, he has no Business here." Six hundred pounds a year would be "but as a Drop in the Ocean—the Man is lost—he is Nothing—less than Nothing and Vanity—and his Contemplation of his own comparative Littleness, is Vexation of Spirit." Sewell found London such a friendless, godless city as to be no place for him and thought that "the cold, inhospitable, Lilliputian Region of Halifax will finally bring me up," as indeed it did. In spite of political turmoil as fiery as that of a great capital, Boston was a simple, austere little city by contrast with London where the slack observance of Sunday and the dissipations and self-indulgence shocked Puritan standards. The loyalist Joshua Chandler wrote: "This kingdom, without a miracle in its favour, must soon be lost; you can have no idea of their corruption, of their Debauchery and Luxury, their Pride, their Riches; their Luxury has ruined them; it is not in the Power of

Human Nature to save them. If they are saved it must be some Heavenly Power." "The temptations," said another exile, Samuel Curwen, "are too great for that degree of philosophy and religion ordinarily possessed by the bulk of mankind." To him England seemed to be sunk in selfish, degenerate sloth and to be in danger of failing in a crisis to make "manly noble exertions." Yet he saw how vain were the colonial hopes of a change in which the people of England should overthrow a "tyrant" king. He heard instead gossip that Britain and France would agree to divide between them the colonies, France taking Canada and New England while Great Britain should retain those farther south.

So far from thinking themselves provincial, the exiled colonists joined the rebels in deriding the narrow outlook of the English. The masses seemed to them ignorant and torpid in regard to great national questions. In the colonies an able writer, Francis Hopkinson, jeered at the English shopkeepers and mechanics as childishly ignorant about politics. The maker of pins "believes in the Athanasian Creed, reverences the splendour of Parliament—and makes pin-heads." He sees a map of England four feet square and one of America two feet square and asks how can America be larger than England. To him England has all that is of any value in the world; the Thames is the greatest river, the British Constitution the most glorious; he reverences the squire who has met the Prime Minister and he feels himself in touch with the great when he sees the squire's lady in church. What more could a maker of pin-heads desire? While this was, of course, the satire of the disloyal side, the loyalists themselves found London a vast, dreary, unfriendly city, with savage manners. Madame von Riedesel, the wife of the leader of the German troops under Burgoyne, says that she saw two naked men covered with blood boxing in a London street, and that her landlady called her to the window to see this "most delightful spectacle." In Bristol, because of her foreign dress, a hundred sailors followed her shouting that she was a French prostitute. The loyalist exiles were amazed at the brutal scenes at elections, at the disorders permitted even in the law courts, at the loud boasts and threats against the Americans whose country, so many believed, was little more than a dumping ground for convicts. At Exeter Curwen found himself suspected of being an American spy. A group of loyalists walking in the streets of Bristol were attacked by a foul-mouthed virago as "damned American rebels." The loyalists, exiles from a land of plenty where food and fuel were cheap, shivered in London before a meagre fire, or perhaps had no fire at all, and thought longingly of blazing hearths where they had burned oak and walnut. "Of all the countries in the world," wrote homesick Ward Chipman, "this is the worst to be in without a good deal of money." He added that even then it had not "half the rational social enjoyments and pleasures that our own country affords . . . such as we have been used to." The supposedly dour Puritans of New England, coming from a really free and gay society, found that in England on every side there were restraints. Curwen, one of this forlorn group, says that not until after efforts extending over two or three weeks did he secure leave to see the British Museum. As early as in 1776 a New England Club of Loyalists was formed in London. They were certain of victory and feared that the king might be too lenient in dealing with the rebels who should have their turn as outcasts.

The loyalists seemed superfluous in a society highly organized and indifferent to poverty-stricken strangers. They did not understand the gradations of rank that still play a part in English society. In New England to be engaged in trade was no disgrace, but in Old England the upper classes despised trade and were apt to look upon all colonists as traders with the "low cunning" of a petty commercial class. Curwen found doors closed to him as a trader that were opened when he made it clear that he was also a judge of admiralty. It was, however, the enforced idleness, the detachment from the life of the world about them, that, more than anything else, made the loyalists heart-sick. "To stay longer in England," wrote Samuel Quincy, a former solicitor-general of Massachusetts, "absent from my friends and family, with a bare subsistence, inactive, without prospects, and useless to myself and the world, was death to me." The man who wrote this had given up everything for his political faith. His father was a stern revolutionary and the two, separated by the civil war, never met again. In the desolation of London money had wings and poverty was a cruel companion. Needy exiles with a grievance, haunting official anterooms, are rarely welcome and, Curwen said, they found "the hand of charity very cold. . . . Blessed is he (saith Pope) that expecteth nothing for he shall never be disappointed." Many a time the delays and insolence of office made them wonder whether, after all, their sacrifices had not been due to a mistake. They did not belong to the school of loyalty that still talked of Charles I as a martyr and held a solemn religious service on the anniversary of his death.

It thus happened that the exiles, loyalists though they were, resented the tone of England towards the colonies. These, they admitted, had been too certain that they could bring England to her knees by destroying her trade, too fond of boasting of the nobility of their cause and of the strength and grandeur of the forces arrayed against tyranny, too sure that they could aid to bring about in England itself a revolution that should destroy George III. But English arrogance, some of these loyalists thought, was even worse. Curwen, with no occupation, travelled much and was a keen observer. He found that at the inns gentry would not mingle with persons whom they did not know, nor take part in general conversation, so that it was with boisterous members of the turf or the obscurer travellers that he chiefly talked. Once, however, at Tewkesbury, when an officer "gave himself great liberties respecting America" and said many "ungenerous and foolish and false things," Curwen's American companion "thoroughly silenced and humbled" him.

The loyalists had in truth a double patriotism, the one imperial, the other American, and often the American proved the stronger. At Bristol, a company of the exiles pass an evening pleasantly "talking treason and justifying American independence" and are anxious to show the "conceited islanders" who talked of "our colonies" and "our plantations" that they must learn to respect the brave men whom the English were fighting. The earlier exiles were, like Charles Fox, more glad than sorry when Burgoyne's army was forced to surrender at Saratoga. What now, they asked, of "the raw, undisciplined beggarly rabble" supposed to make up the colonial armies? The prevailing infirmity in England was "an overwhelming conceit of English bravery, accompanied with a contempt for other nations." There is little to support the theory that the masses in England had no wish to coerce America. The general view, as Curwen noted, was that the Americans were cowards and the French idiots. "You will," he says "scarce meet one that entertains the least shadow of a doubt that government must succeed in the utmost extent of its views." He adds with grim truth that they were celebrating the triumph before they had won the victory. It must be added that he noted a liberty of opinion not found in the colonies. At St. Peter's, Exeter, he heard Canon Barlow say that the war was unjust, that since the Americans were a religious people they might expect a blessing "and we the reverse." Probably any one in Vir-

ginia, or Massachusetts, who rebuked his own side so freely
would have experienced a midnight raid and a coat of tar
and feathers.

While not a few loyalists lost their identity as Americans
and became again English, some returned in the end to
America. Curwen, like many others, in time suspected that
he had abandoned his country, his friends and his means
to live, for a chimera, and that insults, reproaches and
even a dress of tar and feathers, were possibly more tolerable
than the exile that made him long for "that state of
quietude where the weary are at rest." His wife had preferred to stay in Massachusetts rather than to face the long
discomfort of an ocean voyage and he had been obliged to
furnish a substitute to fight in his place in the colonial
army. Curwen came back but when he saw his former home
he found that his imagination had tricked him. After the
magnificence of England, everything in America seemed
"low, mean and diminutive" and he was pained by a trans-
formation in society in which the baser elements had gained
wealth and honour, while the refined and honourable,
fallen into distress and indigence, were glad "to be unknown
and unnoticed to escape insult and plunder."

Critical as Curwen had been of England, he found in
America grievous injustice and abuses. In some states it
was the government that realized large sums from loyalists;
about two-thirds of all property in New York had belonged
to loyalists and for this the state received more than three
million dollars. In some other states, however, such property
became private spoil. Curwen was a fair-minded man and
we may believe him when he states that in his own Massachusetts the loyalists were hunted down from no higher
motive than greed for plunder. The state commissioners
named to deal with loyalist property were, he says, knaves
who failed to hand over funds on which they had laid hands.
The booty that they seized was great. Loyalists who had

been eminent in colonial life attracted special resentment. We have seen what bitterness the governor of Massachusetts, Sir Francis Bernard, aroused when he urged the British government to send troops to Boston to check the violence that had followed the disputes over the Stamp Act. When he took office in 1760 he had been so popular that in the first session under him the Assembly had made him a gift of Mount Desert Island, to-day a summer resort. His temper was, however, arbitrary and his lack of insight and tact had served to stimulate colonial unrest. Though he left the colony in 1769 and never returned, he remained titular governor for two years longer. Copley painted his portrait which still adorns the hall of Christ Church in Oxford. Bernard was a good classical scholar and a friend and benefactor of Harvard College but his policy of repression made many enemies and it was easy to sustain a claim that his property should be confiscated. He lost a beautiful country house at Jamaica Pond with sixty acres of park and garden and many exotic shrubs and plants.

The property of the Pepperell family offered even more attractive booty. The first Sir William Pepperell had led the colonial forces in the capture of Louisbourg in 1745 and had been made a baronet. In the course of a hundred years the family had acquired great estates, a fine house and garden in Boston, a vast property in Maine with thirty miles of frontage on the sea, and many thousands of acres elsewhere. While all these estates were confiscated not two-pence in the pound of the confiscation reached in the end the public treasury. Bitterness against the loyalists was thus often an excuse for robbery, met naturally by an answering hate due to injustice. As early as in 1779, New York had declared guilty of felony fifty-nine persons, all members of the Church of England; their property was forfeited; if found in the state they were to suffer death. Among them were two former governors, Dunmore and

Tryon, and also Sir Henry Clinton, Carleton's predecessor as Commander-in-Chief. No process of reasoning could make traitors to a republic of these three highly placed men, since they were not colonists but officials sent out from England. The motive of the act was to give a title to the seizure of property. It was put into force after peace had been signed and brought many thousands of pounds to the state.

CHAPTER XX

WHEN the early loyalists migrated on an extensive scale from Boston to Nova Scotia their enemies believed that exiles to this region met their deserts since, in that bleak land, they would drag out the residue of a life "more intolerable than death." It was, however, a beautiful country with a long and romantic history. At Port Royal, now Annapolis, French settlement had begun when the site of Boston was still a savage wild. During a century French and English had struggled for Nova Scotia and in 1713 France had finally yielded her claim. When, in 1755, to make Nova Scotia safe, the British deported its French inhabitants many from New England so little considered it a desolate land that they were eager to secure the vacated Acadian farms. Enterprising speculation for lands in Nova Scotia was led, it seems, by shrewd Benjamin Franklin, chiefly among his fellow citizens in Philadelphia. Anthony Wayne, a famous name in American history, spent a year in Nova Scotia with a view to securing lands about the Bay of Fundy and on the south coast. The speculators asked for a modest grant of two million acres. Fort Roseway, destined later to have a melancholy history as the loyalist town of Shelburne, was to become the capital and to be called Jerusalem by its devout sponsors in Philadelphia. Choosing so sacred a name they must have counted on good fruits in the land of promise. In 1760 they received a grant of a million acres, with the result that so many thousands of farmers went from the English colonies to Nova Scotia as to make Nova Scotia a literal outpost of New England. Halifax had liked the Stamp Act hardly more than Boston and extreme spirits had threatened death and damnation to the agent for the stamps. Since most of the members of the legislature were from New England, their sympathies tended to run with the rebel colonies. Two members supported the revolution and their constituencies sent four delegates to the Continental Congress. To the last Samuel Adams was convinced that Nova Scotia wished to be a state in the Union. While British power on the sea made this impossible, by land, too, Nova Scotia was well under control by its British garrison and by loyalist sentiment. The republican element, forced out of the country, appealed to Congress for compensation and in the end received three townships on the south side of Lake Erie where, however, the danger from Indians made life unsafe. New York and Maine also offered lands to these exiles; but only after more than half a century did the United States settle such claims.

Though Nova Scotia had been modelled on the other English colonies and especially Virginia, it was so recent a British conquest that it had remained in closer touch with England and more definitely English than they. Halifax has still a Georgian flavour in its public buildings. In its earliest days when the Church of England was the state church the British government bore the cost of a great wooden church, St. Paul's, Halifax, to seat nine hundred people and modelled on Marylebone Chapel in London. In 1758, with ceremony copied from the sedate assembly at Westminster, an elected legislature had met. In 1767 there were about thirteen thousand people in the country. Some exiled Acadians had come back, not to their former lands but to make new homes in the fertile wilderness. The British Isles furnished settlers: Scots Highlanders, sturdy Protestants from the north of Ireland, hardy Yorkshiremen.

In 1774, a pair of English travellers noted what fine people were, in particular, the settlers from England—strong, tall, ready of speech and courteous in manners. Abusive language and profanity, "the greatest scandal and reproach of Britain," were hardly known. The children had an engaging address. But, while the fishing industry was full of promise, the travellers thought the farming backward. Since markets were remote there was little stimulus to industry, and we have what is no doubt an exaggerated description of the farmers as lying abed until seven or eight and then beginning the day with a glass of rum, resting at midday from eleven to two o'clock, and quitting work at four. Equality of condition had resulted in a genuine democracy. There seemed to be little difference between masters and servants. The curse of Nova Scotia, which then included New Brunswick, was that lands had been granted freely to speculators who made promises of development but in most cases did nothing. When the real settlers came, these grants caused disputes and delays in securing titles.

The Whigs in Boston re-named this land of loyalist exile "Nova Scarcity" and were delighted to think of the Tories in a region of perpetual fog, whose rocky, barren, sodden acres could produce only a spongy moss instead of grass and where winter endured for so long that "there were nine months of winter and three months of cold weather every year." "Hell or Halifax" was a cry of the time and the Whigs hoped that they should mean much the same thing. An exultant Whig wrote of Nova Scotia:

"Of all the vile countries that ever were known
In the frigid or torrid or temperate zone,
From accounts I had there is not such another;
It neither belongs to this world nor the other."

This is, of course, a libel. Even then the Annapolis Valley was notable for its beautiful orchards; the soil was fertile; all kinds of grain did well; and the maligned climate was agreeable, as many a jaded New Englander finds to this day in happy summer holidaying.

The loyalist Winslows who migrated to Nova Scotia were colonial aristocrats. Though the people who had gone out in the *Mayflower* in 1620 to found New England were mostly of humble origin, Edward Winslow, one of their leaders, was a man of birth and education and apparently of some means, for he took with him three servants. He became governor of the Plymouth colony where during a century and a half the family was held in high honour. When Winslow went to England in 1635 Laud sent him to the Fleet Prison, because he, a layman, had solemnized marriage as a civil magistrate and had taught publicly in church. Later, after the execution of Charles I, he was so favoured by Oliver Cromwell that he remained in England. He died on shipboard when named in 1655 to superintend the expedition against the Spanish in the West Indies that made Jamaica an English colony. In spite of the family tradition his remote descendant, Edward who, after the Revolution, went into exile in Nova Scotia, was critical of the Puritan temper. "I was brought up," he wrote, "in a land of psalmody. For several years together there was nothing heard but old men and women bawling psalms and young men and women screeching hymns." On one occasion, when he asked a teacher of music why he was making a kitten squeal by pulling its tail, the man replied that he hoped to get a note that should help him to form a tune. Winslow's uncle, General John Winslow, had created a melancholy link of the family name with Nova Scotia, their future home. In 1755 he was the officer who, with acute dislike for his task, had gathered at Grand Pré hundreds of unhappy Acadians and shipped them away into scattered and homeless exile. Some of them he befriended on his own estate. He died on the eve of the revolution. The later Winslows were cheerful and humorous. There must have been a pleasant society in the little town of Plymouth for during his whole long life Edward Winslow cherished with deep affection his Plymouth friends, many of whom went with him into exile.

The revolution broke up this society. For a time Winslow's father was able to keep Plymouth quiet when other towns were in confusion but the family did not hesitate to take the loyalist side. Edward Winslow acted as guide to Lord Percy's forces that on an April day in 1775 went out from Boston to rescue the tired British army that had fought at Lexington. In March, 1776, after reconciliation had proved impossible, the young man sailed away from Boston with the hundreds of sad exiles to Halifax, but he was soon back with Howe at New York as Muster-Master-General for enlisting loyalist regiments. His old father remained meanwhile at Plymouth and for years, as he said, received every species of insult and abuse that rancour and malice could invent. A neighbour, Colonel Warren, who was under some obligation to Winslow, proved so vindictive that Winslow's daughter Sarah described him as "the completest Devil that ever was suffered to live." Winslow had stayed on at Plymouth hoping that the dispute would soon end as he wished it to end but life there became intolerable and in December, 1781, he took refuge at New York with his aged wife, two daughters and three black servants. He left behind, as his daughter wrote, a fine house, beautifully furnished, and a once happy society, to face a dreary outlook. His property was, of course, confiscated. The abandoned house is still among the finest in Plymouth.

At New York, though the gathered loyalists refused long to believe it, the fatal day of exile was near. Meanwhile the British fleet and army had made the place secure and the Winslows had quieter days than those of the torturing attentions of their neighbours at Plymouth. It is amusing, in view of the New York of to-day, that they had "a pretty box," a "delightful retreat," in the Bowery with two acres of land and the pleasure of rural life. The father wrote that he was much happier there than in the city itself at the lower end of the island where they had lived pleasantly enough for a time but which now he seldom visited. He had a good garden, quantities of the best cherries, a cow that gave plenty of milk, a horse and carriage and a round of afternoon and evening visitors. But adverse fate was closing in. After the surrender of Cornwallis at Yorktown, an ironical advertisement somehow appeared in what was still British New York offering for sale certain books; one "the right of Great Britain to the Dominion of the Sea, a poetic Fiction"; another "Thirteen Volumes on British Possessions in North America, abridged by a royal hand to a single pocket duodecimo."

During six or seven years the younger Edward Winslow, with headquarters at New York, had a trying task in organizing loyalist regiments. The regular officers of the army tended to treat these colonial and civilian recruits with a rather scornful air. They had difficulties in getting adequate equipment, the best being reserved for the regulars. Often capable, educated loyalists likely to be specially useful, because versed in the ways of the country, were left unemployed while, so Winslow thought, "coxcombs, fools and blackguards" of the regular service received favours. We find him asking why, in Heaven's name, every sergeant of the regular army should be cared for, while special capacity was ignored because not in the charmed military circle. Regular officers protested that equal rank and pensions should not be granted to "provincials." Often military tribunals gave harsh judgments on breaches of discipline and etiquette which the colonial soldier might not understand or to which he was not used. It is the old story renewed as late as in the Great War of 1914 of the expert's contempt for the amateur. When British regiments occupied territory they were apt to plunder rebel and loyalist property with equal impartiality. Winslow had seen Howe and Clinton fall into what he called "a stupor of sluggishness." In 1780, when the cause was not yet lost, Winslow is hoping for "a General that's neither a Rebel or [sic] a Histerical Fool at the Head of the British Army in America and when that happens I have no doubt that the war will terminate as every true friend to the constitution wishes."

Winslow had no pay beyond the allowance for his travelling expenses and yet on his shoulders lay the burden of rescuing his desolate family. "My finances, damn them" he wrote in 1779, ". . . Could I help when I met my precious old father and sister giving them everything I had and more too." An erroneous account had appeared in the newspapers of the younger Winslow's death and burial. Heart-broken the father was sitting on a rock at Prudence Island in Narragansett Bay, watching a boat under a flag of truce, beating in against an adverse wind. When it neared the shore the old man recognized his son. But he could hardly believe it and pulled from his pocket a newspaper that contained the sad announcement, "looked at it— looked at me; then he cried 'My God, he died,'" and fell to the ground in a faint as did also his daughter who was with him. "There were present" says Winslow, "rebel officers and rebel soldiers, king's officers and king's soldiers, sailors of both denominations and negroes. . . . All formalities usual with flags was [sic] forgotten, every man turned from us, walked different ways and were [sic] profoundly silent."

By the spring of 1783 to get away to Nova Scotia had become the rage at New York and petitions poured in to Carleton for grants of land. Already in 1782 two ship-loads of loyalists had gone to Nova Scotia. Carleton's view was generous of what a grateful country owed to these sufferers. Each family, so he wrote to the governor of Nova Scotia

in 1782, should have 500 acres, a single man 300; 2000 acres
for a church and 1000 for a school should be set aside in
each township and no fees or rents of any kind should be
charged. Carleton did not realize that such large grants
in a roadless country would separate the holders widely and
be more likely to block than to aid settlement. To the mind
of the time, however, land was always a coveted asset.
Even the commander-in-chief of the British army, the
Duke of York, secured a claim for twenty thousand acres
in Nova Scotia. It was relatively easy for Carleton to load
ships at New York with exiles, but not so easy for Governor
Parr at Halifax to find shelter and food when a load of
stricken people was landed on his shores, sometimes in
bleak days of winter. Since a man familiar with what the
exiles required should be on the spot in Nova Scotia, Carleton found him in the younger Edward Winslow. In April,
1783, Winslow sailed away to what was to be the scene of
his long life. "Your task," said Carleton, "is arduous; exe-
cute it as a man of honour. The season for fighting is over;
bury your animosities and persecute no man. Your ship is
ready. God bless you."

The antecedents of many loyalists now sent to Nova
Scotia were not unlike those of the Winslows—men of
position and education. In this respect they differed from
all but a few of the loyalists who fled by land to Canada
chiefly from the colony of New York. The contrast is seen
in the records preserved. The refugees in Canada were for
the most part inarticulate while from those who went to
Nova Scotia we have abundant and sorrowful comments
on the character of their persecutors and vivid descriptions
of sufferings and hopes. When, in the summer of 1783,
Edward Winslow Jr. reached Nova Scotia with the mission
of securing lands for exiled loyalists, his prospects were, as
he said, "blacker than Hell." But he went into the new
scene in a spirit of hopeful enthusiasm. "I am . . . in per-

fect health and in high spirits, nor shall any rascally vicissitudes which happen in this blackguard world lower them." God, he said, "had been so civil" as to consign to his care the wife and little ones whom he took with him and he added "I hope I have convinced Him that He could not have put them in better hands." He landed at Annapolis and secured across the river at Granville a tolerable farmhouse of two rooms "where we are snug as porkers." "We are," he said, "monstrous poor. I have not a spade, hoe, axe or any article of any kind. . . . A waggon would be of immense consequence . . . If I'd a boat I would not envy the Great Mogul." He needed one to cross the river to Annapolis and for fishing. If his friend Townshend would lend him his seine, "he'll make my fortune and I'll pay for it in fish and cranberries." He secured something better when in July he was given the post of secretary to General Henry Fox, the commander at Halifax. "Had I received a message from the Great Ruler of the World," he said, "allowing me to choose an appointment at this critical time I should have pointed out the very one . . . provided for me."

This appointment, with an assured though small income, lifted Winslow out of the extremes of poverty. These exiled aristocrats, sprung, as was Winslow himself, from the landed classes in England to which Oliver Cromwell belonged, had been exclusive in their social relations. A town in Massachusetts was likely to have a society as nicely graded as that of an English county. A loyalist exiled to Nova Scotia, John Wentworth, former governor of New Hampshire and a relative of the great Marquis of Rockingham, had lived in state at his little capital, Portsmouth. His house lay in a park of six hundred acres; he had a garden of forty acres, cultivated five hundred and owned a hundred thousand, and had his own flour and saw mills. The aristocracy of Portsmouth formed a charmed exclusive circle. When Wentworth travelled in his coach to Boston he required accommodation for twelve horses and eight servants. His magnificence helped, no doubt, to make the less favoured class jealous and early in the trouble he was forced to take refuge in Nova Scotia where in 1792 he became governor and later he was made a baronet. Another loyalist, Jonathan Sewell, even when living in a lodging-house in Bristol, has a footman in attendance. Winslow sends from Halifax to his wife at Granville a Scotch boy whom she is to train as her personal servant; he is to wear livery, green with white cape and cuffs, and to stand behind her chair at meals even when she is alone. Though he may not be sufficiently skilful to do her hair, he may keep his fingers in practice by doing that of the children daily. "He combs and ties my hair very well and I should be sorry he should lose that part of his education." He is not to be allowed to frequent the kitchen, where it seems there is a plurality of servants, for the women there will spoil him. "Such as he is I commend him to you—to make him exactly what you please and may God give you success." His "precious," "most adored" wife may let a friend have some of his port wine but she must keep most of it for use when he is out of debt. Though, for the moment, only rascals and misers seem to flourish and the industrious and the generous seem to be "delivered over in a lump to the Devil to be buffetted, . . . we will get to the windward of him yet."

The soldier, Henry Edward Fox, under whom Winslow served, was the younger brother of Charles James Fox and is described by Horace Walpole as the only good son of the unpopular Henry Fox, Lord Holland. He refused to be dragged into the world of high play that ruined the fortunes of his brother Charles and had a fine career as a soldier during the two revolutions of his time. He served in America when in his teens and fought at Lexington and Bunker Hill and in the British recapture of New York. It has a certain interest that the son of this soldier on the loyalist side was later British minister at Washington at a time of strained relations which he eased by tact and charm like that of his uncle and his father. While Charles Fox was denouncing in London the war, his brother in America served through its long course and at its close, though still only twenty-eight years of age, was sent to command in Nova Scotia. A too indulgent father had done his best to spoil his sons. Lord Holland wrote of the boy Henry that he "has a little horse to ride . . . He lives with the horse, stinks, talks and thinks of nothing but the stables." Fine qualities in the Foxes overcame, however, their upbringing. "All the attempts," said Edward Winslow, "to describe the attentions and kindness of General Fox would be in vain." He had a deep pity for the suffering of the humblest of the refugees and a quick eye for fraud and villainy. At Halifax there was need of alertness. Well-to-do men, with no real claim, called themselves loyalists and demanded supplies for their families and also grants of land. Vicious and indolent vagrants made claims but found help refused until they reformed. The misery was great. Winslow looking out on a throng before his house in Halifax found the scenes heart-breaking. By the beginning of 1784 refugees had come in such numbers that he had some thirty thousand people seeking food while, at the same time, the storehouses were empty and no provisions could be bought in the market. It added to the misery that the British government chose that moment to send out ship-loads of the riff-raff of London, thought good enough to go to the colonies. In bitter weather the loyalists were obliged to live in fragile huts. Starving men clamoured in vain for food for their helpless families and numbers died.

We get some light on loyalist and military society in Halifax when Edward Winslow received there his father's family. After a sorrowful parting at New York with friends

whom they were unlikely to see again, the family arrived
on September 14, 1783. The voyage from New York lasted
fifteen days without an hour of good weather. All were
seasick except the old father who, his daughter says, was
not afraid of anything except that he should not get victuals
enough, a needless anxiety, she adds, since "no others of the
party had any inclination to partake of his delicacies." In
spite of frantic demand and high rents the son's care had
secured them "a good house on the Parade" in the best part
of the town. All had health and we are assured that they
tried "not to reflect on past trials or to anticipate new ones,
but to remember enjoyable blessings still left." Soon there
were social clubs, a Saturday club, dinners, fortnightly
assemblies and balls. We have a glimpse of the social
cleavage of the time when we find that no one connected
with the army or navy was admitted to the Town Assembly,
in retaliation for a similar exclusion from their balls by the
officers, who looked down upon the civilians. The tone of
this military society in a garrison town displeased Winslow
whose official position involved contact with persons of
military rank. "I declare I cannot enjoy the nonsensical
parade and idle amusements of this town . . . Blast all
their visitations and ridiculous compliments. . . . 'Tis a
disgrace to human nature that an honest man should be
obliged to make a respectful Bow to a fool that he despises
or a villain that he detests . . . to mix in company with
abandoned prostitutes and infamous female gamblers, however exalted their station. This is really my case at many
houses, and damn me if I had not rather have the gout
and stay at home."

The elder Winslow died on June 9, 1784, and at the public
funeral all that was high in Halifax society showed him
honour. The sorrowing son wrote to Chipman; "I cannot
write. I thought I could bear anything—but by Heaven
this is too much." Time softened his grief and in September

he wrote to his wife; "Let what will happen, we will bear it handsomely. There's Christian doctrine for you and faith, Mary, (whatever the world may say of me) when put to a severe test I am a Christian." The exiles included men of striking force of character and good education; more than two hundred were graduates of Harvard College which, indeed, then lost perhaps most of its men of mark. It is significant that few, it seems none, of the prominent clergy of New England are found as loyalists in Nova Scotia, while leading clergy from New York are there. Laud's tyranny helped to turn the clergy of New England against the Defender of the Faith in England. It may seem an act of retaliation that when, in 1784, loyalist Samuel Seabury sought the consecration as Bishop of Connecticut that would make him the first bishop of the Church of England in North America, its prelates, led by the Archbishop of Canterbury, refused his request and it was the bishops of the Episcopal Church in Scotland who conceded the laying on of hands that completed the organization of the church in the republic.

The second bishop of the Anglican Church in North America was Charles Inglis, former rector of Trinity Church, New York, who was made Bishop of Nova Scotia in 1787 and was consecrated in England. The episcopal tradition was followed by his son who became the third bishop of the diocese. Another clergyman, Jonathan Odell, former rector at Burlington, New Jersey, had the temper of the nonjuring clergy at the time of the revolution in England in his boundless respect for the royal authority to which he owned allegiance. When forced to fly in 1776 he lay concealed for a time in an attic without light, entered by crawling through a small aperture concealed behind the shelves of a linen closet. He reached the British lines at New York and there served the loyalist side not only as a chaplain but as a writer of pungent political satire. No important leaders on the opposite side escaped his biting comment. Ambition, hypocrisy, treason, fraud and lies inspire them. Congress is composed of weak poltroons. Washington does not escape:

"Myriads of wives and fathers at thy hand
These slaughtered husbands, slaughtered sons demand . . .
Go, wretched author of thy country's grief,
Picture of villainy, of villains chief;
Seek with thy cursed crew the central gloom,
E'er Truth's avenging sword begin thy doom."

At New York, Odell served Carleton as secretary, and in 1783 he is found with his friends, Winslow and Chipman, seeking a home in New Brunswick. He became in 1783 first Provincial Secretary, an office that he held for thirty years and his son for thirty more.

The Sewalls were descended from Samuel Sewall, Chief Justice of Massachusetts. During the mad panic about witchcraft in 1692 he had taken part in condemning nineteen witches; but when, four years later, he saw the folly and cruelty of his acts he made confession of his error in public meeting and prayed "that God might not visit his sin upon him, his family or upon the land." The stern righteousness in this "last of the Puritans" survived in his grandson Jonathan. He had been for a time private secretary to General Gage, but he took refuge in England as early as in 1775. In New England the family had spelled the name with an "a"—Sewall—but he changed the "a" to "e," saying that he would not bear the same name as the rebel members of his family. Jonathan Sewell wrote from London in 1776 to Edward Winslow; "As to Massachusetts Bay, I wish it well, but I wish never to see it again till I return at the Millenium . . . The Mad Conduct of my Countrymen has given me a Dose I shall never get over. God mend them & bless them—but let me never, never be cursed with a residence among them again. I hate the Climate, where Re-

bellion and Fanaticism are engendered." He writes from
Bristol in 1778 to his friend Ward Chipman expressing the
delusive hope that Clinton at New York will soon bring on
a battle that will end the rebellion. In April, 1782, he is
still certain that Great Britain must finally prevail; her
"arm is not shortened that she cannot save." France should
recover Canada; it was a mistake ever to have annexed it.
Britain, France and Spain should divide North America
among themselves and guarantee each others' frontiers.
Since an English university is too expensive for his means.
Sewell is so sure of final victory that he plans to send his
sons to King's College at New York, destined, he thinks,
to remain a British city. He had urged his intimate friend,
John Adams, to stand by the loyalists, but Adams refused:
"Sink or swim," he said, "live or die, survive or perish with
my country is my unalterable determination." The two
men met once again,—in London, however, and not in the
United States, where Sewell vowed he would never set foot
until the unjust acts against the loyalists were repealed.
He became Judge of Admiralty and died at St. John, New
Brunswick, in 1796. His son Jonathan, born in Cambridge,
Massachusetts, in 1766, became in time chief-justice of
Lower Canada where his Toryism, the mark of the loyalist
mind, was the object of the most vehement assaults of the
French Canadian leader, Papineau. Though he accepted a
mark of reconciliation in an honorary degree from Harvard
University, situated in his birth-place, Cambridge, he never
restored the letter "a" to his name.

The aristocrats at Halifax derided the manners of those
who had driven them out. They hear that French and
Colonial officers quarrel, that duels are frequent as are also
rough-and-tumble fights between their men. Miss Winslow
writes in 1784 that Halifax already surpasses Boston in elegance. "The first assembly was amazing brilliant, the
Ladies Dress superb beyond what the New Englanders had

seen before . . . a profusion of waving Plumes and flow-
ers." Edward Winslow delighted to tell how in revolutionary
Boston "a daughter of Hitchborn, the boat builder, married
to Bruce, the butcher, . . . exclaimed bitterly and loudly
that it was not now as in the old Times; then they were
judicious in the choice of company but now, forsooth, assemblies were like operas, everybody that could pay was admitted." Winslow adds that, five years earlier, before the
new order had brought prosperity, Miss Bruce probably
thought that an opera was something to eat. "Some of our
true old charter saints," he says, "publicly roll in chariots
with kept mistresses." His fellow exile, Sewell, describes
these new rich as "damned, fanatical, republican, New
England, Rebellious, ungenerous, ungrateful scoundrels."

Against men of the type of Winslow and Sewell adverse
fortune beat in vain. They might say with Milton:

> Or knock the breast; no weakness, no contempt,
> Dispraise or blame; nothing but well and fair,
> And what may quiet us."
> "Nothing is here for tears, nothing to wail

In Nova Scotia, to which the many loyalist ships headed
across the open sea, John Parr, a former officer, had in 1782
been made governor by his patron, Lord Shelburne. Like
so many appointed to office in that age of patronage, his
zeal for the politics of his patron was greater than his
capacity for the duties of his office. His stout, unwieldy
person unfitted him for rough travel by land and he never
set foot in the part of the territory under his rule soon known
as New Brunswick, to which so many loyalists turned. But,
in spite of a short temper, he was really anxious to do his
duty and he had a heavy task. No instructions had come
to him as to what he should do with his refugees. With
rising dismay he saw the numbers grow from about seven
thousand in May, 1783, to thirty thousand by the following

January. They were not easy to manage. There was not an office in the government but they demanded as of right. Parr discovered what is true of all political exiles that the loyalists rated "their pretensions much above their intrinsic value." All of them desired to secure land on the sea-coast or on a navigable river and they were, he says plaintively, "a people very difficult to please." His surveyors are ill from being out in all weathers and, except for exorbitant pay, the loyalists will not even carry the chains for the surveyors marking the limits of their lands; an angel would not satisfy them. There was little unity of type among the loyalists. To refugees from the Carolinas those from New York were utter strangers. Some brought with them what to Parr seemed riches, while on the other hand two hundred and sixty "miserable wretches" came from St. Augustine, in Florida, "without a shilling, naked, and destitute of almost every necessary of life." Some three thousand negroes seem an incongruous element and later, at heavy expense, the doubtful experiment was made of sending some of them to Sierra Leone in Africa. "Dregs and Banditti" from New York, Boston and other seaports, discontented and turbulent spirits who committed "villainies," stand in contrast with Quakers from Pennsylvania, and an aristocracy of judges and other officials who had led colonial society.

The most considerable settlements in Nova Scotia were Halifax, the little secure fortress on the south coast, and Annapolis, on the Bay of Fundy. Each of them lay on a beautiful land-locked basin. Though Annapolis Royal, the French Port Royal, was the older place, situated at the outlet of a fertile valley, Halifax was now the capital and Annapolis remained and still is a quiet village. The influx to Halifax of loyalists in 1782 and 1783 almost overwhelmed it. Since the surrounding country was not fertile it was necessary for the homeless to seek land elsewhere. Far away across the Bay of Fundy from Annapolis was a timbered country, well watered, especially by the fine river St. John, and almost unpeopled. Here was virgin land for the loyalists. Though a part of Nova Scotia, it lay remote from the seat of government at Halifax, and in 1784 became a separate colony as New Brunswick. To Cape Breton Island and Prince Edward Island went perhaps as many as a thousand loyalists.

The first settlements involved much distress and failure. Near the south-west corner of Nova Scotia lay a beautiful harbour twelve miles long that had been called by the pleasant name of Port Roseway. Salmon, halibut, cod and other fish abounded in its waters and there was safe anchorage for the largest vessels. On the shore was a dense growth of trees, suitable for ship-building and for trade in timber. The land seemed fertile and the sea gave promise of fisheries and of a whaling industry. Loyalists in New York had heard of this favoured spot and, in the autumn of 1782, one hundred and twenty heads of families, looking for new homes, united to send a committee to make enquiries on the spot. The committee sent back glowing reports, the government of Nova Scotia was friendly, the land could be secured, and the new-comers would receive welcome and help.

Out of this came a notable migration. In the spring of 1783 a fleet of more than twenty ships left New York with nearly five hundred loyalist families and their belongings, among them a considerable number of well-to-do persons with negro servants. There were carpenters and other mechanics to aid in building the new town. Benjamin Marston, who was employed in laying it out, wrote to his friend Winslow that his head was full of triangles, squares and other figures and that he was thankful for the employment as it had saved him from starving. Some of the exiles brought with them horses and carriages, though the forest-clad, roadless shores of the beautiful bay might well cause

misgivings as to the use of elegant equipages. The government aided the new-comers. A town with broad streets
was laid out, building sites were allotted and the hum of
busy life was heard on a spot hitherto almost deserted.
Soon, however, the grants of land were found to have been
too generous and later comers received lots of only about
one-sixteenth the original size, with the result of such protest that one surveyor, charged with villainy, fled because
he was in danger of being hanged, while another in panic
drowned himself. When Governor Parr visited the place in
July, 1783, the dancing at a ball in his honour on the *Sophie*
war-ship lasted until five in the morning. He re-named the
town Shelburne, in honour of his patron, the British Prime
Minister. He had not a doubt, he said, that it would "in
a short time become the most flourishing town for trade of
any in this part of the World." It was certain that the
former colonies, which formed the United States, would be
excluded, under the Navigation Acts, from trade with the
British West Indies and it was hoped that much of the trade
of Boston, New York and Philadelphia would go to the seaports of Nova Scotia. Parr saw or imagined some fourteen
hundred houses either finished or well forward and a
hundred ships in the harbour. So enthusiastic was he that
he secured five hundred acres of land in the neighbourhood
and intended to build there a house with the prospect that
Shelburne might become the capital. Meanwhile a road
was planned along the coast to Halifax. A costly barracks
was built for troops. When, by the autumn, nearly ten
thousand people had gathered at Shelburne, the government
undertook to ration for some years the large population so
as to give time for the secure founding of the settlement.
Within a year or two substantial residences were erected.
There were at least two coffee-houses, a fashionable parade,
some twelve schools and the complex organization of a
mature society. A city, it was exultantly believed, had

sprung up suddenly, under the magic of enterprise and hope.

Soon, however, the horizon clouded. The soil was not fertile, and the place was remote from the main currents of life in the colony. Some of the well-to-do exiles who built showy houses had exhausted capital needed for other things. Many of the settlers were military men accustomed to the discipline and gradation in rank of the army but with no temper or training for a life that required the initiative and free play of democratic habits. It was found that the harbour, unlike that of Halifax, was frozen in winter. Disappointed men are apt to be quarrelsome and dissensions broke out. "A damnable Scot from New York," a vulgar person, so Marston says, made much trouble. There were disputes about religion, typical of the age of Wesley's revival: the "New Lights" prophesied that a certain leader who had abandoned them should be carried off by the Devil on a day that they named. There were disputes as to titles to land and charges of breach of faith against the government. As always amongst British peoples in the eighteenth century, there were many grog-shops and much drunkenness. Soldiers who had formed lawless habits on rough campaigns committed crimes that were punished brutally. The penalty of death was inflicted for trifling theft; there were whippings at the cart's tail and at whipping-posts, and also hangings. The many negroes were especially troublesome. The brutal spectacle was often seen of half-naked negro women, streaming with blood, whipped through the streets. When the county of Shelburne was created and there was an election to the assembly at Halifax, the "Blues" and the "Greens" engaged in a hot contest. No fewer than three newspapers appeared in the faction-ridden community.

When, in 1787, the government ceased the paying of rations, Shelburne collapsed and the population slowly dispersed. A good many returned to the United States. Others scattered, whither no man could tell, and there was left a deserted town, with streets of empty houses and great barracks falling into ruins. Six years after his first glowing experiences Governor Parr again visited the place and found two-thirds of the houses uninhabited. Soon fire marked the deserted streets with blackened chimneys and cavernous cellars. Some of the settlers had gone away in such despair or haste that they left in the houses furniture and even trunks with mouldering clothing which it was a point of honour with neighbours not to disturb. There are not many tales sadder than such a record of blighted hopes and the sadness was heightened by the fair but deceptive beauty of the scene. One poor settler who lingered amid the desolation said "poverty brought me here and poverty keeps me here." It has been noted that few songs owe their origin to the loyalists. There is little wonder that desolate exiles did not sing the Lord's song in a strange land.

While Shelburne failed, an important loyalist city was created on the west side of the adjacent long inlet of the sea, the Bay of Fundy, with the turbulent tides that in some places rise forty or fifty feet. The St. John River flows out of the State of Maine and in a course of four hundred and fifty miles at last reaches the sea over a rocky ledge making at low tide a picturesque fall but even at half tide level with the ocean. This spot has a romantic history. Champlain gave the name of St. John in 1604. Later the French built here a fort and fought each other for the profits of the fur trade and the fisheries. This was the scene of the romantic rivalries of Charnisay and La Tour. When in 1648 Charnisay sailed out with six ships and six hundred men across the bay from Port Royal, the present Annapolis, and laid siege to Fort St. John, La Tour, who had a Huguenot wife, escaped to Protestant Boston and soon came back and drove off his assailant. Two years later when Charnisay again appeared and La Tour was absent, his wife made a brave defence until betrayed by a sentinel. Charnisay hanged the whole garrison before the eyes of the heroic lady and the shock killed her. Charnisay himself was soon drowned and the episode ends with the almost incredible romance of the marriage of the widower La Tour to the widow Charnisay in 1653. In the next year Oliver Cromwell appeared in the history of St. John by sending an expedition which held the fort until 1670. During the Revolutionary War colonial privateers swooped down on it and on other places on the bay and this caused in 1777 the building of Fort Howe, named after the British leader who had abandoned Boston in the previous year and a little later occupied New York. This fort, crowning a hill at the entrance of the river, made it and its *hinterland* secure during the rest of the war; and now in 1783 at this spot was created the most important and enduring of all the loyalist settlements.

The St. John River is navigable for about a hundred miles of its lower course and in the rainy season for another hundred. It then winds through a country still forest clad, a paradise for sport, and on a long stretch forms the boundary between New Brunswick and the State of Maine. Naturally the region had attracted both settlers and speculators. The government at Halifax made reckless grants of land, surveys were scanty and in default of a secure title "squatters" had occupied chosen spots along the river and gained a rough but adequate livelihood by cutting timber, by tilling soil in places fertile, by trading in furs and by fishing. A region so attractive and so thinly peopled could take many settlers and by 1782 enquirers were inspecting it. Since no other available spot seemed to offer equal opportunities, in 1783 St. John became like Shelburne an object of desire. At New York Carleton was receiving thousands of refugees; at New York were gathered many loyalist regiments now to be disbanded; and the busy summer of 1783 saw a migration that proved to be one of the anchors of the British tradition in North America. The ships of the time were small and so ill equipped for crowded passenger traffic that cold, discomfort, privation, and the disease that they fostered, caused acute suffering and many deaths.

The movement began early in 1783, for Carleton, all but overwhelmed by numbers, knew that a long harassing season lay before him and was anxious to be eased as soon as possible. A fleet of twenty transports for the St. John was at last ready and on April 26 it sailed from Sandy Hook carrying some three thousand refugees. The voyage occupied three weeks and we may imagine the relief of that desolate company when on May 18 they disembarked at the mouth of the St. John River. There was little to cheer them in the new scene. Barren rocks, swampy pools, a great tract of burnt forest on the right bank with black gaunt skeletons of trees and stumps that stretched on to a dense wilderness, formed the outward aspect of St. John. The exiles were hurried from the transports, anxious to be rid of one human cargo in order to return to New York for another. Some of them moved on quickly up the river and these were the more fortunate since they escaped the crowding at its mouth. When on May 29 the ships sailed away, their going seemed to break the last tie with the outer world. "I watched the sails disappear in the distance," says one of the exiles, "and such a feeling of loneliness came over me that, although I had not shed a tear through all the war, I sat down in the damp moss with my baby in my lap and cried aloud." It was, however, spring, with nature's beauty inspiring hope. Active building began at once. The government supplied boards, shingles and bricks; many stones lay at hand for the building of chimneys; and imminent winter encouraged ceaseless activity. Though they had for tools little more than axes and saws, by the late autumn most of these first comers had either gone up the river or were roughly housed on small plots at St. John. In a sense it is true that the modern city of some fifty thousand people was born on a single day and May 18 is still celebrated as a public holiday. Human activity on the spot has never ceased since that hour. Two years later, on May 18, 1785, the settlement became the first incorporated city in the modern Canada.

Meanwhile at New York Carleton had to provide for an unexpected increase of refugees. It was not unnatural for those who had abandoned their homes during the war to think that now with the return of peace they might be allowed to live among former neighbours. This, however, was not to be until time had soothed passions. Governor Clinton in New York proclaimed his belief that loyalists were a vile scum to whom no pity nor mercy should be shown. When a loyalist returned to visit his parents at a village in New York called Wallkill his former friends shaved his eyebrows, coated him with tar and feathers, put round his neck a pig-yoke with a cow-bell attached, clapped on his head a crown of tar with feathers set in it, and displayed him as a fit companion for the traitor Benedict Arnold and the imps of the Devil. Boston, not to be outdone, declared that the loyalists were ingrates and traitors who should never be allowed to have "lot or portion among us." Delaware declared that loyalists were worse than thieves or murderers and should be expelled as long as nature furnished the necessary energy. With such fury raging the necessity for exile grew and assuredly Carleton had trying tasks during that dismal summer at New York.

A second contingent of loyalists reached St. John late in June and by chill October some ten thousand had arrived. Soldiers in the former loyalist battalions were dis-

banded on landing. While those who came by what was
called the Spring Fleet had had the summer for prepara-
tion, the late comers by the Fall Fleet faced winter at once.
There was such confusion as to titles to lands and to needed
supplies that Governor Parr far away at Halifax became
in the mind of the many newcomers a sinister incompetent.
He was in truth hardly equal to so trying a task. On September 27 some three thousand five hundred refugees arrived,—about two thousand men, the rest women and children. The men were chiefly loyalist soldiers. They had had
a trying voyage. One ship was wrecked with a loss of ninety
lives. While some managed to push on up the river, most
remained at St. John during the harsh winter in cabins
hastily built, and in tents thatched with spruce boughs and
banked with snow. There was poignant suffering, to see
which Winslow said almost killed him. Men, who had dared
and lost all, now felt indignation due to official slackness:
"We served all the war; were promised land; we like the
country; let us have a spot of our own and keep bad men
from injuring us." We are told that "strong men cried like
children and exhausted by cold and famine lay down in
their snow-bound tents to die." The last of the transports
arrived as late as in December. By that time the loyalist
business in New York was wound up and Carleton had
sailed for England.

There is some sunshine in the picture. In the summer of
1783 Edward Winslow, seeking a new home, had gone to
the St. John River. He and what he described as a party
of "young Bucks" ascended the river, with banks lined by
giant trees in summer foliage. He was, he says, "prodi-
giously pleased with the country"; "delighted beyond expression." He secured for himself a fine expanse of land on
the upper river at what he thought the most beautiful spot
he had ever known. There were park-like stretches of
forest with so little undergrowth at some points that a

coach might be driven under the tall trees. "As fine a
country as I ever saw in my life," said General Timothy
Ruggles, a fellow exile, and when Ward Chipman saw it
after farming had begun, no one, he thought, "ever beheld
a more delightful grass country, better cattle or better
grain, or more abundant crops." There were some hundreds
of settlers at scattered points on the river. After the first
shock the exiles met hardship with gaiety. Winslow visited
a camp of the King's American Dragoons on the river and
says that he never saw more cheerfulness and good humour
than prevailed among the men: "They are encamped on
one of the pleasantest spots I ever beheld and they are
enjoying a great variety of luxuries such as Partridges, Salmon, Bass, Trout, Pigeons." Soon the men were occupied
in cutting roads through the forest. In April, 1785, Winslow
wrote of his own lands on the river: "I am in the midst of
as cheerful a society as any in the world." There was no
danger, he said, of starving, or freezing, or from savages,
or bears, or "Tygers."

At the river's mouth St. John was growing quickly into
a city. Beautiful weather aided progress in 1784. In June,
a year after the loyalists landed, an astonished visitor saw
there fifteen hundred frame and four hundred log houses.
He could hardly believe his eyes at such unparalleled exertions. In 1788 it could claim two thousand houses, "many
of which are large and spacious" and some boasted that
it was "one of the best cities in the world." A traveller
in 1791 describes "elegant shops" and "genteel houses."
When he went up the river to Fredericton he visited what
he calls a "beautiful seat" and found Scots with excellent
farms and live stock but longing for the heather of their
native land. At Fredericton there were spacious barracks
and many houses of "noble appearance." He heard wonderful tales of fishing and shooting. By the beautiful river
floated down to the sea great pine trees, tall and straight,

suitable for the ships of the Royal Navy. A mast measured by this curious visitor was one hundred and twenty-eight feet long. Three thousand salmon were killed in a single day but not by sportsmen: they were netted or speared. The largest salmon brought a shilling. One settler had a record of seven bears in one day. Moose weighing fifteen hundred pounds had, the sportsmen thought, a finer flavour than the best beef and there was a great variety of fish and of endless snipe, partridge, and other wild birds. But there was also haunting poverty.

"The river glided by," wrote Winslow later, "without material advantage to me for I had hardly credit for an axle." Cases of bitter hardship so endured, with former services unnoticed and forgotten, that he wrote "By Heaven, I feel a noble indignation." He would continue to do his duty, he said, "altho' Hell's in front and perdition in my rear." These Puritans have a saving sense of humour. When "Miss Fanny" bears sixteen puppies they call a court martial which decides that all shall have the right to live. They write longing letters to old absent friends. Winslow enjoys "the satisfaction of scribbling whole volumes" and his sister writes to Chipman that she has ten million things that it would take a month to say. Mather Byles says to Winslow in 1786 that when he reads his affectionate paragraphs "it choakes me a little to be sure—something like an egg in the neck of a quart bottle, if you know what that is."

Their thoughts turned to those who had caused their exile. John Adams they respected but for his relative Samuel they had hard words. He was, wrote Winslow, low bred and a cheat, cunning, specious, sanctimonious, a vulgar man who appealed to the ignorant and, in order to play the demagogue, neglected his business and let his family suffer for the common necessaries of life. John Hancock was his dupe. Ignorant, awkward and suspicious, Hancock yielded

to the flattery of Adams and supplied money from his prosperous business. Adams was a defaulter and it was Hancock's money that saved him; he wrote Hancock's speeches
and by busy activity in his behalf brought him to the front.
In spite of such severe comment exiled aristocrats resumed,
in some cases, former friendships in New England. None
the less were their judgments severe on loyalists who returned to the United States. They were skulkers, deserters,
who had gone back to become hewers of wood and drawers
of water.

Since the settlers blamed busy, fussy Governor Parr
for delays and confusion, they were resolved to have a government of their own on the spot. There was cleavage between them and earlier settlers from New England who
had some of the proprietary airs of the older settler. While
these men were fully represented in the legislature at Halifax, inevitably the newcomers were not. Inevitably, too,
educated men such as Winslow and Chipman felt that they
were better fitted to govern than certain officials at Halifax,
one of whom, the attorney-general, Winslow describes as
an "ignorant harmless nincompoop," while the solicitor-
general was "a great lubberly insolent Irish rebel." Oddly
enough local feeling was reinforced by opinion in London.
While it is true that experience teaches, it is not always
that its pupils adopt the wisest of its lessons. We might
suppose that one lesson of the American Revolution was
that free peoples living far across the ocean from London
must regulate their own internal affairs and tax themselves.
This was, however, not what officials had learned. To them
the rebellion was a deplorable example of the license of
democracy. Accordingly, in what was left of the Empire,
lines must be drawn more tightly. Thus we find, as early
as in 1778, plans in London to keep individual colonies
weak and as small as possible. Nova Scotia should be divided into several units whose legislatures should have no

powers of taxation. After all colonies were for the advantage of the mother country and should be regulated with that end in view. When independence was conceded to the United States the remaining British colonies in the north should all be placed under "the sole direction and control of a Governor-General."

It thus happened that the demand at St. John for immediate separation from Nova Scotia was accepted in London almost before it was formally made. Accordingly, the year 1784 saw the creation of the new colony and the first legislature met at St. John in 1785. It had been proposed to adopt the name New Ireland, an appropriate third in the trinity with New England and New Scotland (Nova Scotia). Since, however, just at this time, Ireland made its declaration of legislative independence, a product of the American Revolution, the name was rejected and by a lack of taste shown in earlier times in the names New York and New Jersey it was decided to call the province New Brunswick. The British royal house bore the name of the German duchy of Brunswick. Its then ruler, being in debt, had sold a considerable number of his subjects to George III for service on the loyalist side in America and this venal act is called up by the name of the new province. Winslow and others hoped that the young General Henry Fox should be the first governor. He had visited the region in 1783 and was pleased at the outlook. When the post was offered to him it was also made known that a governor-general was to be appointed for all the British provinces. Fox was ready to stay for a few years if his former chief at New York, Guy Carleton, was made governor-general. This, however, was not done for two years and to the sorrow of Winslow and his friends Fox returned to England.

In the end the appointment was given to Sir Guy's brother, Thomas Carleton, who accepted it in 1784 on the condition, never fulfilled, that he should go to Quebec as

governor in the next year. Winslow, or some one else
vitally interested in the country, should, of course, have
been appointed but, to the mind of the governing circle in
London, a colonist was not fit for station so high. Thomas
Carleton was the normal type of the rather stilted British
officer of the time, with a chilly manner and little tact
and capacity to unbend. He was an ardent patriot, a sincere member of the Church of England, a friend of well-
guarded education for the upper classes and a generous
contributor to what he thought good causes. He had, however, a rather wooden mind, nervous as to "the American
spirit of innovation," suspicious of democracy and bent on
keeping "the lower orders" in their place. Though active
at times, he was really indolent and firm in the conviction
that office brought privileges as much as duty. He had
fought in Germany in the time of Frederick the Great; and
later, when serving in the Russian army against the Turks,
he had spent a winter in St. Petersburg. He had also
travelled in Italy and France. He held his post from 1784
to 1817, thirty-three years. He left the province, however, in
1803, and did not return during the remaining fourteen
years of his tenure. The age assuredly had a tender regard for the comfort of those whom it honoured with office. Like many old soldiers Carleton was fond of growing
vegetables in his large garden at the new capital where he
enjoyed a quiet life in a quiet town.

This capital was not the seaport St. John but another
new place far up the river and called Fredericton. Leaders,
otherwise all but forgotten, have given their names to
obscure places that became important. The name New York
commemorates that Duke of York who, as James II, lost
his throne for the sake of his religion. "Tommy Townshend,"
who became secretary of state after the fall of North,
later, as Lord Sydney, gave his name to the great city in
Australia. The capital of New Brunswick was named after

a prince of the Brunswick line, Frederick, Duke of York, the handsome second son of George III. Though he failed later as a leader in the field, he was then popular and tried as commander-in-chief of the British army to correct abuses that had grown up under his predecessor, Amherst. Few men such as he, of mediocre talent, are honoured in the names of two capitals; Fredericton, the capital of New Brunswick, and York (now Toronto) the capital of Ontario, were named after the young duke. A tall column at the end of Waterloo Place, on perhaps the finest site in London, is a further tribute to him.

There had been acute differences of opinion as to the site of the new capital. St. John, on the coast, was easily accessible and like Halifax was secure from attack as long as Britain had command of the sea. Fredericton lies at a distance of eighty-four miles from the mouth of the river, then difficult to ascend on account of shoals and currents, but in time made navigable for the larger ships of the time. Along the banks and especially in the higher reaches were vast, depressing burnt areas from forest fires and the danger of fire from dry fallen trees and moss was always real. St. John pleaded that to have the law courts at a capital far up the river from the chief centre of commerce would involve costs so heavy as to deprive the poor of their rights. The opposing opinion that prevailed was due to the desire to carry settlement to the interior, to plant farmers on the banks of the long, beautiful river, to cut timber and to protect the workers from attack by Indians. There was also fear of aggression by the United States. To open communications overland with Canada seemed also important. In due course, when the elder Carleton brother who ruled in Canada was ill, the younger at Fredericton made on snow-shoes a long journey overland to Quebec that involved camping eight nights in the forest in a region peopled by only a few Indians. To the wisdom of the time, nervous about the frontier, fearful that invaders might march from Maine by way of the north to the sea and attack Nova Scotia, it seemed necessary to build some costly forts in this wild country. The garrison of British regulars quartered at Fredericton seems, however, to a critical eye to have been useless for purposes of war in a region all but unpeopled and to have been inevitably idle in the tranquil days of peace except for ceremonial parade in mounting guard for the governor and in doing some quiet labour at his farm. In Nova Scotia there was military outlay that led to Burke's outburst in Parliament on "that nook of penury and cold": "Good God," he said, "what sums the nursing of that ill-thriven, hard-visaged and ill-favoured brat has cost to the whole nation. Sir, this colony has stood us in the sum of not less than £700,000."

The new province secured its measure of self-government. Thomas Carleton was instructed to follow the usual colonial pattern and set up a legislature. But while the franchise was liberal, the power of the elected assembly was restricted. Subject to the veto of the crown, the governor appointed to all the offices and fixed the salaries in the public service. He had the revenue at his disposal that came from the lease and the sale of crown lands, revenue at first greater than any that the legislature could raise by taxation. He controlled the Customs and the Post Office. His council, which formed a sort of cabinet, consisted chiefly of educated men, the flower of New England. The members of the second chamber were his nominees, while the popular chamber did not greatly matter since its powers were limited. In the background was the secretary of state in England whose word was final. George III himself was personally interested. To him went even the names of the students for a proposed college and he was expected to show interest in specimens of the handwriting of former negro slaves under instruction in Nova Scotia.

In such a system a popular election seems almost super-fluous but the first electoral contests in this loyalist commu-nity came in 1785. Some of the disbanded soldiers had formed idle, unruly habits; rum was cheap; there were many grog-shops; and violent passions came to the front. The riots were such that Carleton had to call out the military. The elected assembly did not meet until January, 1786. It was so much the child of the ideas of George III that, as in the days of Wilkes, it met with closed doors and the people were left to guess at the proceedings. It proclaimed religious toleration while, at the same time, giving the Church of England a privileged position—a magnanimous act of descendants of Puritans whom that church had driven from England.

The loyalist leaders were convinced that they could create the finest community in all America and the most gentlemanlike in all the world "if not damned by bad men and bad measures." They persuaded themselves that their exile made for their real happiness. Why, they asked, is it thought misfortune to leave New York or Connec-ticut to remain the happy subjects of the best of kings? Like the founders of Shelburne they expected a great trade with the West Indies, such as had developed in the rebel-lious colonies, and they too insisted that the old Navigation Acts should so apply as to exclude from this trade the United States, now a foreign nation. They had resources in fisheries and timber and a fertile soil for varied grains, things that other parts of the Empire needed. Too many forgot, however, the element of time needed to make use of nature's bounty. Roads must be built and meanwhile what were called roads meant "thumping, swimming, wal-lowing and tumbling" over trails and spelled isolation. Saw-mills for timber multiplied on the St. John and other rivers, and care was taken that each county should have a stream down which timber could be floated. Tall forests fell to the axe. Markets, however, were distant, costs were heavy, and only a few prospered in this difficult trade. Men who had gone into the farther interior faced hardships that, as one of them said, if known, would fill the mind with horror. While the governor ruled, the scheming politician was abroad and made mischief. "Gentlemen," it was said, "gardened and shoemakers legislated."

The loyalist colony settled down to the slow progress that has given New Brunswick about half a million people. Fredericton long remained all but a village, with the vivid politics of a small community. British troops remained there in garrison. The governor kept up vice-regal ceremony and opened the small parliament with pomp copied from Westminster. When the Church of England secured a bishop, the result followed that the present city of fewer than ten thousand people is adorned by a small but beautiful cathedral. The healthful climate gave to many long life. Edward Winslow, soldier, settler, official, became in the end a judge and to some of his sturdy contemporaries seemed in 1815 to have died young at sixty-nine. Chipman, his lively friend, also held high office and became a judge. They and many other graduates of Harvard University represented its best in their devotion to duty. Time has so softened the old asperities that intercourse with the larger population of republican New England has had marked influence upon the little colony that in its early days gave to the king devotion so defiant. The result is that the New Brunswick and the Nova Scotia of to-day have in their society many graduates of Harvard University as, in a different spirit, they had a century and a half ago.

CHAPTER XXI

EXILE IN THE CANADIAN WILDERNESS

IT was inevitable that the great northern region under the British flag should be a refuge for loyalists. Though the Canada even of that time extended far westward, it was chiefly in the region lying between the sites of the two great cities of to-day, Detroit and Montreal, that the desolate exiles were to make their new homes. Farther east lay the older Canada peopled by the French, with a few scattered English, chiefly soldiers or traders in the towns, who were birds of passage. For Canada the American Revolution meant that the French should remain French and that beyond the western border near Montreal of the one-time French colony should grow up a new society as stiff in the traditions of England as were the Canadians in those of France.

The early friction in the English colonies about taxation by England had caused a dribbling exile to Canada long before the dispute involved civil war. As we have seen, a resident in a town in Massachusetts who, during the fury against the Stamp Act, ventured on open protest or even to stand aloof might have his house surrounded at night by a threatening mob and be warned to get away lest something worse should happen. Even then and also later, after the destruction of tea at Boston in 1773, there was a migration to French Canada of loyalists harassed by the menacing attentions of patriot neighbours. In 1774, a year before the fight at Lexington that meant war, we find loyalists protesting to the government at Quebec their sac-

444

rifices and expecting aid in their dire need. When Lexington was followed not many days later by Ethan Allen's dramatic seizure of the British fort at Ticonderoga the route to Canada by Lake Champlain was closed and the early loyalists had to find obscurer ways by rivers and by forest paths to the haven in the north. Inevitably such refugees were chiefly from the colony of New York that stretched its long frontier opposite Canada, on the St. Lawrence, on Lake Ontario, and on the Niagara River. The British had so controlled the Canadian side that during the long war Canada remained a safe haven for loyalists.

Before the struggle ended, many of the Iroquois had crossed the Niagara River and were living in Canada. Since, to the mind of the negotiators in the refined centre of Paris, the Indian tribes were only primitive savages, the treaty of peace made no mention of them, to their chagrin. In the end five of the depleted Six Nations made what terms they could with the young republic. The Mohawk chief Brant was resolved to "Sink or Swim" with the British and Governor Haldimand so valued his loyalty that he made extensive grant of lands in Upper Canada for his people. The chief one was a great tract stretching for six miles on each side of the Grand River that flows southward into Lake Erie. Some restless warriors went off to join warlike tribes in the west. It was chiefly Mohawks who remained wards of Canada and only after another century were they conceded the right to vote. As white settlers came in, they were induced to sell their lands, of which the quantity was greater than their needs. They were not robbed; the capital was invested for their benefit and they still receive the annual revenue. They remain a rather forlorn remnant living on a fragment of their original grants. Most of them adhere to the Church of England and they still treasure with pride communion plate presented to them by Queen Anne and the Prayer Book and

Gospels translated into their own tongue by Brant himself. Some still retain, however, the pagan faith of their remote ancestors. Brantford, a thriving industrial city, has grown up on their former reserve. Brant himself played some part in the politics of Canada at a later date.

Among the loyalist exiles were hundreds of embittered men driven as outlaws from their homes and many of them long separated from their families. Some were rough frontiersmen who had known and been tainted by the ruthless Indian wars; others were of Highland origin with the barbaric traditions of clan warfare; still others were peace-loving farmers, mechanics, and tradesmen, hunted out by rebellious committees. When the war was over there was for these loyalists no return to their former homes. In such revengeful mood were their foes that in 1784 the jail at Albany was full of prisoners suspected of loyalism and some were brutally flogged. After Sir Guy Carleton left Canada in 1778 the burden of the loyalists, by that time heavy, fell on his successor, Haldimand. Political exiles are apt to be fretful, to be conscious of suffering and to suspect a lack of sympathy from the more fortunate. Sympathy the kindly governor, himself an exile from his own country, gave, but he could not bring ease to all the sufferers in a lost cause and there were complaints of neglect. Among the exiles themselves the governor found what he called "a lack of Brotherly love." The genteel held aloof from the plebeian. When he enlisted loyalist companies, every man, he said, wished to be an officer. The government paid the cost of billeting many loyalists in French villages. As a rule they were quiet and docile, and plaintive as to their losses, but the habitants in whose cottages they were quartered sometimes complained that these imposed guests wore out their welcome by remaining for two years at a time. Some took up land of which the military authorities made generous grants. The British govern-

ment bought a large tract of land near the mouth of the
Richelieu River and here loyalists built their own houses
of timber from the adjacent forest. The cost of such care
was heavy. Major Nairne, who was in charge of the loyalists in Verchères and other villages on the south shore
opposite Montreal, rendered a single account for twenty
thousand pounds, only one of several from this one point.
Clearly, however, there was little room for the loyalists in
the settled parts of French Canada, with its closely knit
social organization and its people alien to the loyalists in
creed and speech. When regiments were disbanded after the
war, some loyalists settled in the remote Gaspé peninsula
where to-day many of their descendants are hardy fishermen. But the chief movement was westward to what was
soon to be Upper Canada. Some of Sir John Johnson's soldiers settled on the north shore of the St. Lawrence above
Montreal, and on Lake Ontario, while Butler's Rangers
went chiefly to the Niagara peninsula and to the lands
stretching westward to Detroit.

At the close of the American Revolution what came then
to be known as Upper Canada (the present Ontario) was
a vast wilderness. In Nova Scotia and in Quebec, regions
long in course of settlement, were farms that had in some
cases been cultivated for more than a hundred years, but
in Upper Canada the loyalist exiles had to confront the
problems of the untouched forest. Though fur-traders
and voyageurs had passed up the St. Lawrence beyond
Montreal and along the north shores of Lake Ontario and
Lake Erie, only at a few points of vantage, at the head of
the river, where now is Kingston, and at Niagara and Detroit, was there much trace of man's effort. There had been
little exploration of the interior with a view to settlement.
Rumour said that it was a dreary wilderness, covered with
swamps, infested by wild beasts and venomous serpents,

and that only the savage Indians could bear the rigours of the harsh climate. The great forest trees showed, however, that the soil was rich. We have a record of one tree with a trunk eleven feet in diameter. While such monsters proved the land's fertility they also hampered agriculture for they made difficult and costly the task of clearing the ground.

The new settlers reached Upper Canada by varied routes. A few exiles from the southern colonies and from Florida, once more Spanish after a score of years of British occupation, came by way of the Mississippi and its tributaries to Detroit and from there could pass easily into Canada. Others by devious journeyings reached the southern shore of Lake Erie and crossed it to form a few scattered settlements on the Canadian side. Farther east loyalists, chiefly from New York, crossed the Niagara River and settled side by side with disbanded soldiers of Butler's Rangers. From Niagara, around the western end of Lake Ontario and then eastward along its north shore, population spread slowly to meet other settlers coming westward by way of the great river to Upper Canada. In the summer of 1783 ships laden with loyalists from New York reached the River St. Lawrence by way of the Gulf, directed, it may be, to this long and difficult route by the fear that already too many were going to Nova Scotia. By October five vessels had arrived at Sorel. While many were going still farther, the season was late and they spent the winter at this spot and at Yamachiche, on the north shore, fed and housed by the government under the direction of military officers. In the following summer they resumed their long journey. From Lachine, just above Montreal, they had to ascend the river in flat boats. When rapids made rowing impossible the men, often in water to their waists, towed the heavy boats near shore. Such work had been done for more prosperous travellers by French Canadians, inured to its hardships, but this service was costly and as a rule poverty compelled the ex-

iles themselves to this trying labour for which they had
had no training. The journey to the head of the rapids
on the St. Lawrence was made in brigades of perhaps a
dozen bateaux, and occupied ten or twelve days. All day
long and day after day, men rowed or dragged the boats up
the majestic river, never less than a mile wide, sweeping
to the sea in resistless force. At night the tired company
camped by the river bank, often too heart-heavy and desolate to note the smell of the pine trees, the deer bounding
to cover from the water's edge, the fascinating romance
of wild nature; too weary to enjoy the glowing camp fire,
the rush of waters and the changing tints of the swift-flow-
ing river. Many of the men were former soldiers accustomed
to the labour of pitching the tents. Among these were
some of the German mercenaries, chiefly from Hesse, sold
by their prince to George III for service in America, and
now content to face the hardships of a freer life in the
new world.

Each head of a loyalist family had what was called a
location ticket giving him the right to a grant of land in a
certain area marked off on a surveyor's plan. The exact location in this area might be determined by lot—a piece of
paper drawn from a battered hat. Every one desired
frontage on the water. We may picture the arrival of a
loyalist "brigade" at its allotted site. Vague directions might
involve that to stay at this point was a mistake since another claimant might appear. When the flotilla of boats
carrying perhaps a dozen families drew to the shore, the
children we may be sure would be the first to climb out
and to run among the trees. The white tents are pitched
and, with what hope and courage they can command, the
exiles survey the scene of their future labours. Before
them is the boundless forest with, in some places, trees
that surpass in size the oaks and elms of the old world
of their ancestors. There are no roads. The streams are

unbridged. The only highway is the water. The group casts lots for the site on which each family is to make its home and then the possessor pitches his tent on the spot where in due course are to be built first a shanty of one room, made of logs, to be replaced in time by a frame house and perhaps in due course by one of the many brick houses of the prosperous farmers of to-day. The loyalist private was entitled to a hundred acres with frontage on the water, two hundred in the remoter region in the rear, and fifty additional acres for his wife and for each child. Each son and daughter, on coming of age, was entitled to two hundred acres. A field officer had as many as a thousand acres. The lavish extravagance of these grants hampered settlement. Each owner was supposed to cut a road across his property,—to cut a road with vast forest trees barring the way, a road perhaps through swampy land to be crossed in the end only by laying logs side by side to form what was known as corduroy. The road might lead to a brimming river across which for a length of years no bridge might be built. The early bridges of wood on shaky piles were well fitted to try even robust nerves.

It was perhaps a tribute to the German mercenaries in the war that at first Upper Canada was divided into districts with German names, Luneburgh, Mecklenburgh, Nassau and Hesse, names that the first legislature was happily inspired to change to the Eastern, the Midland, the Home and the Western divisions. Kingston at the eastern end of Lake Ontario and Queenston at the west show reverence for the royal house. Though posterity refuses to remember Adolphus, Amelia, Elizabeth and Ernest, children of George III, loyalism put their names on the map where also those of Wolfe and Amherst and Gage in military circles and of two lord chancellors, the Tory Thurlow and the Whig Camden, reveal the colonial tie with England's history. The loyalists were not afraid to

plant new Londons, Edinburghs, and Dublins in the un-
tenanted wilderness. Even the name Niagara of the village
at the mouth of that river gave way for a time to the old-
world name of Newark.

The British government took a generous view of its
need to care for the suffering people. During many years
such help involved the support of thousands of families.
The government furnished the loyalists with clothing, with
axes, saws, farm implements, and muskets; it built and
equipped flour-mills and saw-mills; it provided seed to
sow, and sometimes a cow for a pair of families; it made
gifts of tents and boats and even of church bells. The task
was difficult. Loyalists were widely scattered; means of
transport were primitive; and in that day, even more than
in our own, departments of government were apt to be in-
efficient. Until Upper Canada received a separate government in 1792, the central authority was remote at Quebec.
With a postal service hardly yet existent, complaints travelled slowly and redress was even more tardy. The result
was that some families were left without resources in the
lonely forest. Nature had, however, her rich stores, in fish at
times in amazing abundance, and in wild life. Though often,
we may be sure, skill was lacking to exploit these treasures,
this time might cure. Naturally there were complaints of
injustice. The very generosity of government led to such
habits of dependence that some loyalists, when urged to
industry, were resentful that, after their sacrifices, they
must learn to shift for themselves.

We may dismiss the legend that most of the loyalists had
been reared in luxury. While inevitably among them were
leaders with social prestige and high intelligence, the great
mass of the newcomers in Upper Canada were accustomed
to the normal hardships of people in the new world who
work for their living either on the farm or in the shop.
Those who had come from towns where there were houses,

streets, the outward mechanism of civilized life, knew little of labour on the land. For them now the elemental problems were to secure shelter, food and clothing. Though in the end they turned the wilderness into a land of ordered well-being under the flag they loved, at first their life was bleak. Nearly all were so wholly of the new world that any among them born in the British Isles were regarded with surprise and curiosity. Their accent in speech was that of the part of the United States from which they came and this was chiefly New York. Accordingly, the origins of the present ardently British Province of Ontario are, in large measure, to be found in the State of New York.

The forest with its great trees, some of them of heavy hard wood, walnut, maple, oak and elm, was rather the enemy than the friend. Only the softer woods would float down the streams to markets. There was no means of moving the fallen trunks of hard woods, and their massive bulk cluttered land required for crops. Sometimes logs of walnut were split into rails for fences. Another remedy was in fire. Trees of hard woods now valuable were dragged, often without aid of horses or oxen, into piles and burned, usually a long slow process. The ashes were useful as a fertilizer and for the alkali needed in making soap. Sometimes a spark in the heaps of drying branches, would start a devastating forest fire. The smaller trunks were used to build the log cabin, in which to construct a chimney of stone and clay that should serve the needed purpose was a difficult problem for the uninitiated. In summer buzzing insects were a terrible pest, in winter only heavy labour could keep up a supply of fuel to fight the bitter cold. Since transport was costly, few houses had the iron stoves now so universal. The house was warmed from an open fire-place in which were burned logs sometimes so huge that a horse or ox was needed to drag them to the door. The fire was carefully banked at night; if it went out, so hard was it to start a new one that a tramp of half a mile through the dark forest might be necessary in order to get live coals from a neighbour. Cooking was done either before the great wood fire or in an oven outside the house made of stones and clay such as one sees still in the Province of Quebec. To find the means to sharpen an axe was not easy until the government supplied grindstones. The ground was sometimes harrowed by the heavy branch, in foliage, of a tree dragged at the butt end.

The life of the forest involved danger of loss from wild beasts especially wolves that might kill cattle and sheep and pigs. When communications failed, in the stress of winter, or when food furnished by the government was not at hand, blank starvation confronted the exiles and a few of the less provident starved to death. In such circumstances a pound of flour was of more value than an acre of land. The forest was capricious in the supply of game and often the settler lacked ammunition. Malaria, called by the settlers "fever and ague" and due to the condition of the soil, long weakened many families. Since there were almost no doctors, unaided nature was the principal healer. Often the settler had himself to play the surgeon and set a broken limb or to be dentist when teeth were extracted.

Worst of all was the deadly isolation of life on the edge of the forest. People brought up perhaps in luxury dressed now in deerskin or homespun and lived on a level with rough backwoodsmen. The children of both classes were apt to share a common ignorance and manners were coarsened. With some, drink was a great evil. It was so easy to distil a raw whiskey from grain that this deadly liquor could be bought for sixpence a quart or even less. It was sometimes used medicinally as a remedy for fever and ague and to flavour milkless porridge given even to children. We need not wonder that drunkenness was a primal curse among the settlers. It would be untrue, however, to represent this life as chiefly gloomy. Though there was acute suffering, within a few years the worst difficulties were overcome. Work usually makes men cheerful and the loyalists had it in abundance. The log cabin was in time followed by a plastered house of timber and boards, with bedsteads and tables and chairs to replace rough shelves and benches and cross sections of trees for seats. There were compensations in the new life. The forest was conquered, good crops were reaped from land enriched by the mould of ages; in time clergy and schoolmasters and physicians and storekeepers came for the benefit of mind and body and the exchange of products. Defoe's tale of "Robinson Crusoe" is fascinating, largely because it shows man in primitive conditions exacting from nature the service he requires.

The untamed forest had its charm. In the springtime a sugar of delicate flavour was to be extracted from the sap of the maple tree. It was pleasant to follow the Indian trails under the arching trees by stream and gleaming lakes in the fresh spring or amid the glowing tints of autumn. Such delights were of course only for those in rugged health. In the rivers flowing into Lake Ontario salmon, now the valued and elusive object of privileged sport, were then so plentiful that in season the settlers not only on waters by the sea but in Upper Canada could rely upon them for food. They came in such shoals that women and children speared them with pitchforks. A settler describes how his canoe was raised in the water by a school of salmon so dense that with difficulty he could use his paddle. In due time their coming suddenly ceased for reasons unknown. For big game there were deer and bears, the bears robbers of the farm yard to be guarded against. The settlers trapped foxes for their furs. Wolves were such a pest that government paid a reward for their destruction. In the spring, flocks of wild pigeons containing numbers running into millions, and so vast as now to seem incredible, were killed so recklessly that this beautiful bird has disappeared. Wild ducks by thousands were to be found in the land-locked waters of the Bay of Quinté and on that at Toronto. There were wild geese, huge wild turkeys, and an abundance of partridges. The pioneer became almost inevitably a sportsman and the instinct runs to this day in the blood of his descendants. We may well be surprised at the rapidity of development. An officer, Patrick Campbell, travelling from Montreal to Kingston in 1791, describes flour-mills and saw-mills; on some farms as many as one hundred acres were already cleared. A certain Captain Fraser had a large house, extensive barns and flocks of poultry. Mrs. Fraser showed Campbell ten large fat hogs just killed for food in winter and added that twenty hogs and two fat oxen were the winter's supply. At dinner there were venison steaks and the host and his guest drank port wine until they could drink no more.

While such a life appealed to the strong, nature taught some rude lessons. "All our golden promises are vanished in smoke," one of the loyalists wrote after the labours of a year; "We have nothing but his Majesty's rotten pork and unbaked flour to subsist on. It is the most inhospitable clime that ever mortal sat on (sic)." In 1787 and 1788 the crops failed and since, at the same time, the allowance to the settlers came to an end, the result was in some quarters a despairing cry for bread. Fish swarming in the rivers did not prevent acute famine. Starving families ate even unripe grain in the fields. From nuts ground they made a kind of gruel and when spring came they fed on young buds. Distressed people haunted the routes of travel by water, holding out appealing hands to passing boats. The famine was not widespread but a few starved to death. These are, however, only dark spots in what is mainly a story of hard labour rewarded by an ample inheritance. The records show that many of these settlers lived to vigorous old age.

Still, on granite and marble stones, sometimes on decaying wood, memorials in old cemeteries, too often neglected, show that not a few of the exiles lived to nearly a hundred years. Hard work in the open air invigorated more often than it killed. We hear the pioneers lamenting in old age the soft life of their descendants and contrasting the pleasure-seeking and apparent flippancy of easier times with the stern joys and the glad fellowship in toil of the early days. Some of them indeed wondered whether they had acted wisely in leaving their former homes. The truth is that probably they had no chance even at the outset, since if known in local politics as Tories their Whig neighbours might have attacked them. Roger Conant, member of a good family in Massachusetts, a loyalist who had forfeited thirteen thousand acres, tells us that he and loyalist friends of his type agreed that their course was mistaken and foolish.

Man's labour, however weak, changed the face of Upper Canada. Along a frontage on lake and river of five hundred miles there were soon gashes in the forest monotony of green that had remained little altered during we know not how many thousands of years. Here and there peeped out the brown roof of a settler's house with stumps dotting the scanty fields. Villages soon appeared. Devout people by united effort built churches of wood, austere in type, but in some cases spacious temples compared with the narrow housing of most of those who frequented them. Kingston became quickly a fortified town where a military society echoed the tone of distant garrison's in England. At the other end of the lake at Niagara were also soldiers and a fort lying within territory ceded to the United States but still flying the British flag during a dozen years after the treaty of peace. The British claimed that redress in regard to the terms of the treaty must be made before they would surrender the many frontier posts on the American side

that they had held throughout the war. The fur-traders at
Montreal were glad of the dispute since, during the years
that it lasted, they controlled the avenues of trade to the
west and shifted permanently the centre of the fur trade
from Albany to Montreal.

The British in Upper Canada never engaged in war with
the native tribes. These became, indeed, docile wards,
restive and dangerous only when maddened by fire-water.
A primitive culture is apt to crumble before one that has
learned to make wider use of the forces of nature. There
was no chemistry in the Indian villages to solve the mystery
of gunpowder; no knowledge to turn raw ores into the
tempered iron of the axe or the gun, or the copper of the
needed kettle. Of these the European retained a monopoly.
Opinion differs in the estimate of the Indian's character;
to some he is always the brutal savage, treacherous and
bloodthirsty; to a more tolerant school he is simply human,
with measure of good and evil in his nature equal to that
of civilized man; with indeed a simplicity of honesty remote
from the corrupt wiles of the European. Mrs. Simcoe, wife
of the first governor of Upper Canada, saw him at Kingston
sauntering about the town as nonchalant and indifferent
as a London loafer; "unwarlike, idle, drunken, dirty." He
had little of the sense of property that makes begging a
disgrace and, expecting perhaps some gift, he would sit for
hours by loyalist doors without the regard for time that
the business of civilization makes necessary. While sometimes a needed friend when, for a low wage, his skill in
hunting supplied the loyalist larder, he was of little use in
the steady, disciplined labour of cutting down trees or dig-
ging in the soil. This he had never learned; if in native life
such work was achieved, it was likely to be the squaw who
did it.

At first, but for only a few years, some loyalists had the
slave labour of the negro, especially in the region about

Niagara. During the hundred years prior to the American
revolution British slave traders had carried to the American
colonies and to the West Indies about two million slaves,
an average of twenty thousand in each year. Imagination
can hardly picture the horrors of this traffic. It was at its
height when the revolution began and was vastly profitable,—profitable enough to overcome the waste involved
that for every slave placed on a plantation in, for instance,
Virginia, one other seized in Africa died during the horrors
of the passage. When the loyalists could, they took with
them their slaves, not as persons but as property and they
carried some thousands to their new homes. While most
went to Nova Scotia, a few reached Upper Canada, and
there in the first days of loyalist settlement slaves were
sometimes put up for sale. Advertisement offered a strong
young negro who could do hard work, and a young woman
with accomplishments so varied that she could cook, wash,
take care of poultry and even dress the lady's hair.

It is to the credit of those who ruled Upper Canada that
they ended quickly this traffic. In 1772, on the eve of the
American Revolution, England herself had decreed by
the famous judgment of Lord Mansfield, concurred in by the
other judges, that a slave so happy as to set foot on the
soil of Great Britain became by that act a free man. The rule
was not applied to the American colonies where slavery
remained a festering malady that in the end caused civil
war. Mansfield's judgment fortified in the minds of Englishmen such a horror of the brutal institution that its
enemies, Granville Sharp, Wilberforce and others did not
toil in vain. In 1793 the newly formed legislature of Upper Canada passed an Act forbidding the further bringing
of slaves into the country. A slave, moreover, might not be
held in bondage for more than nine years and the children
of slaves were to be free when they reached the age of
twenty-five. In consequence slavery gradually disappeared

as the old slaves died and the young ones became free, and it resulted that after 1793 Canada was a refuge for slaves. Once across the frontier from the United States they gained unchallenged freedom. No newcomer might be a slave. An obscure British legislature sitting in a wooden shanty on the border of the wilderness had outlawed the slave trade years before this was achieved by Great Britain herself.

The Canadian wilderness had only inadequately the means of communication that are a force so pregnant in the growth of civilization. Roads and ships are chief instruments of culture. Though China that attained civilization had and has few roads, it had easy movement for ships on its crowded rivers and its long sea-coast. Greece owed her sprightly culture to her access to the sea. Rome's ships enabled her to master the shores of the Mediterranean and her genius for building roads carried her overland to Germany and to the conquest of Britain. At first the scattered settlements of Upper Canada had the slightest means of communication by land. Gigantic trees, marshes, unbridged rivers made the way difficult. The native tribes that had wandered in its forests, during we know not how many centuries, followed only narrow trails and bridged no rivers. When moving by land they carried their burdens on their backs along routes so dim in the encircling forest that only eyes highly trained could follow as guides the marks on trees. The Indian had little inventive talent. While the wheel may well be taken as the symbol of man's advance by land, by what seems a strange blindness, in neither of the two American continents did the natives ever acquire an invention known to early peoples in Europe, even to the primitive Britons whom Rome conquered. During thousands of years the peasant of Italy had his wheeled cart; the Roman legions had their war-chariots; but in all America there was no cart or chariot and thus no need of roads for wheeled vehicles.

On water, however, the Indian achieved one great triumph; he made the beautiful canoe of birch bark that gave him free movement on river and lake in contrast with his clumsy immobility on land. To make a canoe involved ingenuity and skill that may well arouse our wonder when we remember how few were the Indian's tools. He had no knife, nor chisel, nor other steel implement. His axe or hatchet was made of stone. He had no saw. His sharpest edged tool was of flint or obsidian. He had only wooden nails and his ropes and cord consisted of what the forest gave to him in the ready-made sinewy growth of vines, bark and branches. Yet he managed to cut from the birch tree the great sheets of bark that made the water-tight skin of his canoe and to shape its light skeleton of wood. He whittled with a stone tool from a piece of split wood the paddle by which his swelling muscles propelled his creation. The European could so little rival the Indian in this field that it may be doubted whether, during the long years of contact with the Indian and with the advantage of better tools, any of the French or English in Canada have ever learned to make a canoe of birch bark, though civilized skill has indeed now learned to copy the Indian's model in other and more enduring material.

With highways by land lacking in Upper Canada, highways by water were the more quickly used. The fine timber of the country invited ship-building. Before the end of the seventeenth century ships of more than a hundred and twenty tons had been built on the St. Lawrence and the industry hardly flagged until it was ended by the ship of steel. To sail Lake Ontario, ships must be built above the rapids on the St. Lawrence, and to go further and sail the upper lakes they must be built above the great torrent of Niagara. During the war in which France lost Canada, British and French ships had fought on Lake Ontario and

by the time of the American Revolution there was a score
of vessels on the lakes. Most were armed and it was the
British command of the lakes that enabled them to hold
the frontier posts long after the war had ended. The early
ships were roughly made. Mrs. Simcoe noted in 1792 the
crudity of the work in the shipyard at Kingston. Nearly
everything used but the timber had to be brought the long
distance from England; the workmen were unskilled and
the tools inadequate for the more delicate tasks. The
sailors too were for the most part amateurs who knew little
of navigation and kept no log. Though time cured this
defect when men trained in the Royal Navy were brought
to the lakes, earlier experience caused tragedies on the inland waters. Charts, lighthouses and other guides to navigation were at first unknown and wrecks were frequent,
sometimes with heavy loss of life. When in 1780 the
Ontario, twenty-two guns, set out from Niagara carrying a
detachment of the King's Own she was never heard of
again, with, it is said, a loss of a hundred and seventy-two
lives.

Meanwhile far away in London was being debated the
problem of a vast Canada that should stretch westward
from the Atlantic Ocean at first for nearly two thousand
miles and later for four thousand. Since Quebec, the old
capital, far in the east, was French and new-comers pushing westward beyond Montreal spoke English and had
English traditions, a new ruling centre must be created in
the west. In a later volume we shall look at the debates
in the House of Commons on this topic, debates in which
Fox and Burke took part, as they had taken part in the debates on Canada in 1774 when all North America to the
Mississippi and the Gulf of Mexico was still British territory. In the Ottawa River nature offered a suitable mark

of division and that river became the frontier between Lower Canada to be ruled from Quebec and Upper Canada which must find its own capital.

An Indian group of huts at the mouth of the river now called the Humber, flowing into Lake Ontario on the north shore opposite Niagara, was known by the name of Toronto. The river served the useful purpose of providing a short route by canoe to Lake Huron from Lake Ontario and thus saving the long journey by way of Lake Erie and Detroit. Though La Salle had used this route near the end of the seventeenth century, it was not until the year 1749 that, to protect their trade, the French built a post at Toronto and called it Fort Rouillé, after the colonial minister of the time. The fort had a short life for in 1759, during the war with Great Britain, the French abandoned and destroyed it. At Toronto a spacious bay all but land-locked by an island of sand offered a secure haven for shipping. Only a few wandering Indians and hunters and traders had frequented the spot when in 1760, after the surrender of Montreal, the hardy frontier soldier Robert Rogers paused here on his way to take possession of the west and noted what the French had already discovered that the place was well situated for trade. When, in 1793, long after the visit of Rogers, the first governor, John Graves Simcoe, pitched his tent on the shore of the bay, he was pondering a grave problem. In the previous year he had, with impressive ceremony, copied from Westminster, opened the tiny legislature of Upper Canada in the village at the mouth of the Niagara River. When, however, he looked across that river, he had misgivings. There, not half a mile away, lay a fort commanding with its cannon the little Canadian capital. Though it was within the United States, over it still floated the British flag, which, however, as Simcoe well knew, must soon be replaced by the Stars and Stripes of the republic. Renewed war was, he thought, certain to come, as it did, and in such a case the little capital of Upper Canada would soon lie in ruins. Far across the wide lake lay a snug haven, the advantage of which the French had already seen, and there Simcoe fixed the capital of what is now the most populous and the richest of the Canadian provinces. Simcoe's foresight did not save the little town that he called York, since, when war came, both the first capital at Niagara and the second at Toronto were devastated by invaders from the United States, acts which had their opposing counterpart in the burning by the British of Washington the capital of the republic.

CHAPTER XXII

LOYALIST INDEMNITIES

THE British government undertook not only to aid the loyalists to settle in new homes but also to pay them compensation for losses in property and income. If we may blame the lack of insight that caused the revolution, we may also admire the generous consideration of the defeated mother country for those who had suffered in her behalf. While food and supplies were given at once, inevitably it took some years to enquire into and to determine the value of the property lost. In truth the best help that the British government gave was not by compensation for losses but in its expenditure of the equivalent of about nine million dollars in what is now Canada to support the exiles until they could shift for themselves. This problem of immediate help was really simpler than that of enquiry into claims for compensation. In July, 1783, Parliament named commissioners, numbering ultimately five, to relieve loyalists in need, to aid refugees in England to go to America in order to recover their property and, above all, to enquire into losses from Florida to Canada. The enquiries lasted for about five years. As late as in 1792 claims were still being met by grants of land.

The commissioners rented for their use a house in Lincoln's Inn Fields, in London, and there the most important claims were presented. A committee of loyalists, with one from each of the former colonies, aided the commissioners with their knowledge of local conditions. Sir William Pepperell, grandson of the hero of Louisbourg, and dent in England. Since the exiles had suffered more heavily they were to be paid more,—ninety per cent. of claims between ten and thirty thousand pounds, eighty-five per cent. on additions up to fifty thousand pounds and eighty per cent. on still larger sums. Even for those who had no claim that they had been driven into exile but who had lost property the scale was generous. They were to receive eighty per cent. up to thirty thousand pounds and less for larger sums. Most claimants were paid in full, since few had losses of more than ten thousand pounds. On proved loss of income fifty per cent. was paid up to four hundred pounds and then forty per cent. up to fifteen hundred pounds. The outlay for these purposes and for relief was not less than thirty million dollars. We get some idea of the magnitude of the losses of some of the loyalists when we find Sir John Johnson, who fled from the State of New York to Montreal, receiving the equivalent of more than two hundred thousand dollars, about one-third of the real value of what he had lost. Beverley Robinson claimed $334,000 and received $128,000. Frederick Philipse Jr. claimed $777,000 and received $210,000. Oliver De Lancey claimed $390,000 and received $125,000. Loyalists who had remained in or returned to the United States filed claims amounting to $6,911,000 and were allowed $2,745,000. About one-third of the $30,000,000, spent in behalf of loyalists or paid to them for losses, went to loyalists from New York.

We shall never know with certainty how many loyalists found new homes in the northern land. The highest estimate is about sixty thousand. Rather more than three thousand loyalists made claims for losses but many of these did not, of course, settle in Canada. Not more than about six thousand names have been preserved of loyalist families in Canada and we can only guess the number of the nameless who linked their fortunes with more conspicuous per-

Joseph Galloway, an eminent loyalist leader and writer, served on this committee. The commissioners were staggered at the amounts demanded. Before the end of March, 1784, claims for seven million pounds had been filed. The Penns, who lost the vast estates in Pennsylvania inherited from their ancestor, William Penn, received in the end half a million pounds. Lord Fairfax lost literally millions of acres. While with one or two exceptions the few claimants for large sums dwelt in England, most of the lesser claimants dwelt in America. Since they could not cross the sea to urge their claims it was necessary that commissioners should go to them. Accordingly Colonel Thomas Dundas and Jeremy Pemberton proceeded to Nova Scotia and Canada. John Anstey, a London barrister, was sent to New York. One or other of the commissioners sat at Halifax, Shelburne, St. John, Quebec, Montreal and Niagara. Though wide notice was given to persons to file their claims, it is doubtful if such notices ever reached some of the remoter settlers.

The work of the commissioners in America occupied more than four years. Usually the claimant, when summoned to meet the sitting commissioners in a private room, was placed on oath, and then questioned. If he had deeds of lost lands or other business papers, he produced them and he was required to deduct from the value of the lost property debts owing by himself in the colony concerned, for which his property had been, of course, liable. Then the commissioners examined persons who might have knowledge of the claimant's position. Every claim was sifted and some patriots were found to lack the virtue of moderation in stating their losses. The commissioners would make allowances only for actual, realized losses. They would not allow anything, for instance, to a lawyer for income that he might have earned had he not been exiled during the war. Claims for lands seized, or for an office that had been granted for life, were allowed, but the claimant must prove that the cause of the loss was his loyalty. Such rigorous methods of a law court wounded the feelings of a good many men, conscious of heavy sacrifices and expecting sympathy.

The provision that loyalists were to be paid for losses in personal effects as well as in lands caused much perplexity. What had they lost? We have seen the loyalists fleeing in panic from Boston on March 17, 1776, and now some of them produced careful lists of what had been left in their deserted houses. What was a commissioner who had a sense of humour to do with a bill that included a dozen towels, a frying pan, a "large Brass Kettel," a dozen coffee cups, two good suits of clothes, and a "marreners Compas," abandoned on that momentous day? The spelling of this claimant indicates that Boston had not yet done its perfect work of culture. The commissioners were asked to ponder the value of bedsteads, chests of drawers, chairs, feather-beds, sheets and table linen; of medicines and books; of puncheons of "New England rum"; of saddles and bridles. What could be said of the value of hay and buckwheat left unharvested, of potatoes planted and never gathered, of horses and cows and pigs and sheep lost beyond recovery? When a claim was put in for a negro slave killed by the "rebels" we find that the price of negroes ran from forty to seventy pounds. It was a far cry from this loss to one of six hundred acres of land on the Mississippi, or of a ship taken by the rebels, "a trading vessel from Jamaica to Floriday."

It is fair to lay stress upon the varied and difficult character of the claims because suffering patriots charged undue delay in their relief. In truth long waiting was inevitable. The commissioners, high-minded and industrious men, spent laborious years at their tasks. They had need to be alert against the guile of patriotism hungry for reward by a grateful country in terms of cash. Lord Dun-

more who had burned part of Norfolk, in Virg[...] compensation for vast areas of lands to which h[...] doubtful. The Bayards of New York, of whom i[...] said that, like their illustrious French namesake, th[...] *sans peur*, if not, like him, *sans reproche*, put in[...] claims for losses. No doubt they had suffered. The[...] Charles Inglis, afterwards first Bishop of Nova Scotia,[...] clared that William Bayard was so long confined "in[...] miserable Garret" in New Jersey as to injure his health[...] But, after the British took New York, Bayard and his brother made large profits through an agency for selling prizes brought into that harbour and through other channels of trade. In such circumstances reticence as to losses would have seemed fitting.

The commissioners had to probe these claims and must have learned much about human nature. No doubt many loyalists, whose losses were real, made no claims at all. Men who had served in the ranks sometimes trusted their officers to look after their claims and found the officers broken reeds. It was not easy for a settler in remoter Upper Canada to go to Montreal or Niagara to make his claim in person on oath, nor, could he have done so, was it easy to produce evidence to convince the commissioners. To forget losses was often easier than to secure compensation. The path of patriotism is after all the path of sacrifice. Those whose claims were admitted had little cause for complaint, though to men in a hard struggle to secure a new footing in life, the delay was trying.

The work of the commission was done while Pitt was Prime Minister. In 1788, five years after the peace, he announced in the House of Commons that up to ten thousand pounds all accepted claims would be paid in full. In respect of amounts beyond this sum, Pitt drew a proper distinction between the loyalists driven from their homes in America and the owners of confiscated property who had been resi-

Joseph Galloway, an eminent loyalist leader and writer, served on this committee. The commissioners were staggered at the amounts demanded. Before the end of March, 1784, claims for seven million pounds had been filed. The Penns, who lost the vast estates in Pennsylvania inherited from their ancestor, William Penn, received in the end half a million pounds. Lord Fairfax lost literally millions of acres. While with one or two exceptions the few claimants for large sums dwelt in England, most of the lesser claimants dwelt in America. Since they could not cross the sea to urge their claims it was necessary that commissioners should go to them. Accordingly Colonel Thomas Dundas and Jeremy Pemberton proceeded to Nova Scotia and Canada. John Anstey, a London barrister, was sent to New York. One or other of the commissioners sat at Halifax, Shelburne, St. John, Quebec, Montreal and Niagara. Though wide notice was given to persons to file their claims, it is doubtful if such notices ever reached some of the remoter settlers.

The work of the commissioners in America occupied more than four years. Usually the claimant, when summoned to meet the sitting commissioners in a private room, was placed on oath, and then questioned. If he had deeds of lost lands or other business papers, he produced them and he was required to deduct from the value of the lost property debts owing by himself in the colony concerned, for which his property had been, of course, liable. Then the commissioners examined persons who might have knowledge of the claimant's position. Every claim was sifted and some patriots were found to lack the virtue of moderation in stating their losses. The commissioners would make allowances only for actual, realized losses. They would not allow anything, for instance, to a lawyer for income that he might have earned had he not been exiled during the war. Claims for lands seized, or for an office that had been granted for life, were allowed, but the claimant must prove that the cause of the loss was his loyalty. Such rigorous methods of a law court wounded the feelings of a good many men, conscious of heavy sacrifices and expecting sympathy.

The provision that loyalists were to be paid for losses in personal effects as well as in lands caused much perplexity. What had they lost? We have seen the loyalists fleeing in panic from Boston on March 17, 1776, and now some of them produced careful lists of what had been left in their deserted houses. What was a commissioner who had a sense of humour to do with a bill that included a dozen towels, a frying pan, a "large Brass Kettel," a dozen coffee cups, two good suits of clothes, and a "marreners Compas," abandoned on that momentous day? The spelling of this claimant indicates that Boston had not yet done its perfect work of culture. The commissioners were asked to ponder the value of bedsteads, chests of drawers, chairs, feather-beds, sheets and table linen; of medicines and books; of puncheons of "New England rum"; of saddles and bridles. What could be said of the value of hay and buckwheat left unharvested, of potatoes planted and never gathered, of horses and cows and pigs and sheep lost beyond recovery? When a claim was put in for a negro slave killed by the "rebels" we find that the price of negroes ran from forty to seventy pounds. It was a far cry from this loss to one of six hundred acres of land on the Mississippi, or of a ship taken by the rebels, "a trading vessel from Jamaica to Floriday."

It is fair to lay stress upon the varied and difficult character of the claims because suffering patriots charged undue delay in their relief. In truth long waiting was inevitable. The commissioners, high-minded and industrious men, spent laborious years at their tasks. They had need to be alert against the guile of patriotism hungry for reward by a grateful country in terms of cash. Lord Dunmore who had burned part of Norfolk, in Virginia, claimed compensation for vast areas of lands to which his title was doubtful. The Bayards of New York, of whom it has been said that, like their illustrious French namesake, they were *sans peur,* if not, like him, *sans reproche,* put in heavy claims for losses. No doubt they had suffered. The Rev. Charles Inglis, afterwards first Bishop of Nova Scotia, declared that William Bayard was so long confined "in a miserable Garret" in New Jersey as to injure his health. But, after the British took New York, Bayard and his brother made large profits through an agency for selling prizes brought into that harbour and through other channels of trade. In such circumstances reticence as to losses would have seemed fitting.

The commissioners had to probe these claims and must have learned much about human nature. No doubt many loyalists, whose losses were real, made no claims at all. Men who had served in the ranks sometimes trusted their officers to look after their claims and found the officers broken reeds. It was not easy for a settler in remoter Upper Canada to go to Montreal or Niagara to make his claim in person on oath, nor, could he have done so, was it easy to produce evidence to convince the commissioners. To forget losses was often easier than to secure compensation. The path of patriotism is after all the path of sacrifice. Those whose claims were admitted had little cause for complaint, though to men in a hard struggle to secure a new footing in life, the delay was trying.

The work of the commission was done while Pitt was Prime Minister. In 1788, five years after the peace, he announced in the House of Commons that up to ten thousand pounds all accepted claims would be paid in full. In respect of amounts beyond this sum, Pitt drew a proper distinction between the loyalists driven from their homes in America and the owners of confiscated property who had been resi-

dent in England. Since the exiles had suffered more
heavily they were to be paid more,—ninety per cent. of
claims between ten and thirty thousand pounds, eighty-five
per cent. on additions up to fifty thousand pounds and eighty
per cent. on still larger sums. Even for those who had no
claim that they had been driven into exile but who had
lost property the scale was generous. They were to receive eighty per cent. up to thirty thousand pounds and less
for larger sums. Most claimants were paid in full, since
few had losses of more than ten thousand pounds. On
proved loss of income fifty per cent. was paid up to four
hundred pounds and then forty per cent. up to fifteen hundred pounds. The outlay for these purposes and for relief
was not less than thirty million dollars. We get some idea
of the magnitude of the losses of some of the loyalists when
we find Sir John Johnson, who fled from the State of New
York to Montreal, receiving the equivalent of more than
two hundred thousand dollars, about one-third of the real
value of what he had lost. Beverley Robinson claimed
$334,000 and received $128,000. Frederick Philipse Jr.
claimed $777,000 and received $210,000. Oliver De Lancey
claimed $390,000 and received $125,000. Loyalists who had
remained in or returned to the United States filed claims
amounting to $6,911,000 and were allowed $2,745,000.
About one-third of the $30,000,000, spent in behalf of loyal-
ists or paid to them for losses, went to loyalists from New
York.

We shall never know with certainty how many loyalists
found new homes in the northern land. The highest estimate is about sixty thousand. Rather more than three
thousand loyalists made claims for losses but many of these
did not, of course, settle in Canada. Not more than about
six thousand names have been preserved of loyalist families
in Canada and we can only guess the number of the nameless who linked their fortunes with more conspicuous per-

sons. It was long a matter of pride for loyalists to attach to their names the distinguishing letters "U.E." that enshrined their devotion to a United Empire and we may conclude that persons certain of loyalist ancestry were anxious to make the fact known. Whatever their numbers, the loyalists shaped for generations the political thought of the Maritime Provinces and of Upper Canada.

Ever since the founding of Halifax in 1749 Nova Scotia had desired government like that of the English colonies in America, with an elected legislature and English law. In 1758 the colony secured this, on the model of Virginia, and the loyalists who settled by the sea found at once a political system, with the heat and freedom of elections like those of their former homes. But Upper Canada was still a part of the Province of Quebec, under the French civil law and the despotic rule of a military governor with a nominated council. Such a system under which government was for, but never by, the people was alien to the loyalist habit of mind. French feudal law that made the tiller of the soil a vassal under the authority of a seigneur would certainly not do for these freeholders from the English colonies. They were accustomed to elect a legislature with a real authority in public affairs. Nearly all of them were Protestants and they were not willing that the Roman Church should occupy the privileged position conceded to it by the Quebec Act. With the migration of the loyalists the English in Canada were no longer a few restless and perhaps vulgar traders. Thousands of patriots had come who knew how to suffer for their convictions, and their coming meant the creation of a new political system. At its head, much to his surprise, was to be, in the end, Carleton himself.

CHAPTER XXIII

THE CURTAIN FALLS

GENERAL HALDIMAND had kept watch at Quebec since the summer of 1778. When he sailed for England in the autumn of 1784 he had, says the *Quebec Gazette,* "an affectionate and respectful adieu" from the whole population. In England he received knighthood, a costly honour for a poor man, since the fees amounted to nearly eight hundred pounds. His diary, written in the French of his youth, records his life in London society and reflects the spirit of his class at the close of the American Revolution; mild gambling at whist, with gains or losses never exceeding than two or three guineas, dinners, balls, involving late hours, receptions at court and in great houses. George III and his queen were always gracious at the many levées; "You are always a soldier and always right," the king said to him. Haldimand saw the king turn coldly away from Charles Fox whose sense of duty took him to a levée. He finds pleasure in good pictures and music, meets many officers who had served in America, and shows a shrewd and sometimes a mordant insight into men and manners. General Gage, a shadow in thinness of body, he found much disturbed over the examination of his accounts in America after the lapse of eleven years.

The three men Murray, Carleton, and Haldimand, who had ruled Canada for the long period since the British conquest meet sometimes in society and each is critical of the others. For some unexplained reason Haldimand thought Murray "a bad fellow." Both were disturbed at the pros-

pect of Carleton's return to Canada. An exiled chief-justice
of New York, William Smith, was intimate with Carleton
and might, so Canada's former rulers feared, copy there
colonial New York with an elected legislature. Murray
called Smith Carleton's "nurse," and Haldimand thought
him "a rebel at heart" now "unmasked as a fool," probably
because he had no belief in benevolent despotism as a final
form of government. So unmoved by events was the military mind. When Carleton and Haldimand meet at levées
they discuss the absorbing topic of the incomes and pensions
of returned officers. Carleton maintained a "profound silence" about his future policy that seemed ominous. His
insistence on being governor general over all the remaining British colonies caused delay and he did not reach
Quebec until the second year after Haldimand retired.

Haldimand saw much of "Joseph" as he called the Mohawk chief, Brant. Like many others he was in London
after the revolution, seeking pay and pensions from the
government. Haldimand gave aid in having his portrait
both painted and engraved. He grew, however, rather weary
of one who did not, it seems, fit easily into the world of
fashion in London, and after reading a "weak, shallow"
speech by Joseph to Lord Sydney, Haldimand declares that
"I do not wish to be mixed up with these people any longer."
He meets Lord Cornwallis, about to set out to rule India
and in no way disgraced in the public mind because of his
surrender at Yorktown. General Clinton who had cut so
poor a figure in the American war was making "enormous
pretensions" in London. Both he and his predecessor Howe
had lived sumptuously at New York, drawing daily rations
for a hundred people to use as they pleased and taking an
unlimited supply of firewood, when in harsh winter days
it was very scarce. Clinton had been able to return to
England with, as was reported, a large fortune made from
his savings. Haldimand contrasted this with his own moder-

ation, though in truth as a soldier of fortune he had not
fared badly. He had been able to acquire extensive lands
in Florida, Maryland, New Brunswick and near Quebec.
At Quebec he had partly rebuilt at the public cost the gov-
nernor's residence and at his own cost had built a house at
Montmorency Falls. On arriving at Quebec he had purchased Carleton's furniture and taken over his personal
staff. He told Carleton that when he returned to Canada he
might have free use of the carriages, a post-chaise and
twelve horses that he had left at Quebec, an indication of
sumptuous allowances to keep up his state; and he added
that hé hoped Carleton would buy his house at Montmorency. This Carleton at once repudiated as Lady Maria
would not at any price risk the children in the rocky heights
about the falls. She decided too that Carleton should buy
nothing stored by Haldimand, a touch, so Haldimand
thought, of meanness. Of what he had left behind, in the
prospect of sale to his successor, he seems to have recovered little and he draws the cynical but probably sound
moral: "when leaving a place not to return, nothing should
be left behind, nor should any one be trusted."

Haldimand moved in a rather greedy military society,
conscious that power lay in the hands of a few influential
persons and on the alert to pay court to them. He had now
the high rank of lieutenant-general and was urgent in asking not only for the salary but also for the allowances that
usually went with the rank. He was, however, still tech-
nically a foreigner, for his naturalization had never been
completed, and Amherst, final conqueror of Canada and
until recently commander-in-chief, reminded him that,
under the law, a foreigner could not be considered as per-
forming the duties in England with which allowances went.
Haldimand's comment is that Amherst "is a man who
never uses his credit for any one and certainly he does not
like foreigners." Horace Walpole disliked him and called

him a log of wood whose stupidity and incapacity were beyond belief. When Haldimand and his fellow Swiss officer, General Prevost, father of a later governor in Canada, reminded Amherst of their services and claimed his interest and protection they received only evasive answers, Haldimand, however, walks with Amherst in the Park, dines with him and maliciously accepts at his table the unwilling offer of a rare bottle of old madeira; he and a swarm of officers attend weekly receptions at Amherst's house, where, on one occasion, every one is bored and on another some complain that there is no opportunity for gambling at whist. It is a society absorbed in its own interests and amusements, satisfied with its own standards and possessed by an insular sense of superiority to anything that might be found elsewhere in the world. The hard selfishness of this circle causes in Haldimand the comment: "the better I know this country the more do I see that it is a supreme folly to trust to the generosity of the nation. Our services are forgotten the moment there is no longer need for them." We know that there were other aspects of this world that good Dr. Johnson loved and John Wesley enlightened.

Haldimand, the foreigner, saw perhaps only the polished surface of a caste that lived as if it was rich even though it might be poor. A friend advised him that, to maintain his position, he should keep up such state in his manner of living as to involve for his bachelor establishment at least seven servants on full time including a man to tend the horses, one to go behind the carriage, a coachman and a groom. It was impossible for the glittering world in which Haldimand moved to believe that the plain people who had created the United States could hold together as a nation. Reports in which Haldimand delighted reached London that already in 1787, four years after the peace, there were in Boston loyal toasts to George III. Signs of dissolution after the strain of the war had indeed appeared

but these were checked by the new constitution of the
United States that came into force in 1789 and made Washington, who had been the nation's great leader in time of
war, its guiding head in time of peace. It was rather Europe
that tended to break up. In that year of hope for the
United States revolution began in France. In the next year
came the menace of a British war with Spain over claims on
the Pacific coast in what is now British Columbia, a region
that Haldimand's imagination could not have pictured as
a part of Canada.

And so life passed pleasantly enough for the old warrior.
While he had taken an active part in one revolution he had
no place in that new surging world that was to see a king
and queen of France go to the scaffold, and to involve
nearly a quarter of century of upheaval and war, until the
ambitious plans of Napoleon ended in his exile to St. Helena.
We find Haldimand in reminiscent mood reading some of
the vast collection of papers that he had carried with him
to London and that are now lodged in the British Museum.
He had kept up ties with his native Switzerland and, perhaps weary of the London parade, began to build for himself a house in Yverdun, but he did not live to finish it.
He died there in the house of his brother on June 5, 1791.
There is a tablet in his honour in Henry VII's chapel in
Westminster Abbey.

The American Revolution produced a new type of political society. While the federations in ancient Greece and
in modern Switzerland consisted of small communities,
that of the United States included thirteen independent
colonies fronting on the Atlantic for a thousand miles, extending for a similar distance into the interior and aiming
to include the whole continent. Revolution, so-called, in
England, under Cromwell and William of Orange, had not
altered the structure of society, but the framers of the

federal constitution had no such structure and had to
create something wholly new. For them there were no precedents. They had doubts, difficulties and antagonisms.
They had been reared in the English political system, the
liberties of which they believed had been warped by a tyrant
king, and now they must exclude any such danger and furnish guarantees of enduring liberty. With no tradition behind them, they were obliged to frame their ideals in the
rigid clauses of an instrument of government that has
endured, little changed, for a century and a half and, except
that of Great Britain, is now the oldest among the great
nations of the world. Though it was created in an age of
slow movement for a people as yet few in number and isolated from the rest of the world, under it now is ruled a
world power the most populous of the nations of the west
except Russia. Naturally, especially in regard to foreign
affairs, the constitution creaks in such changed conditions.

Revolutions, said Aristotle, are not for trifles though
they may arise out of trifles. The American Revolution was
not due to a single problem of taxation, nor to restrictions
on trade, nor to grievances that involved real hardship, but
to something behind each particular dispute. The era of
colonial beginnings was over; foundations had been well
and truly laid; and now the teeming life of a new world
that had become self-reliant required complete freedom to
shape its own destiny. The time arrives in the lives of
nations when far-reaching change is imminent. While a few
may see this at the critical moment, it would have needed
all but impossible imagination and tact in British statesmen to grasp and accept the outlook of the colonies. The
present is so much with leaders in political life that decisions are made for to-day without realizing what they
may involve for many to-morrows. Violence in Boston in
1765 startled the complacent sense in England of complete
authority over the colonies. After this Property was

shocked when mobs destroyed cargoes of tea owned by Englishmen. The refusal of compensation caused armed force to step in and armed force so led to war that the mother country was committed to a fatal policy of conquest. Coercion, however, even though for the time victorious, could never have led to reconciliation across three thousand miles of ocean. At home in England it could indeed make Cornwall obey London, as at home in the United States it forced a rebellious south to obey a victorious north. But space itself, miles of ocean, condemned efforts to conquer the colonies into enduring subordination. A British victory would only have postponed the final conflict. A better way was found later in the second British Empire, with the result that communities overseas many times more populous than the thirteen English colonies are now both completely free and also remain linked with the motherland in the closest ties of friendship and coöperation.

English-speaking Canada and the republic of the United States were the outcome of strife so bitter that survivals of the passions of that stormy time are still real in both countries. To millions of people in the United States, Britain remains the relentlessly selfish power, always watching to lay greedy hands upon some new portion of the earth. Her actions in all parts of the world and her offers of friendship are watched with suspicion. Against no other country is it still so easy to arouse animosity. Events of a century and a half ago are still vivid memories in the United States. Europe, on the other hand, has had so many upheavals as almost to forget all but the most recent. England treasures no bitterness in regard to the American Revolution while Lexington and Bunker Hill arouse emotions in the United States that have some influence in the politics of today.

In Canada there remains a tradition of the hardships of

the loyalists, whose clinging to the British monarchy resulted in their exile from the United States. Their sufferings stimulated a devotion to the king, more uncompromising than that of the British themselves in the home land. Suspicions of American designs has played its part in more than one political crisis in Canada. Of this we may say that resentment is not a happy temper to inspire a young state, though no doubt in this temper it was that Massachusetts itself had been founded to escape from the tyranny of Laud. Since the loyalists were driven from their homes by men who spoke in extravagant terms of democracy and liberty as cures for the ills of society, it followed that in Canada during more than fifty years, one party, at least, prided itself on denying that there could be any virtue in democracy and despised whatever seemed republican.

Those who now cross the frontier between the United States and Canada are soon aware of a change of atmosphere. Though conditions of life are similar, since in each land is now a ruling democracy with its merits and its defects, traditions are different. To one side Washington seems the greatest leader and hero perhaps that the world has ever known; Adams, Jefferson, and later presidents are great national figures; descendants of men who signed the Declaration of Independence have a mark of distinction; the Fourth of July still stirs emotions. Across the northern frontier all this has little meaning. Washington is remembered with respect but with no special reverence; other Presidents, except Lincoln, are barely known by name; the Fourth of July passes unnoticed and flamboyant phrases in the Declaration of Independence, familiar to every school boy in the United States, are apt, if noticed at all, to excite humorous derision. In their differences the two nations, with the same language and in large degree the same origin, express the present-day outcome of the American Revolution. Still are heard, though now more rarely, old phrases of antagonism. Those in the United States, so far as they continue to exist, are directed not against Canada herself but against the tie that she retains with Britain, still disliked as the old enemy of liberty. In Canada too, harsh traditions still survive. Yet here as in so many aspects of human affairs is a paradox. The intercourse between the two peoples is on a scale not to be found elsewhere in the world. Every year some millions of one country or the other cross the international frontier and memories have so softened in the greater and the lesser nation that now they are probably more deeply friendly than any other two peoples in the world. This, indeed, in spite of surface antagonisms, may be said of the whole British Empire and the United States. The doubter may make comparisons with the attitude to each other of the nations in Europe and in Asia; France with Germany; Germany with Russia; China with Japan.

AUTHORITIES

Abbreviations:
C.A.   Report on Canadian Archives
C.H.R.   The Canadian Historical Review
D.A.B.   Dictionary of American Biography
D.N.B.   Dictionary of National Biography
R.S.C.   Transactions of the Royal Society of Canada
S. and D.   Adam Shortt and A. G. Doughty (eds.): *Documents relating to the constitutional history of Canada* (2nd edition, 2 vols. Ottawa, 1908)

The following authorities are those likely to be directly useful. Though many others have been consulted, lists too elaborate tend rather to confuse than to aid the reader.

GENERAL WORKS ON THE PERIOD

J. Holland Rose, *et al., The Cambridge History of the British Empire:* Vol. I, *The old empire from the beginning to 1783,* and Vol. VI, *Canada and Newfoundland* (Cambridge 1929–30) has lists of authorities. So also has Edward Channing, *History of the United States* (Vol. III, New York, 1912). Of English writers Sir G. O. Trevelyan's six volumes on the revolution lean to the Whig side, while Sir J. W. Fortescue's *History of the British Army* has the opposite quality. The current literature relating to Canada and the American Revolution is reviewed in *The American Historical Review* and in *The Canadian Historical Review.*

CHAPTER I

THE AMERICAN REVOLUTION

ON the situation in England L. B. Namier, *The structure of politics at the accession of George III* (2 vol., London, 1929), and his *England in the age of the American Revolution* (London, 1930). The Declaration of Equality in 1926 is printed in A. B. Keith, *Speeches and documents on . . . the British Dominions, 1918–1931* (Oxford, 1931). Lord E. Fitzmaurice, *Life of William, Earl of Shelburne* (2 vol. London, 1912). O. A. Sherrard, *A life of John Wilkes* (London, 1930). R. Postgate, *That devil Wilkes* (London, 1930). Earl of Ilchester, *Henry Fox, first Lord Holland* (London, 1920). Lord John Russell, *Correspondence of John, Fourth Duke of Bedford* (Vol. III, London, 1846). H. W. V. Temperly, *The Peace of Paris,* in Vol. 1 of *The Cambridge History of the British Empire.*

CHAPTER II

THE CANADIANS AT HOME

THE political, economic, and social life of Canada is dealt with in 23 volumes edited by Adam Shortt and A. G. Doughty, *Canada and its prov-*

inces, with a list of authorities in XXIII (Toronto, 1917). W. S. Wallace, *Dictionary of Canadian biography* (Toronto, 1926) gives authorities; so does L. J. Burpee, *The Oxford encyclopædia of Canadian history* (Oxford, 1926), who includes the history of Canadian cities. On geography, L. J. Burpee (ed.), *An historical atlas of Canada* (Toronto, 1927); J. W. Rogers, Vol. V, Part III (Oxford, 1911) of Sir C. P. Lucas, *Historical geography of the British Empire;* E. Reclus, *Nouvelle géographie universelle* (Vol. XV, Paris, 1890).

The Articles of Capitulation in 1760, the reports of Murray, Burton and Gage in 1762, and the text of the Treaty in 1763 are in S. and D. C.A., 1888 and 1905 have material relating to Canadians who went to France after the cession to Great Britain. R. H. Mahon, *Life of the Hon. James Murray . . .* (London, 1921), covers the career of the first British governor. Voluminous papers relating to Murray are described in C.A. 1913. The earlier phases of Murray's career with authorities are given in G. M. Wrong, *The rise and fall of New France* (2 Vol. New York, 1928) and in *The fall of Canada* (Oxford, 1914). W. Knox, *An historical journal of the campaigns in North America* (New ed., edited by A. G. Doughty, 3 vol., Toronto, 1914–16) is by a British officer at the time of the conquest. Philippe Aubert de Gaspé's romance *Les anciens canadiens* (Quebec, 1863), translated into English by C. G. D. Roberts, *The Canadians of old* (London, 1890), is the classic picture of the Canadians by an author who lived (1786–1871) when manners had little changed. Thomas Anburey, *Travels through the interior parts of North America* (new ed. 2 vol., Boston, 1923), a good observer, was at Quebec with Burgoyne in 1776. On the seigneur and his people W. B. Munro, *The seigniorial system in Canada* (New York, 1907) and his *Documents relating to the seigniorial tenure in Canada* (Toronto, 1908), G. M. Wrong, *A Canadian manor and its seigneurs* (Toronto, reprint, 1926) is the story of the seigniory at Murray Bay.

J. C. Bracq, *The evolution of French Canada* (New York, 1924), in French *L'évolution du Canada français* (Paris, n.d.) has adequate notes on authorities. L'Abbé A. Gosselin, *L'église du Canada après la conquête, première partie, 1760–1775* (Quebec, 1916). Léon Gérin, *L'habitant de Saint-Justin, contribution à la géographie sociale du Canada* (R.S.C., 2nd series, Vol. IV, pp. 139–216) is a penetrating study of family life in a French Canadian village. *Au Canada,* preface de M. Gabriel Hanotaux (Paris, 1922), contains valuable impressions of French visitors to Canada. L'Abbé Lionel Groulx, *L'Enseignement français au Canada* (Montreal, 1931); his *Lendemain de Conquête* (Montreal, 1920); and *Vers l'Emancipation* (première période, Montreal, 1920). André Siegfried, *Canada, les deux races* (Paris, 1906): in English, *The race question in Canada* (London, 1907) is by a French observer severely critical of the French in Canada, while Wilfrid Bovey, *Canadien, a study of the French Canadians* (London, 1933) is appreciative. M. Barbeau and E. Sapir, *Folk songs of French Canada* (New Haven, 1925).

CHAPTER III

THE PERPLEXITIES OF THE FIRST BRITISH GOVERNOR OF CANADA

THE instructions to Murray and later governors are in C.A. 1904; Murray's *Ordinances* are in C.A., 1918, and his report on the mutiny is in *Murray Papers.* That to Shelburne in 1766 is printed in W. Kingsford, *History of Canada,* Vol. V. (Toronto, 1892). S. and D. for many documents. Amherst's note on the mutiny is in J. C. Webster, *The journal of Jeffery Amherst* (Toronto, 1931). *The Quebec Gazette,* the only newspaper then in Canada, begun June 21, 1764, relates chiefly to matters of trade and to official announcements. On the evolution of British rule, H. E. Egerton and W. L. Grant (eds.), *Canadian constitutional development* (London, 1907); W. P. M. Kennedy (ed.), *Documents of the Canadian constitution, 1759–1915* (Oxford, 1918) and *The constitution of Canada* (Oxford, 1922). C. W. Alvord and C. E. Carter, *The critical period, 1763–1765* (Collections of the Illinois State Historical Society, British series, Vol. I, 1915). Chester Martin, *Empire and Commonwealth* (Oxford, 1929) describes the setting up of a legislature in Nova Scotia in 1758, the only British legislature in North America to survive the American Revolution. M. A. Thomson, *The Secretaries of State, 1681–1782* (Oxford, 1932) and A. H. Basye, *The Lords Commissioners of Trade and Plantations, commonly known as The Board of Trade, 1748–1782* (New Haven, 1925) describing the system in London related to the control of the colonies. Useful special studies: S. Morley Scott, *Civil and military authority in Canada, 1764–1766* (C.H.R., Vol. IX); W. S. Wallace, *The beginnings of British rule in Canada* (*Ibid.*, Vol. VI); D. A. McArthur, *The British Board of Trade and Canada* (Report of the Canadian Historical Association, Ottawa, 1932); a clear account, among many, of the attack on Walker, is printed in C.A., 1888; the incident is described by A. L. Burt, *The mystery of Walker's ear* (C.H.R., Vol. III, 1922), and in *The old province of Quebec* (Toronto, 1933). D.N.B. on Egremont, Halifax, Dartmouth, Hillsborough, and others.

CHAPTER IV

THE INDIAN RISING AGAINST THE BRITISH

A. C. FLICK (ed.), *The papers of Sir William Johnson* (Vol. IV, V, Albany, 1921–31). W. L. Stone, *The life and times of Sir William Johnson* (2 vol., Albany, 1865). Arthur Pound, in collaboration with Richard E. Say, *A biography of Sir William Johnson* (New York, 1930); also *Johnson of the Mohawks* (New York, 1930). On the Indian war, Francis Parkman, *The conspiracy of Pontiac* (first published 2 vol., Boston, 1851) remains unchallenged as a brilliant narrative. J. W. Fortescue, *History of the British Army* (Vol. III, London, 1902) is a soldier's judgment of the military operations. He pays special tribute to the gallantry of Bouquet's small force that relieved Fort Pitt. On the events at Detroit: W. R. Riddell. *The last Indian council of the French at Detroit* (R.S.C., Ser. 3, Vol. XXV, 1931); M. Agnes Burton (ed.), *Journal of Pontiac's conspiracy, 1763* (Detroit, 1913); Charles Moore, *The Gladwin manuscript with an introductory sketch of the conspiracy* (Michigan Pioneer and Historical Collections, Vol. XXVII, 1897) traces the career of the chief British officer at Detroit, F. B. Hough, *The diary of the siege of Detroit* (Albany, 1860). Bouquet's voluminous papers are lodged in the British Museum; copies are in the Canadian Archives, Ottawa, and there is a Calendar in the *Report* of the Archivist for 1889. In *New York Colonial Documents*, Vol. VII and in the *Publications of the Michigan Pioneer and Historical Society*, Vol. XIX, extensive extracts, including letters of Amherst, are printed.

Major Robert Rogers is noticed, with authorities, in D.N.B. He tells his own story in his *Journals* (London, 1765; new ed., edited by F. B. Hough, Albany, 1863). He wrote, or took part in writing, a play illustrating the harsh attitude of the British trader to the Indians: *Ponteach* (1766), reprinted in *Representative plays, by American dramatists*, edited by M. J. Moses (New York, 1918) and by A. Nevins, *Ponteach, or the Savages of America, a tragedy by Robert Rogers*, with an introduction and a biography of the author (Chicago, 1914). Rogers published in 1765 *A concise account of North America* that secured the attention of George III. J. C. Webster (ed.), *The journal of Jeffery Amherst* (*op. cit.*); and his *Journal of John Montresor's expedition to Detroit in 1763* (R.S.C., 3rd Ser., Vol. XXII, 1928). J. C. Long, *Lord Jeffery Amherst* (New York, 1933). N. V. Russell, *The battle of Bloody Run* (C.H.R., 1931). For the massacre at Michilimackinac, Alexander Henry, *Travels and adventures in Canada and the Indian territories between the years 1760-1766* (New York, 1809; new ed. edited by J. Bain, Toronto, 1901); Alvord and Carter, *The critical period, 1763-65* (*op. cit.*) relates to the rising; and their *Mississippi Valley in British Politics* (2 vol. Cleveland, 1917) gives the political background. The outlook of the fur-trader, who succeeded the French *coureur-de-bois*, is seen in Alexander Henry, and also in Jonathan Carver, *Travels through the interior part of North America in the years 1766, 1767, and 1768* (London, 1781). H. A. Innis, *The fur-trade in Canada, an introduction to Canadian economic history* (Yale University Press, 1930). C. Hale Sipe, *The Indian wars of Pennsylvania*, a copious work, has material on Pontiac's war (Harrisburg, 1929). W. C. McLeod, *The American Indian frontier* (New York, 1928) gives a remorseless picture of European contact with the natives. Sir C. P. Lucas, *History of Canada, 1763-1812* (Oxford, 1909), Charles Moore, *The North-West under three flags, 1635-1796* (New York, 1900), and A. L. Burt (*op. cit.*) have narratives of the rising. On grants in Prince Edward Island, L. B. Namier, *England in the age of the American Revolution* (*op. cit.*).

CHAPTER V

THE AMERICAN COLONIST AND THE ENGLISHMAN

JAMES TRUSLOW ADAMS, *Revolutionary New England, 1691-1716* (Vol. II of *The history of New England*, Boston, 1921-27); his *Provincial Society, 1690-1776* (New York, 1927); and *The Adams family* (Boston, 1930) are three penetrating studies with full authorities. H. L. Osgood, *The American colonies in the eighteenth century* (4 vol., New York, 1924). M. D. George, *London life in the eighteenth century* (London, 1925) describes conditions in the capital; her *England in Johnson's day* (London, 1928) consists of extracts from contemporary writers on all phases of life in England. A. S. Turberville (ed.), *Johnson's England* (2 vol., London, 1933). L. B. Namier (*op. cit.*). Constantia Maxwell, *The English traveller in France* (London, 1932) shows the Englishman's attitude to foreigners. Walpole, Johnson and Wesley illustrate different aspects of the life of the time in England.

CHAPTER VI

THE BRITISH POLITICAL SYSTEM UNDER GEORGE III

THE most effective revelation of the king is in his own correspondence: J. W. Fortescue, *George III, king of England, correspondence from 1760 to December 1783* (6 vol., London, 1927-28). F. A. Mumby (ed.), *George III and the American Revolution* (London, 1923) is a useful selection from contemporary writings. On politics: L. B. Namier (*op. cit.*); Sir G. O. Trevelyan, *Early history of Charles James Fox* (many reprints), and on British later insistence on colonial subordination, Sir George Cornwall Lewis, *Administration of Great Britain from 1783 to 1830* (London, 1884) and J. W. Kaye, *Life and correspondence of Lord Metcalfe* (London, 1858), giving the opinions of Lord Stanley.

CHAPTER VII

THE CONTROL BY ENGLAND OF COLONIAL TRADE

H. E. EGERTON, *A short history of British colonial policy* (revised ed., London, 1908) covers the subject adequately. So does G. L. Beer, *The origins of the British system, 1578–1660* (New York, 1922); *The Old colonial system, 1665–1754* (2 vol., New York, 1912); and *British colonial policy, 1754–1765* (New York, 1922). A. M. Schlesinger, *The colonial merchants and the American Revolution* (New York, 1922). G. B. Herz, *The old colonial system* (Manchester, 1905) is a penetrating study. A. H. Basye, *The Lord Commissioners of Trade (op. cit.).* The organization of British smuggling is shown in Lord Teignmouth and C. G. Harper, *The smugglers* (2 vol., London, 1923). On the destruction of tobacco, etc., in England, Munro and Grant, *Acts of the Privy Council, Colonial Series, 1633–1680,* and later volumes.

CHAPTER VIII

THE TAXING OF THE COLONIES

THE brief debate in Parliament is in *Parliamentary History,* Vol. XVI, p. 34 *sqq.* The text of the Stamp Act, often reprinted, is in S. E. Morison, *Sources and documents illustrating the American Revolution* (Oxford, 1923). W. T. Laprade, *The Stamp Act in British politics* (American Historical Review, July, 1930). Franklin's autobiography, for his interview with Grenville and for Grenville's opinions. W. J. Smith (ed.), *The Grenville Papers* (4 vols., London, 1852–3). Burke is the most acute commentator on the period. G. S. Kimball (ed.), *Correspondence of William Pitt with colonial governors* (2 vol., New York, 1906). E. B. Greene, *The provincial governor in the English colonies of North America* (Harvard, 1906). C. E. Carter (ed.), *Thomas Gage, 1721–1787. Correspondence with the Secretaries of State, 1763, 1765 . . .* (2 vol. New Haven, 1931, 1933.) W. C. Abbott, *New York in the American Revolution* (New York, 1929). Mary Hulton, *Letters of a Loyalist lady* (Cambridge, Mass., 1927) shows the violence in Boston from an early time. W. E. H. Lecky, *History of England in the eighteenth century* (many editions) and L. Tyerman, *The Life of the Rev. George Whitefield* (2 vol., London, 1876) illustrate this spirit in religion. W. B. Kerr, *The Stamp Act in Quebec* (English Historical Review, October, 1932) and his *Merchants of Nova Scotia and the American Revolution* and *Nova Scotia in the critical years, 1775–6* (C.H.R., Vol. XIII, 1932) shows opinions on the Act in colonies that remained British. H. E. Egerton, *The causes and character of the American Revolution* (Oxford, 1932) stresses, with adequate authorities, the unyielding temper on both sides. Dora Mae Clark, *English opinion and the American Revolution* (New Haven, 1930).

CHAPTER IX

TEA

FITZMAURICE, *Life of Shelburne (op. cit.)* tells the little that is known about the debate on taxing tea, etc. Taylor and Pringle (ed.), William Pitt, First Earl of Chatham, *Correspondence* (4 vol., London, 1838–40). *The Grenville Papers (op. cit.).* F. Sherson, *The lively Lady Townshend and her friends* (London, 1928) helps to explain the folly of Charles Townshend. D.N.B. and D.A.B. for persons named in the text.

CHAPTER X

THE TURNING TO INDEPENDENCE

THE many excellent histories of the time make unnecessary a list of authorities for the brief narrative of the text. The voluminous debates in Parliament on the Boston Port Bill are in *Parliamentary History*, Vol. XVII. C. H. Van Tyne, *op. cit.*, and his *War of Independence* (Boston, 1929) have full references to authorities. For the mental atmosphere of the time M. C. Tyler, *The literary history of the American Revolution* (2 vol., New York, 1897). Mumby, (*op. cit.*) is a useful collection of extracts.

CHAPTER XI

CANADA A STRONGHOLD AGAINST DEMOCRACY

ON constitutional matters the authorities under Chapter III. C.A., 1888 (French military officers preparing to serve in Canada); 1905, (Carleton's Instructions); 1912 and 1913, (papers of Inglis, the first Anglican bishop). A. L. Burt, *Sir Guy Carleton and his first council* (C.H.R., Vol. IV). A. G. Bradley, *Lord Dorchester* (revised ed., London and Toronto, 1926) is based on Carleton's papers in the Royal Institution, now in Ann Arbor, Mich. William Wood, *The Father of British Canada: a Chronicle of Carleton* (Toronto, 1916) has a list of authorities. W. S. Wallace, *The Masères Letters* (Toronto, 1919). The article on Masères in D.N.B. has a list of his numerous writings on Canada. On the Church, R. R. Owsley, *The Anglican Episcopate of Canada and Newfoundland* (London, 1928). Shortt and Doughty *Canada and its provinces* (*op. cit.*), Vol. XI. An adequate history of the Anglican Church in Canada is much to be desired.

CHAPTER XII

THE PLANNING OF A VASTER CANADA

THE Quebec Act has been the subject of highly specialized study. R. Coupland, *The Quebec Act, a study in statesmanship* (Oxford, 1925) has adequate references to authorities. An earlier study is Victor Coffin, *The Province of Quebec and the American Revolution* (Madison, Wis., 1896). J. Wright (ed.), *Cavendish's debates of the House of Commons in the year 1774 on the bill for making more effectual provision for the government of the Province of Quebec* (London, 1839). The debates in the Lords are briefly noted in *Parliamentary History*, Vol. XVII. The only summary of Chatham's speech in the Lords is in the *Correspondence of the Earl of Chatham* (*op. cit.*). The Report of the Historical Manuscripts Commission on *The Dartmouth Papers* (2 vol., London, 1887, 1895). The Petition of the City of London against the Act is printed in W. Kingsford, *The history of Canada*, Vol. V, p. 230 (Toronto, 1892). When Lord Camden introduced, on May 17, 1775, a bill to repeal the Quebec Act, he was opposed by Lord Lyttelton, whose speech was printed (London, 1775). William Knox, *Justice and policy of the late Act of Parliament for the . . . governance of the Province of Quebec* (London, 1774), and his *Extra official state papers* (2 vol. London, 1789). The many pamphlets relating to the Act have no special value. The documents in S. and D. and in W. P. M. Kennedy, *Constitutional documents* and his *Constitution of Canada* (*op. cit.*). Louise Phelps Kellogg, *A footnote to the Quebec Act* (C.H.R., Vol., 13, 1932) explains the reasons for including the Illinois country in the Province of Quebec. William Smith, *The struggle for the laws of Canada* (C.H.R., Vol. I, 1920).

CHAPTER XIII

CIVIL WAR

IN contrast with the brief debates on the Stamp Act, those on the events of 1775 are voluminous (*Parliamentary History*, Vol. XVIII). Fortescue, *Correspondence of George III* (*op. cit.*). The *Works* of John Adams and *Letters* of his wife Abigail illustrate the spirit of the time, especially in New England. *The Dartmouth Papers* (*op. cit.*) have much urging both severity and moderation. Historical Manuscripts Commission, *MSS. of Mrs. Stopford-Sackville* have papers on the siege of Boston and on Burgoyne. Gage's *Correspondence* (*op. cit.*). George III rebuked Gage's moderation. C.A., 1926, calendars Admiralty and other letters of the time. F. J. Hinkhouse, *The preliminaries of the American Revolution as seen in the English press, 1763–1775* (New York, 1926). M. W. Willard, *Letters on the American Revolution* (Boston, 1925) consists chiefly of letters written in America and printed in English monthly newspapers. Dora Mae Clark, *British opinion and the American Revolution* (*op. cit.*). *Diary of Frederick Mackenzie . . .* (Harvard, 1930) describes the Concord Expedition. R. Frothingham, *The siege of Boston* (Boston, 1903).

CHAPTER XIV

THE COLONIES INVADE CANADA

THE fullest account based on adequate research is J. H. Smith, *Our struggle for the fourteenth colony: Canada and the American Revolution* (2 vol., New York, 1907). The Canadian General Staff's History of Canada's naval and military forces has in Vol. II *The war of the American Revolution* (Ottawa, 1920). C.A. 1883, 1884, 1886, 1890, 1904, and 1914–15. The protest of George III on April 10, 1775 is printed in F. Mumby (*op. cit.*). Francis Masères, *Additional papers concerning the Province of Quebec* (London, 1776). W. B. Munro, (see Chap. II) describes opinion among the people. On Ticonderoga: John Pell, *Ethan Allen* (New York, 1929) and Allen French, *The taking of Ticonderoga in 1775: the British story* (Cambridge, Mass., 1928). On the attitude of the Canadians to the invaders the various local histories show welcome at first and later hostility: see, for instance, J. E. Bellemère, *Histoire de Nicolet, 1669–1924* (Arthabaska, Quebec, 1924), and J. E. Roy, *Histoire de la seigneurie de Lauzon* (5 vol., Levis, Quebec 1897–1905). On the attitude of the church: H. Têtu and C. O. Gagnon: *Mandements des Evêques de Québec* (6 vol., Quebec, 1888); A. Gosselin, *L'Eglise du Canada après la Conquête, 1775–1789* (Vol. II, Quebec, 1916). S. and D. Vol. I. has many papers. The diary of Foucher, a notary in St. John's during the siege, is printed in the *Bulletin des Recherches Historiques,* March and April, 1934. H. A. J. B. Verreau, *Invasion du Canada: collection des Mémoires* (2 vol., Montreal, 1870–73). On Arnold's expedition: J. H. Smith, *Arnold's march from Cambridge to Quebec* (New York, 1903); John Codman, *Arnold's expedition to Quebec* (New York, 1901). On the siege of Quebec: the publications of the Quebec Literary and Historical Society, 1868, 1871, 1875 and especially *The Blockade of Quebec in 1775–76 by the American Revolutionists* (2 vol., 1905–06). G. M. Wrong, *A Canadian manor* (*op. cit.*) gives letters and a diary of the time. The *Annual Register* for 1776 reflects Burke's tone of sympathy for the American cause. On Franklin at Montreal, L. A. Leonard, *A Life of Charles Carroll of Carrollton*, containing his journal (New York, 1918). Peter Guilday, *The life and times of John Carroll* . . . (New York, 1922). Franklin has left no account. On the American retreat by way of Lake Champlain, O. Sherwin, *Benedict Arnold* (New York, 1931). G. W. Allen, *The naval history of the American Revolution* (2 vol., New York, 1913).

CHAPTER XV

THE END OF THE REVOLUTIONARY WAR

FORTESCUE, Trevelyan, and Channing (*op. cit.*) for the general history. Recent works are C. H. Van Tyne, *The war of Independence* (New York, 1929) and F. E. Whitton, *The American War of Independence* (London, 1929). The *Memoirs of Richard Cumberland* (Vol. II, London, 1807) for a favourable view of Germain. R. W. Pettingill, *Letters from America, 1776–1779* (Boston, 1924). In spite of frivolous titles, F. J. Hudleston, *Gentleman Johnny Burgoyne* (London, 1928); and R. Partridge, *Sir Billy Howe* (London, 1932) are serious works. H. Nickerson, *The turning-point of the Revolution, or Burgoyne in America* (New York, 1928) is well documented. Jane Clark, *Responsibility for the failure of the Burgoyne campaign* (American Historical Review, April, 1930), and her *Command of the Canadian Army for the Campaign of 1777* (C.H.R., Vol. X). A. L. Burt, *Carleton and Germain* (C.H.R., Vol. XI) describes their dispute. C. A., 1885, has their letters. On Howe's failure to meet Burgoyne the authorities are in Van Tyne (*op. cit.*), and H. E. Egerton, *The American Revolution* (Oxford, 1923). The correspondence of Germain with Howe is in the Stopfort-Sackville Papers (*op. cit.*). Burgoyne defended himself in *A statement of the expedition from Canada* . . . (London, 1780). Germain's papers are now in the W. L. Clements Library, Ann Arbor, Michigan. M. von Eelking, *Memoirs and letters and journals of Maj.-Gen. Riedesel* . . . (Tr. by W. L. Stone, 2 vol., Albany, 1868); also Freiherrin von Riedesel, *Letters and journals* (Albany, 1867). J. P. Baxter (ed.), *The British invasion from the North* (Albany, 1877) contains the copious diary of Lieut. Digby. Authorities on Brant are given in D.N.B. and in L. A. Wood, *The War Chief of the Six Nations* (Toronto, 1914). F. D. Reville, *History of the county of Brant* (Brantford, 1920) has a sketch. F. W. Halsey, *The old New York frontier* (New York, 1901) counts the Butlers and Grant as inhuman monsters, while Howard Swiggett, *War out of Niagara: Walter Butler and the Tory Rangers* (New York, 1933) softens this judgment. R. Coupland, *The American Revolution and the British Empire* (London, 1930) describes the bad state of the navy under Sandwich. G. R. Barnes and J. H. Owen (eds.), *The private papers of John, Earl of Sandwich* (2 vol., Navy Records Soc., 1932, 1933) put him in a light more favourable than that of the Whig historians. W. M. James, *The British navy in adversity, a study of the American War of Independence* (London, 1926). G. W. Allen, *The naval history of the American Revolution* (*op. cit.*). Charles, First Marquis Cornwallis, *Correspondence* (3 vol., London, 1859). Fortescue, *Correspondence of George III* (*op. cit.*). Luzerne's letters are in C.A. 1912. Sir N. W. Wraxall, *Historical memoirs of my own time* (reprint, London, 1904) depicts London after Yorktown.

CHAPTER XVI

THE CANADIAN SCENE

HALDIMAND's voluminous papers in some 200 volumes are in the British Museum. Copies are at Ottawa calendared in C.A. 1887, 1888, and 1889.

His copious diary is printed in 1889. J. N. McIlwraith, *Sir Frederick Haldimand* (Toronto, 1904; reprint, 1926). F.-J. Audet, *Sir Frederick Haldimand* (R.S.C., Vol. XVI, 1923). W. Kingsford, *History of Canada* (Vol. VI, Toronto, 1893) sets out fully Haldimand's problem of canals.

CHAPTER XVII

PEACE AND FRONTIERS

FORTESCUE, *Correspondence of George III* and Fitzmaurice, *Shelburne* (*op. cit.*). Lord John Russell, *Memorials and correspondence of Charles James Fox* (2 vol., London, 1853); A. H. Smyth, *The writings of Benjamin Franklin* (10 vol., New York, 1905) and C. F. Adams, *The works of John Adams* (10 vol., Boston, 1856) are well indexed. Oswald's *Journal* is printed in Franklin's *Works,* and extracts are in Sir G. C. Lewis, *Essays on the administration of Great Britain* (*op. cit.*). C.A., 1921, has a calendar of Oswald's correspondence with Shelburne (volumes 71 and 72 of *Shelburne Papers*). G. K. Guttridge, *David Hartley, M.P., The advocate of conciliation* (Berkeley, Cal., 1926). Temple Bodley, *George Rogers Clark* (Boston, 1926). A. L. Burt, *The old province of Quebec* (*op. cit.*). W. A. S. Hewins (ed.), *The Whitefoord Papers* (Oxford, 1898). Eunice Wead, *British public opinion of peace with America in 1782* (American Historical Review, Vol. XXXIV), S. F. Bemis, *Canada and the peace settlement of 1782-3* (C.H.R., Vol. XIV). G. W. Brown, *The St. Lawrence in the boundary settlement of 1783* (C.H.R., Vol. IX); Charles G. Paullin (ed. by John K. Wright), *Atlas of the Historical Geography of the United States* (New York, 1932) reproduces the Mitchell map used for the treaty of 1783, showing the various boundaries claimed. Dudley Mills, *British diplomacy in Canada* (United Empire, New Series, Vol. II) gives maps and full comment on the boundary. D.N.B. for Oswald and Hartley.

CHAPTER XVIII

THE LOYALIST MIGRATION

S. AND D. have many documents. Loyalist material in C.A. is described by W. W. Campbell, *Report on MS. lists relating to the United Empire Loyalists* (Ottawa, 1909). These papers contain little of narrative interest. W. S. Wallace, *The United Empire Loyalists* (Toronto, 1914) and H. E. Egerton (see Chap. XXII) have good lists of authorities. C. H. Van Tyne, *The Loyalists in the American Revolution* (New York, 1902). A. G. Bradley, *The United Empire Loyalists* (London, 1932). Henry Belcher, *The first American civil war* (2 vol., London, 1911) champions the loyalists. A. C. Flick, *Loyalism in New York during the American Revolution* (New York, 1901). A. C. Flick (ed.), *History of the State of New York* (10 vol., Vol. III, *Whig and Tory*, Vol. IV. *The new state*, New York. 1933). James H. Stark, *The Loyalists of Massachusetts and the other side of the story* (Boston, 1910). E. A. Jones, *The Loyalists of Massachusetts, their memorial petitions and claims* (Boston, 1930). N.M. Tiffany, *Letters of James Murray, Loyalist* (Boston, 1901). O. T. Barck, Jr., *New York City during the war for Independence* (New York, 1931). E. W. Spaulding, *New York in the critical period, 1783-1787* (New York, 1932). V. H. Paltsits (ed.), *Minutes of the Commissioners for detecting and defeating conspiracies in the State of New York, Albany County Sessions, 1778-1781* (3 vol. Albany, 1909-10). Wilbur C. Abbott, *New York in the American*

Revolution (New York, 1929). G. A. Gilbert, *The Connecticut Loyalists* (Amer. Hist. Rev., Vol. IV). E. Alfred Jones, *The Loyalists of New Jersey* (Coll. of New Jersey Historical Society, Vol. X, 1927). W. H. Siebert, *The Loyalists of Pennsylvania* (Columbus, Ohio, 1920) and *The Loyalists in East Florida, 1774 to 1785* (2 vol., Florida State Historical Society, 1929). J. S. Harrell, *Loyalism in Virginia* (Durham, N. C., 1926). Lorenzo Sabine, *Biographical sketches of loyalists in the American Revolution* (Boston, 1864). Egerton Ryerson, *The Loyalists of America and their times* (2 vol., Toronto, 1880). E. E. Beardsley, *Life and correspondence of the Right Rev. Samuel Seabury* (Boston, 1881). Historical MSS. Commission, *Report on American MSS. in the Royal Institution* has in Vol. IV (London, 1904) instances of harsh treatment of Loyalists after the peace.

CHAPTER XIX

EXILE IN ENGLAND

LEWIS EINSTEIN, *Divided Loyalties* (London, 1933) has biographies of Copley, Rumford and other loyalists. Rumford's letters to Lord George Germain are in the *Stopford-Sackville Papers,* Vol. II (*op. cit.*). Authorities for Jonathan Boucher are given in D.N.B. and D.A.B. G. E. Ellis, *Memoir of Sir Benjamin Thompson, Count Rumford* (Boston, 1871). Allen French, *General Gage's Informers* (Ann Arbor, 1932) charges Thompson with treachery. W. O. Raymond, *The Winslow Papers* (see Chap. XX) has many references to Thompson, Sewell and other loyalists in England. Samuel Curwen, *Journals and Letters, 1775–84* (New York, 1842) is one of the few personal narratives of a Loyalist in England.

CHAPTER XX

THE LOYALISTS BY THE SEA

J. B. BREBNER, *Acadia, New England's Outpost* (New York, 1927), a scholarly account of Nova Scotia. D. G. Harvey, *Early settlement and social conditions in Prince Edward Island* (Dalhousie Review, Halifax, Jan. 1932). John Robinson and Thomas Rispin, *A journey through Nova Scotia* (New York, 1774). W. O. Raymond (ed.), *The Winslow Papers* (St. John, N.B., 1901), the most vivid and varied collection of loyalist papers. The original manuscripts are now chiefly in the New Brunswick Archives at St. John. The papers of Ward Chipman, Winslow's intimate friend, are in Ottawa. T. Watson Smith, *The Loyalists at Shelburne* (Vol. V, Coll. of Nova Scotia Hist. Soc., 1887–88). J. P. Edwards, *The Shelburne that was and is not;* and *The vicissitudes of a loyalist city* (Dalhousie Review, July, October, 1922). L. T. Mayo, *John Wentworth, Governor of New Hampshire, 1767–1775* (Harvard, 1921). Sir A. Archibald, *Sir John Wentworth* (Coll. Nova Scotia Hist. Soc., Vol. XX). R. S. Reyson, *Charles Inglis, a chapter in beginnings* (Queen's Quarterly, 1925). W. O. Raymond, *The river St. John* (St. John, 1910) and in Vol. XIII of *Canada and its provinces.* P. Campbell, *Travels in the interior inhabited parts of North America in the year 1791-2* (Edinburgh, 1792), a careful description of St. John and the state of settlement on the river. M. G. Otty, *The river of the loyalists* (Can. Geog. Jour., Jan., 1931). Marion Gilroy, *The partition of Nova Scotia, 1784* (C.H.R., Vol. XIV, 1933). J. W. Lawrence, *The judges of New Brunswick and their times* (St. John, 1907) includes Winslow and Chipman. Benjamin Marston's *Journal* is in Vol. I of the publications of the New Brunswick Historical Society, which contain many papers on the Loyalists. C. W. Rife, *Edward Winslow, Junior, Loyalist pioneer* (Report of the Can. Historical Assn., 1928) C.A., 1884, contains report by Robert Morse on Nova Scotia in 1784; 1912 and 1913 have letters of Inglis, first Bishop of Nova Scotia; 1921 has Parr's Correspondence with Shelburne. There are other papers on Nova Scotia in 1885, 1894, 1895 (correspondence of Thomas Carleton), 1904; 1914–15 has a map made in 1784–87 of the St. John river; 1891 has a report on the river (about 1783) by Captain John Munro.

CHAPTER XXI

EXILE IN THE CANADIAN WILDERNESS

W. H. SIEBERT, *The American Loyalists in the Province of Quebec* (R.S.C., 3rd ser. Vol. VII and VIII). P. Campbell, (*op. cit.*) gives a detailed account of his journey in 1791 from Montreal to Kingston and visits to loyalist settlements. In the extensive publications of the Ontario Historical Society are many papers relating to loyalists. The *Reports of the Ontario Bureau of Archives* contain many papers, chiefly relating to grants of lands. *The Centennial of the settlement of Upper Canada by the United Empire Loyalists, 1784–1884* (Toronto, 1885). W. Canniff, *History of the Settlement of Upper Canada (Ontario)* (Toronto, 1869) has value chiefly for its record of individual loyalists. A Canuck [Michael G. Scherck], *Pen pictures of early pioneer life in Upper Canada* (Toronto, 1905) is an account of pioneer occupations, education and amusements covering every phase of pioneer life. E. C. Guillet, *Early life in Upper Canada* (Toronto, 1933). E. A. Cruikshank, *The fur-trade, 1763–1787* (*Transactions* of the Canadian Institute, Toronto, 1894–95); *Records of Niagara, 1778–1787* (Niagara Historical Society, 1927); and *The settlement of the United Empire Loyalists on the Upper St. Lawrence and Bay of Quinté in 1784* (Ontario Historical Society, 1934). Thomas Conant, *Life in Canada* (Toronto, 1903). W. S. Herrington, *Pioneer life among the loyalist settlements of Upper Canada* (Toronto, 1915); and *The history of the county of Lennox and Addington* (Toronto, 1913). R. W. Cumberland, *Pioneer problems in Upper Canada . . .* and *The U.E. Loyalist settlements between Kingston and Adolphustown* (Queen's Quarterly, 1923). A. L. Burt, *The old province of Quebec* (*op. cit.*). Percy J. Robinson, *Toronto during the French régime* (Toronto, 1933).

CHAPTER XXII

LOYALIST LOSSES

PITT's outline of the terms of compensation is in *Parliamentary History*, XXVII, p. 610 *sqq.* H. E. Egerton, *The Royal Commission on the losses and services of American Loyalists, 1783 to 1785*, being the notes of D. P. Coke, M.P., one of the commissioners (The Roxburghe Club, 1915), a well-edited volume sumptuous in form. There is on pp. LIII–LV a list of works on the loyalists. J. Eardley Wilmot, *Historical view of the Commission for enquiring into the losses, services, and claims of the American Loyalists* (London, 1815) is a summing up by the Chairman of the Commission. The *Report of the Bureau of Archives for Ontario* (Toronto, 1904) gives the claims of Canadian Loyalists made to the two commissioners sent to Canada. The original is in the Library of Congress at Washington. William Knox, *New establishments for the American Loyalists* (London, 1783). A. M. Davis, *The confiscation of John Chandler's estate* (Boston, 1905).

INDEX

Abercrombie, General James, 305.

Adams, Abigail, 190; anger at coercion of Boston, 267–8; on fight at Bunker Hill, 274, 374.

Adams, John, President of the United States, 43, 117–8, 121, 129, 135, 192, 215; denounces Quebec Act, 258; at Continental Congress, 261–9; 301, 363, 366; at Paris, treating for peace, 352–64; 390, 400; loyalist opinion of, 436; 477.

Adams, Samuel, 148, 212, 214, 217–8, 372, 376; urges severity for loyalists, 381–2, 387, 411; loyalist contempt for, 436–7.

Allen, Ethan, takes Ticonderoga, 280–1; made prisoner, 288; 309, 385–6, 445.

Amherst, Jeffery, Baron, 23; scornful tone to Indians, 74, 80, 88–96; harsh terms to Indians, 104–6; asks for Jesuit Estates, 114; 140, 222, 348, 450; at War Office, 472–3.

Andros, Thomas, 384–5.

Anstey, John, commissioner for loyalist claims, 465.

Arbuthnot, Admiral, 334.

Arnold, Benedict, at Ticonderoga, 280; invasion of Canada and siege of Quebec, 293–302; at Montreal, 310, 314; on Lake Champlain, 318–9; treason of, 336.

Asquith, H. H., Prime Minister, 161.

Bâby, settler at Detroit, 98.

Baldwin, Robert, Canadian statesman, 160.

Barlow, Canon, 406.

Barré, Colonel Isaac, 120, 158, 178, 219; on Quebec Act, 249–53.

Bayard, William, loyalist, 467.

Bedford, Grosvenor, 177.

Bedford, John Russell, Duke of, 142, 154, 209.

Belêtre, Captain, in command at Detroit, 83–6.

Bentham, Jeremy, 352.

Bernard, Sir Francis, Governor of Massachusetts, 408.

Berridge, preacher, 188.

Bigot, François, Intendant, 29, 32.

Blackstone, Sir W., 130.

Bliss, Daniel, loyalist, 270.

Bolingbroke, Henry St. John, Viscount, 142–3.

Boswell, James, biographer of Dr. Johnson, 125, 159.

Boucher, Rev. Jonathan, loyalist, 187, 190–1, 399–400.

Bouchette, Jean Baptiste, seaman, 292.

Bouquet, Colonel Henry, ends Pontiac's rising, 104–5; 110, 344.

Braddock, General Edward, 78, 82, 90, 95.

Bradstreet, Colonel John, treats with Indians at Detroit, 109–10.

Brant, Joseph (Thayendanegea), 78; charged with savagery, 328–32; moves to Canada, 445–6; in London, 471.

Brant, Mary, 78.

Breckenridge, Hugh Henry, 387.

Briand, Jean Olivier, Bishop of Quebec, 237, 281–5, 319.

Brooke, Rev. John, Chaplain at Quebec, 233–4.

Brougham, Henry Peter, Baron, 148.

Brown, John, Colonial envoy to Canada, 280.

Brown, Major, Colonial Officer, 291.

Buckingham, Duchess of, 122.

Burgoyne, General Sir John, 148, failure and surrender at Saratoga, 317–23; 337, 382–3.

Burke, Edmund, 5, 15, 118, 124, 128–37, 143; his debts, 151, 153–8, 175; on Stamp Act, 183; M. P., 195; 198, 200; on C. Townshend, 205–6, 208; on Quebec Act, 252–3; 287, 304, 317, 330–1, 358, 384, 388, 441, 461.

Burke, William, on Quebec Act, 253.

491